DATE DUE

NORTH ATLANTA HIGH SCHOOL
MEDIA CENTER
2875 NORTHSIDE DRIVE NE
ATLANTA, GA 30305

DEMCO

THE CONSTITUTION OF ENGLAND

NATURAL LAW AND
ENLIGHTENMENT CLASSICS

Knud Haakonssen
General Editor

Jean Louis De Lolme

NATURAL LAW AND
ENLIGHTENMENT CLASSICS

The Constitution of England; Or, An Account of the English Government

Jean Louis De Lolme

Edited and with an Introduction
by David Lieberman

LIBERTY FUND

Indianapolis

Introduction, annotations, bibliography, index
© 2007 by Liberty Fund, Inc.

Printed in the United States of America

C   I   2   3   4   5   6   7   8   9   10
P   I   2   3   4   5   6   7   8   9   10

Frontispiece: Line engraving of Jean Louis De Lolme, by Heath,
after Stoddart, published 1784. Reproduced by permission
of the National Portrait Gallery, London.

Library of Congress Cataloging-in-Publication Data
Lolme, Jean Louis de, 1740–1806. [Constitution de l'Angleterre. English]
The Constitution of England; or, An account of the English government/
Jean Louis DeLolme; edited and with an introduction by David Lieberman.
p.   cm.—(Natural law and enlightenment classics)
Translation of: Constitution de l'Angleterre.
Includes bibliographical references and index.
ISBN 978-0-86597-464-7 (hc: alk. paper)   ISBN 978-0-86597-465-4 (pbk: alk. paper)
1. Constitutional history—Great Britain.   2. Constitutional law—Great Britain.
3. Great Britain—Politics and government.   I. Lieberman, David.   II. Title.
III. Title: Account of the English government.
KD3934.L636 2007
342.4202—dc22   2007013521

LIBERTY FUND, INC.
8335 Allison Pointe Trail, Suite 300
Indianapolis, Indiana 46250-1684

CONTENTS

INTRODUCTION

Jean Louis De Lolme's *The Constitution of England,* which first appeared in French in 1771, was a major contribution to eighteenth-century constitutional theory and enjoyed wide currency in and beyond the eras of the American and French Revolutions. Its authority and judgment were invoked in parliamentary debate and in partisan political polemic. John Adams, the American revolutionary leader, constitutional advocate, and later president, praised the work as "the best defence of the political balance of three powers that ever was written."[1] Even De Lolme's contemporary critics were forced to acknowledge "a work which has been honored with the public approbation and which certainly possesses great merit."[2]

Notwithstanding the reputation and influence that *The Constitution of England* earned its author, the details of De Lolme's life remain poorly documented. We rely chiefly on the scanty biographical information provided in his publications and the anecdotal and variable reminiscences assembled by others in the years following his death in 1806.[3]

1. John Adams, *A Defence on the Constitutions of Government of the United States of America,* 3 vols. (Philadelphia, 1797), 1:70.

2. *Answer to Mr. De Lolme's Observations on the Late National Embarrassment by Neptune* (London, 1789), 10.

3. The most rigorous effort to authenticate the details of De Lolme's life and writings is provided by Edith Ruth in *Jean Louis de Lolme und sein Werk über die Verfassung Englands,* Historische Studien, Heft 240 (Berlin, 1934). Also of importance is Jean-Pierre Machelon, *Les idées politiques de J. L. de Lolme* (Paris, 1969). The article on De Lolme by Adam I. P. Smith in the *Oxford Dictionary of National Biography* (Oxford, 2004) contains less detail than the earlier biography by G. P. Macdonell in the original *Dictionary of National Biography* (Oxford, 1888).

De Lolme's Life and Early Writings

De Lolme was born in Geneva in 1741. The title page of the 1784 edition of *The Constitution of England* distinguished him as a "Member of the Council of the Two Hundred in the Republic of Geneva." Service on this political body placed De Lolme within the ranks of Geneva's most prominent families. By reputation a brilliant student, he followed family tradition and was trained in the law, beginning his professional career in the 1760s, first as a notary and later as an advocate. His customary classical education and more specialized legal learning were plainly of value to his future writing on government and constitutional liberty. But most fateful was the political training De Lolme acquired in his native city in these early years. "As a native of a free Country, I am no stranger to those circumstances which constitute or characterise liberty," he explained to his English readers. The "Republic of which I am a member" was the setting "in which I formed my principles."[4]

In its outward political forms, eighteenth-century Geneva was a republic of self-governing citizens. For the contemporary enthusiasts of republican liberty, Geneva and its independence offered a welcome exception to a European state system dominated by large and potent monarchies. In practice, however, Geneva's government had long been an oligarchy of elite families. Political authority operated through a series of citizen councils. Although sovereignty was formally held by a General Council of all citizens, political rule was effectively exercised by two "small councils"—the Council of the Twenty-Five and the Council of the Two Hundred—under the control of the wealthiest and most powerful families. It was these smaller bodies that in practice determined Geneva's legal and fiscal policies and selected the leading officeholders.

Throughout the eighteenth century, Geneva's rulers faced organized challenges from excluded groups and, in moments of gravest political crisis, depended upon foreign support, particularly from the French monarchy, to sustain their power. Significant episodes of protest occurred in 1707, 1718, 1734–38, 1763–68, 1770, 1781–82, and 1789. These typically centered

---

4. See below, *Constitution of England,* introduction, p. 20.

on a program of republican revival that called for the restoration of the sovereignty of the General Council, an enlargement of the number of citizens entitled to serve on the small councils, and a more equitable legal and fiscal treatment of the great number of propertied residents who lacked the benefits of full citizenship. In the period just before De Lolme's birth, these conflicts had led Geneva's government to summon military support from France and the cantons of Berne and Zurich to help "mediate" the political crisis between ruling elite and popular ascendancy. The resulting 1738 Act of Mediation stabilized oligarchic control, notwithstanding a number of political concessions to the authority of the General Council. As De Lolme later explained in *The Constitution of England,* the reforms proved largely cosmetic. By limiting the General Council's legislative role to the formal approval of measures initiated only by the Council of the Twenty-Five, the governing elites easily subverted popular constraints on its rulership. "The Citizens had thus been successively stripped of all their political rights," he observed, "and had little more left to them than the pleasure of being called a Sovereign Assembly."[5]

By the time of De Lolme's early adulthood, Geneva weathered even more serious political instability in the years 1763–68, when the forces of reform, the "Représentants" (or Party of Remonstrance), again challenged patrician rulership, now organized politically as a party of conservative "Négatifs." Geneva's most famous native son, Jean-Jacques Rousseau, whose writings had been condemned by the Council of the Twenty-Five in 1762, entered the controversy with a scathing critique of Geneva's ruling oligarchy published in 1764 as *Lettres de la montagne* (Letters from the mountain). On this occasion, the popular cause proved successful in forcing substantive concessions from the Council of the Twenty-Five, which in 1768 granted the General Council additional powers to control the other governing bodies. "The Citizens," De Lolme enthusiastically recorded, through "an uncommon spirit of union and perseverance . . . succeeded in a great measure to repair the injuries which they had been made to do to themselves."[6]

5. See below, book 2, chapter 5, pp. 174–75, note a.
6. Ibid.

Here De Lolme wrote not in his usual capacity as an observer and theorist of government, but as an engaged political participant. He embraced the Représentants' call for reform and republican renewal in several anonymous polemics that contributed to the vibrant public debate that Geneva's rulers found impossible to contain. The most important of these publications was the 1767 *La purification des trois points de droit souillés par un anonyme* (The purification of three soiled points of law by an anonymous author). The unrestrained tone of this attack on the constitutional authority of the ruling Négatifs produced a prompt rebuke from the Genevan government, accompanied by the recommendation that its author quit his native city. Soon after, the banished citizen of Geneva arrived in the foreign land where he was to spend the bulk of his remaining years and whose constitution served as his most important subject matter.

The Constitution of England

De Lolme left no record concerning why he chose England as his destination. But in the major publications that quickly followed his brief career in Genevan politics, he made clear that he had come to perceive in the English constitution a unique system of government in which political liberty was sustained in a manner that sharply contrasted with the experience of other states, not least the city from which he was banished. As De Lolme put the point in 1772 in his first major publication in the English language, "I have studied History and seen most of the Republics of Europe, and I do not hesitate to affirm that there is, or has been, no Government upon Earth where the property, and especially the person, of the Subject, is by far so secure as it is" in England.[7] The exploration and analysis of this defining theme received its influential rendering in 1775, in *The Constitution of England; or, An Account of the English Government,* a translation and enlargement of the original French edition.

De Lolme's subtitle—"An account of the English government in which it is compared both with the Republican form of government and occa-

---

7. *A Parallel Between the English Constitution and the Former Government of Sweden* (London, 1772), 26.

sionally with the other Monarchies in Europe"—indicates the scope and ambition of the study.[8] His goal was both to explain how the English constitution produced the liberty for which it was deservedly celebrated and to deploy this information to explain why liberty proved so notoriously vulnerable elsewhere. Having experienced firsthand in Geneva the ease with which political power could be manipulated and abused, he turned to the sharply contrasting case in which "Liberty has at length disclosed her secret to Mankind, and secured an Asylum to herself."[9]

De Lolme's famous explanation for this exceptional situation centered on the manner in which public power had been distributed into separate and balanced institutional hands, such that the "freedom of the Constitution" was the product of "an equilibrium between the ruling Powers of the State."[10] This thesis, presented most compactly in the opening chapters of book 2, dominated all the historical examples and political arrangements he assembled for discussion. In England, executive power had become the exclusive monopoly of a hereditary monarch; legislative power of a bicameral Parliament. Both powers in themselves were formidable. But the executive, being utterly dependent on the legislative power for its funding, was "like a ship completely equipped, but from which the Parliament can at pleasure draw off the water, and leave it aground."[11] The members of the legislature, though able to control the funding of the executive, were equally unable to exercise the executive power itself. They thus created laws always knowing that another power would be enforcing their enactments, even over themselves. "All Men in the State," De Lolme explained, "whatever may be their rank, wealth, or influence," recognized "that they must . . . continue to be *Subjects;* and are thus compelled really to love, to defend, and to promote, those laws which secure the liberty of the Subject."[12]

---

8. In the fourth edition (1784), De Lolme slightly modified his subtitle by deleting the qualifying phrase "occasionally with." The change reflected the expansion of his comparative treatment of the European monarchies; see the discussion below on pp. xix–xxi.

9. See below, book 2, chapter 21, p. 342.

10. Ibid., chapter 1, p. 139.

11. See below, book 1, chapter 6, p. 65.

12. See below, book 2, chapter 1, p. 148, note a.

In treating English liberty in these terms, De Lolme followed Montesquieu—"a man of so much genius"[13]—whose 1748 *De l'esprit des lois* likewise presented the English constitution as a unique political form and the generic guide to the nature of political liberty. The account involved a substantial reinterpretation of the institutional components of England's political system.[14] Whereas previous writers related liberty to the relative weakness of the Crown in comparison with the Continent's more absolute monarchs, De Lolme emphasized the remarkable executive capacity of English kings, "sufficient to be as arbitrary as the Kings of France" but for the powerful constraint imposed by "the right of taxation . . . possessed by the People."[15] England's constitutional balance was conventionally understood in terms of its tripartite legislature, the King-in-Parliament, which combined elements of democracy (House of Commons), aristocracy (House of Lords), and monarchy (king)—a balanced and "mixed constitution" of classical proportions. De Lolme focused on a different equilibrium that balanced legislative capacity against other political power. Similarly, where traditional accounts presented the democratic status of the House of Commons as the linchpin of English liberty, De Lolme again firmly reoriented the discussion. The significance of the Commons' legislative power was its control over "the initiative in legislation." This reversed the dominant model of ancient and modern republics, whereby the legislative power of the populace was limited to the approval or rejection of measures proposed by the powerful.[16] Furthermore, the most significant democratic elements of the constitution were not parliamentary elections, but the "institution of the Trial by Jury" and "the Liberty of the Press," which rendered England "a more Democratical State than any other we are acquainted with."[17]

De Lolme also followed Montesquieu concerning the nature of political

---

13. Ibid., chapter 18, p. 317, note a.

14. I summarize here an interpretation of eighteenth-century constitutional theory set out more fully in my "The Mixed Constitution and the Common Law," in *The Cambridge History of Eighteenth-Century Political Thought,* ed. Mark Goldie and Robert Wokler (Cambridge: Cambridge University Press, 2006).

15. See below, book 2, chapter 20, p. 329.

16. Ibid., chapter 4, p. 162.

17. Ibid., chapter 17, p. 280, note a.

liberty itself. Many "writers of the present age"—not least his fellow countryman Rousseau—identified liberty with the power to participate in lawmaking and therefore located political liberty in the institutions of republican self-government. In contrast, De Lolme identified liberty with personal security under law: "in a state where the laws are equal for all, and sure to be executed."[18] It was this emphasis on the legally preserved security of the subject that made the operations of law and the constitutional structuring of "the judicial power" so central to the analysis of political freedom. De Lolme, admittedly, did not include judicial power within the key constitutional equilibrium between legislative and executive authority. Nonetheless, *The Constitution of England* devoted lavish attention to the role of legal process and independent courts in England's political development. Many of these topics concerned matters that De Lolme acknowledged to fall outside those specifically constitutional arrangements by which "the Powers that concur to form the Government constantly balance each other."[19] But they were fundamental to the analysis of constitutional freedom, since so much of England's liberty depended not only on those "very extensive" laws that defined the subject's liberties, but equally on "the manner in which they are executed."[20]

Having revealed the logic of England's political order, De Lolme was equipped to explain why liberty had proved so precarious in other governments. No target was so momentous as republican Rome, often in early modern political theory the very model of political achievement and public freedom. Ancient Rome figured as the ever-present negative counterpoint to De Lolme's treatment of England. Despite the numerous expedients and violent conflicts that characterized Rome's efforts to preserve its liberty, none had succeeded in protecting the citizenry from the abuses and manipulations of the politically powerful. Their failure could not be understood in the common terms of corruption through imperial growth, commercial luxury, or, later, the excessive ambitions of its leaders. The problems were structural and foundational. The liberty of the citizen was

18. Ibid., chapter 5, p. 170.
19. See below, book 1, chapter 12, p. 115.
20. See below, book 2, chapter 16, p. 231.

violated because public power always combined those legislative and executive capacities which needed separation and balance.

So extensive was De Lolme's critique of the rival model of republican
liberty that he feared his study might be misunderstood as an endorsement
of "every kind of Monarchy."[21] Instead, the analysis of England's constitutional logic also disclosed the structural defects of the European monarchies and the failings of alternative strategies for combining royal prerogatives and political freedom. England's constitution ensured that the
power of an English king operated "by means totally different" from that
of other monarchs, who enjoyed both legislative and executive authority.[22]
Elsewhere, the effort to prevent the abuse of royal power typically involved
a strategy of taking powers from the king and distributing them to the
nobility or "the Representatives of the People."[23] But this simply replaced
one institutional mixture of legislative and executive authority with another, and thus substituted royal tyranny with tyranny from other sites of
power. "It may be laid down as a maxim," De Lolme maintained, "that
Power, under any form of Government, must exist, and be trusted somewhere."[24] It was the now-revealed secret of *The Constitution of England* to
show how vast executive power could be concentrated in a single monarchic
hand, where it could be vigilantly watched and balanced by a no less potent
legislature.

Later Writings

De Lolme lived for well over thirty years after the original publication of
Constitution de l'Angleterre. But there is a distinct sense of anticlimax attending his later literary productions. He produced one more large-scale
work that attracted critical notice and enjoyed frequent reprinting, the
splendidly titled *The History of the Flagellants; or, the advantages of the Discipline; being a Paraphrase and Commentary on the Historia Flagellantium
of the Abbé Boileau, Doctor of the Sorbonne, Canon of the Holy Chapel etc.*

21. Ibid., chapter 17, p. 260.
22. Ibid., p. 302.
23. See below, book 2, chapter 19, p. 322.
24. Ibid., p. 320.

by somebody who is not Doctor of the Sorbonne, published in London in 1777. This narrative reworking of materials assembled in Jacques Boileau's 1700 *Historia flagellantium* offered a case study in the pathologies of religious extremism, showing how the sectarian practice of self-mortification in fact violated the Christian teaching its adherents believed themselves to be serving. The combination of the work's familiar Enlightenment themes and provocative subject matter ensured healthy sales. *The History of the Flagellants* reached its fourth edition in 1783, at which stage De Lolme revised and relaunched the publication as *Memorials of Human Superstition,* which appeared in successive editions in 1784 and 1785.

The majority of De Lolme's literary productions, however, comprised more ephemeral and less ambitious writings in which he exploited his established reputation as a scholar of English government and history to comment on issues of the moment. In 1786 he composed a historical survey of the political relations between England and Scotland up to the period of the 1707 Union of the Parliaments of the two kingdoms, along with a companion account of the relations between England and Ireland that urged similar constitutional unification. The *Essay Containing a few strictures on the Union of Scotland with England; and on the present situation of Ireland* first served as an introduction to a new edition of Daniel Defoe's *History of the Union* and was reissued the following year as the freestanding work *The British Empire in Europe.* In 1788 he published a series of brief tracts condemning parliamentary taxes on windows, shops, and peddlers and offering proposals *"for the Improvement of the Metropolis."* That same year, he attracted greater attention for his contribution to the partisan debate over the Regency Crisis that followed in the wake of George III's mental collapse in 1788–89. De Lolme's *The Present National Embarrassment Considered* was twice printed and sustained vituperative criticism from "Neptune" in the 1789 *Answer to Mr. De Lolme's Observations on the Late National Embarrassment.*

For De Lolme's early-nineteenth-century editors and admirers, this corpus of political writing seemed a poor return on the talent and erudition displayed in *The Constitution of England.* Why had De Lolme not achieved more? In the substantial advertisement that first appeared in the 1781 edition of *The Constitution of England,* De Lolme himself explained his disap-

pointments at the outset of his literary career in London. An English translation of the French text was ready for publication several years prior to its
1775 first edition. The delay resulted from De Lolme's failure to find a patron for the work or a sympathetic bookseller, notwithstanding the book's
"favourable reception" and "successive editions" on "the Continent."[25] Instead, De Lolme was forced to publish by subscription, an expedient that
further postponed any significant financial reward for the undertaking.
These frustrations and privations, it was proposed, readily explained his
later career. "The fact is mortifying to record," Isaac Disraeli concluded in
1812, "that the author who wanted every aid, received less encouragement
than if he had solicited subscriptions for a raving novel or an idle poem.
De Lolme . . . became so disgusted with authorship that he . . . ceased almost to write."[26] Others attributed his chronic indebtedness and inability
to secure regular patronage to darker defects of character and propriety. His
political adversary Neptune reported that "he is even supposed to pride
himself in a contempt of all decency in private life," while more approving
observers acknowledged his secrecy and evasiveness and the frequency with
which he appeared "slovenly to a degree that indicated indigence."[27]

Whatever the accuracy of these assessments, De Lolme's English career
mostly reflects the common harshness and insecurity of the eighteenth-
century literary market for any author who lived by his pen without the
benefit of settled party connection or a prosperous patron. In this respect,
the later career of the "English Montesquieu," as Isaac Disraeli styled him,
shared a fate common to London's political scribes of this period. De
Lolme's own writings, as well as the biographical anecdotes supplied by
others, contain frequent reference to plans for books and journals that were
never realized. At the same time, there is no reason to suppose that all of
De Lolme's writing appeared under his own name or that we can definitively determine the extent of his literary corpus. One important discovery,

25. See below, Advertisement, p. 9.

26. Isaac Disraeli, *The Calamities and Quarrels of Authors* (1st ed., 1812; London,
1867), 200–201.

27. *Answer to Mr. De Lolme's Observations*, 14; Thomas Busby, *Arguments and Facts
Demonstrating that the Letters of Junius were written by John Lewis De Lolme, LL.D. Advocate . . .* (London, 1816), 13.

recently made by Michael Sletcher of Yale University, is De Lolme's editorship of two British reprints of the documentary collection *The Constitutions of the Several Independent States of America; The Declaration of Independence; The Articles of Confederation . . .* and related materials. The editions, apparently unknown to earlier scholars, were published in London in 1782 and in 1783 and contained what De Lolme described as "the Magna Charta of the United American States . . . the code of their fundamental laws."[28] On the other hand, modern scholarship has firmly put to rest one long-standing and contested attribution of authorship: the claim that De Lolme secretly authored the famous "Letters of Junius" that appeared in London's *Public Advertiser* between 1769 and 1772 and which De Lolme cited approvingly in *The Constitution of England.*[29] The case for authorship was presented at exhaustive length by Thomas Busby in 1816 and more quickly dispatched by John Cannon in 1978.[30]

De Lolme's final years were spent in his native Geneva. As with so much of his biography, the details of his departure from England are not known. He received an inheritance that enabled him to pay his creditors and to return to the setting that first inspired his influential political speculations. He died on July 13, 1806, and was buried in Seewen-sur-le-Ruffiberg in the Swiss Canton of Schwitz.

Editions of *The Constitution of England*

For the preparation of this edition, Åsa Söderman completed a detailed survey of the principal English editions of *The Constitution of England* published in De Lolme's lifetime. Her research revealed for the first time

28. *The Constitutions of the Several Independent States of America; The Declaration of Independence; The Articles of Confederation . . . with an Advertisement by J. L. De Lolme* (London, 1783), v. The original version of this collection of documents was published in Philadelphia "by Order of Congress." The London editions of 1782 and 1783 contain the identical editorial advertisement by De Lolme; however, De Lolme's authorship is identified only in the 1783 edition. I am indebted to Michael Sletcher for his generosity in sharing this discovery with me and in allowing me to publicize it in these pages.

29. See below, book 1, chapter 13, p. 127, note a.

30. See Thomas Busby, *Arguments and Facts demonstrating that the letters of Junius were written by John Lewis De Lolme* (London, 1816); and John Cannon, *The Letters of Junius* (Oxford, England: Clarendon Press, 1978), 540–41, 546.

the extensive changes to the text De Lolme made in the ten-year period from 1775 to 1784.

De Lolme's study was first published as *Constitution de l'Angleterre ou État du gouvernement anglais comparé avec la forme républicaine et avec les autres monarchies de l'Europe* in Amsterdam in 1771. Later French-language editions appeared in Amsterdam (1774, 1778), London (1785), Geneva (1787, 1788, 1789, 1790), Breslau (1791), and Paris (1819, 1822).

The original 1775 English edition, published in London as *The Constitution of England; or, an Account of the English Government; in which it is compared with the Republican Form of Government and occasionally with the Other Monarchies in Europe,* comprised more than a translation of the earlier French version. De Lolme reorganized some of the chapter divisions and introduced three substantial chapters to book 2 (chapters 15–17). These additions extended the treatment of England's constitutional development and legal system and reinforced De Lolme's central thesis concerning the many beneficial consequences of the crown's monopoly of executive power.

Three further editions of the English text were published in London during De Lolme's lifetime (1777, 1781, and 1784), along with pirate printings in Dublin (1776 and 1777). These publications became the vehicle through which De Lolme further revised and expanded his discussion. Major changes to the later French editions (Geneva, 1788, and Breslau, 1791), for example, included translations and insertions of the new material added previously to the English editions. De Lolme updated his study in a variety of ways, responding critically to recent political events, such as the restoration of royal absolutism in Sweden in 1772 (book 2, chapter 17, p. 258, note c) and the French military intervention in Geneva in 1782 (book 2, chapter 5, pp. 174–75, note a), and to important recent publications, such as Adam Smith's 1776 *An Inquiry into the Nature and Causes of the Wealth of Nations* (book 2, chapter 17, pp. 288–89). He was especially diligent in refining the language of the text. No section of the book was overlooked in the effort to clarify the argument through changes of expression and wording.

In addition to these frequent and often minor alterations, De Lolme introduced major revisions to the third (1781) and fourth (1784) editions.

He added the dedication and advertisement, as well as two new chapters to book 1 (chapters 10–11), two new chapters to book 2 (chapters 19–20), and substantial new material to book 2, chapter 17 (pp. 267–74). The new chapters in book 1 added significant detail to the treatment of England's legal institutions. The additions to book 2 greatly extended De Lolme's contrast between the nature of the monarchic power under the English constitution and the more typical examples of monarchy in continental Europe. (The new chapter 19, for example, largely incorporated material from De Lolme's 1772 publication *A Parallel between the English Constitution and the former Government of Sweden; containing some observations on the late Revolution in that kingdom and Examination of the causes that secure us against both Aristocracy and Absolute Monarchy.*) At the same time, these additions rendered the work more repetitive and much less tightly ordered. As De Lolme candidly reported, the new chapters of book 1 on English law "proved much longer than I intended at first" (chapter 11, p. 114), and the unexpected swelling of book 2, chapter 17, had been so great "as almost to make it a kind of a separate Book by itself" (advertisement postscript, p. 16). The 1784 version of De Lolme's text was used in the subsequent and numerous editions of *The Constitution of England* published in the late eighteenth and the nineteenth centuries.

In addition to the French and English editions, German translations were published in Amsterdam (1772), Leipzig (1776, 1848), and Altona [Hamburg] (1819). A Spanish translation was published in Ovieda in 1812.

David Lieberman

A NOTE ON THE TEXT

This edition of *The Constitution of England* presents the 1784 version of De Lolme's text. My principal aim as editor has been to make the work more accessible to a modern reader by clarifying the many (now obscure) historical episodes, political institutions, and practices, and by identifying the classical and modern authorities De Lolme invoked. Editorial annotations to De Lolme's main text appear as numbered footnotes. Annotations to De Lolme's original notes are enclosed in double square brackets inserted into the body of the note. Page breaks in the 1784 edition are indicated by the use of angle brackets. (For example, page 112 begins after <112>.) In checking and translating De Lolme's quotations from classical sources, I have consulted, where available, editions in the Loeb Classical Library. I have been aided by the translations in William Hughes Hughes's edition of *The Constitution of England* (London, 1834).

Like many early modern writers, De Lolme was casual in his references to other authors, often trusting memory. Furthermore, he relied on versions of texts that have since been superseded. I have not tried to correct De Lolme's citations and instead have only noted those instances where the quotations in his text involve significant variation from an original source. Obvious typographical errors in the text have been silently corrected.

Before 1752, England retained the Julian (or "Old Style") calendar, in which the New Year is taken to begin on March 25. I have adjusted dates so that the New Year starts on January 1. This is awkward when dealing with events relating to the Glorious Revolution, which to contemporaries occurred in 1688 and to moderns in 1689. To deal with these few episodes, I have used the inelegant formula: 1688/89.

ACKNOWLEDGMENTS

My greatest debt is to Knud Haakonssen, who first proposed that this volume be included in the series under his general editorship and who thereafter remained a frequent and much-needed source of guidance, patience, and support. Åsa Söderman's detailed and exacting survey of the principal early editions of *The Constitution of England*, discussed more fully in the editorial introduction, provided the critical starting point for the preparation of this edition. Michael Sletcher showed fine generosity in sharing his discovery of a previously unreported publication by De Lolme, also detailed above.

I imposed on the expertise of many friends and scholars to elucidate particular references in De Lolme's text and am delighted to acknowledge the help of Thomas Brady, Jan deVries, Eliga Gould, Lindsay Farmer, Richard Kagan, Ernest Metzger, Carlos Noreña, James Oldham, and Richard Whatmore. Several graduate students at the Boalt Hall School of Law provided skillful research assistance: Benjamin Bechstedt, Brad Bryan, Tucker Culbertson, and, above all, Pablo Rueda Saiz, whose dedication and contributions were invaluable. As on past occasions, I have benefited from the wonderful resources and staff of several libraries at the University of California at Berkeley: the Bancroft Library, the Robbins Collection, and the Garret W. McEnerney Law Library. I am especially grateful for the expertise and many kindnesses of the Law Library's associate director, Marci Hoffman.

THE CONSTITUTION OF ENGLAND

THE

CONSTITUTION

OF

ENGLAND,

OR

AN ACCOUNT

OF THE

ENGLISH GOVERNMENT;

In which it is compared, both with the REPUBLICAN
Form of GOVERNMENT, and the other
MONARCHIES in EUROPE.

By J. L. DE LOLME, Advocate,

Member of the Council of the Two HUNDRED in the
Republic of GENEVA.

THE FOURTH EDITION,
Corrected and Enlarged.

Ponderibus librata suis.———

OVID. Met. L. I. 13.[1]

LONDON,
Printed for G. ROBINSON, N° 25, Paternoster-Row;
and J. MURRAY, N° 32, Fleet-street.
MDCCLXXXIV.

1. "Poised by its own weight," Ovid (Publius Ovidius Naso) *Metamorphoses,* bk. 1.13.

TO THE

KING.

SIRE,

The approbation with which the Public have been pleased to favour this Work, together with the nature of the subject, embolden me to lay the present fourth and enlarged Edition of the same at your Majesty's feet, both as an homage, and an expression of the desire I entertain, the Book may for a few minutes engage the attention of a person of your deep and extensive knowledge.

Your Majesty's reign has, for many years past, afforded proofs in more respects than one, that, though human wisdom may not always be able to anticipate difficulties, yet, assisted by fortitude, it can succeed in terminating them in a more favourable manner than it seemed at first possible to be expected, or even in bringing them to an happy issue. According to the common course of Nature, your Majesty has only yet seen the less considerable part of the years of which your reign is to be composed: that the part which now opens before your Majesty, may be attended with a degree of satisfaction proportionate to your Majesty's public and private virtues, to your disinterested government, and religious regard for your royal engagements, is the fond hope of

Your Majesty's
Most humble and
Most devoted Servant,
And these many Years
Subject by Choice,

May, 1784.

J. L. DE LOLME.

CONTENTS[1]

1. The page numbers in the Contents are those of the Liberty Fund edition.

ADVERTISEMENT[1]

The Book on the English Constitution, of which a new Edition is here offered to the Public, was first written in French, and published in Holland. Several persons have asked me the question, how I came to think of treating such a subject? One of the first things in this Country, that engages the attention of a Stranger who is in the habit of observing the objects before him, is the peculiarity of its Government: I had moreover been lately a witness of the broils which had for some time prevailed in the Republic in which I was born, and of the revolution by which they were terminated. Scenes of that kind, in a State which, though small, is independent, and contains within itself the principles of its motions, had naturally given me some competent insight into the first real principles of Governments: owing to this circumstance, and perhaps also to some moderate share of natural abilities, I was enabled to perform the task I had undertaken, with tolerable success. I was twenty-seven years old when I first came to this Country: after having been in it only a year, I began to write my work, which I published about nine months afterwards: and I have since been surprised to find that I had committed so few errors of a certain kind: I certainly was fortunate in avoiding to enter deeply into those articles with which I was not sufficiently acquainted.

The Book met with rather a favourable reception on the Continent; several successive Editions having been made of it. And it also met here with approbation, even from Men of opposite parties; which, in this Country, was no small luck for a Book on systematical politics.[2] Allowing that there

---

1. This advertisement first appeared in the 1781 edition.
2. De Lolme's original French version of the book was first published in Amsterdam in 1771 and at the time of this advertisement had been republished in 1774 and 1778.

was some connection and clearness, as well as novelty, in the arguments, I
think the work was of some peculiar utility, if the epoch at which it was
published, is considered; which was, though without any design from me,
at the time when the disputes with the Colonies were beginning to take a
serious turn, both here and in America. A work which contained a specious,
if not thoroughly true, confutation of those political notions by the help
of which a disunion of the Empire was endeavoured to be promoted (which
confutation was moreover noticed by Men in the highest places) should
have procured to the Author some sort of real encouragement; at least the
publication of it should not have drawn him into any inconvenient situation. When my enlarged English Edition was ready for the press, had I
acquainted Ministers that I was preparing to boil my tea kettle with it, for
want of being able conveniently to afford the expence of printing it, I do
not pretend to say what their answer would have been; but I am firmly of
opinion, that, had the like arguments in favour of the existing Government
of this Country, against republican principles, been shewn to Charles the
First, or his Ministers, at a certain period of his reign, they would have
very willingly defrayed the expences of the publication.—In defect of encouragement from Great Men (and even from Booksellers) I had recourse
to a subscription; and my having expected any success from such a plan,
shews that my knowledge of this Country was at that time but very incomplete (*a*). <iv>

Separate German translations appeared in Amsterdam in 1772 and in Leipzig in 1776.
The English translation was first published in London in 1775, and at the time of this
advertisement it had been republished in 1776 (Dublin) and 1777 (London and Dublin).
For further details concerning these and later editions, see the editorial introduction,
pp. xix–xxi.

(*a*) In regard to two Subscribers in particular, I was, I confess, sadly disappointed.—
Though all the Booksellers in London had at first refused to have any thing to do with
my English Edition (notwithstanding the French Work was extremely well known), yet,
soon after I had thought of the expedient of a Subscription, I found that two of them,
who are both living, had begun a translation, on the recommendation, as they told me,
of a noble Lord, whom they named, who had, till a few years before, filled one of the
highest offices under the Crown. [[De Lolme's nineteenth-century editors identified the
"noble Lord" as William Nassau de Zuylestein, Earl of Rochford, who served as secretary
of state from 1768 to 1775.]] I paid them ten pounds, in order to engage them to drop
their undertaking, about which I understood they already had been at some expence.
Had the Noble Lord in question favoured me with his subscription, I would have

After mentioning the advantages with which my Work has not been favoured, it is however just I should give an account of those by which it has been attended. In the first place, as is above <v> said, Men of high rank have condescended to give their approbation to it; and I take this opportunity of returning them my most humble acknowledgments. In the second place, after the difficulties by which the publication of the Book had been attended and *followed*, were overcome, I began to share with Booksellers in the profits arising from the sale of it. These profits I indeed thought to be but scanty and slow: but then I considered this was no more than the common complaint made by every Trader in regard to his gain, as well as by every Great Man in regard to his emoluments and his pensions. After a course of some years, the net balance formed by the profits in question, amounted to a certain sum, proportioned to the bigness of the performance. And, in fine, I must add to the account of the many favours I

---

celebrated the generosity and munificence of my Patron; but as he did not think proper so to do, I shall only observe that his recommending my Work to a Bookseller, cost me ten pounds.

At the time the above subscription for my English Edition was advertising, a copy of the French Work was asked of me for a Noble Earl, then invested with a high office in the State; none being at that time to be found at any Bookseller's in London. I gave the only copy I had (the consequence was, that I was obliged to borrow one, to make my English Edition from); and I added, that I hoped his Lordship would honour me with his subscription. However, my hopes were here again confounded. As a gentleman, who continues to fill an important office under the Crown, accidentally informed me about a year afterwards, that the Noble Lord here alluded to, had lent him my French work, I had no doubt left that the copy I had delivered, had reached his Lordship's hand; I therefore presumed to remind him by a letter, that the Book in question had never been paid for; at the same time apologizing for such liberty from the circumstances in which my late English Edition had been published, which did not allow me to lose one copy. I must do his Lordship (who is moreover a Knight of the Garter) the justice to acknowledge, that, no later than a week afterwards, he sent two half-crowns for me to a Bookseller's in Fleet-street. A Lady brought them in a coach, who took a receipt. As she was, by the Bookseller's account, a fine Lady, though not a Peeress, it gave much concern that I was not present to deliver the receipt to her myself.

At the same time I mention the noble Earl's great punctuality, I think I may be allowed to say a word of my own merits. I waited, before I presumed to trouble his Lordship, till I was informed that a pension of four thousand pounds was settled upon him (I could have wished much my own Creditors, had, about that time, shewn the like tenderness to me), and I moreover gave him time to receive the first quarter.

have received, that I was allowed to carry on the above business of selling my book, without any objection being formed <vi> against me from my not having served a regular apprenticeship, and without being molested by the Inquisition.—Several Authors have chosen to relate, in Writings published after death, the personal advantages by which their performances had been followed: as for me, I have thought otherwise; and, fearing that during the latter part of my life I may be otherwise engaged, I have preferred to write now the account of my successes in this Country, and to see it printed while I am yet living.

I shall add to the above narrative (whatever the Reader may be pleased to think of it) a few observations of rather a more serious kind, for the sake of those persons who, judging themselves to be possessed of abilities, find they are neglected by those having it in their power to do them occasional services, and suffer themselves to be mortified by it. To hope that Men will in earnest assist in setting forth the mental qualifications of others, is an expectation which, generally speaking, must needs be disappointed. To procure one's notions and opinions to be attended to, and approved, by the circle of one's acquaintance, is the universal wish of Mankind. To diffuse these notions farther, to numerous parts of the Public, by means of the press or by others, becomes an object of real ambition: nor is this ambition always proportioned to the real abilities of those who feel it; very far from it. When the approbation of Mankind is in question, all per-<vii>sons, whatever their different ranks may be, consider themselves as being engaged in the same career: they look upon themselves as being candidates for the very same kind of advantage: high and low, all are in that respect in a state of primaeval equality; nor are those who are likely to obtain some prize, to expect much favour from the others.

This desire of having their ideas communicated to, and approved by, the Public, was very prevalent among the Great Men of the Roman Commonwealth, and afterwards with the Roman Emperors; however imperfect the means of obtaining these ends might be in those days, compared with those which are used in our's. The same desire has been equally remarkable among modern European Kings, not to speak of other parts of the World; and a long catalogue of Royal Authors may be produced. Ministers, especially after having lost their places, have shewn no less inclination than

their Masters, to convince Mankind of the reality of their knowledge. Noble Persons of all denominations, have increased the catalogue. And to
speak of the Country in which we are, there is it seems no good reason to
make any exception in regard to it; and Great Men in it, or in general those
who are at the head of the People, are we find sufficiently anxious about
the success of their Speeches, or of the printed performances which they
<viii> sometimes condescend to lay before the Public; nor has it been every
Great Man wishing that a compliment might be paid to his personal knowledge, that has ventured to give such lasting specimens.

Several additions were made to this Work, at the time I gave the first English
Edition of it.[3] Besides a more accurate division of the chapters, several new
notes and paragraphs were inserted in it; for instance in the 11th chapter of
the 2d Book; and three new chapters, the 15th, 16th, and 17th, amounting
to about ninety pages, were added to the same Book. These three additional
chapters, never having been written by me in French, have been inserted
in the third Edition made at Amsterdam, translated by a person whom the
Dutch Bookseller employed for that purpose: as I never had an opportunity
to peruse a copy of that Edition, I cannot say how well the Translator has
performed his task. Having now parted with the copy-right of the Book,
I have farther added four new chapters to it (10, 11, B. I. 19, 20, B. II.) by
way of taking a final leave of it; and in order the more completely to effect
this, I may perhaps, give, in a few months, a French Edition of the same
(which I cannot tell why I have not done sooner) in which all the above
mentioned additions, translated by myself, shall be inserted. <ix>

In one of the former additional Chapters (the 17th, B. II.) mention is
made of a peculiar circumstance attending the English Government, considered as a Monarchy, which is the solidity of the power of the Crown.
As one proof of this peculiar solidity, it is remarked, in that Chapter, that
all the Monarchs who ever existed, in any part of the World, were never
able to maintain their ground against certain powerful subjects (or a combination of them) without the assistance of regular forces at their constant
command; whereas it is evident that the power of the Crown, in England,

3. See the editorial introduction, pp. xix–xxi.

is not at this day supported by such means; nor even had the English Kings a guard of more than a few scores of Men, when their power, and the exertions they at times made of it, were equal to what has ever been related of the most absolute Roman Emperors.

The cause of this peculiarity in the English Government is said in the same Chapter, to lie in the circumstance of the great or powerful Men, in England, being divided into two distinct Assemblies, and at the same time, in the principles on which such division is formed. To attempt to give a demonstration of this assertion otherwise than by facts (as is done in the Chapter here alluded to) would lead into difficulties which the reader is little aware of. In general, the Science of Politics, considered as an *exact Science,* that is to say, as a Science capable of actual demonstration, is infinitely deeper than the reader so much perhaps as suspects. The know-<x>ledge of Man, on which such a Science, with its preliminary *axioms* and *definitions,* is to be grounded, has hitherto remained surprisingly imperfect: as one instance, how little Man is known to himself, it might be mentioned that no tolerable explanation of that continual human phaenomenon, laughter, has been given, as yet; and the powerful, complicate, sensation which each sex produces in the other, still remains an equally inexplicable mystery.

To conclude the above digression (which may do very well for a Preface) I shall only add, that those Speculators who will amuse themselves in seeking for the *demonstration* of the political Theorem above expressed, will thereby be led through a field of observations which they will at first little expect; and in their way towards attaining such demonstration, will find the Science, commonly called Metaphysics, to be at best but a very superficial one, and that the Mathematics, or at least the mathematical reasonings hitherto used by Men, are not so completely free from error as has been thought (*a*). <xi>

(*a*) Certain errors that are not discovered, are in several cases, compensated by others, which are equally unperceived.

Continuing to avail myself of the indulgence an Author has a right to claim in a Preface, I shall mention, as a farther explanation of the peculiarity in the English Government above alluded to, and which is again touched upon in the postscript to this

Out of the four Chapters added to the present Edition, two (the 10th and 11th, B. I.) contain among other things, a few strictures on the Courts of Equity; in which I wish it may be found I have not been mistaken: of the two others, the one (19th, B. II.) contains a few observations on the attempts that may in different circumstances be made, to set new limits on the authority of the Crown; and in the 20th, a few general thoughts are introduced on the right of taxation, and on the claim of the American Colonies in that respect. Any farther observations I may hereafter make on the English Government, such as comparing it with the other Governments of Europe, and examining what difference in the manners of the inhabitants of this Country may have resulted from it, must come in a new Work, if I ever undertake to treat these subjects. In regard to the American disputes, what I may hereafter write on that account, will be introduced in a Work which I may at some future time publish, under the title of *Histoire de George Trois, Roi d'Angleterre,* or, perhaps, of *Histoire d'Angleterre, depuis l'année* 1765 (that in which < xii > the American Stamp duty was laid) *jusques à l'année* 178—meaning that in which an end shall be put to the present contests. (*a*).

Nov. 1781.

POSTSCRIPT[4]

Notwithstanding the intention above expressed, of making no additions to the present Work, I have found it necessary, in the present new Edition, to render somewhat more complete the xviith Chapter, B. II. p. 387. *On the peculiar foundations of the English Monarchy, as a Monarchy,* as I found its tendency not to be very well understood; and in fact, that Chapter contained little more than hints on the subject mentioned in it: the task, in the course of writing, has increased beyond my expectation, and has swelled the Chapter to about sixty pages beyond what it was in the former Edition,

---

Advertisement, that a Government may be considered as a great Ballet or Dance, in which, the same as in other Ballets, every thing depends on the disposition of the figures.

(*a*) A certain Book written in French, on the subject of the American disputes, was, I have been told, lately attributed to me, in which I had no share.

4. This postscript first appeared in the 1784 edition. See chapter XVII, p. 256.

so as almost to make it a kind of a separate Book by itself. The reader will now find in it several remarkable new instances to prove the fact of the peculiar *stability* of the executive power of the British Crown; and especially a much more complete delineation of the advantages that result from this stability in favour of public liberty (*a*). <xiii>

These advantages may be enumerated as follows. I. The numerous restraints the governing authority is able to bear, and extensive freedom it can afford to allow the Subject, at its expence. II. The liberty of speaking and writing, carried to the great extent it is in England. III. The unbounded freedom of the Debates in the Legislature. IV. The power to bear the constant union of all orders of Subjects against its prerogative. V. The freedom allowed to all individuals to take an active part in Government concerns. VI. The strict impartiality with which Justice is dealt to all Subjects, without any respect whatever of persons. VII. The lenity of the criminal law, both in regard to the mildness of punishments, and the frequent remitting of them. VIII. The strict compliance of the governing Authority with the letter of the law. IX. The needlessness of an armed force to support itself by, and as a consequence, the singular subjection of the Military to the Civil power.

The above mentioned advantages are peculiar to the English Government. To attempt to imitate them, or transfer them into other Countries, with that degree of extent to which they are carried <xiv> in England, without at the same time transferring the whole Order and conjunction of circumstances in the English Government, would prove unsuccessful attempts. Several articles of English liberty already appear impracticable to be preserved in the new American Commonwealths. The Irish Nation have of late succeeded to imitate several very important regulations in the English Government, and are very desirous to render the assimilation complete: yet, it is possible, they will find many inconveniencies to arise from their endeavours, which do not take place in England, notwithstanding the very great general similarity of circumstances in the two kingdoms in many

(*a*) For the sake of these Readers who like exactly to know in what one Edition of a Book differs from another, I shall mention, that five new pages have also been added in the xviiith Chapter, viz. page 482–486 [[see book II, pp. 309–11]], besides a few short notes in the course of the Work: for instance in page 140, 384, &c. [[see book I, p. 106, and book II, p. 254]]

respects, and even also, we might add, notwithstanding the respectable power and weight the Crown derives from its British dominions, both for defending its prerogative in Ireland, and preventing anarchy. I say, the similarity in *many respects* between the two kingdoms; for this resemblance may perhaps fail in regard to some important points: however, this is a subject about which I shall not attempt to say any thing, not having the necessary information.[5]

The last Chapter in the Work, concerning the nature of the *Divisions that take place in this Country,* I have left in every English Edition as I wrote it at first in French. With respect to the exact manner of the Debates in Parliament, mentioned in that Chapter, I should not be able to say more at present than I was at that time, as I never had an opportunity to hear the Debates in either House. In re-<xv>gard to the Divisions in general to which the spirit of party gives rise, I did perhaps the bulk of the People somewhat more honour than they really deserve, when I represented them as being free from any violent dispositions in that respect: I have since found, that, like the bulk of Mankind in all Countries, they suffer themselves to be influenced by vehement prepossessions for this or that side of public questions, commonly in proportion as their knowledge of the subjects, is imperfect. It is however a fact, that their political prepossessions and party spirit are not productive in this Country, of those dangerous consequences which might be feared from the warmth with which they are sometimes manifested. But this subject, or in general the subject of the political quarrels and divisions in this Country, is not an article one may venture to meddle with in a single Chapter; I have therefore let this subsist, without touching it.

I shall however observe, before I conclude, that there is an accidental circumstance in the English Government, which prevents the party spirit by which the Public are usually influenced, from producing those lasting and rancorous divisions in the Community, which have pestered so many other free States, making of the same Nation as it were two distinct People,

---

5. The constitutional status of Ireland was transformed by British parliamentary legislation of 1782–83, which repealed the Irish Parliament's previous legislative subordination to the British Parliament. The newly independent Irish Parliament enacted a variety of measures that brought the kingdom closer to the British model of government.

in a kind of constant warfare with each other. The circumstance I mean, is, the frequent reconciliations (commonly to quarrel again afterwards) that take place between the Leaders of parties, by which the most violent and ignorant <xvi> Class of their partizans are bewildered, and made to lose the scent. By the frequent coalitions between *Whig* and *Tory* Leaders, even that party distinction, the most famous in the English History, has now become useless: the meaning of the words has thereby been rendered so perplexed that nobody can any longer give a tolerable definition of them; and those persons who now and then aim at gaining popularity by claiming the merit of belonging to either party, are scarcely understood. The late *Coalition* between two certain Leaders has done away and prevented from settling, that violent party spirit to which the administration of Lord Bute had given rise, and which the American disputes had carried still farther.[6] Though this Coalition has met with much obloquy, I take the liberty to rank myself in the number of its advocates, so far as the circumstance here mentioned.

May, 1784. <1>

6. De Lolme here refers to the government led by the Tory leader Lord North and the Whig leader Charles James Fox. The Fox-North Coalition was one of several ministerial groupings of Whig and Tory party leaders that succeeded the controversial administration of Lord Bute in the 1760s.

THE
CONSTITUTION
OF
ENGLAND

⚘ INTRODUCTION ⚘

The spirit of Philosophy which peculiarly distinguishes the present age, after having corrected a number of errors fatal to Society, seems now to be directed towards the principles of Society itself; and we see prejudices vanish, which are difficult to overcome, in proportion as it is dangerous to attack them (*a*). This rising freedom of sen-<2>timent, the necessary forerunner of political freedom, led me to imagine that it would not be unacceptable to the Public, to be made acquainted with the principles of a Constitution on which the eye of curiosity seems now to be universally turned; and which, though celebrated as a model of perfection, is yet but little known to its admirers.

(*a*) As every popular notion which may contribute to the support of an arbitrary Government, is at all times vigilantly protected by the whole strength of it, political prejudices are, last of all, if ever, shaken off by a Nation subjected to such a Government. A great change in this respect, however, has of late taken place in France, where this book was first published, and opinions are now discussed there, and tenets avowed, which, in the time of Lewis the Fourteenth, would have appeared downright blasphemy: it is to this an allusion is made above. [[De Lolme's note appeared in the first English edition of 1775 and clarifies that the opening reference to unphilosophical "prejudices" was directed at France, not England. He mistakenly reports that "this book was first published in France"; the original 1771 French edition was published in Amsterdam.]]

19

I am aware that it will be deemed presumptuous in a Man who has passed the greatest part of his life out of England, to attempt a delineation of the English Government; a system which is supposed to be so complicated as not to be understood, or developed, but by those who have been initiated in the mysteries of it from their infancy.

But, though a foreigner in England, yet, as a native of a free Country, I am no stranger to those circumstances which constitute or characterise liberty. Even the great disproportion between the Republic of which I am <3> a member, and in which I formed my principles, and the British Empire, has perhaps only contributed to facilitate my political inquiries.[1]

As the Mathematician, the better to discover the proportions he investigates, begins with freeing his *equation* from *coefficients*, or such other quantities as only perplex without properly constituting it,—so it may be advantageous to the inquirer after the causes that produce the equilibrium of a government, to have previously studied them, disengaged from the apparatus of fleets, armies, foreign trade, distant and extensive dominions, in a word from all those brilliant circumstances which so greatly affect the external appearance of a powerful Society, but have no essential connection with the real principles of it.

It is upon the passions of Mankind, that is upon causes which are unalterable, that the action of the various parts of a State depends. The machine may vary as to its dimensions, but its movement and acting springs still remain intrinsically the same; and that time cannot be considered as lost, which has been spent in seeing them act and move in a narrower circle. <4>

One other consideration I will suggest, which is, that the very circumstance of being a foreigner, may of itself be attended, in this case, with a degree of advantage. The English themselves (the observation cannot give them any offence) having their eyes open, as I may say, upon their liberty, from their first entrance into life, are perhaps too much familiarised with its enjoyment, to enquire, with real concern, into its causes. Having acquired practical notions of their government, long before they have med-

---

1. The relationship between De Lolme's experience of Genevan politics and his treatment of the English constitution is sketched in the editorial introduction, pp. x–xiii.

itated on it, and these notions being slowly and gradually imbibed, they at
length behold it without any high degree of sensibility; and they seem to
me, in this respect, to be like the recluse inhabitant of a palace, who is
perhaps in the worst situation for attaining a complete idea of the whole,
and never experienced the striking effect of its external structure and elevation; or, if you please, like a Man who, having always had a beautiful and
extensive scene before his eyes, continues for ever to view it with
indifference.

But a stranger, beholding at once the various parts of a Constitution
displayed before him, which, at the same time that it carries liberty to its
height, has guarded against in-<5>conveniences seemingly inevitable, beholding in short those things carried into execution, which he had ever
regarded as more desirable than possible, he is struck with a kind of admiration; and it is necessary to be thus strongly affected by objects, to be
enabled to reach the general principle which governs them.

Not that I mean to insinuate that I have penetrated with more acuteness
into the Constitution of England than others; my only design in the above
observations, was to obviate an unfavourable, though natural, prepossession; and if, either in treating of the causes which originally produced the
English liberty, or of those by which it continues to be maintained, my
observations should be found new or singular, I hope the English reader
will not condemn them, but where they shall be found inconsistent with
History, or with daily experience. Of readers in general I also request, that
they will not judge of the principles I shall lay down, but from their relation
to those of human nature: a consideration which is almost the only one
essential, and has been hitherto too much neglected by the Writers on the
subject of government. <6>

Causes of the liberty of the English Nation.— Reasons of the difference between the Government of England, and that of France.—In England, the great power of the Crown, under the Norman kings, created an union between the Nobility and the People.

When the Romans, attacked on all sides by the Barbarians, were reduced to the necessity of defending the centre of their Empire, they abandoned Great Britain as well as several other of their distant provinces. The Island, thus left to itself, became a prey to the Nations inhabiting the shores of the Baltic; who, having first destroyed the ancient inhabitants, and for a long time reciprocally annoyed each other, established several Sovereignties in the southern part of the Island, afterwards called England, which at length were united, under Egbert, into one Kingdom.

The successors of this Prince, denominated the Anglo-Saxon Princes, among whom Alfred the Great and Edward the Confessor are particularly celebrated, reigned for about two hundred years; but, though our knowledge of the prin-<7>cipal events of this early period of the English History is in some degree exact, yet we have but vague and uncertain accounts of the nature of the Government which those Nations introduced.

It appears to have had little more affinity with the present Constitution, than the general relation, common indeed to all the Governments established by the Northern Nations, that of having a King and a Body of Nobility; and the ancient Saxon Government is "left us in story" (to use the

expressions of Sir William Temple on the subject) "but like so many an-
tique, broken, or defaced pictures, which may still represent something of
the customs and fashions of those ages, though little of the true lines, proportions, or resemblance" (*a*).

It is at the era of the Conquest, that we are to look for the real foundation
of the English Constitution.[1] From that period, says Spelman, *novus sec-
lorum nascitur ordo*.[2] (*b*) William of Normandy, having defeated Harold,

---

(*a*) See his Introduction to the History of England. [[William Temple, *Introduction
to the History of England* (1695). Composed in the period after William of Orange (William III) and Mary's accession to the English throne, most of Temple's history was devoted to the reign in England of William of Normandy.]]

1. In the paragraphs that follow, De Lolme introduces one of his major themes concerning the creation of England's political freedom. England's constitutional history
begins with the Norman Conquest of 1066, which introduced oppressive feudal law and
near-absolute royal powers. The concentration of so much political capacity in the hands
of the monarch ultimately served constitutional liberty by uniting the English nobility
and the people in opposition to absolute power.

2. "A new series of ages arises."

(*b*) See Spelman, *Of Parliaments*. [[De Lolme refers to Henry Spelman's essay "Of
Parliaments," which appeared in the 1723 *Reliquiae Spelmannianae: The Posthumous
Works of Sir Henry Spelman Kt*. Spelman (1563?–1641), a distinguished legal antiquarian,
published several studies indicating a major transformation of English law at the time
of the Norman Conquest.]]—It has been a favourite thesis with many Writers, to pretend that the Saxon Government was, at the time of the Conquest, by no means subverted; that William of Normandy legally acceded to the Throne, and consequently to
the engagements, of the Saxon Kings; and much argument has in particular been employed with regard to the word *Conquest,* which, it has been said, in the feudal sense only
meant *acquisition.* These opinions have been particularly insisted upon in times of popular opposition: and, indeed, there was a far greater probability of success, in raising
among the People the notions familiar to them of legal claims and long established customs, than in arguing with them from the no less rational, but less determinate, and
somewhat dangerous, doctrines, concerning the original rights of Mankind, and the
lawfulness of at all times opposing force to an oppressive Government.

But if we consider that the manner in which the public Power is formed in a State,
is so very essential a part of its Government, and that a thorough change in this respect
was introduced into England by the Conquest, we shall not scruple to allow that a new
Government was established. Nay, as almost the whole landed property in the Kingdom
was at that time transferred to other hands, a new System of criminal Justice introduced,
and the language of the law moreover altered, the revolution may be said to have been
such as is not perhaps to be paralleled in the History of any other Country.

Some Saxon laws, favourable to the liberty of the people, were indeed again established under the successors of William; but the introduction of some new modes of

and made <8> himself master of the Crown, subverted the ancient fabric of the Saxon Legislation: he <9> exterminated, or expelled, the former occupiers of lands, in order to distribute their possessions among his followers; and established the feudal system of Government, as better adapted to his situation, and indeed the only one of which he possessed a competent idea. <10>

This sort of Government prevailed also in almost all the other parts of Europe. But, instead of being established by dint of arms and all at once, as in England, it had only been established on the Continent, and particularly in France, through a long series of slow successive events; a difference of circumstances this, from which consequences were in time to arise, as important as they were at first difficult to be foreseen.

The German Nations who passed the Rhine to conquer Gaul, were in a great degree independent. Their Princes had no other title to their power, but their own valour and the free election of the People; and as the latter had acquired in their forests but contracted notions of sovereign authority, they followed a Chief, less in quality of subjects, than as companions in conquest.

Besides, this conquest was not the irruption of a foreign army, which only takes possession of fortified towns. It was the general invasion of a whole People, in search of new habitations; and as the number of the Con-

---

proceeding in the Courts of Justice, and of a few particular laws, cannot, so long as the ruling Power in the State remains the same, be said to be the introduction of a new Government; and, as when the laws in question were again established, the public power in England continued in the same channel where the Conquest has placed it, they were more properly new modifications of the Anglo-Norman Constitution, than they were the abolition of it; or, since they were again adopted from the Saxon Legislation, they were rather imitations of that legislation, than the restoration of the Saxon Government.

Contented, however, with the two authorities I have above quoted, *(Spelman and Temple)* I shall dwell no longer on a discussion of the precise identity, or difference, of two Governments, that is, of two ideal systems, which only exist in the conceptions of men. Nor do I wish to explode a doctrine, which, in the opinion of some persons, giving an additional sanction and dignity to the English Government, contributes to increase their love and respect for it. It will be sufficient for my purpose, if the Reader shall be pleased to grant that a material change was, at the time of the Conquest, effected in the Government then existing, and is accordingly disposed to admit the proofs that will presently be laid before him, of such change having prepared the establishment of the present English Constitution.

querors bore a great proportion to that of the conquered, who were at the same time enervated by long peace, the expedition was no sooner completed than <11> all danger was at an end, and of course their union also. After dividing among themselves what lands they thought proper to occupy, they separated; and though their tenure was at first only precarious, yet, in this particular, they depended not on the King, but on the general assembly of the Nation (*a*).

Under the Kings of *the first race,* the fiefs, by the mutual connivance of the Leaders, at first became annual; afterwards, held for life. Under the descendants of Charlemain, they became hereditary (*b*). And when at length Hugh Capet effected his own election to the prejudice of Charles of Lorrain, intending to render the Crown, which in fact was a fief, hereditary in his own family (*c*), he established the hereditariship of fiefs as a general principle; and from <12> this epoch, authors date the complete establishment of the feudal system in France.

On the other hand, the Lords who gave their suffrages to Hugh Capet, forgot not the interest of their own ambition. They completed the breach of those feeble ties which subjected them to the royal authority, and became every where independent. They left the King no jurisdiction either over themselves, or their Vassals; they reserved the right of waging war with each

(*a*) The fiefs were originally called, *terrae jure beneficii concessae;* and it was not till under Charles *le Gros* the term *fief* began to be in use.—See BENEFICIUM, *Gloss. Du Cange.* [["Lands granted by right of free (gratuitous) donation." De Lolme cites here, and in the following note, material from Charles du Fresne Du Cange's authoritative *Glossarium mediae et infimae Latinitatis* (Glossary of medieval and late Latin), which first appeared in 1678.]]

(*b*) *Apud Francos vero, sensim pedetentimque, jure haereditario ad haeredes transierunt feuda; quod labente saeculo nono incipit.* [["The custom slowly and progressively prevailed among the Franks, that the fiefs passed by hereditary right directly to the heirs. This commenced in the course of the ninth century."]] See FEUDUM—Du Cange.

(*c*) Hottoman has proved beyond a doubt, in his *Francogallia,* that under the two first races of Kings, the Crown of France was elective. The Princes of the reigning family had nothing more in their favour, than the custom of chusing one of that house. [[De Lolme refers to François Hotman's controversial 1573 *Francogallia.* Hotman, a Huguenot opponent of French royal absolutism, argued that the monarch in France enjoyed limited powers under the design of the historic French constitution and that the kingship remained elective under the Merovingian and Carolingian dynasties (the "two first races" of French kings).]]

other; they even assumed the same privilege, in certain cases, with regard to the King himself (*a*); so that if Hugh Capet, by rendering the Crown hereditary, laid the foundation of the greatness of his family, and of the Crown itself, yet he added little to his own authority, and acquired scarcely any thing more than a nominal superiority over the number of <13> Sovereigns who then swarmed in France (*b*).

But the establishment of the feudal system in England, was an immediate and sudden consequence of that conquest which introduced it. Besides, this conquest was made by a Prince who kept the greater part of his army in his own pay, and who was placed at the head of a people over whom he was an hereditary Sovereign: circumstances which gave a totally different turn to the Government of that kingdom.

Surrounded by a warlike, though a conquered Nation, William kept on foot part of his army. The English, and after them the Normans themselves, having revolted, he crushed both; and the new King of England, at the head of victorious troops, having to do with two Nations laying under a reciprocal check from the enmity they bore to each other, <14> and moreover equally subdued by a sense of their unfortunate attempts of resistance, found himself in the most favourable circumstances for becoming an absolute Monarch; and his laws, thus promulgated in the midst as it were of

(*a*) The principal of these cases was when the King refused to appoint Judges to decide a difference between himself and one of his first Barons; the latter had then a right to take up arms against the King; and the subordinate Vassals were so dependent on their immediate Lords, that they were obliged to follow them against the Lord Paramount. St. Louis [["St. Louis" is the French king Louis IX, who reigned from 1226 to 1270]], though the power of the Crown was in his time much increased, was obliged to confirm both this privilege of the first Barons, and this obligation of their Vassals.

(*b*) "The Grandees of the Kingdom," says Mezeray, "thought that Hugh Capet ought to put up with all their insults, because they had placed the Crown on his head: nay, so great was their licentiousness, that on his writing to Audebert, Viscount of Perigueux, ordering him to raise the siege he had laid to Tours, and asking him, by way of reproach, who had made him a Viscount? that Nobleman haughtily answered, *Not you, but those who made you a King*. [Non pas vous, mais ceux qui vous ont fait Roi.]" [[De Lolme cites François Eudes de Mézeray's multivolume *Abrégé chronologique de l'histoire de France*. The history was first published in Paris in 1668 and was later republished and expanded in several French-language editions. English editions of the work appeared in the late seventeenth and the eighteenth centuries under the title *A General Chronological History of France*.]]

thunder and lightning, imposed the yoke of despotism both on the victors and the vanquished.

He divided England into sixty thousand two hundred and fifteen military fiefs, all held of the Crown; the possessors of which were, on pain of forfeiture, to take up arms, and repair to his standard on the first signal: he subjected not only the common people, but even the Barons, to all the rigours of the feudal Government: he even imposed on them his tyrannical forest laws (*a*).

He assumed the prerogative of imposing taxes. He invested himself with the whole executive power of Government. But what <15> was of the greatest consequence, he arrogated to himself the most extensive judicial power, by the establishment of the Court which was called *Aula Regis;* a formidable tribunal, which received appeals from all the Courts of the Barons, and decided in the last resort on the estates, honour, and lives of the Barons themselves, and which, being wholly composed of the great officers of the Crown, removeable at the King's pleasure, and having the King himself for President, kept the first Nobleman in the Kingdom under the same controul as the meanest subject.

Thus, while the Kingdom of France, in consequence of the slow and gradual formation of the feudal government, found itself, in the issue, composed of a number of parts simply placed by each other, and without any reciprocal adherence, the Kingdom of England on the contrary, in consequence of the sudden and violent introduction of the same system, became a compound of parts united by the strongest ties, and the regal Authority, by the pressure of its immense weight, consolidated the whole into one compact indissoluble body.

(*a*) He reserved to himself an exclusive privilege of killing game throughout England, and enacted the severest penalties on all who should attempt it without his permission. The suppression, or rather mitigation of these penalties, was one of the articles of the *Charta de Foresta,* which the Barons afterwards obtained by force of arms, *Nullus de cetero amittat vitam, vel membra, pro venatione nostrâ.* Ch. de Forest. Art. 10. [["No man henceforth shall lose either life or limb for killing our deer." The Charter of Forests, adopted in 1215 during the reign of King John and reconfirmed by later English monarchs, was traditionally associated with Magna Charta as a fundamental statement of English liberties. De Lolme invokes the measure as evidence of the absolute power of the Norman kings in England, which the later Charter of Forests was designed to curtail. He explores the theme more fully below, book 1, chapter 2.]]

To this difference in the original Constitution of France and England, that is, in the original power of their Kings, we are to attri-<16>bute the difference, so little analogous to its original cause, of their present Constitutions. This it is which furnishes the solution of a problem which, I must confess, for a long time perplexed me, and explains the reason why, of two neighbouring Nations, situated almost under the same climate, and having one common origin, the one has attained the summit of liberty, the other has gradually sunk under an absolute Monarchy.

In France, the royal Authority was indeed inconsiderable; but this circumstance was by no means favourable to the general liberty. The Lords were every thing; and the bulk of the Nation were accounted nothing. All those wars which were made on the King, had not liberty for their object; for of this the Chiefs already enjoyed but too great a share: they were the mere effect of private ambition or caprice. The People did not engage in them as associates in the support of a cause common to all; they were dragged, blindfold and like slaves, to the standard of their Leaders. In the mean time, as the laws by virtue of which their Masters were considered as Vassals, had no relation to those by which they were themselves bound as subjects, the resistance of which they were made <17> the instruments, never produced any advantageous consequence in their favour, nor did it establish any principle of freedom that was in any case applicable to them.

The inferior Nobles, who shared in the independence of the superior Nobility, added also the effects of their own insolence to the despotism of so many Sovereigns; and the People, wearied out by sufferings, and rendered desperate by oppression, at times attempted to revolt. But being parcelled out into so many different States, they could never perfectly agree, either in the nature, or the times of their complaints. The insurrections, which ought to have been general, were only successive and particular. In the mean time the Lords, ever uniting to avenge their common cause as Masters, fell with irresistible advantage on Men who were divided; the People were thus separately, and by force, brought back to their former yoke; and Liberty, that precious offspring, which requires so many favourable circumstances to foster it, was every where stifled in its birth (*a*). <18>

(*a*) It may be seen in Mezeray, how the Flemings, at the time of the great revolt which was caused, as he says, "by the inveterate hatred of the Nobles (les Gentils-hommes)

At length, when by conquests, by escheats, or by Treaties, the several Provinces came to be *re-united* (*a*) to the extensive and continually increasing dominions of the Monarch, they became subject to their new Master, already trained <19> to obedience. The few privileges which the Cities had been able to preserve, were little respected by a Sovereign who had himself entered into no engagement for that purpose; and as the *re-unions* were made at different times, the King was always in a condition to over-

---

against the people of Ghent," were crushed by the union of almost all the Nobility of France.—*See Mezeray, Reign of Charles* VI. [[De Lolme cites Mézeray, *Abrégé chronologique de l'histoire de France;* see above, p. 27, note b.]]

(*a*) The word *re-union* expresses in the French law, or History, the reduction of a Province to an immediate dependence on the Crown. The French lawyers, who were at all times remarkably zealous for the aggrandisement of the Crown (a zeal which would not have been blameable, if it had been exerted only in the suppression of lawless Aristocracy) always contended, that when a province once came into the possession of the King, even any private dominion of his before he acceded to the Throne, it became *re-united* for ever: the *Ordonnance* of Moulins, in the year 1566, has since given a thorough sanction to these principles. The re-union of a province might be occasioned, first, by the case just mentioned, of the accession of the possessor of it to the throne: thus, at the accession of Henry IV. (the sister of the late King being excluded by the Salic law) Navarre and Bearn were *re-united.* Secondly, by the felony of the possessor, when the King was able to enforce by dint of arms, the judgment passed by the Judges he had appointed: thus the small Lordship of Rambouillet was seized upon by Hugh Capet; on which authors remark that it was the first dominion that was re-united: and the duchy of Normandy was afterwards taken in the same manner by Philip Augustus from John King of England, condemned for the murder of Arthur Duke of Britanny. Thirdly, by the last will of the possessor: Provence was re-united in this manner, under the reign of Lewis XI. Fourthly, by intermarriages: this was the case of the county of Champagne, under Philip the Fair; and of Britanny under Francis I. Fifthly, by the failure of heirs of the blood, and sometimes of heirs male: thus Burgundy was seized upon by Lewis XI. after the death of Charles the Bold, Duke of that Province. Lastly, by purchases: thus Philip of Valois purchased the Barony of Montpellier; Henry IV. the Marquisat of Saluces; Lewis XIII. the Principality of Sedan, &c.

These different Provinces, which, with others united, or *re-united,* after a like manner, now compose the French Monarchy, not only thus conferred on their respective Sovereigns different titles, but also differed from each other with respect to the laws which they followed, and still follow: the one are governed by the Roman law, and are called *Pays de Droit écrit;* the others follow particular customs, which in process of time have been set down in writing, and are called *Pays de Droit Coutumier.* In those Provinces the people had, at times, purchased privileges from their Princes, which in the different Provinces were also different, according to the wants and temper of the Princes who granted them.

whelm every new Province that accrued to him, with the weight of all those he already possessed. <20>

As a farther consequence of these differences between the times of the *re-unions,* the several parts of the Kingdom entertained no views of assisting each other. When some reclaimed their privileges, the others, long since reduced to subjection, had already forgotten their's. Besides, these privileges, by reason of the differences of the Governments under which the Provinces had formerly been held, were also almost every where different: the circumstances which happened in one place, thus bore little affinity to those which fell out in another; the spirit of union was lost, or rather had never existed: each Province, restrained within its particular bounds, only served to insure the general submission; and the same causes which had reduced that warlike, spirited Nation, to a yoke of subjection, concurred also to keep them under it.

Thus Liberty perished in France, because it wanted a favourable culture and proper situation. Planted, if I may so express myself, but just beneath the surface, it presently expanded, and sent forth some large shoots; but having taken no root, it was soon plucked up. In England, on the contrary, the seed lying at a great depth, and being covered with an enormous weight, seemed at first to be smothered; <21> but it vegetated with the greater force; it imbibed a more rich and abundant nourishment; its sap and juice became better assimilated, and it penetrated and filled up with its roots the whole body of the soil. It was the excessive power of the King which made England free, because it was this very excess that gave rise to the spirit of union, and of concerted resistance. Possessed of extensive demesnes, the King found himself independent; vested with the most formidable prerogatives, he crushed at pleasure the most powerful Barons in the Realm: it was only by close and numerous confederacies, therefore, that these could resist his tyranny; they even were compelled to associate the People in them, and make them partners of public Liberty.

Assembled with their Vassals in their great Halls, where they dispensed their hospitality, deprived of the amusements of more polished Nations, naturally inclined, besides, freely to expatiate on objects of which their hearts were full, their conversation naturally turned on the injustice of the public impositions, on the tyranny of the judicial proceedings, and, above all, on the detested forest laws. <22>

Destitute of an opportunity of cavilling about the meaning of laws the
terms of which were precise, or rather disdaining the resource of sophistry,
they were naturally led to examine into the first principles of Society; they
enquired into the foundations of human authority, and became convinced,
that Power, when its object is not the good of those who are subject to it,
is nothing more than the *right of the strongest,* and may be repressed by the
exertion of a similar right.

The different orders of the feudal Government, as established in England, being connected by tenures exactly similar, the same maxims which
were laid down as true against the Lord paramount in behalf of the Lord
of an upper fief, were likewise to be admitted against the latter, in behalf
of the owner of an inferior fief. The same maxims were also to be applied
to the possessor of a still lower fief: they farther descended to the freeman,
and to the peasant; and the spirit of liberty, after having circulated through
the different branches of the feudal subordination, thus continued to flow
through successive homogeneous channels; it forced a passage to itself into
the remotest ramifications, and the principle of primeval equa-<23>lity became every where diffused and established. A sacred principle, which neither injustice nor ambition can erase; which exists in every breast, and, to
exert itself, requires only to be awakened among the numerous and oppressed classes of Mankind.

But when the Barons, whom their personal consequence had at first
caused to be treated with caution and regard by the Sovereign, began to be
no longer so, when the tyrannical laws of the Conqueror became still more
tyrannically executed, the confederacy, for which the general oppression
had paved the way, instantly took place. The Lord, the Vassal, the inferior
Vassal, all united. They even implored the assistance of the peasants and
cottagers; and that haughty aversion with which on the Continent the Nobility repaid the industrious hands which fed them, was, in England, compelled to yield to the pressing necessity of setting bounds to the Royal
authority.

The People, on the other hand, knew that the cause they were called
upon to defend, was a cause common to all; and they were sensible, besides, that they were the necessary supporters of it. Instructed by the example of their Leaders, they spoke and stipulated <24> conditions for

themselves: they insisted that, for the future, every individual should be intitled to the protection of the law; and thus did those rights with which the Lords had strengthened themselves, in order to oppose the tyranny of the Crown, become a bulwark which was, in time, to restrain their own.

A second advantage England had over France:
—it formed one undivided State.

It was in the reign of Henry the First, about forty years after the Conquest, that we see the above causes begin to operate. This Prince having ascended the throne to the exclusion of his elder brother, was sensible that he had no other means to maintain his power than by gaining the affection of his subjects; but, at the same time, he perceived that it must be the affection of the whole nation: he, therefore, not only mitigated the rigour of the feudal laws in favour of the Lords, but also annexed as a condition to the Charter he granted, that the Lords should allow the same freedom to their respective Vassals. Care was even taken to <25> abolish those laws of the Conqueror which lay heaviest on the lower classes of the People (*a*).

Under Henry the Second, liberty took a farther stride; and the ancient *Trial by jury,* a mode of procedure which is at present one of the most valuable parts of the English law, made again, though imperfectly, its appearance.

(*a*) Amongst others, the law of the *Curfeu.* [[The Norman law of curfew, limiting the movement of the inhabitants of towns at night, was relaxed during the reign of William the Conqueror's son Henry I.]] It might be matter of curious discussion to inquire what the Anglo-Saxon Government would in process of time have become, and of course the Government of England be, at this present time, if the event of the Conquest had never taken place; which, by conferring an immense as well as unusual power on the Head of the feudal System, compelled the Nobility to contract a lasting and sincere union with the People. It is very probable that the English Government would at this day be the same as that which long prevailed in Scotland, where the King and Nobles engrossed, jointly, or by turns, the whole power in the State, the same as in Sweden, the same as in Denmark, Countries whence the Anglo-Saxons came.

But these causes, which had worked but silently and slowly under the two Henrys, who were Princes in some degree just, and of great capacity, manifested themselves, at once, under the despotic reign of King John. The royal prerogative, and the forest laws, having been exerted by this Prince to a degree <26> of excessive severity, he soon beheld a general confederacy formed against him: and here we must observe another circumstance, highly advantageous, as well as peculiar to England.

England was not, like France, an aggregation of a number of different Sovereignties: it formed but one State, and acknowledged but one Master, one general title. The same laws, the same kind of dependence, consequently the same notions, the same interests, prevailed throughout the whole. The extremities of the kingdom could, at all times, unite to give a check to the exertions of an unjust power. From the river Tweed to Portsmouth, from Yarmouth to the Land's End, all was in motion: the agitation increased from the distance like the rolling waves of an extensive sea; and the Monarch, left to himself, and destitute of resources, saw himself attacked on all sides by an universal combination of his subjects.

No sooner was the standard set up against John, than his very Courtiers forsook him. In this situation, finding no part of his kingdom less irritated against him than another, having no detached province which he could engage in his defence by promises of pardon, <27> or of particular concessions, the trivial though never-failing resources of Government, he was compelled, with seven of his attendants, all that remained with him, to submit himself to the disposal of his subjects; and he signed at Running Mead (*a*) the Charter of the Forest, together with that famous charter, which, from its superior and extensive importance, is denominated *Magna Charta*.

By the former, the most tyrannical part of the forest laws was abolished; and by the latter, the rigour of the feudal laws was greatly mitigated in favour of the Lords. But this Charter did not stop there; conditions were also stipulated in favour of the numerous body of the people who had concurred to obtain it, and who claimed, with sword in hand, a share in that security it was meant to establish. It was hence instituted by the Great

(*a*) Anno 1215.

Charter, that the same services which were remitted in favour of the Barons, should be in like manner remitted in favour of their Vassals. This Charter moreover established an equality of weights and measures throughout England; it exempted the Merchants from arbitrary imposts, and gave <28> them liberty to enter and depart the Kingdom at pleasure: it even extended to the lowest orders of the State, since it enacted, that the *Villain,* or Bondman, should not be subject to the forfeiture of his implements of tillage. Lastly, by the twenty-ninth article of the same Charter, it was enacted, that no Subject should be exiled, or in any shape whatever molested, either in his person or effects, otherwise than by judgment of his peers, and according to the law of the land (*a*): an article so important, that it may be said to comprehend the whole end and design of political societies; and from that moment the English would have been a free People, if there were not an immense distance between the making of laws, and the observing of them.

But though this Charter wanted most of those supports which were necessary to insure respect to it, though it did not secure to the <29> poor and friendless any certain and legal methods of obtaining the execution of it (provisions which numberless transgressions alone could, in process of time, point out), yet it was a prodigious advance towards the establishment of public liberty. Instead of the general maxims respecting the rights of the People and the duties of the Prince (maxims against which ambition perpetually contends, and which it sometimes even openly and absolutely denies), here was substituted a written law, that is, a truth admitted by all parties, which no longer required the support of argument. The rights and privileges of the individual, as well in his person as in his property, became settled axioms. The Great Charter, at first enacted with so much solemnity,

(*a*) "Nullus liber homo capiatur, vel imprisonetur, vel dissesietur de libero tenemento suo, vel libertatibus vel liberis consuetudinibus suis; aut utlagetur, aut exuletur, aut aliquo modo destruatur; nec super eum ibimus, nec super eum mittemus, nisi per legale judicium parium suorum, vel per legem terrae. Nulli vendemus, nulli negabimus, aut differemus, justitiam vel rectum." *Magna Chart.* cap. xxix. [["No freeman shall be taken, or imprisoned, or be disseised of his freehold, or liberties, or free customs, or be outlawed, or exiled, or any otherwise destroyed; nor will we pass upon him, nor condemn him, but by lawful judgment of his peers, or by law of the land. We will sell to no man, we will not deny or defer to any man, either justice or right."]]

and afterwards confirmed at the beginning of every succeeding reign, became like a general banner perpetually set up for the union of all classes of the people; and the foundation was laid on which those equitable laws were to rise, which offer the same assistance to the poor and weak, as to the rich and powerful (*a*). <30>

Under the long reign of Henry the Third, the differences which arose between the King and the Nobles, rendered England a scene of confusion. Amidst the vicissitudes which the fortune of war produced in their mutual conflicts, the People became still more and more sensible of their importance, and so did in consequence both the King and the Barons also. Alternately courted by both parties, they obtained a confirmation of the Great Charter, and even the addition of new privileges, by the statutes of Merton and of Marlebridge.[1] But I <31> hasten to reach the grand epoch of the reign of Edward the First; a Prince, who, from his numerous and prudent laws, has been denominated the English Justinian.

Possessed of great natural talents, and succeeding a Prince whose weakness and injustice had rendered his reign unhappy, Edward was sensible that nothing but a strict administration of justice could, on the one side,

---

(*a*) The reader, to be more fully convinced of the reality of the causes to which the liberty of England has been here ascribed, as well as of the truth of the observations made at the same time on the situation of the people of France, needs only to compare the Great Charter, so extensive in its provisions, and in which the Barons stipulated in favour even of the Bondman, with the treaty concluded between Lewis the Eleventh and several of the Princes and Peers of France, intitled, *A Treaty made at St. Maur, between the Dukes of Normandy, Calabre, Bretagne, Bourbonnois, Auvergne, Nemours; the Counts of Charolois, Armagnac, and St. Pol, and other Princes of France, risen up in support of the public good, of the one part; and King Lewis the Eleventh of the other,* October 29, 1465. In this Treaty, which was made in order to terminate a war that was called the war for the Public good (*pro bono Publico*), no provision was made but concerning the particular power of a few Lords: not a word was inserted in favour of the people. This treaty may be seen at large in the *pieces justificatives* annexed to the *Mémoires de Philippe de Comines.* [[*Mémoires de Philippe de Comines,* cited here by De Lolme, was subtitled *"l'histoire des rois de France Louis XI. et Charles VIII."* The author, Philippe de Comines (or Commynes) (1447–1511), served as a key advisor to Louis XI. His *Mémoires* became a standard source of information concerning French politics in the late medieval period.]]

1. In 1225 the Magna Carta and the Charter of Forests were reenacted under Henry III, and these revised versions of the charters became authoritative in the English legal tradition. The Statute of Merton (1236) and Statute of Marlebridge (1267) covered a variety of matters concerning the legal privileges of the nobility and the crown.

curb a Nobility whom the troubles of the preceding reign had rendered
turbulent, and on the other, appease and conciliate the people, by securing
the property of individuals. To this end, he made jurisprudence the principal object of his attention; and so much did it improve under his care,
that the mode of process became fixed and settled; Judge Hale going even
so far as to affirm, that the English laws arrived at once, & *quasi per saltum,* [2]
at perfection, and that there has been more improvement made in them
during the *first* thirteen years of the reign of Edward, than all the ages since
his time have done.[3]

But what renders this aera particularly interesting, is, that it affords the
first instance of the admission of the Deputies of Towns and Boroughs
into (*a*) Parliament.[4] <32>

Edward, continually engaged in wars, either against Scotland or on the
Continent, seeing moreover his demesnes considerably diminished, was
frequently reduced to the most pressing necessities. But though, in consequence of the spirit of the times, he frequently indulged himself in particular acts of injustice, yet he perceived that it was impossible to extend a
general oppression over a body of Nobles, and a People, who so well knew
how to unite in a common cause. In order to raise subsidies therefore, he
was obliged to employ a new method, and to endeavour to obtain through
the consent of the People, what his Predecessors had hitherto expected
from their own power. The Sheriffs were ordered to invite the Towns and
Boroughs of the different Counties to send Deputies to Parliament; and

(*a*) I mean their legal origin; for the Earl of Leicester, who had usurped the power
during part of the preceding reign, had called such Deputies up to Parliament before.

2. "And as though by a leap."

3. The influential common law judge and jurist Matthew Hale celebrated Edward I's
legal achievements in chapter 7 of his *History of the Common Law of England.* The history
was composed in the 1670s and first published in 1713.

4. In the paragraphs that follow, De Lolme discusses the controversial question of
whether the representatives of the Commons formed part of England's original constitutional order. He acknowledges the weakness of the Commons within the structure of
medieval government in England but emphasizes how much more authority the Commons then enjoyed in comparison with the other monarchic governments of Europe.

it is from this aera that we are to date the origin of the House of Commons (*a*).

It must be confessed, however, that these Deputies of the People were not, at first, possessed of any considerable authority. They <33> were far from enjoying those extensive privileges which, in these days, constitute the House of Commons a collateral part of the Government: they were in those times called up only to provide for the wants of the King, and approve of the resolutions taken by him and the assembly of the Lords (*b*). But it was nevertheless a great point gained, to have obtained the right of uttering their complaints, assembled in a body and in a legal way—to have acquired, instead of the dangerous resource of insurrections, a lawful and regular mean of influencing the motions of the Government, and thenceforth to have become a part of it. Whatever disadvantage might attend the station at first allotted to the Representatives of the People, it was soon to be compensated by the preponderance the <34> People necessarily acquire, when they are enabled to act and move with method, and especially with concert (*c*).

(*a*) Anno 1295.

(*b*) The end mentioned in the Summons sent to the Lords, was *de arduis negotiis regni tractaturi, & consilium impensuri:* the Summons sent to the Commons was, *ad faciendum & consentiendum.* The power enjoyed by the latter was even inferior to what they might have expected from the Summons sent to them: "In most of the ancient Statutes they are not so much as named; and in several, even when they are mentioned, they are distinguished as petitioners merely, the Assent of the Lords being expressed in contradistinction to the Request of the Commons." See on this subject the Preface to the Collection of the Statutes at large, by Ruffhead, and the authorities quoted therein. [[The first Latin passage means: "Concerning weighty affairs of the kingdom to deliberate and afford counsel"; the second: "To do and consent." De Lolme cites the standard eighteenth-century collection of English legislation edited by Owen Ruffhead, *The Statutes of the Realm, from Magna Charta to the end of the Last Parliament,* which was first published, in eight volumes, in 1769.]]

(*c*) France had indeed also her assemblies of the General Estates of the Kingdom, in the same manner as England had her Parliament; but then it was only the Deputies for the Towns within the particular domain of the Crown, that is, for a very small part of the Nation who, under the name of the *Third Estate,* were admitted in those Estates; and it is easy to conceive that they acquired no great influence in an assembly of Sovereigns who gave the law to their Lord Paramount. Hence, when these disappeared, the maxim became immediately established, *The will of the King is the will of the Law.* In old French, *Qui veut le Roy, si veut la Loy.*

And indeed this privilege of naming Representatives, insignificant as it might then appear, presently manifested itself by the most considerable effects. In spite of his reluctance, and after many evasions unworthy of so great a King, Edward was obliged to confirm the Great Charter; he even confirmed it eleven times in the course of his reign. It was moreover enacted, that whatever should be done contrary to it, should be null and void; that it should be read twice a year in all Cathedrals; and that the penalty of excommunication should be denounced against any one who should presume to violate it (*a*). <35>

At length, he converted into an established law a privilege of which the English had hitherto had only a precarious enjoyment; and, in the statute *de Tallagio non concedendo,* he decreed, that no tax should be laid, nor impost levied, without the joint consent of the Lords and Commons (*b*). A most important Statute this, which, in conjunction with Magna Charta, forms the basis of the English Constitution. If from the latter the English are to date the origin of their liberty, from the former they are to date the establishment of it; and as the Great Charter was the bulwark that protected the freedom of individuals, so was the Statute in question the engine which protected the Charter itself, and by the help of which the People were thenceforth to make legal conquests over the authority of the Crown.

This is the period at which we must stop, in order to take a distant view, and contemplate the different prospect which the rest of Europe then presented. <36>

The efficient causes of slavery were daily operating and gaining strength. The independence of the Nobles on the one hand, the ignorance and weakness of the people on the other, continued to be extreme: the feudal government still continued to diffuse oppression and misery; and such was the confusion of it, that it even took away all hopes of amendment.

(*a*) Confirmationes Chartarum, cap. 2, 3, 4. [[Confirmation of the Charters (1297).]]

(*b*) "Nullum tallagium vel auxilium, per nos, vel haeredes nostros, in regno nostro ponatur seu levetur, sine voluntate & assensu Archiepiscoporum, Episcoporum, Comitum, Baronum, Militum, Burgensium, & aliorum liberorum hom' de regno nostro." Stat. an. 24 Ed. I. [["No tallage or aid shall be taken or levied by us or our heirs in our realm, without the good will and assent of archbishops, bishops, earls, barons, knights, burgesses, and other freemen of the land."]]

France, still bleeding from the extravagance of a Nobility incessantly engaged in groundless wars, either with each other, or with the King, was again desolated by the tyranny of that same Nobility, haughtily jealous of their liberty, or rather of their anarchy (*a*). The people, oppressed by those who ought to have guided and protected them, loaded with insults by those who existed by their labour, revolted on all sides. But their tumultuous insurrections had scarcely any other object than that of giving vent to <37> the anguish with which their hearts were full. They had no thoughts of entering into a general combination; still less of changing the form of the Government, and laying a regular plan of public liberty.

Having never extended their views beyond the fields they cultivated, they had no conception of those different ranks and orders of Men, of those distinct and opposite privileges and prerogatives, which are all necessary ingredients of a free Constitution. Hitherto confined to the same round of rustic employments, they little thought of that complicated fabric, which the more informed themselves cannot but with difficulty comprehend, when, by a concurrence of favourable circumstances, the structure has at length been reared, and stands displayed to their view.

In their simplicity, they saw no other remedy for the national evils, than the general establishment of the Regal power, that is, of the authority of one common uncontrouled Master, and only longed for that time, which, while it gratified their revenge, would mitigate their sufferings, and reduce to the same level both the oppressors and the oppressed.

The Nobility, on the other hand, bent solely on the enjoyment of a momentary independ-<38>ence, irrecoverably lost the affection of the only Men who might in time support them; and equally regardless of the dictates of humanity and of prudence, they did not perceive the gradual and continual advances of the royal authority, which was soon to overwhelm them

---

(*a*) Not contented with oppression, they added insult. "When the Gentility," says Mezeray [[for Mézeray, see above, p. 27, note b, and p. 29, note a]], "pillaged and committed exactions on the peasantry, they called the poor sufferer, in derision, *Jaques bonhomme* (Good man James). This gave rise to a furious sedition, which was called the *Jaquerie*. It began at Beauvais in the year 1357, extending itself into most of the Provinces of France, and was not appeased but by the destruction of part of those unhappy victims, thousands of whom were slaughtered."

all. Already were Normandy, Anjou, Languedoc, and Touraine, re-united
to the Crown: Dauphiny, Champagne, and part of Guienne, were soon to
follow: France was doomed at length to see the reign of Lewis the Eleventh;
to see her general Estates first become useless, and be afterwards abolished.

It was the destiny of Spain also, to behold her several Kingdoms united
under one Head: she was fated to be in time ruled by Ferdinand and Charles
the Fifth (*a*). And Ger-<39>many, where an elective Crown prevented the
re-unions (*b*), was indeed to acquire a few free Cities; but her people, parcelled into so many different dominions, were destined to remain subject
to the arbitrary yoke of such of her different Sovereigns as should be able
to maintain their power and independence. In a word, the feudal tyranny
which overspread the Continent, did not compensate, by any preparation
of distant advantages, the present calamities it caused; nor was it to leave
behind it, as it disappeared, any thing but a more regular kind of Despotism. <40>

But in England, the same feudal system, after having suddenly broken
in like a flood, had deposited, and still continued to deposit, the noble seeds
of the spirit of liberty, union, and sober resistance. So early as the times of

(*a*) Spain was originally divided into twelve Kingdoms, besides Principalities, which
by Treaties, and especially by Conquests, were collected into three Kingdoms; those of
Castile, Aragon, and Granada. Ferdinand the Fifth, King of Aragon, married Isabella,
Queen of Castile; they made a joint Conquest of the Kingdom of Granada, and these
three Kingdoms, thus united, descended, in 1516, to their grandson Charles V. and
formed the Spanish Monarchy. At this aera, the Kings of Spain began to be absolute;
and the States of the Kingdoms of Castile and Leon, "assembled at Toledo, in the month
of November 1539, were the last in which the three orders met, that is, the Grandees,
the Ecclesiastics, and the Deputies of the Towns." *See Ferrera's General History of Spain.*
[[De Lolme refers to *Historia de España* by Juan de Ferreras (1652–1735), which was published in sixteen volumes from 1700 to 1727.]]

(*b*) The Kingdom of France, as it stood under Hugh Capet and his next Successors,
may, with a great degree of exactness, be compared with the German Empire, as it exists
at present, and also existed at that time: but the Imperial Crown of Germany having,
through a conjunction of circumstances, continued elective, the German Emperors,
though vested with more high-sounding prerogatives than even the Kings of France,
laboured under very essential disadvantages: they could not pursue a plan of aggrandisement with the same steadiness as a line of hereditary Sovereigns usually do; and the
right to elect them, enjoyed by the greater Princes of Germany, procured a sufficient
power to these, to protect themselves, as well as the lesser Lords, against the power of
the Crown.

Edward, the tide was seen gradually to subside; the laws which protect the person and property of the individual, began to make their appearance; that admirable Constitution, the result of a threefold power, insensibly arose (*a*); and the eye might even then discover the verdant summits of that fortunate region that was destined to be the seat of Philosophy and Liberty, which are inseparable companions. <41>

(*a*) "Now, in my opinion," says Philipe de Comines, in times not much posterior to those of Edward the First, and with the simplicity of the language of his times, "among all the Sovereignties I know in the world, that in which the public good is best attended to, and the least violence exercised on the people, is that of England." *Memoires de Comines,* tom. I. lib. v. chap. xix. [[For *Mémoires de Comines,* see above, p. 37, note a.]]

The Subject continued.

The Representatives of the Nation, and of the whole Nation, were now admitted into Parliament: the great point therefore was gained, that was one day to procure them the great influence which they at present possess; and the subsequent reigns afford continual instances of its successive growth.

Under Edward the Second, the Commons began to annex petitions to the bills by which they granted subsidies: this was the dawn of their legislative authority. Under Edward the Third, they declared they would not, in future, acknowledge any law to which they had not expressly assented. Soon after this, they exerted a privilege in which consists, at this time, one of the great balances of the Constitution: they impeached, and procured to be condemned, some of the first Ministers of State.[1] Under Henry the Fourth, they refused to grant subsidies before an answer had been given to their petitions. In a word, every event of any consequence was attended with an increase of the power of the Commons; increases indeed but <42> slow and gradual, but which were peaceably and legally effected, and were the more fit to engage the attention of the People, and coalesce with the ancient principles of the Constitution.

Under Henry the Fifth, the Nation was entirely taken up with its wars against France; and in the reign of Henry the Sixth began the fatal contests between the houses of York and Lancaster. The noise of arms alone was

---

1. De Lolme refers to the parliamentary impeachment and conviction of Lord Latimer in 1377, which was conventionally treated as the first recorded instance of the impeachment process.

now to be heard: during the silence of the laws already in being, no thought was had of enacting new ones; and for thirty years together, England presents a wide scene of slaughter and desolation.

At length, under Henry the Seventh, who, by his intermarriage with the house of York, united the pretensions of the two families, a general peace was re-established, and the prospect of happier days seemed to open on the Nation. But the long and violent agitation under which it had laboured, was to be followed by a long and painful recovery. Henry, mounting the throne with sword in hand, and in great measure as a Conqueror, had promises to fulfil, as well as injuries to avenge. In the mean time, the People, wearied out by the calamities they had undergone, and longing only <43> for repose, abhorred even the idea of resistance; so that the remains of an almost exterminated Nobility beheld themselves left defenceless, and abandoned to the mercy of the Sovereign.

The Commons, on the other hand, accustomed to act only a second part in public affairs, and finding themselves bereft of those who had hitherto been their Leaders, were more than ever afraid to form, of themselves, an opposition. Placed immediately, as well as the Lords, under the eye of the King, they beheld themselves exposed to the same dangers. Like them, therefore, they purchased their personal security at the expence of public liberty; and in reading the history of the two first Kings of the house of Tudor, we imagine ourselves reading the relation given by Tacitus, of Tiberius and the Roman Senate (*a*).

The time, therefore, seemed to be arrived, at which England must submit, in its turn, to the fate of the other Nations of Europe. All those barriers which it had raised for the defence of its liberty, seemed to have only been able to postpone the inevitable effects of Power. <44>

But the remembrance of their ancient laws, of that great charter so often and so solemnly confirmed, was too deeply impressed on the minds of the English, to be effaced by transitory evils. Like a deep and extensive ocean, which preserves an equability of temperature amidst all the vicissitudes of

---

(*a*) *Quanto quis illustrior, tanto magis falsi ac festinantes.* [["The more exalted the personage, the grosser his hypocrisy and his haste." De Lolme cites the *Annals,* book I, chapter 7, of the Roman historian Publius, or Gaius, Cornelius Tacitus (ca. 56–ca. 117 C.E.).]]

seasons, England still retained those principles of liberty which were so universally diffused through all orders of the People, and they required only a proper opportunity to manifest themselves.

England, besides, still continued to possess the immense advantage of being one undivided State.

Had it been, like France, divided into several distinct dominions, it would also have had several National Assemblies. These Assemblies, being convened at different times and places, for this and other reasons, never could have acted in concert; and the power of withholding subsidies, a power so important when it is that of disabling the Sovereign and binding him down to inaction, would then have only been the destructive privilege of irritating a Master who would have easily found means to obtain supplies from other quarters.

The different Parliaments or Assemblies of these several States, having thenceforth no <45> means of recommending themselves to their Sovereign but their forwardness in complying with his demands, would have vied with each other in granting what it would not only have been fruitless, but even highly dangerous, to refuse. The King would not have failed soon to demand, as a tribute, a gift he must have been confident to obtain; and the outward form of consent would have been left to the People only as an additional means of oppressing them without danger.

But the King of England continued, even in the time of the Tudors, to have but one Assembly before which he could lay his wants, and apply for relief. How great soever the increase of his power was, a single Parliament alone could furnish him with the means of exercising it; and whether it was that the members of this Parliament entertained a deep sense of their advantages, or whether private interest exerted itself in aid of patriotism, they at all times vindicated the right of granting, or rather refusing, subsidies; and, amidst the general wreck of every thing they ought to have held dear, they at least clung obstinately to the plank which was destined to prove the instrument of their preservation. <46>

Under Edward the Sixth, the absurd tyrannical laws against High Treason, instituted under Henry the Eighth, his predecessor, were abolished.[2]

2. The Treasons Act of 1547, passed in the first year of Edward VI's reign, repealed

But this young and virtuous Prince having soon passed away, the blood-thirsty Mary astonished the world with cruelties, which nothing but the fanaticism of a part of her subjects could have enabled her to execute.

Under the long and brilliant reign of Elizabeth, England began to breathe anew; and the Protestant religion, being seated once more on the throne, brought with it some more freedom and toleration.

The Star-Chamber, that effectual instrument of the tyranny of the two Henries, yet continued to subsist; the inquisitorial tribunal of the High Commission was even instituted; and the yoke of arbitrary power lay still heavy on the subject. But the general affection of the people for a Queen whose former misfortunes had created such a general concern, the imminent dangers which England escaped, and the extreme glory attending that reign, lessened the sense of such exertions of authority as would, in these days, appear the height of Tyranny, and served at that time to justify, as they still do excuse, a Princess <47> whose great talents, though not her principles of government, render her worthy of being ranked among the greatest Sovereigns.

Under the reign of the Stuarts, the Nation began to recover from its long lethargy. James the First, a prince rather imprudent than tyrannical, drew back the veil which had hitherto disguised so many usurpations, and made an ostentatious display of what his predecessors had been contented to enjoy.

He was incessantly asserting, that the authority of Kings was not to be controuled, any more than that of God himself. Like Him, they were om-nipotent; and those privileges to which the people so clamorously laid claim, as their inheritance and birthright, were no more than an effect of the grace and toleration of his royal ancestors (*a*).

---

several Henrician laws granting the crown new legal powers, including provisions of the 1534 statute concerning high treason.

(*a*) See his Declaration made in Parliament, in the years 1610 and 1621. [[De Lolme refers to two extended criticisms of parliamentary deliberations by James I that extolled the divine origins and power of kings and gained reputation as unqualified statements of royal absolutism. See "Speech to Parliament of . . . 1610" and "His Majesties Dec-laration, Touching his Proceedings in the Late . . . Parliament," in King James VI and I, *Political Writings,* ed. Johann P. Sommerville (Cambridge: Cambridge University Press, 1994), 179–203, 250–67.]]

Those principles, hitherto only silently adopted in the Cabinet, and in the Courts of Justice, had maintained their ground in consequence of this very obscurity. Being now announced from the Throne, and resounded <48> from the pulpit, they spread an universal alarm. Commerce, besides, with its attendant arts, and above all that of printing, diffused more salutary notions throughout all orders of the people; a new light began to rise upon the Nation; and that spirit of opposition frequently displayed itself in this reign, to which the English Monarchs had not, for a long time past, been accustomed.

But the storm, which was only gathering in clouds during the reign of James, began to mutter under Charles the First, his successor; and the scene which opened to view, on the accession of that Prince, presented the most formidable aspect.

The notions of religion, by a singular concurrence, united with the love of liberty: the same spirit which had made an attack on the established faith, now directed itself to politics: the royal prerogatives were brought under the same examination as the doctrines of the Church of Rome had been submitted to; and as a superstitious religion had proved unable to support the test, so neither could an authority pretended unlimited, be expected to bear it.

The Commons, on the other hand, were recovering from the astonishment into which <49> the extinction of the power of the Nobles had, at first, thrown them. Taking a view of the state of the Nation, and of their own, they became sensible of their whole strength; they determined to make use of it, and to repress a power which seemed, for so long a time, to have levelled every barrier. Finding among themselves Men of the greatest capacity, they undertook that important task with method and by constitutional means; and thus had Charles to cope with a whole Nation put in motion and directed by an assembly of Statesmen.

And here we must observe how different were the effects produced in England, by the annihilation of the power of the Nobility, from those which the same event had produced in France.

In France, where, in consequence of the division of the People and of the exorbitant power of the Nobles, the people were accounted nothing, when the Nobles themselves were suppressed, the work was compleated.

In England, on the contrary, where the Nobles ever vindicated the rights of the People equally with their own,—in England, where the People had successively acquired <50> most effectual means of influencing the motions of the Government, and above all were undivided, when the Nobles themselves were cast to the ground, the body of the People stood firm, and maintained the public liberty.

The unfortunate Charles, however, was totally ignorant of the dangers which surrounded him. Seduced by the example of the other Sovereigns of Europe, he was not aware how different, in reality, his situation was from theirs: he had the imprudence to exert with rigour an authority which he had no ultimate resources to support: an union was at last effected in the Nation; and he saw his enervated prerogatives dissipated with a breath (*a*). By the famous act, called the Petition of <51> Right, and another posterior Act,[3] to both which he assented, the compulsory loans and taxes, disguised under the name of *Benevolences,* were declared to be contrary to law; arbitrary imprisonments, and the exercise of the martial law, were abolished; the Court of High Commission, and the Star-Chamber, were suppressed

(*a*) It might here be objected, that when, under Charles the First, the regal power was obliged to submit to the power of the People, the king possessed other dominions besides England, viz. Scotland and Ireland, and therefore seemed to enjoy the same advantage as the Kings of France, that of reigning over a divided Empire or Nation. But, to this it is to be answered, that, at the time we mention, Ireland, scarcely civilized, only increased the necessities, and consequently the dependance, of the King; while Scotland, through the conjunction of peculiar circumstances, had thrown off her obedience. And though those two States, even at present, bear no proportion to the compact body of the Kingdom of England, and seem never to have been able, by their union with it, to procure to the King any dangerous resources, yet, the circumstances which took place in both at the time of the Revolution, or since, sufficiently prove that it was no unfavourable circumstance to English liberty, that the great crisis of the reign of Charles the First, and the great advance which the Constitution was to make at that time, should precede the period at which the King of England might have been able to call in the assistance of two other Kingdoms.

3. The 1628 Petition of Right, promulgated by Parliament, technically was not an act or statute, but a statement of liberties that the king's current policies violated. The "posterior Act" refers to several statutes enacted in 1641–42 in the years immediately prior to the outbreak of civil war.

(*a*); and the Constitution, freed from the apparatus of despotic powers with which <52> the Tudors had obscured it, was restored to its ancient lustre. Happy had been the People if their Leaders, after having executed so noble a work, had contented themselves with the glory of being the benefactors of their Country. Happy had been the King, if obliged at last to submit, his submission had been sincere, and if he had become sufficiently sensible, that the only resource he had left was the affection of his subjects.

But Charles knew not how to survive the loss of a power he had conceived to be indisputable: he could not reconcile himself to limitations and restraints so injurious, according to his notions, to sovereign authority. His discourse and conduct betrayed his secret designs; distrust took possession of the Nation; certain ambitious persons availed themselves of it to promote their own views; and the storm, which seemed to have blown over, burst forth anew. The contending fanaticism of persecuting sects, joined in the conflict between regal haughtiness and the ambition of individuals; the tempest blew from every point of the compass; the Constitution was rent asunder, and Charles exhibited in his fall an awful example to the Universe. <53>

The Royal power being thus annihilated, the English made fruitless attempts to substitute a republican Government in its stead. "It was a curious spectacle," says Montesquieu, "to behold the vain efforts of the English to establish among themselves a Democracy."[4] Subjected, at first, to the power of the principal Leaders in the Long Parliament, they saw that power expire, only to pass, without bounds, into the hands of a Protector. They saw it afterwards parcelled out among the Chiefs of different bodies of troops; and thus shifting without end from one kind of subjection to another, they

---

(*a*) The Star-Chamber differed from all the other Courts of Law in this: the latter were governed only by the common law, or immemorial custom, and Acts of Parliament; whereas the former often admitted for law the proclamations of the King in Council, and grounded its judgments upon them. The abolition of this Tribunal, therefore, was justly looked upon as a great victory over regal Authority. [[De Lolme's characterization here is too casual. Star Chamber was not the only court in England that did not adhere to common law customs and procedures; however, it was distinctive in its relation to the royal prerogative and the perceived threats of monarchic tyranny. The legislation abolishing the court was enacted in 1641.]]

4. Montesquieu's comments appeared in his 1748 *The Spirit of the Laws,* book 3, chapter 3.

were at length convinced, that an attempt to establish liberty in a great Nation, by making the people interfere in the common business of Government, is of all attempts the most chimerical; that the authority *of all,* with which Men are amused, is in reality no more than the authority of a few powerful individuals who divide the Republic among themselves; and they at last rested in the bosom of the only Constitution which is fit for a great State and a free People; I mean that in which a chosen number deliberate, and a single hand executes; but in which, at the same time, the public satisfaction <54> is rendered, by the general relation and arrangement of things, a necessary condition of the duration of Government.

Charles the Second, therefore, was called over; and he experienced, on the part of the people, that enthusiasm of affection which usually attends the return from a long alienation. He could not however bring himself to forgive them the inexpiable crime of which he looked upon them to have been guilty. He saw with the deepest concern that they still entertained their former notions with regard to the nature of the royal prerogative; and, bent upon the recovery of the ancient powers of the Crown, he only waited for an opportunity to break those promises which had procured his restoration.

But the very eagerness of his measures frustrated their success. His dangerous alliances on the Continent, and the extravagant wars in which he involved England, joined to the frequent abuse he made of his authority, betrayed his designs. The eyes of the Nation were soon opened, and saw into his projects; when, convinced at length that nothing but fixed and irresistible bounds can be an effectual check on the views and efforts of Power, they resolved <55> finally to take away those remnants of despotism which still made a part of the regal prerogative.

The military services due to the Crown, the remains of the ancient feudal tenures, had been already abolished: the laws against heretics were now repealed; the Statute for holding parliaments once at least in three years was enacted; the *Habeas Corpus* Act, that barrier of the Subject's personal safety, was established; and, such was the patriotism of the Parliaments, that it was under a King the most destitute of principle, that liberty received its most efficacious supports.[5]

5. De Lolme refers to the following measures: the 1660 statute for the Abolition of

At length, on the death of Charles, began a reign which affords a most exemplary lesson both to Kings and People. James the Second, a prince of a more rigid disposition, though of a less comprehensive understanding, than his late brother, pursued still more openly the project, which had already proved so fatal to his family. He would not see that the great alterations which had successively been effected in the Constitution, rendered the execution of it daily more and more impracticable: he imprudently suffered himself to be exasperated at a resistance he was in no condition to overcome; <56> and, hurried away by a spirit of despotism and a monkish zeal, he ran headlong against the rock which was to wreck his authority.

He not only used, in his declarations, the alarming expressions of Absolute Power and Unlimited Obedience—he not only usurped to himself a right to dispense with the laws; but moreover sought to convert that destructive pretension to the destruction of those very laws which were held most dear by the Nation, by endeavouring to abolish a religion for which they had suffered the greatest calamities, in order to establish on its ruins a mode of faith which repeated Acts of the Legislature had proscribed; and proscribed, not because it tended to establish in England the doctrines of Transubstantiation and Purgatory, doctrines in themselves of no political moment, but because the unlimited power of the Sovereign had always been made one of its principal tenets.

To endeavour therefore to revive such a Religion, was not only a violation of the laws, but was, by one enormous violation, to pave the way for others of a still more alarming nature. Hence the English, seeing that their liberty was attacked even in its first principles, had recourse to that remedy which reason and na-<57>ture point out to the People, when he who ought to be the guardian of the laws becomes their destroyer: they withdrew the allegiance which they had sworn to James, and thought themselves absolved from their oath to a King who himself disregarded the oath he had made to his People.

But, instead of a revolution like that which dethroned Charles the First, which was effected by a great effusion of blood, and threw the state into a

---

Military Tenures, the 1672 Declaration of Indulgence, the 1664 Triennial Act, and the 1679 Habeas Corpus Amendment Act.

general and terrible convulsion, the dethronement of James proved a matter of short and easy operation. In consequence of the progressive information of the People, and the certainty of the principles which now directed the Nation, the whole were unanimous. All the ties by which the
People were bound to the throne, were broken, as it were, by one single
shock; and James, who, the moment before, was a Monarch surrounded
by subjects, became at once a simple individual in the midst of the Nation.

That which contributes, above all, to distinguish this event as singular
in the annals of Mankind, is the moderation, I may even say, the legality
which accompanied it. As if to dethrone a King who sought to set himself
<58> above the Laws, had been a natural consequence of, and provided for
by, the principles of Government, every thing remained in its place; the
Throne was declared vacant, and a new line of succession was established.[6]

Nor was this all; care was had to repair the breaches that had been made
in the Constitution, as well as to prevent new ones; and advantage was taken
of the rare opportunity of entering into an original and express compact
between King and People.

An Oath was required of the new King, more precise than had been
taken by his predecessors; and it was consecrated as a perpetual formula of
such oaths. It was determined, that to impose taxes without the consent of
Parliament, as well as to keep up a standing army in time of peace, are
contrary to law. The power which the Crown had constantly claimed, of
dispensing with the laws, was abolished. It was enacted, that the subject,
of whatever rank or degree, had a right to present petitions to the King (a).

6. De Lolme's characterization of the removal of James II follows the purposefully
moderate language of the 1688/89 Bill of Rights, which similarly emphasized the vacancy
of the crown that resulted when James II "abdicated the government."

(a) The Lords and Commons, previous to the Coronation of King William and
Queen Mary, had framed a Bill which contained a declaration of the rights which they
claimed in behalf of the People, and was in consequence called the *Bill of Rights*. This
Bill contained the Articles above, as well as some others, and having received afterwards
the Royal assent, became an Act of Parliament, under the title of *An Act declaring the
Rights and Liberties of the Subject, and settling the Succession of the Crown.*—A. 1 William
and Mary, Sess. 2. Cap. 2. [[As a measure adopted by the Lords and Commons in the
period after the "abdication" of James II but before the coronation of William and Mary,
the 1688/89 Bill of Rights could not receive royal assent and therefore did not qualify as

Lastly, <59> the key-stone was put to the arch, by the final establishment of the Liberty of the Press[7] (*a*).

The Revolution of 1689 is therefore the third grand aera in the history of the Constitution of England. The great charter had marked out the limits within which the Royal authority ought to be confined; some outworks were raised in the reign of Edward the First; but it was at the Revolution that the circumvallation was compleated.

It was at this aera, that the true principles of civil society were fully established. By the expulsion of a King who had violated his oath, the doctrine of Resistance, that ultimate resource of an oppressed People, was confirmed beyond a doubt. By the exclusion given to a <60> family hereditarily despotic, it was finally determined, that Nations are not the property of Kings. The principles of Passive Obedience, the Divine and indefeasible Right of Kings, in a word, the whole scaffolding of false and superstitious notions by which the Royal authority had till then been supported, fell to the ground, and in the room of it were substituted the more solid and durable foundations of the love of order, and a sense of the necessity of civil government among Mankind.

---

an Act of Parliament. Its subsequent inclusion in the 1689 statute "settling the succession of the crown" served to overcome this legal obstacle. The Bill of Rights, to which De Lolme refers frequently, served as a constitutional cornerstone of the Glorious Revolution, which transferred the crown from the Catholic James II to the Protestant William and Mary.]]

(*a*) The liberty of the press was, properly speaking, established only four years afterwards, in consequence of the refusal which the Parliament made at that time to continue any longer the restrictions which had before been set upon it. [[Liberty of the press was not directly treated in any of the legislation enacted at the time of the Glorious Revolution. De Lolme's note refers to the parliamentary decision of 1695 not to renew the Licensing Act of 1685 that guided the system of prepublication censorship of printed materials. De Lolme's dating of the development ("only four years afterwards") appears to confuse the final lapsing of the Licensing Act in 1695 with the 1692 statute that renewed the act for a two-year period.]]

7. De Lolme returns to the topic of liberty of the press in book 2, chapter 12, where he explains at length the novelty and importance of this form of public freedom.

Of the Legislative Power.

In almost all the States of Europe, the will of the Prince holds the place of law; and custom has so confounded the matter of right with the matter of fact, that their Lawyers generally represent the legislative authority as essentially attached to the character of King; and the plenitude of his power seems to them necessarily to flow from the very definition of his title. <61>

The English, placed in more favourable circumstances, have judged differently: they could not believe that the destiny of Mankind ought to depend on a play of words, and on scholastic subtilties; they have therefore annexed no other idea to the word *King,* or *Roy,* a word known also to their laws, than that which the Latins annexed to the word *Rex,* and the northern Nations to that of *Cyning.*

In limiting therefore the power of their King, they have acted more consistently with the etymology of the word; they have acted also more consistently with reason, in not leaving the laws to the disposal of the person who is already invested with the public power of the State, that is, of the person who lies under the greatest and most important temptations to set himself above them.

The basis of the English Constitution, the capital principle on which all others depend, is that the Legislative power belongs to Parliament alone; that is to say, the power of establishing laws, and of abrogating, changing, or explaining them.

The constituent parts of Parliament are the King, the House of Lords, and the House of Commons.

The House of Commons, otherwise the Assembly of the Representatives of the Nation, <62> is composed of the Deputies of the different Counties, each of which sends two; of the Deputies of certain Towns, of which London, including Westminster and Southwark, sends eight,— other Towns, two or one: and of the Deputies of the Universities of Oxford and Cambridge, each of which sends two.

Lastly, since the Act of Union,[1] Scotland sends forty-five Deputies; who, added to those just mentioned, make up the whole number of five hundred and fifty-eight. Those Deputies, though separately elected, do not solely represent the Town or County that sends them, as is the case with the Deputies of the United Provinces of the Netherlands, or of the Swiss Cantons; but, when they are once admitted, they represent the whole body of the Nation.

The qualifications required for being a Member of the House of Commons are, for representing a County, to be born a subject of Great Britain, and to be possessed of a landed estate of six hundred pounds a year; and of three hundred, for representing a Town, or Borough.

The qualifications required for being an elector in a County, are, to be possessed, in that County, of a Freehold of forty shillings <63> a year (*a*). With regard to electors in Towns or Boroughs, they must be Freemen of them; a word which now signifies certain qualifications expressed in the particular Charters.

When the King has determined to assemble a Parliament, he sends an order for that purpose to the Lord Chancellor, who, after receiving the same, sends a writ under the great seal of England to the Sheriff of every County, directing him to take the necessary steps for the election of Members for the County, and the Towns and Boroughs contained in it. Three days after the reception of the writ, the Sheriff must, in his turn, send his precept to the Magistrates of the Towns and Boroughs, to order them to make their

---

(*a*) This Freehold must have been possessed by the elector one whole year at least before the time of election, except it has devolved to him by inheritance, by marriage, by a last will, or by promotion to an office.

1. The 1707 Act of Union created the "Parliament of Great Britain," which replaced the previously independent parliaments of England and Scotland.

election within eight days after the reception of the precept, giving four days notice of the same. And the Sheriff himself must proceed to the election for the County, not sooner than ten days after the receipt of the writ, nor later than sixteen.

The principal precautions taken by the law, to insure the freedom of elections, are, <64> that any Candidate, who after the date of the writ, or even after the vacancy, shall have given entertainments to the electors of a place, or to any of them, in order to his being elected, shall be incapable of serving for that place in Parliament. That if any person gives, or promises to give, any money, employment, or reward, to any voter, in order to influence his vote, he, as well as the voter himself, shall be condemned to pay a fine of five hundred pounds, and for ever disqualified to vote and hold any office in any corporation; the faculty however being reserved to both, of procuring their indemnity for their own offence, by discovering some other offender of the same kind.

It has been moreover established, that no Lord of Parliament, or Lord Lieutenant of a County, has any right to interfere in the elections of members; that any officer of the excise, customs, &c. who shall presume to intermeddle in elections, by influencing any voter to give or withhold his vote, shall forfeit one hundred pounds, and be disabled to hold any office. Lastly, all soldiers quartered in a place where an election is to be made, must move from it, at least one day before the election, to the distance of two miles or more, and re-<65>turn not till one day after the election is finished.

The House of Peers, or Lords, is composed of the Lords Spiritual, who are the Archbishops of Canterbury and of York, and the twenty-four Bishops; and of the Lords Temporal, whatever may be their respective titles, such as Dukes, Marquises, Earls, &c.

Lastly, the King is the third constitutive part of Parliament: it is even he alone who can convoke it; and he alone can dissolve, or prorogue it. The effect of a dissolution is, that from that moment the Parliament completely ceases to exist; the commission given to the Members by their Constituents is at an end; and whenever a new meeting of Parliament shall happen, they must be elected anew. A prorogation is an adjournment to a term appointed by the King; till which the existence of Parliament is simply interrupted, and the function of the Deputies suspended.

When the Parliament meets, whether it be by virtue of a new summons, or whether, being composed of Members formerly elected, it meets again at the expiration of the term for which it had been prorogued, the King either goes to it in person, invested with the insignia of his dignity, or appoints proper persons to <66> represent him on that occasion, and opens the session by laying before the Parliament the state of the public affairs, and inviting them to take them into consideration. This presence of the King, either real or represented, is absolutely requisite at the first meeting; it is it which gives life to the Legislative Bodies, and puts them in action.

The King, having concluded his declaration, withdraws. The Parliament, which is then legally intrusted with the care of the National concerns, enters upon its functions, and continues to exist till it is prorogued, or dissolved. The House of Commons, and that of Peers, assemble separately: the former, under the presidence of the Lord Chancellor; the latter, under that of their Speaker: and both separately adjourn to such days as they respectively think proper to appoint.

As each of the two Houses has a negative on the propositions made by the other, and there is, consequently, no danger of their encroaching on each other's rights, nor on those of the King, who has likewise his negative upon them both, any question judged by them conducive to the public good, without exception, may be made the subject of their respec-<67>tive deliberations. Such are, for instance, new limitations, or extensions, to be given to the authority of the King; the establishing of new laws, or making changes in those already in being. Lastly, the different kinds of public provisions, or establishments, the various abuses of administration, and their remedies, become, in every Session, the object of the attention of Parliament.

Here, however, an important observation must be made. All Bills for granting Money must have their beginning in the House of Commons: the Lords cannot take this object into their consideration but in consequence of a bill presented to them by the latter; and the Commons have at all times been so anxiously tenacious of this privilege, that they have never suffered the Lords even to make any change in the Money Bills which they have sent to them; and the Lords are expected simply and solely either to accept or reject them.

This excepted, every Member, in each House, may propose whatever question he thinks proper. If, after being considered, the matter is found to deserve attention, the person who made the proposition, usually with some others adjoined to him, is desired to set it down in writing. If, after more complete discussions of the <68> subject, the proposition is carried in the affirmative, it is sent to the other House, that they may, in their turn, take it into consideration. If the other House reject the Bill, it remains without any effect: if they agree to it, nothing remains wanting to its complete establishment, but the Royal Assent.

When there is no business that requires immediate dispatch, the King usually waits till the end of the Session, or at least till a certain number of bills are ready for him, before he declares his royal pleasure. When the time is come, the King goes to Parliament in the same state with which he opened it; and while he is seated on the Throne, a Clerk, who has a list of the Bills, gives or refuses, as he reads, the Royal Assent.

When the Royal Assent is given to a public Bill, the Clerk says, *le Roy le veut.*[2] If the bill be a private Bill, he says, *soit fait comme il est désiré.*[3] If the Bill has subsidies for its object, he says, *le Roy remercie ses loyaux Subjects, accepte leur bénévolence, & aussi le veut.*[4] Lastly, if the King does not think proper to assent to the Bill, the Clerk says, *le Roy s'advisera;*[5] which is a mild way of giving a refusal.

It is, however, pretty singular, that the King of England should make use of the French <69> language to declare his intentions to his Parliament. This custom was introduced at the Conquest (*a*), and has been continued,

---

(*a*) William the Conqueror added to the other changes he introduced, the abolition of the English language in all public, as well as judicial, transactions, and substituted to it the French that was spoke in his time: hence the number of old French words that are met with in the style of the English laws. It was only under Edward III, that the English language began to be re-established in the Courts of Justice. [[De Lolme refers to a statute of 1356, enacted in the reign of Edward III, that replaced French with English as the language for pleadings in court and with Latin as the language for written court records.]]

2. "The king wills it."

3. "Let it be as it is desired."

4. "The king thanks his loyal subjects, accepts their benevolence, and also wills it."

5. "The king will consider it."

like other matters of form, which sometimes subsist for ages after the real substance of things has been altered; and Judge Blackstone expresses himself, on this subject in the following words. "A badge, it must be owned (now the only one remaining) of Conquest; and which one would wish to see fall into total oblivion, unless it be reserved as a solemn memento to remind us that our liberties are mortal, having once been destroyed by a foreign force."[6]

When the King has declared his different intentions, he prorogues the Parliament. Those Bills which he has rejected, remain without force: those to which he has assented, become the expression of the will of the highest power acknowledged in England: they have the same binding force as the *Edits enrégistrés* have <70> in France (*a*), and as the *Populiscita* had in an-

(*a*) They call in France, *Edits enrégistrés,* those Edicts of the King which have been registered in the Court of Parliament. The word Parliament does not however express in France, as it does in England, the Assembly of the Estates of the Kingdom. The French *Parlemens* are only Courts of Justice: that of Paris was instituted in the same manner, and for the same purposes, as the *Aula Regis* was afterwards in England, viz. for the administration of public Justice, and for deciding the differences between the King and his Barons: it was in consequence of the Judgments awarded by that Court, that the King proceeded to seize the dominions of those Lords or Princes against whom a sentence had been passed, and when he was able to effect this, united them to the Crown. The *Parliament* of Paris, as do the other Courts of Law, grounds its judgments upon the *Edits* or *Ordonnances* of the King, when it has once registered them. When those *Ordonnances* are looked upon as grievous to the Subject, the Parliament refuses to register them: but this they do not from any pretension they have to a share in the Legislative authority; they only object that they are not satisfied that the *Ordonnance* before them is really the will of the King, and then proceed to make remonstrances against it: sometimes the King defers to these; or, if he is resolved to put an end to all opposition, he comes in person to the *Parliament,* there holds what they call *un Lit de Justice,* declares that the *Ordonnance* before them is actually his will, and orders the proper Officer to register it. [[De Lolme here distinguishes the different functions and authority exercised by the institution named "Parliament" in England and in France. The French "Parlements" functioned primarily as judicial bodies. The capacity of the Parliament of Paris to criticize and delay the official registration of proposed royal legislation was not to be confused with the "share in the Legislative authority" enjoyed by the two houses of Parliament in England. The "Lit de Justice" (literally, "Bed of Justice") denoted the session of the Parlement of Paris, under the presidency of the king, for the registration of royal edicts.]]

6. Blackstone's comments appeared in his chapter "Of the Parliament" in William Blackstone, *Commentaries on the Laws of England,* 4 vols. (1765–69), 1:177. De Lolme's own account of Parliament's composition and procedures drew heavily on this chapter.

cient Rome:[7] in a word, they are LAWS. And, though each of the constituent parts of the Parliament might, at first, have prevented the existence
of those laws, the united will of all the Three is now necessary to repeal
them. <71>

7. *Populiscita* (or "decrees of the people") was not a standard term of Roman law.
De Lolme presumably refers to legislation approved by any one of Rome's popular assemblies (*comitia curiata, comitia centuriata, comitia tributa*), in contradistinction to the
plebiscitum (or "decrees of the plebs") adopted by the *concilium plebis.*

༄ CHAPTER V ༄

Of the Executive Power.

When the Parliament is prorogued or dissolved, it ceases to exist; but its laws still continue to be in force: the King remains charged with the execution of them, and is supplied with the necessary power for that purpose.

It is however to be observed that, though in his political capacity of one of the constituent parts of the Parliament, that is, with regard to the share allotted to him in the legislative authority, the King is undoubtedly Sovereign, and only needs alledge his will when he gives or refuses his assent to the bills presented to him; yet, in the exercise of his powers of Government, he is no more than a Magistrate, and the laws, whether those that existed before him, or those to which, by his assent, he has given being, must direct his conduct, and bind him equally with his subjects. <72>

The first prerogative of the King, in his capacity of Supreme Magistrate, has for its object the administration of Justice.

1°. He is the source of all judicial power in the State; he is the Chief of all the Courts of Law, and the Judges are only his Substitutes; every thing is transacted in his name; the Judgments must be with his Seal, and are executed by his Officers.

2°. By a fiction of the law, he is looked upon as the universal proprietor of the kingdom; he is in consequence deemed directly concerned in all offences; and for that reason prosecutions are to be carried on, in his name, in the Courts of law.

3°. He can pardon offences, that is, remit the punishment that has been awarded in consequence of his prosecution.

II. The second prerogative of the King, is, to be the *fountain of honour,* that is, the distributor of titles and dignities: he creates the Peers of the realm, as well as bestows the different degrees of inferior Nobility. He more-over disposes of the different offices, either in the Courts of law, or elsewhere.

III. The King is the superintendent of Commerce; he has the prerogative of regulating weights and measures; he alone can coin money, and can give a currency to foreign coin. <73>

IV. He is the Supreme head of the Church. In this capacity, he appoints the Bishops, and the two Archbishops; and he alone can convene the Assembly of the Clergy. This Assembly is formed, in England, on the model of the Parliament: the Bishops form the upper House; Deputies from the Dioceses, and from the several Chapters, form the lower House: the assent of the King is likewise necessary to the validity of their Acts, or Canons; and the King can prorogue, or dissolve, the Convocation.

V. He is, in right of his Crown, the Generalissmo of all sea or land forces whatever; he alone can levy troops, equip fleets, build fortresses, and fills all the posts in them.

VI. He is, with regard to foreign Nations, the representative, and the depositary, of all the power and collective majesty of the Nation; he sends and receives ambassadors; he contracts alliances; and has the prerogative of declaring war, and of making peace, on whatever conditions he thinks proper.

VII. In fine, what seems to carry so many powers to the height, is, its being a fundamental maxim, that THE KING CAN DO NO WRONG: which does not signify, however, that the King has not the power of doing ill, or, as it was pretended by certain persons in former <74> times, that every thing he did was lawful; but only that he is above the reach of all Courts of law whatever, and that his person is sacred and inviolable.

The Boundaries which the Constitution has set to the Royal Prerogative.

In reading the foregoing enumeration of the powers with which the laws of England have intrusted the King, we are at a loss to reconcile them with the idea of a Monarchy, which, we are told, is limited. The King not only unites in himself all the branches of the Executive power,—he not only disposes, without controul, of the whole military power in the State,—but he is moreover, it seems, Master of the Law itself, since he calls up, and dismisses, at his will, the Legislative Bodies. We find him therefore, at first sight, invested with all the prerogatives that ever were claimed by the most absolute Monarchs; and we are at a loss to find that liberty which the English seem so confident they possess.

But the Representatives of the people still have, and that is saying enough, they still have in their hands, now that the Constitution is <75> fully established, the same powerful weapon which has enabled their ancestors to establish it. It is still from their liberality alone that the King can obtain subsidies; and in these days, when every thing is rated by pecuniary estimation, when gold is become the great moving spring of affairs, it may be safely affirmed, that he who depends on the will of other men, with regard to so important an article, is, whatever his power may be in other respects, in a state of real dependence.

This is the case of the King of England. He has, in that capacity, and without the grant of his people, scarcely any revenue. A few hereditary duties on the exportation of wool, which (since the establishment of manufactures) are become tacitly extinguished; a branch of the excise, which,

64

under Charles the Second, was annexed to the Crown as an indemnification for the military services it gave up, and which, under George the First, has been fixed to seven thousand pounds; a duty of two shillings on every ton of wine imported; the wrecks of ships of which the owners remain unknown; whales and sturgeons thrown on the coast; swans swimming on public rivers; and a few other feudal relics, now compose the whole appropriated revenue of the King, and <76> are all that remains of the ancient inheritance of the Crown.

The King of England, therefore, has the prerogative of commanding armies, and equipping fleets—but without the concurrence of his Parliament he cannot maintain them. He can bestow places and employments— but without his Parliament he cannot pay the salaries attending on them. He can declare war,—but without his Parliament it is impossible for him to carry it on. In a word, the Royal Prerogative, destitute as it is of the power of imposing taxes, is like a vast body, which cannot of itself accomplish its motions; or, if you please, it is like a ship completely equipped, but from which the Parliament can at pleasure draw off the water, and leave it aground,—and also set it afloat again, by granting subsides.

And indeed we see, that, since the establishment of this right of the Representatives of the People, to grant, or refuse, subsidies to the Crown, their other privileges have been continually increasing. Though these Representatives were not, in the beginning, admitted into Parliament but upon the most disadvantageous terms, yet they soon found means, by joining petitions to their money-bills, to have a share in framing those laws by which they <77> were in future to be governed; and this method of proceeding, which at first was only tolerated by the King, they afterwards converted into an express right, by declaring, under Henry the Fourth, that they would not, thenceforward, come to any resolutions with regard to subsidies, before the King had given a precise answer to their petitions.[1]

In subsequent times we see the Commons constantly successful, by their exertions of the same privilege, in their endeavours to lop off the despotic

---

1. De Lolme refers to an incident in 1400, when the House of Commons took advantage of Henry IV's political weakness to insist that the king respond to their petitions before enacting any of the fiscal legislation sought by the crown.

powers which still made a part of the regal prerogative. Whenever abuses of power had taken place, which they were seriously determined to correct, they made *grievances and supplies,* to use the expression of Sir Thomas Wentworth, *go hand in hand together,* which always produced the redress of them. And in general, when a bill, in consequence of its being judged by the Commons essential to the public welfare, has been joined by them to a money bill, it has seldom failed *to pass in that agreeable company (a).*[2]
<78>

(*a*) In mentioning the forcible use which the Commons have at times made of their power of granting subsidies, by joining provisions of a different nature to bills that had grants for their object, I only mean to shew the great efficiency of that power, which was the subject of this Chapter, without pretending to say any thing as to the propriety of the measure. The House of Lords have even found it necessary (which confirms what is said here) to form, as it were, a confederacy among themselves, for the security of their Legislative authority, against the unbounded use which the Commons might make of their power of taxation; and it has been made a standing order of their House, to reject any bill whatsoever to which a money-bill has been *tacked.* [[The Lords resisted the House of Commons' efforts to extend its control over fiscal legislation at several points during the reign of Charles II (1660–85). The main dispute over "tacking" bills occurred in 1678.]]

2. De Lolme likely refers to comments made by Wentworth soon after his 1632 appointment as lord deputy of Ireland, when he linked "grievances and supplies" in his response to a petition of grievances received from leading Catholic peers and gentry in Ireland.

The same Subject continued.

But this force of the prerogative of the Commons, and the facility with which it may be exerted, however necessary they may have been for the first establishment of the Constitution, might prove too considerable at present, when it is requisite only to support it. There might be the danger, that, if the Parliament should ever exert their privilege to its full extent, the Prince, reduced to despair, might resort to fatal extremities; or that the Constitution, which subsists only by virtue of its equilibrium, might in the end be subverted.

Indeed this is a case which the prudence of Parliament has foreseen. They have, in this respect, imposed laws upon themselves; and without touching their prerogative itself, they <79> have moderated the exercise of it. A custom has for a long time prevailed, at the beginning of every reign, and in the kind of overflowing of affection which takes place between a King and his first Parliament, to grant the King a revenue for his life; a provision which, with respect to the great exertions of his power, does not abridge the influence of the Commons, but yet puts him in a condition to support the dignity of the Crown, and affords him, who is the first Magistrate in the Nation, that independence which the laws insure also to those Magistrates who are particularly intrusted with the administration of Justice (*a*).

(*a*) The twelve Judges.—Their commissions, which in former times were often given them *durante bene placito,* now must always "be made *quamdiu se bene gesserint,* and their salaries ascertained; but upon an address of both Houses it may be lawful to remove them."—Stat. 13. Will. III. c. 2. [[The 1701 Act of Settlement provided the judges of the

This conduct of the Parliament provides an admirable remedy for the accidental disorders of the State. For though, by the wise distribution of the powers of Government, great <80> usurpations are become in a manner impracticable, nevertheless it is impossible but that, in consequence of the continual, though silent efforts of the Executive power to extend itself, abuses will at length slide in. But here the powers, wisely kept in reserve by the Parliament, afford the means of remedying them. At the end of each reign, the civil list, and consequently that kind of independence which it procured, are at an end. The successor finds a Throne, a Sceptre, and a Crown; but he finds neither power, nor even dignity; and before a real possession of all these things is given him, the Parliament have it in their power to take a thorough review of the State, as well as correct the several abuses that may have crept in during the preceding reign; and thus the Constitution may be brought back to its first principles.

England, therefore, by this means, enjoys one very great advantage, one that all free States have sought to procure for themselves; I mean that of a periodical reformation. But the expedients which Legislators have contrived for this purpose in other Countries, have always, when attempted to be carried into practice, been found to be productive of very disadvantageous consequences. Those laws which were <81> made in Rome, to restore that equality which is the essence of a Democratical Government, were always found impracticable:[1] the attempt alone endangered the overthrow of the Republic; and the expedient which the Florentines called *ripigliar il stato,*[2] proved nowise happier in its consequences. This was because all

---

central courts of Westminster Hall with increased security of tenure and thereby strengthened the independence of the judiciary. Whereas earlier judges served "at the pleasure" of the crown, judges now held their positions "for so long as they shall well conduct themselves."]] In the first year of the reign of his present Majesty, it has been moreover enacted, that the commissions of the Judges shall continue in force, notwithstanding the demise of the King; which has prevented their being dependent, with regard to their continuation in office, on the heir apparent. [[De Lolme refers to the statute of 1760, enacted by the first Parliament of George III, that preserved the judges' tenure in office following the death of the monarch who first appointed the judges.]]

1. Republican Rome had frequently enacted sumptuary laws, limiting private consumption and expenditures, in the contentious effort to preserve equality among the citizens.

2. "To recover the state."

those different remedies were destroyed beforehand, by the very evils they were meant to cure; and the greater the abuses were, the more impossible it was to correct them.

But the means of reformation which the Parliament of England has taken care to reserve to itself, is the more effectual, as it goes less directly to its end. It does not oppose the usurpations of prerogative, as it were, in front—it does not encounter it in the middle of its career, and in the fullest flight of its exertion: but it goes in search of it to its source, and to the principle of its action. It does not endeavour forcibly to overthrow it; it only enervates its springs.

What increases still more the mildness of the operation, is, that it is only to be applied to the usurpations themselves, and passes by, what would be far more formidable to encounter, the obstinacy and pride of the usurpers. <82>

Every thing is transacted with a new Sovereign, who, till then, has had no share in public affairs, and has taken no step which he may conceive himself bound in honour to support. In fine, they do not wrest from him what the good of the State requires he should give up: he himself makes the sacrifice.

The truth of all these observations is remarkably confirmed by the events that followed the reign of the two last Henries. Every barrier that protected the People against the excursions of Power had been broke through. The Parliament, in their terror, had even enacted that proclamations, that is the will of the King, should have the force of laws (*a*): the Constitution seemed really undone. Yet, on the first opportunity afforded by a new reign, liberty began to make again its appearance (*b*). And when the Nation, at length recovered from its long supineness, had, at the accession of Charles the

---

(*a*) Stat. 31 Hen. VIII. chap. 8. [[The legislation was enacted in 1539 and empowered the crown to issue proclamations that had the legal force of acts of Parliament and made it treasonous to disobey such edicts.]]

(*b*) The laws concerning Treason, passed under Henry the Eighth, which Judge Blackstone calls "an amazing heap of wild and new-fangled treasons," were, together with the statute just mentioned, repealed in the beginning of the reign of Edward VI. [[Blackstone, *Commentaries on the Laws of England,* 4:424. The legislation repealing many of the treason laws introduced under Henry VIII was enacted by the first Parliament of Edward VI in 1547.]]

First, another opportunity of a change of Sovereign, that enormous mass
<83> of abuses, which had been accumulating, or gaining strength, during
five successive reigns, was removed, and the ancient laws were restored.

To which add, that this second reformation, which was so extensive in
its effects, and might be called a new creation of the Constitution, was
accomplished without producing the least convulsion. Charles the First, in
the same manner as Edward had done in former times (*a*), assented to every
regulation that was passed; and whatever reluctance he might at first manifest, yet the Act called *the Petition of Right* (as well as the Bill which afterwards completed the work) received the Royal Sanction without
bloodshed.[3]

It is true, great misfortunes followed; but they were the effects of particular circumstances. During the time which preceded the reign of the
Tudors, the nature and extent of regal authority having never been accurately defined, the exorbitant power of the Princes of that House had gradually introduced political prejudices of even an extrava-<84>gant kind:
those prejudices, having had a hundred and fifty years to take root, could
not be shaken off but by a kind of general convulsion; the agitation continued after the action, and was carried to excess by the religious quarrels
which arose at that time.

(*a*) Or, which is equally in point, the Duke of Somerset his uncle, who was the Regent
of the Kingdom, under the name of Protector. [[Edward VI ascended the throne at the
age of nine. In response, the Privy Council appointed the Duke of Somerset, Edward's
uncle, to the position of Protector of the Realm.]]

3. The 1628 Petition of Right set out the violations of right created by the crown's
practice of using prerogative powers to raise funds in the absence of parliamentary taxation. De Lolme's emphasis on the ease with which the measure was adopted by Parliament and accepted by the crown gives little acknowledgment of the political clashes
between Charles I and the House of Commons at the opening of his reign.

CHAPTER VIII

New Restrictions.

The Commons, however, have not intirely relied on the advantages of the great prerogative with which the Constitution has intrusted them.

Though this prerogative is, in a manner, out of danger of an immediate attack, they have nevertheless shewn at all times the greatest jealousy on its account. They never suffer, as we have observed before, a money-bill to begin any where but with themselves; and any alteration that may be made in it, in the other House, is sure to be rejected. If the Commons had not most strictly reserved to themselves the exercise of a prerogative on which their very existence depends, the <85> whole might at length have slidden into that other body which they might have suffered to share in it equally with them. If any other persons besides the Representatives of the People, had had a right to make an offer of the produce of the labour of the people, the executive Power would soon have forgot, that it only exists for the advantage of the public (*a*). <86>

(*a*) As the Crown has the undisputed prerogative of assenting to, and dissenting from, what bills it thinks proper, as well as of convening, proroguing, and dissolving, the Parliament, whenever it pleases, the latter have no assurance of having a regard paid to their Bills, or even of being allowed to assemble, but what may result from the need the Crown stands in of their assistance: the danger, in that respect, is even greater for the Commons than for the Lords, who enjoy a dignity which is hereditary, as well as inherent to their persons, and form a permanent Body in the State; whereas the Commons completely vanish, whenever a dissolution takes place: there is, therefore, no exaggeration in what has been said above, that their *very being* depends on their power of granting subsidies to the Crown.

Moved by these considerations, and no doubt by a sense of their duty towards their Constituents, to whom this right of taxation originally belongs, the House of Commons

Besides, though this prerogative has of itself, we may say, an irresistible efficiency, the Parliament has neglected nothing that may increase it, or at least the facility of its exercise; and though they have allowed the general prerogatives of the Sovereign to remain undisputed, they have in several cases endeavoured to restrain the use he might make of them, by entering with him into divers express and solemn conventions for that purpose (a).

Thus, the King is indisputably invested with the exclusive right of assembling Parliaments: <87> yet he must assemble one, at least once in three years; and this obligation on the King, which was, we find, insisted upon by the People in very early times, has been since confirmed by a act passed in the sixteenth year of the reign of Charles the Second.[1]

Moreover, as the most fatal consequences might ensue, if laws which might most materially affect public liberty, could be enacted in Parliaments abruptly and imperfectly summoned, it has been established that the Writs for assembling a Parliament must be issued forty days at least before the first meeting of it. Upon the same principle it has also been enacted, that the King cannot abridge the term he has once fixed for a prorogation, except in the two following cases, viz. of a rebellion, or of imminent dan-

---

have at all times been very careful lest precedents should be established, which might, in the most distant manner, tend to weaken that right. Hence the warmth, I might say the resentment, with which they have always rejected even the amendments proposed by the Lords in their Money Bills. The Lords however have not given up their pretension to make such amendments; and it is only by the vigilance and constant predetermination of the Commons to reject all alteration whatever made in their Money Bills, without even examining them, that this pretension of the Lords is reduced to be an useless, and only dormant, claim. The first instance of a misunderstanding between the two Houses, on that account, was in the year 1671: and the reader may see at length, in Vol. I. of the *Debates of the House of Commons,* the reasons that were at that time alledged on both sides. [[For these political clashes, see above, book 1, chapter 6, p. 66, note a.]]

(a) Laws made to bind such Powers in a State, as have no superior power by which they may be legally compelled to the execution of them (for instance, the Crown, as circumstanced in England) are nothing more than general conventions, or treaties, made with the Body of the People.

1. De Lolme refers to a statute of 1664, which modified the earlier Triennial Act of 1641 and required the king to summon Parliament at least every three years.

ger of a foreign invasion; in both which cases a fourteen days notice must be given (*a*).

Again, the King is the head of the Church; but he can neither alter the established religion, or call individuals to an account for their religious opinions (*b*). He cannot even <88> profess the religion which the Legislature has particularly forbidden; and the Prince who should profess it, is declared incapable of *inheriting, possessing, or enjoying, the Crown of these Kingdoms* (*c*).

The King is the first Magistrate; but he can make no change in the maxims and forms consecrated by law or custom: he cannot even influence, in any case whatever, the decision of causes between subject and subject; and James the First, assisting at the Trial of a cause, was reminded by the Judge, that he could deliver no opinion (*d*).[2] Lastly, though crimes are prosecuted

(*a*) Stat. 30 Geo. II. c. 25. [[The statute—"An Act of the better ordering of the Militia"—was enacted in 1757. De Lolme refers to provisions contained in section 46 of the act.]]

(*b*) The Convocation, or assembly of the Clergy, of which the King is the head, can only regulate such affairs as are merely ecclesiastical; they cannot touch the Laws, Customs, and Statutes, of the Kingdom.—Stat. 25 Hen. VIII. c. 19. [[De Lolme refers to the 1534 "Act for the Submission of the clergy to the King's Majesty," which was one of the series of Henrician statutes that helped secure the separation of the church and clergy in England from the Roman Catholic Church and the constitutional supremacy of the monarch over the Anglican Church.]]

(*c*) 1 Will. and M. Stat. 2. c. 2. [[De Lolme refers to the 1688/89 Bill of Rights that specifically excluded a Roman Catholic, or anyone married to a Roman Catholic, from occupying the throne.]]

(*d*) These principles have since been made an express article of an Act of Parliament; the same which abolished the Star Chamber. "Be it likewise declared and enacted, by the authority of this present Parliament, That neither his Majesty, nor his Privy Council, have, or ought to have any jurisdiction, power, or authority, to examine or draw into question, determine, or dispose of the lands, tenements, goods, or chattels, of any of the subjects of this Kingdom."—Stat. A. 16. ch. i. cap. 10. § 10. [[De Lolme refers (though his citation is incorrect) to the 1641 legislation that limited the legal authority of the king's Privy Council and abolished the court of Star Chamber and other courts associated with the king's prerogative power.]]

2. De Lolme likely refers to a celebrated incident of 1607, posthumously reported in the *Twelfth Part of the Reports of Sir Edward Coke* (1656), when Coke, then chief justice of the Court of Common Pleas, informed James I "that the King in his own person cannot adjudge any case betwixt party and party. . . . but this ought to be determined and adjudged in some Court of Justice, according to the Law and Custom of England" (*The Selected Writings of Sir Edward Coke,* ed. Steve Sheppard, 3 vols. [Indianapolis: Liberty Fund, 2003], 1:479).

in his name, he cannot refuse to lend it to any particular persons who have complaints to prefer. <89>

The King has the privilege of coining money; but he cannot alter the standard.

The King has the power of pardoning offenders; but he cannot exempt them from making a compensation to the parties injured. It is even established by law, that, in a case of murder, the widow, or next heir, shall have a right to prosecute the murderer; and the King's pardon, whether it preceded the Sentence passed in consequence of such prosecution, or whether it be granted after it, cannot have any effect (a).

The King has the military power; but still with respect to this, he is not absolute. It is true, in regard to the sea-forces, as there is in them this very great advantage, that they cannot be turned against the liberty of the Nation, at the same time that they are the surest bulwark of the island, the King may keep them as he thinks proper; and in this respect he lies only under the general restraint of applying to Parliament for obtaining the means of doing it. But in regard to land forces, as they may become an immediate <90> weapon in the hands of Power, for throwing down all the barriers of public liberty, the King cannot raise them without the consent of Parliament. The guards of Charles the Second were declared anti-constitutional (b); and James's army was one of the causes of his being at length dethroned (c).[3]

In these times however, when it is become a custom with Princes to keep those numerous armies which serve as a pretext and means of oppressing

(a) The method of prosecution mentioned here, is called an *Appeal;* it must be sued within a year and a day after the completion of the crime. [[The appeal of murder was one of several (largely obsolete) forms of criminal prosecution in which a private party, as opposed to the state represented by the crown, initiated the proceeding. Since in these cases the king did not prosecute the offense, the power of royal pardon could not be exercised.]]

(b) He had carried them to the number of four thousand Men.

(c) A new sanction has been given to the above restriction, in the sixth Article of the Bill of Rights: "A standing army, without the consent of Parliament, is against law."

3. The size of the king's army during periods of war and the existence of a standing army during periods of peace were frequent objects of political controversy during the reigns of Charles II (1660–85) and James II (1685–88). The "anti-constitutional" nature of Charles II's guards may refer to grievances sent by the House of Commons to the king in 1673 and 1674, protesting Charles's army policies.

the People, a State that would maintain its independence, is obliged, in great measure, to do the same. The Parliament has therefore thought proper to establish a standing body of troops, which amounts to about thirty thousand Men, of which the King has the command.

But this army is only established for one year; at the end of that term, it is (unless re-established) to be *ipso facto* disbanded; and as the question which then lies before Parlia-<91>ment, is not, whether the army *shall be dissolved,* but whether it shall be *established anew,* as if it had never existed, any one of the three branches of the Legislature may, by its dissent, hinder its continuance.

Besides, the funds for the payment of this body of troops, are to be raised by taxes that never are established for more than one year (*a*); and it becomes likewise necessary, at the end of this term, again to establish them (*b*). In a word, this instrument of defence, which the circumstances of modern times have caused to be judged necessary, being capable, on the other hand, of being applied to the most dangerous purposes, has been joined to the State by only a slender thread, the knot of which may be slipped, on the first appearance of danger (*c*). <92>

(*a*) The land-tax, and malt tax.

(*b*) It is also necessary that the Parliament, when they renew the Act called the *Mutiny Act,* should authorise the different Courts Martial to punish military offences, and desertion. It can therefore refuse the King even the necessary power of military discipline.

(*c*) To these laws, or rather conventions, between King and People, I shall add here the Oath which the King takes at his Coronation; a compact which, if it cannot have the same precision as the laws we have related above, yet in a manner comprehends them all, and has the farther advantage of being declared with more solemnity.

> *The archbishop or bishop shall say,* Will you solemnly promise and swear to govern the people of this Kingdom of England, and the dominions thereto belonging, according to the Statutes in Parliament agreed on, and the laws and customs of the same?—*The king or queen shall say,* I solemnly promise so to do.
>
> *Archbishop or bishop.* Will you to your power cause law and justice, in mercy, to be executed in all your judgments?—*King or queen.* I will.
>
> *Archbishop or bishop.* Will you to the utmost of your power maintain the laws of God, the true profession of the gospel, and the protestant reformed religion established by the law? And will you preserve unto the bishops and clergy of this realm, and to the churches committed to their charge, all such rights and privileges as by law do or shall appertain unto them, or any of them?—*King or queen.* All this I promise to do.
>
> *After this the king or queen, laying his or her hand upon the holy gospels, shall say,*

But these laws which limit the King's authority, would not, of themselves, have been sufficient. As they are, after all, only intellectual barriers,
which it is possible that the King might not at all times respect, as the check
which the Commons have on his proceedings, by a refusal of subsidies,
affects too much the whole State, to be exerted on every particular abuse
of his power; and lastly, as <93> even this means might in some degree be
eluded, either by breaking the promises which have procured subsidies, or
by applying them to uses different from those for which they were appointed, the Constitution has besides supplied the Commons with a means
of immediate opposition to the misconduct of Government, by giving
them a right to impeach the Ministers.

It is true, the King himself cannot be arraigned before Judges; because,
if there were any that could pass sentence upon him, it would be they, and
not he, who must finally possess the executive power: but, on the other
hand, the King cannot act without Ministers; it is therefore those Ministers, that is, those indispensable instruments, whom they attack.

If, for example, the public money has been employed in a manner contrary to the declared intention of those who granted it, an impeachment
may be brought against those who had the management of it. If any abuse
of power is committed, or in general any thing done contrary to the public
weal, they prosecute those who have been either the instruments, or the
advisers of the measure (a). <94>

But who shall be the Judges to decide in such a cause? What Tribunal
will flatter itself, that it can give an impartial decision, when it shall see,

---

The things which I have here before promised I will perform and keep: so help
me God. *And then shall kiss the book.* [[De Lolme quotes the revised form of the
Coronation Oath adopted by statute for the accession of Queen Mary and King
William III in 1688/89.]]

(a) It was upon these principles that the Commons, in the beginning of this century,
impeached the Earl of Oxford, who had advised the Treaty of Partition, and the Lord
Chancellor Somers, who had affixed the great-seal to it. [[Admiral Edward Russell, the
Earl of Orford, and Lord Chancellor Sir John Somers were impeached in 1701 as part
of the political attack on the Partition Treaties of 1698 and 1700, which had been secretly
negotiated by Britain, France, and the United Provinces. (De Lolme's note mistakenly
identifies "the Earl of Oxford" for "the Earl of Orford." Robert Harley, the Earl of
Oxford, was impeached in 1717, in a proceeding that did not concern the Partition
Treaty.)]]

appearing at its bar, the Government itself as the accused, and the Representatives of the People, as the accusers?

It is before the House of Peers that the Law has directed the Commons to carry their accusation; that is, before Judges whose dignity, on the one hand, renders them independent, and who, on the other, have a great honour to support in that awful function where they have all the Nation for spectators of their conduct.

When the impeachment is brought to the Lords, they commonly order the person accused to be imprisoned. On the day appointed, the Deputies of the House of Commons, with the person impeached, make their appearance: the impeachment is read in his presence; Counsel are allowed him, as well as time, to prepare for his defence; and at the expiration of this term, the trial goes on from day to day, with open doors, and every thing is communicated in print to the public. <95>

But whatever advantage the law grants to the person impeached for his justification, it is from the intrinsic merits of his conduct that he must draw his arguments and proofs. It would be of no service to him, in order to justify a criminal conduct, to alledge the commands of the Sovereign; or, pleading guilty with respect to the measures imputed to him, to produce the Royal pardon (*a*). It is against the Administration itself that the impeachment is carried on; it should therefore by no <96> means interfere: the King can neither stop nor suspend its course, but is forced to behold, as an inactive spectator, the discovery of the share which he may himself

(*a*) This point in ancient times was far from being clearly settled. In the year 1678, the Commons having impeached the Earl of Danby, he pleaded the King's pardon in bar to that impeachment: great altercations ensued on that subject, which were terminated by the dissolution of that Parliament. It has been since enacted, (Stat. 12 and 13 W. III. c. 2) "that no pardon under the great-seal can be pleaded in bar to an impeachment by the House of Commons." [[De Lolme quotes from Article 3 of the 1701 Act of Settlement, which settled the previously unresolved issue of whether a royal pardon could be pleaded to prevent a Parliamentary impeachment.]]

I once asked a Gentlemen very learned in the laws of this Country, if the King could remit the punishment of a Man condemned in consequence of an impeachment of the House of Commons; he answered me, the Tories will tell you the King can, and the Whigs, he cannot.—But it is not perhaps very material that the question should be decided: the great public ends are attained when a corrupt Minister is removed with disgrace, and the whole System of his proceedings unveiled to the public eye.

have had in the illegal proceedings of his servants, and to hear his own sentence in the condemnation of his Ministers.

An admirable expedient! which, by removing and punishing corrupt Ministers, affords an immediate remedy for the evils of the State, and strongly marks out the bounds within which Power ought to be confined; which takes away the scandal of guilt and authority united, and calms the people by a great and awful act of Justice: an expedient, in this respect especially, so highly useful, that it is to the want of the like, that Machiavel attributes the ruin of his Republic.[4]

But all these general precautions to secure the rights of the Parliament, that is, those of the Nation itself, against the efforts of the executive Power, would be vain, if the Members themselves remained personally exposed to them. Being unable openly to attack, with any safety to itself, the two legislative bodies, and by a forcible exertion of its prerogatives, to make, as it were, a general assault, the executive power might, by subdividing the same prerogatives, <97> gain an entrance, and sometimes by interest, and at others by fear, guide the general will, by influencing that of individuals.

But the laws which so effectually provide for the safety of the People, provide no less for that of the Members, whether of the House of Peers, or that of the Commons. There are not known in England, either those *Commissaries,* who are always ready to find those guilty whom the wantonness of ambition points out, nor those secret imprisonments which are, in other Countries, the usual expedients of Government. As the forms and maxims of the Courts of Justice are strictly prescribed, and every individual has an invariable right to be judged according to Law, he may obey without fear the dictates of public virtue. Lastly, what crowns all these precautions, is its being a fundamental maxim, "That the freedom of speech, and debates and proceedings in Parliament, ought not to be impeached or questioned in any Court or place out of Parliament" (*a*). <98>

The legislators, on the other hand, have not forgot that interest, as well as fear, may impose silence on duty. To prevent its effects, it has been en-

(*a*) Bill of Rights. Art. 9. [[De Lolme refers to the 1688/89 Bill of Rights, which identified this freedom as one of Parliament's "ancient rights and liberties."]]

4. By "his Republic" De Lolme apparently references Machiavelli's native Florence. The repeated failures in Florence to control the abuses of powerful citizens were treated by Machiavelli in his 1525 *History of Florence,* book 3, chapters 5–6.

acted, that all persons concerned in the management of any taxes created since 1692, commissioners of prizes, navy, victualling office, &c. comptrollers of the army accounts, agents for regiments, the clerks in the different offices of the revenue, any persons that hold any new office under the Crown, created since 1705, or having a pension under the Crown, during pleasure, or for any term of years, are incapable of being elected Members. Besides, if any Member accepts an office under the Crown, except it be an Officer in the army or navy accepting a new commission, his seat becomes void; though such Member is capable of being re-elected.[5]

Such are the precautions hitherto taken by the Legislators, for preventing the undue influence of the great prerogative of disposing of rewards and places; precautions which have been successively taken, according as circumstances have shewn them to be necessary; and which we may thence suppose, are owing to causes powerful enough to produce <99> the establishment of new ones, whenever circumstances shall point out the necessity of them (a). <100>

(a) Nothing can be a better proof of the efficacy of the causes that produce the liberty of the English, and which will be explained hereafter, than those victories which the Parliament from time to time gains over itself, and in which the Members, forgetting all views of private ambition, only think of their interest as subjects.

Since this was first written, an excellent regulation has been made for the decision of controverted elections. Formerly the House decided them in a very summary manner, and the witnesses were not examined upon oath. But, by an Act passed a few years ago, the decision is now to be left to a Jury, or Committee, of fifteen Members, formed in the following manner. Out of the Members present, who must not be less than one hundred, forty-nine are drawn by lots: out of these, each Candidate strikes off one alternately, till there remain only thirteen, who with two others, named out of the whole House, one by each Candidate, are to form the Committee: in order to secure the necessary number of a hundred Members, all other business in the House is to be suspended, till the above operations are completed. [[The new procedure for the adjudication of disputed elections to the House of Commons was introduced by statute in 1770.]]

5. In the period after 1688, Parliament frequently debated and enacted legislation designed to preserve the independence and integrity of Parliament by preventing those holding profitable office in the king's administration from serving in the House of Commons. De Lolme refers here to the provisions of the 1701 Act of Settlement and its 1706 statutory revision.

Of private Liberty, or the Liberty of Individuals.

We have hitherto only treated of general liberty, that is of the rights of the Nation as a Nation, and of its share in the Government. It now remains that we should treat particularly of a thing without which this general liberty, being absolutely frustrated in its object, would be only a matter of ostentation, and even could not long subsist, I mean the liberty of individuals.

Private Liberty, according to the division of the English Lawyers, consists, first, of the right of *Property,* that is of the right of enjoying exclusively the gifts of fortune, and all the various fruits of one's industry. Secondly, of the right of *Personal Security.* Thirdly, of the *Loco-motive Faculty,* taking the word Liberty in its more confined sense.[1]

Each of these rights, say again the English Lawyers, is inherent in the person of every Englishman: they are to him as an inheritance, and he cannot be deprived of them, but by virtue of a sentence passed according to the <101> laws of the land. And indeed, as this right of inheritance is expressed in English by one word (*birth-right*) the same as that which expresses the King's title to the Crown, it has, in times of oppression, been often opposed to him as a right, doubtless of less extent, but of a sanction equal to that of his own.

One of the principal effects of the right of Property is, that the King can take from his subjects no part of what they possess; he must wait till they themselves grant it him: and this right, which, as we have seen before,

---

1. De Lolme here adopts the classification of the liberties of the English subject presented by Blackstone in *Commentaries on the Laws of England,* 1:125.

is, by its consequences, the bulwark that protects all the others, has more-over the immediate effect of preventing one of the chief causes of oppression.

In regard to the attempts to which the right of property might be exposed from one individual to another, I believe I shall have said every thing, when I have observed, that there is no Man in England who can oppose the ir-resistible power of the Laws,—that, as the Judges cannot be deprived of their employments but on an accusation by Parliament, the effect of in-terest with the Sovereign, or with those who approach his person, can scarcely influence their decisions,—that, as the Judges themselves have no power to pass sen-<102>tence till the matter of fact has been settled by Men nominated, we may almost say, at the common choice of the parties (*a*), all private views, and consequently all respect of persons, are banished from the Courts of Justice. However, that nothing may be wanting which may help to throw light on the subject I have undertaken to treat, I shall relate, in general, what is the law in civil matters, that has taken place in England.

When the Pandects were found at Amalphi,[2] the Clergy, who were then the only Men that were able to understand them, did not neglect that op-portunity of increasing the influence they had already obtained, and caused them to be received in the greater part of Europe. England, which was destined to have a Constitution so different from that of other States, was to be farther distinguished by its rejecting the Roman Laws.

Under William the Conqueror, and his immediate successors, a multi-tude of foreign Ecclesiastics flocked to the Court of England. Their influ-ence over the mind of the Sovereign, which, in the other States of Europe, as <103> they were then constituted, might be considered as matter of no great importance, was not so in a Country where the Sovereign being all-powerful, to obtain influence over him, was to obtain power itself. The English Nobility saw with the greatest jealousy, Men of a condition so dif-

---

(*a*) Owing to the extensive right of challenging jurymen, which is allowed to every person brought to his trial, though not very frequently used.

    2. The legendary discovery in Amalfi in 1135 of a manuscript copy of Justinian's *Digest* (or "Pandects") of classical Roman law was routinely credited, as here, with the revival of Roman law studies in the medieval period.

ferent from their own, vested with a power to the attacks of which they
were immediately exposed, and thought that they would carry that power
to the height, if they were ever to adopt a system of laws which those same
men sought to introduce, and of which they would necessarily become both
the depositaries and the interpreters.

It happened, therefore, by a somewhat singular conjunction of circumstances, that, to the Roman laws, brought over to England by Monks, the
idea of ecclesiastical power became associated, in the same manner as the
idea of regal Despotism became afterwards annexed to the Religion of the
same Monks, when favoured by Kings who endeavoured to establish an
arbitrary government. The Nobility at all times rejected these laws, even
with a degree of ill humour (a); and the usurper Ste-<104>phen, whose
interest it was to conciliate their affections, went so far as to prohibit the
study of them.[3]

As the general disposition of things brought about, as hath been above
observed, a sufficient degree of intercourse between the Nobility or Gentry,
and the People, the aversion to the Roman Laws gradually spread itself far
and wide; and those laws, to which their wisdom in many cases, and particularly their extensiveness, ought naturally to have procured admittance
when the English laws themselves were as yet but in their infancy, experienced the most steady opposition from the Lawyers: and as those persons
who sought to introduce them, frequently renewed their attempts, there at

(a) The nobility, under the reign of Richard II. declared in the French language of
those times, "Purce que le roialme d'Engleterre n'étoit devant ces heures, ne à l'entent
du Roy notre Seignior, & Seigniors du Parlement, unques ne sera, rulé ne governé par
la loy civil." viz. Inasmuch as the Kingdom of England was not before this time, nor
according to the intent of the King our Lord, and Lords of Parliament, ever shall be,
ruled or governed by the civil law.—*In Rich. Parlamento Westmonasterii, Feb. 3. Anno 2.*
[[The 1378 declaration of the House of Lords was frequently treated by English jurists,
as by De Lolme here, as designed to block the efforts of the clergy and bishops to promote
the advancement of Roman law at the expense of common law.]]

3. The "usurper Stephen" ascended the English throne in 1135, following the death
of his uncle, Henry I, and against the claims of Henry I's daughter, Matilda. He issued
a charter at the beginning of his reign, granting various concessions to the nobility and
clergy.

length arose a kind of general combination amongst the Laity, to confine them to Universities and Monasteries (*a*). <105>

This opposition was carried so far, that Fortescue, Chief Justice of the King's Bench, and afterwards Chancellor under Henry VI. wrote a Book intitled *De Laudibus Legum Angliae,* in which he proposes to demonstrate the superiority of the English laws over the Civil; and, that nothing might be wanting in his arguments on that subject, he gives them the advantage of superior antiquity, and traces their origin to a period much anterior to the foundation of Rome.[4]

This spirit has been preserved even to much more modern times; and when we peruse the many paragraphs which Judge Hale has writ-<106>ten in his History of the Common Law,[5] to prove, that in the few cases in which the Civil Law is admitted in England, it can have no power by virtue of any deference due to the orders of Justinian (a truth which certainly had no need of proof) we plainly see that this Chief Justice, who was also a very great Lawyer, had, in this respect, retained somewhat of the heat of party.

Even at present the English Lawyers attribute the liberty they enjoy, and

(*a*) It might perhaps be shewn, if it belonged to the subject, that the liberty of thinking in religious matters, which has at all times remarkably prevailed in England, is owing to much the same causes as its political liberty: both perhaps are owing to this, that the same Men, whose interest it is in other Countries that the people should be influenced by prejudices of a political or religious kind, have been in England forced to inform and unite with them. I shall here take occasion to observe, in answer to the reproach made to the English, by President Henault, in his much esteemed Chronological History of France [[De Lolme refers to *Nouvel abrégé chronologique de l'histoire de France* by Charles Jean François Hénault (1685–1770), president of the Parliament of Paris. Hénault's *History* first appeared in 1744 and later was reissued in several expanded editions.]], that the frequent changes of religion which have taken place in England, do not argue any servile disposition in the people; they only prove the equilibrium between the then existing Sects: there was none but what might become the prevailing one, whenever the Sovereign thought proper to declare for it; and it was not England, as people may think at first sight, it was only its Government, which changed its religion.

4. Sir John Fortescue composed *De laudibus legum Angliae* (In praise of the laws of England) ca. 1468–71. The work, in the form of a dialogue between the Prince of Wales and the Lord Chancellor, contains extensive discussion of the superiority of English law to Roman ("the Civil") law.

5. For Hale's *History of the Common Law of England,* see above, book 1, chapter 2, p. 38, note 3.

of which other Nations are deprived, to their having rejected, while those
Nations have admitted, the Roman law; which is mistaking the effect for
the cause. It is not because the English have rejected the Roman laws that
they are free; but it is because they were free, or at least because there existed
among them causes which were, in process of time, to make them so, that
they have been able to reject the Roman laws. But even though they had
admitted those laws, the same circumstances that have enabled them to
reject the whole, would have likewise enabled them to reject those parts
which might not have suited them; and they would have seen, that it is very
possible to receive the decisions of the Civil law on the subject of the *ser-*
vitutes ur-<107>*banae & rusticae,*[6] without adopting its principles with respect to the power of the Emperors (*a*).

Of this the Republic of Holland, where the Civil law is adopted, would
afford a proof, if there were not the still more striking one, of the Emperor
of Germany, who, though in the opinion of his People he is the successor
to the very Throne of the *Caesars* (*b*), has not by a great deal so much power
as a King of England; and the reading of the several treaties which deprive
him of the power of nominating the principal offices of the Empire, sufficiently shews that a spirit of unlimited submission to Monarchical power,
is no necessary consequence of the admission of the Roman Civil Law.

The Laws therefore that have taken place in England, are what they call
the *Unwritten Law,* also termed the *Common Law,* and the *Statute Law.*

The *Unwritten Law* is thus called, not because it is only transmitted by
tradition from generation to generation; but because it is not founded on
any known act of the Legislature. It receives its force from immemorial
custom, and, for the most part, derives its origin from <108> Acts of Parliament enacted in the times which immediately followed the Conquest,

---

(*a*) What particularly frightens the English Lawyers is Lib. 1. Tit. 4. Dig.—*Quod
Principi placuerit legis habet vigorem.* [[De Lolme quotes the controversial formula appearing in Justinian's *Digest,* which was commonly renderd by English commentators,
"that which pleases the prince has the force of law." The more technical, modern translation is, "A decision given by the emperor has the force of a statute." See *Corpus Juris
Civilis. Digest,* 1.4.1.]]

(*b*) The German word to express the Emperor's dignity, is, *Caesar,* Kaiser.

6. "Civic and rustic burdens."

(particularly those anterior to the time of Richard the First) the originals of which are lost.

The principal objects settled by the Common Law, are the rules of descent, the different methods of acquiring property, the various forms required for rendering contracts valid; in all which points it differs, more or less, from the Civil Law. Thus, by the Common Law, lands descend to the eldest son, to the exclusion of all his brothers and sisters; whereas, by the Civil Law, they are equally divided between all the children: by the Common Law, property is transferred by *writing;* but by the Civil Law, *tradition,* or actual delivery, is moreover requisite, &c.

The source from which the decisions of the Common Law are drawn, is what is called *praeteritorum memoria eventorum,* [7] and is found in the collection of judgments that have been passed from time immemorial, and which, as well as the proceedings relative to them, are carefully preserved under the title of *Records.* In order that the principles established by such a series of judgments may be known, extracts from them are, from time to time, published under the name of *Reports;* and these re-<109>ports reach, by a regular series, so far back as the reign of Edward the Second, inclusively.

Besides this collection, which is pretty voluminous, there are also some ancient Authors of great authority among Lawyers; such as *Glanvil,* who wrote under the reign of Henry the Second—*Bracton,* who wrote under Henry the Third,—*Fleta,* and *Lyttelton.* Among more modern Authors, is Sir Edward Coke, Lord Chief Justice of the King's Bench under James the First, who has written four books of Institutes, and is at present the Oracle of the Common Law. [8]

7. "The record of past events."
8. De Lolme invokes the following legal authorities: *De Legibus et Consuetudinibus Angliae* (Of the Laws and Customs of England), standardly attributed to Ranulf de Glanvill and composed ca. 1187; *De Legibus et Consuetudinibus Angliae* (Of the Laws and Customs of England), standardly attributed to Henry de Bracton and likely composed in the 1220s and 1230s; *Fleta,* of unknown authorship and composed in the late thirteenth century; Sir Thomas Littleton's *New Tenures,* first printed in 1481; and Sir Edward Coke's four-part *Institutes of the Laws of England,* the first part of which appeared in 1628 and the later parts of which were first printed posthumously in the 1640s.

The Common Law moreover comprehends some particular customs, which are fragments of the ancient Saxon laws, escaped from the disaster of the Conquest; such as that called *Gavelkind,* in the County of Kent, by which lands are divided equally between the Sons; and that called *Borough English,* by which, in some particular districts, lands descend to the youngest Son.

The Civil Law, in the few instances where it is admitted, is likewise comprehended under the Unwritten Law, because it is of force only so far as it has been authorised by immemorial custom. Some of its principles are fol-<110>lowed in the Ecclesiastical Courts, in the Courts of Admiralty, and in the Courts of the two Universities; but it is there nothing more than *lex sub lege graviori;*[9] and these different Courts must conform to Acts of Parliament, and to the sense given to them by the Courts of Common Law; being moreover subjected to the controul of these latter.

Lastly, the Written Law is the collection of the various Acts of Parliament, the originals of which are carefully preserved, especially since the reign of Edward the Third. Without entering into the distinctions made by Lawyers with respect to them, such as *public* and *private* Acts, *declaratory* Acts, or such as are made to extend or restrain the Common Law, it will be sufficient to observe, that being the result of the united wills of the Three Constituent Parts of the Legislature, they, in all cases, supersede both the Common Law and all former Statutes, and the Judges must take cognizance of them, and decide in conformity to them, even though they had not been alledged by the parties (*a*).

The different Courts for the Administration of Justice, in England, are <III>

I. The Court of *Common Pleas.* It formerly made a part of the *Aula Regis;* but as this latter Court was bound by its institution always to follow the person of the King, and private individuals experienced great difficulties in obtaining relief from a Court that was ambulatory, and always in motion,

---

(*a*) Unless they be private Acts. [[In the case of a private act of Parliament, the enactment needed to be formally pleaded and introduced into evidence before the common law judges were required to take notice of it.]]

9. "Law derived from higher law."

it was made one of the articles of the Great Charter, that the Court of Common Pleas should thenceforwards be held in a fixed place (*a*); and since that time it has been seated at Westminster. It is composed of a Lord Chief Justice, with three other Judges; and appeals from its judgments, usually called *Writs of Errour,* are brought before the Court of King's Bench.

II. The Court of Exchequer. It was originally established to determine those causes in which the King, or his servants, or accomptants, were concerned, and has gradually become open to all persons. The confining the power of this Court to the above class of persons, is therefore now a mere fiction; only a man must, for form's sake, set forth in his declaration that he is debtor to the King, whether he be so, or no. The Court of Exchequer is <112> composed of the Chief Baron of the Exchequer, and three other Judges.

III. The Court of King's Bench forms that part of the *Aula Regis* which continued to subsist after the dismembering of the Common Pleas. This Court enjoys the most extensive authority of all other Courts: it has the superintendence over all Corporations, and keeps the various jurisdictions in the Kingdom within their respective bounds. It takes cognizance, according to the end of its original institution, of all criminal causes, and even of many causes merely civil. It is composed of the Lord Chief Justice of the Court of King's Bench, and three other Judges. Writs of errour against the judgments passed in that Court in civil matters, are brought before the Court of the Exchequer Chamber, or, in most cases, before the House of Peers.

IV. The Court of the Exchequer Chamber. When this Court is formed by the four Barons, or Judges of the Exchequer, together with the Chancellor and Treasurer of the same, it sits as a Court of Equity; a kind of institution on which some observations will be introduced in a following

---

(*a*) *Communia Placita non sequantur Curiam nostram, sed teneantur in aliquo loco certo.* Magna Charta, cap. II. [["Common Pleas shall not follow our court, but shall be held in some place certain."]]

Chapter. When this Court is formed by the twelve Judges, to whom sometimes the Lord Chancellor is joined, its office is to <113> deliberate, when
properly referred and applied to, and give an opinion on important and
difficult causes, before judgments are passed upon them, in those Courts
where the causes are depending.

¤ CHAPTER X[1] ¤

On the Law in regard to Civil matters, that is observed in England.

Concerning the manner in which Justice is administered, in civil matters, in England, and the kind of law that obtains in that respect, the following observations may be made.

In the first place, it is to be observed, that the beginning of a civil process in England, and the first step usually taken in bringing an action, is the seizing by public authority the person against whom that action is brought. This is done with a view to secure such person's appearance before a Judge, or at least make him give sureties for that purpose. In most of the Countries of Europe, where the forms introduced in the Roman Civil Law, in the reigns of the latter Emperors, have been imitated, a different method has been adopted <114> to procure a man's appearance before a Court of Justice. The usual practice is to have the person sued, summoned to appear before the Court, by a public officer belonging to it, a week before-hand: if no regard is paid to such summons twice repeated, the Plaintiff, or his Attorney, is admitted to make before the Court a formal reading of his demand, which is then granted him, and he may proceed to execution (*a*).

In this mode of proceeding, it is taken for granted, that a person who declines to appear before a Judge, to answer the demand of another, after

---

1. This chapter first appeared in the 1781 edition.

(*a*) A person against whom a judgment of this kind has been passed (which they call in France *un jugement par défaut*) [["a judgment by default"]] may easily obtain relief: but as he now in his turn becomes in a manner the Plaintiff, his deserting the cause, in this second stage of it, would leave him without remedy.

being properly summoned, acknowledges the justice of such demand; and this supposition is very just and rational. However, the above mentioned practice of securing before-hand the body of a person sued, though not so mild in its execution as that just now described, nor even more effectual, appears more obvious, and is more readily adopted, in those times when Courts of Law begin <115> to be formed in a Nation, and rules of distributive justice to be established; and it is, very likely, followed in England as a continuation of the methods that were adopted when the English laws were as yet in their infancy.

In the times we mention, when laws begin to be formed in a Country, the administration of justice between individuals is commonly lodged in the same hands which are intrusted with the public and military authority in the State. Judges invested with a power of this kind, like to carry on their operations with a high hand: they consider the refusal of a Man to appear before them, not as being barely an expedient to avoid doing that which is just, but as a contempt of their authority: they of course look upon themselves as being bound to vindicate it; and a writ of *Capias* is speedily issued to apprehend the refractory Defendant. A preliminary Writ, or order, of this kind, becomes in time to be used of course, and as the first regular step of a law-suit; and thus, it is likely enough, has it happened that in the English Courts of law, if I am rightly informed, a Writ of *Capias* is either issued before the *original* Writ itself (which contains the summons of the plaintiff, and a formal delineation of his case), or is joined to such Writ, by means <116> of an *ac etiam capias,* and is served along with it.[2] It may be remembered that, in England, the *Aula Regis,* at the head of which the King himself presided, was originally the common Court of Justice for the whole Kingdom, in civil as well as criminal matters, and continued so till the Court of Common-pleas was in time separated from it.

In Rome, where the distribution of civil Justice was at first lodged in the hands of the Kings, and afterwards of the Consuls, the method of seizing the person of a Man against whom a demand of any kind was preferred,

---

2. *Capias* was a judicial writ that authorized the arrest of the defendant. It differed from "the original Writ" in not specifying the alleged injury that formed the subject matter of the suit.

previously to any judgment being passed against him, was likewise adopted, and continued to be followed after the institution of the Praetor's Court, to whom the civil branch of the power of the Consuls was afterwards delegated; and it lasted till very late times; that is, till the times when those capital alterations were made in the Roman civil Law, during the reigns of the latter Emperors, which gave it the form it now has in those Codes or collections of which we are in possession.

A very singular degree of violence even took place in Rome, in the method used to secure the persons of those against whom a legal demand was preferred. In England, the way <117> to seize upon the person of a Man under such circumstances, is by means of a public Officer, supplied with a Writ or order for that purpose, supposed to be directed to him (or to the Sheriff his employer) from the King himself. But in Rome, every one became a kind of public officer in his own cause, to assert the Praetor's prerogative; and, without any ostensible legal licence or badge of public authority, had a right to seize by force the person of his opponent, wherever he met him. The practice was, that the Plaintiff (*Actor*) first summoned the person sued (*Reum*) with a loud voice, to follow him before the Court of the Praetor (*a*). When the Defendant refused to obey such summons, the Plaintiff, by means of the words *licet antestari*,[3] requested the bystanders to be witnesses of the fact, as a remembrance of which he touched the ears of each of them; and then proceeded to seize the person of his opponent, by throwing his arms round his neck (*obtorto collo*), thus endeavouring to drag him before the Praetor. When the person sued was, through age or sickness, disabled from following the Plaintiff, the latter was directed by the law of the Twelve Tables to supply him with a horse (*jumentum dato*). <118>

The above method of proceeding was however in after-times mitigated, though very late and slowly. In the first place, it became unlawful to seize a man in his own house, as it was the abode of his domestic Gods. Women of good family (*Matronae*) were in time protected from the severity of the

---

(*a*) *Ad Tribunal sequere, in Ius ambula*. [["Follow to the judgment-seat, walk into court."]]

3. "Are you willing to witness the arrest?"

above custom, and they could no longer be dragged by force before the Tribunal of the Praetor. The method of placing a sick or aged person by force upon a horse, seems to have been abolished during the latter times of the Republic. Emancipated Sons, and freed Slaves, were afterwards restrained from summoning their Parents, or late Masters, without having expressly obtained the Praetor's leave, under the penalty of fifty pieces of gold. However, so late as the time of Pliny, the old mode of summoning, or carrying by force, before a Judge, continued in general to subsist; though, in the time of Ulpian, the necessity of expressly obtaining the Praetor's leave was extended to all cases and persons; and in Constantine's reign, the method began to be established of having legal summonses served only by means of a public Officer appointed for that purpose.[4] After that time, other changes in the former law were introduced, from which the mode of proceeding <119> now used on the Continent of Europe, has been borrowed.

In England likewise, some changes we may observe, have been wrought in the law and practice concerning the arrests of sued persons, though as slowly and late as those effected in the Roman Republic or Empire, if not more so; which evinces the great impediments of various kinds that obstruct the improvement of laws in every Nation. So late as the reign of king George the First, an Act was passed to prohibit the practice of previous personal Arrest, in cases of demands under two pounds sterling;[5] and since that time, those Courts, justly called *of Conscience,* have been established, in which such demands are to be summarily decided, and simple summonses, without arrest, can only be used.[6] And lately, another Bill has been passed on the motion of Lord Beauchamp, whose name deserves to be recorded, by which the like prohibition of arrest is extended to all cases of debt under ten pounds sterling: a Bill the passing of which was of twenty,

---

4. De Lolme here reports on several centuries of legal development, from the time of Pliny the Younger (62–113), through the period of Ulpian's service as Praetorian prefect (222–28), and to the reign of Constantine I (306–37).

5. De Lolme refers to a statute of 1725 titled "An act to prevent frivolous and vexatious arrests." The legislation prevented arrest for debts of less than 20 shillings in value.

6. Courts of conscience (or courts of request) were created by statute for the recovery of small debts.

or even a hundred times, more real importance than the rise or fall of a favourite or a Minister, though it has perhaps been honoured with a less degree of attention by the Public.[7] <120>

Another peculiarity in the English Civil Law, is the great refinements, formalities, and strictness that prevail in it. Concerning such refinements, which are rather imperfections, the same observation may be made that has been introduced above in regard to the mode and frequency of civil arrest in England; which is, that they are continuations of methods adopted when the English Law began to be formed, and are the consequences of the situation in which the English placed themselves when they rejected the ready made Code of the Roman civil Law, compiled by order of Justinian, which most Nations of Europe have admitted, and rather chose to become their own Lawmakers, and raise from the ground the structure of their own national civil Code; which Code, it may be observed, is as yet in the first stage of its formation, as the Roman Law itself was during the times of the Republic, and in the reigns of the first Emperors.

The time at which the power of administering justice to individuals, becomes separated from the military power (an event which happens sooner or later in different Countries) is the real aera of the origin of a regular system of laws in a Nation. Judges being now deprived of the power of the sword, or, which <121> amounts to the same, being obliged to borrow that power from other persons, endeavour to find their resources within their own Courts, and, if possible, to obtain submission to their decrees from the great regularity of their proceedings, and the reputation of the impartiality of their decisions.

At the same time also, Lawyers begin to croud in numbers to Courts which it is no longer dangerous to approach, and add their refinements to the rules already set down either by the Legislature or the Judges. As the employing of them is, especially in the beginning, matter of choice, and they fear, that, if bare common sense were thought sufficient to conduct a

7. De Lolme refers to the 1779 Insolvent Debtors Act. Lord Beauchamp, who sponsored the legislation in the House of Commons, was Francis Ingram Seymour Conway (1743–1822), eldest son of the Earl of Hertford.

law-suit, every body might imagine he knows as much as they do, they contrive difficulties to make their assistance needful. As the true science of the Law, which is no other than the knowledge of a long series of former rules and precedents, cannot as yet exist, they endeavour to create an artificial one to recommend themselves by. Formal distinctions and definitions are invented to express the different kinds of claims Men may set up against one another; in which almost the same nicety is displayed as that used by Philosophers in classing the different subjects, <122> or *kingdoms,* of natural History. Settled forms of words, under the name of *Writs,* or such like, are devised to set those claims forth; and, like introductory passes, serve to usher Claimants into the Temple of Justice. For fear their Clients should desert them after their first introduction, like a sick man who rests contented with a single visit of the Physician, Lawyers contrive other ceremonies and technical forms for the farther conduct of the process and the *pleadings;* and in order still more safely to bind their Clients to their dominion, they at length obtain to make every error relating to their professional regulations, whether it be a *misnomer,* a *mispleading,* or such like transgression, to be of as fatal a consequence as a failure against the laws of strict Justice. Upon the foundation of the above mentioned definitions and metaphysical distinctions of cases and actions, a number of strict rules of law are moreover raised, with which none can be acquainted but such as are complete masters of those distinctions and definitions.

To a person who in a posterior age observes for the first time such refinements in the distribution of Justice, they appear very strange, and even ridiculous. Yet, it must be confessed, that during the times of the first institution of <123> Magistracies and Courts of a civil nature, ceremonies and formalities of different kinds, are very useful to procure to such Courts, both the confidence of those persons who are brought before them, and the respect of the Public at large; and they thereby become actual substitutes for military force, which, till then, had been the chief support of Judges. Those same forms and professional regulations are moreover useful to give uniformity to the proceedings of the Lawyers and of the Courts of Law, and to insure constancy and steadiness to the rules they set down among themselves. And if the whole system of the refinements we mention continues to subsist in very remote ages, it is in a great measure owing (not to mention other causes) to their having so coalesced with the essential parts of the Law as to make danger, or at least great difficulties, to be apprehended from a separation; and they may, in that respect, be compared with a scaffolding used in the raising of a house, which, though only intended to set the materials and support the builders, happens to be suffered for a long time afterwards to stand, because it is thought the removing of it might endanger the building. <124>

Very singular law formalities and refined practices of the kind here alluded to, had been contrived by the first Jurisconsults in Rome, with a view to amplify the rules set down in the Laws of the Twelve Tables; which being but few, and engraved on brass, every body could know as well as they: it even was a general custom to give those laws to children to learn, as we are informed by Cicero.[8]

Very accurate definitions, as well as distinct branches of cases and actions, were contrived by the first Roman Jurisconsults; and when a Man had once made his election of that peculiar kind of *action* he chose to pursue his claim by, it became out of his power to alter it. Settled forms of words, called *Actiones legis,*[9] were moreover contrived, which Men must absolutely use to set forth their demands. The party himself was to recite the appointed words before the Praetor; and should he unfortunately happen to miss or add a single word, so as to seem to alter his real case or demand, he lost his suit thereby. To this an allusion is made by Cicero, when he says, "We have a civil law so constituted, that a Man becomes non-suited, who has not proceeded in the manner he should have <125> done" (*a*). An observation of the like nature is also to be found in Quintilian, whose expressions on the subject are as follow: "There is besides another danger; for if but one word has been mistaken, we are to be considered as having failed

---

(*a*) *Ita Ius civile habemus constitutum, ut causâ cadat is qui non quemadmodum oportet egerit.* De Invent II. 19. [[De Lolme translates and cites Marcus Tullius Cicero, *De inventione,* book 2, chapter 19.]]

8. The Twelve Tables, dating from the mid-fifth century B.C.E., were the first published materials of ancient Roman law. Cicero's comments appeared in Marcus Tullius Cicero, *De legibus,* book 2, chapter 23 (title 59).

9. "Processes of law."

in every point of our suit" (*a*). Similar solemnities and appropriated forms of words were moreover necessary to introduce the reciprocal answers and replies of the Parties, to require and accept sureties, to produce witnesses, &c.

Of the above *Actiones legis,* the Roman Jurisconsults and Pontiffs had carefully kept the exclusive knowledge to themselves, as well as of those Days on which religion did not allow Courts of Law to sit (*b*). One Cn. Flavius, secretary to Appius Claudius, having happened to divulge the secret of those momentous forms (an act for which he was afterwards preferred by the People), Jurisconsults contrived fresh ones, which they began to keep written with secret cyphers; but a Member of their own Body again betrayed them, and the new Collection which he published, was called *Ius* <126> *Aelianum,* from his name, Sex. Aelius, in the same manner as the former collection had been called, *Ius Flavianum.*[10] However, it does not seem that the influence of Lawyers became much abridged by those two Collections: besides written information of that sort, practice is also necessary; and the public Collections we mention, like the many books that have been published on the English law, could hardly enable a Man to become a Lawyer, at least sufficiently so as to conduct a law suit (*c*).

(*a*) *Est etiam periculosum, quum si uno verbo sit erratum, totâ causâ cecidisse videamur.* Inst. Orat. III. 8. VII. 3. [["For it is a most dangerous practice, since, if we make a mistake in a single word, we are likely to lose our whole case." Quintilian (Marcus Fabius Quintilianus), *Institutio oratoria,* 8.3.17.]]

(*b*) *Dies Fasti & Nefasti.* [["Dies fasti" were the days on which the praetor administered justice; "dies nefasti" were the days on which it was unlawful for the praetor to act.]]

10. Several Latin authors, including Livy and Pliny, relate how Cneius Flavius achieved fame and high office by revealing to the community legal procedures and requirements that previously were known only by the Roman patricians and jurists. The disclosed material became known as the *Ius Flavium* (ca. 304 B.C.E.). The *Ius Aelianum* (ca. 198 B.C.E.), named for Sextus Aelius Catus, likewise was based on the unauthorized disclosure of previously secret legal materials.

(*c*) The Roman Jurisconsults had extended their skill to objects of *voluntary* jurisdiction as well as to those of *contentious* jurisdiction, and had devised peculiar formalities, forms of words, distinctions, and definitions, in regard to the contracting of obligations between Man and Man, in regard to stipulations, donations, spousals, and especially last wills, in regard to all these things they had displayed surprising nicety, refinement, accuracy, and strictness. The English Lawyers have not bestowed so much pains on the

Modern Civilians have been at uncommon pains to find out and produce the ancient law *formulae* we mention; in which they really have had
surprising success. Old Comic Writers, such as Plautus and Terence, have
supplied them with several; the settled words, for instance, used to claim
the property of a Slave, frequently occur in their Works (*a*). <127>

---

objects of *voluntary* jurisdiction, nor any thing like it. [[De Lolme's meaning here is
somewhat obscure. He apparently contrasts the refinement and detail of Roman law
covering certain voluntary agreements (such as contracts and testaments) with the relative paucity of common law on these topics. English courts routinely handled disputes
involving such voluntary agreements. However, a unified common law of contracts and
wills was a development of the nineteenth century.]]

(*a*) The words addressed to the Plaintiffs by the person sued, when the latter made
his appearance on the day for which he had been compelled to give sureties, were as
follow, and are alluded to by Plaut. *Curcul.* I. 3. v. 5. [[De Lolme quotes the comedy
Curculio (1.3,5–9) by the master comic dramatist Titus Maccius Plautus (ca. 254–184
B.C.E.).]] "Where art thou who hast obliged me to give sureties? Where art thou who
summonest me? Here I stand before thee, do thyself stand before me." To which the
Plaintiff made answer, "Here I am." The defendant replied, "What dost thou say?" When
the Plaintiff answered, I say . . . (*Aio*) and then followed the form of words by which
he chose to express his action. *Ubi tu es, qui me vadatus es? Ubi tu es qui me citasti? Ecce
ego me tibi sisto; tu contra & te mihi siste, &c.*

If the action, for instance, was brought on account of goods stolen, the settled penalty
or damages for which was the restitution of twice the value, the words to be used were,
AIO *decem aureos mihi furto tue abesse, teque eo nomine viginti aureos mihi dare oportere.*
[["I say that through your theft I am minus ten aurei, and that on that account you ought
to pay me twenty aurei."]] For work done, such as cleaning of cloaths, &c. AIO *te mihi
tritici modium de quo inter nos convenit ob polita vestimenta tua, dare oportere.* [["I say you
ought to pay me a bushel of wheat, according to the agreement between us for cleaning
your clothes."]] For recovering the value of a Slave killed by another Citizen, AIO *te
hominem meum occidisse, teque mihi quantum ille hoc anno plurimi fuit dare oportere.* [["I
say that you killed my slave, and that you ought to pay me what his highest value amounts
to this year."]] For damages done by a vicious animal, AIO *bovem Maevii servum meum,
Stichum, cornu petiisse & occidisse, eoque nomine Maevium, aut servi aestimationem praes-
tare, aut bovem mihi noxae dare, oportere;* or AIO *ursum Maevii mihi vulnus intulisse, &
Maevium quantum aequius melius mihi dare oportere, &c. &c.* [["I say that Maevius's ox
gored and killed my slave Stichus, and that on that account Maevius ought either to pay
the estimated value of the slave, or else surrender to me the ox, as an equivalent for the
injury; or, I say that Maevius's bear has wounded me, and that Maevius ought to make
the most ample equitable compensation."]]

It may be observed, that the particular kind of remedy which was provided by the
law for the case before the Court, was expresly pointed out in the formula, used by a
Plaintiff; and in regard to this no mistake was to be made. Thus, in the last quoted

Extremely like the above *Actiones legis* are the *Writs* used in the English Courts of law. Those Writs are framed for, and adapted to, every branch or denomination of actions, such <128> as *detinue, trespass, action upon the case, accompt and covenant,* &c. The same strictness obtains in regard to them as did in regard to the Roman law *formulae* above mentioned:[11] there is the same danger in misapplying them, or in failing in any part of them; and to use the words of an English Law-writer on the subject, "Writs must be rightly directed, or they will be nought . . . In all writs, care must be had that they be laid and formed according to their case, and so pursued in the process thereof" (*a*).

The same formality likewise prevails in the English *pleadings* and conduct of the process, as obtained in the old Roman law proceedings; and in the same manner as the Roman Jurisconsults had their *Actionis postulationes & editiones,* their *inficiationes, exceptiones, sponsiones, replicationes, duplicationes, &c.* so the English Lawyers have their *counts, bars, re-*<129>*plications, rejoinders, sur-rejoinders, rebutters, sur-rebutters,* &c.[12] A scrupulous accuracy in observing certain rules, is moreover necessary in the management of those pleadings: the following are the words of an English Law-writer on the subject: "Though the art and dexterity of pleading, was in its nature and design only to render the fact plain and intelligible, and to bring the matter to judgment with convenient certainty, it began to degenerate from its primitive simplicity. Pleaders, yea and Judges, having become too

---

formula, the words *quantum aequius melius* [["most ample equitable remedy"]], shew that the Praetor was to appoint inferior Judges, both to ascertain the damage done, and determine finally upon the case, according to the direction he previously gave them; these words being exclusively appropriated to the kind of actions called *Arbitrariae,* from the above mentioned Judges or Arbitrators. In actions brought to require the execution of conventions that had no name, the convention itself was expressed in the formula; such is that which is recited above, relating to work done by the Plaintiff, &c. &c.

(*a*) Jacob's Law Dictionary. See *Writ.* [[De Lolme cites, with some variation, Giles Jacob, *A New Law-Dictionary* (1729), s.v. "Writ."]]

11. Writs were the legal documents obtained to initiate a suit at common law. *"Detinue, trespass,"* etc., were the names of specific types of legal process—or "forms of action"—used by the common law for the determination of legal rights and the redress of legal injuries.

12. De Lolme invokes the technical terms for the required steps by which lawyers presented and developed their clients' cases in formal court proceedings.

curious in that respect, pleadings at length ended in a piece of nicety and curiosity, by which the miscarriage of many a cause, upon small trivial objections, has been occasioned" (*a*).

There is however a difference between the Roman *Actiones legis,* and the English Writs; which is, that the former might be framed when new ones were necessary, by the Praetor or Judge of the Court, or, in some cases, by the body of the Jurisconsults themselves,—whereas *Writs,* when wanted for such new cases as may offer, can only be devised by a distinct Judge or Court, exclusively invested with such power, viz. the High Court of Chancery. The issuing of Writs already existing, for the different cases to which they belong, is also ex-<130>presly reserved to this Court; and so important has its office on those two points been deemed by Lawyers, that it has been called, by way of eminence, the Manufactory of Justice, (*Officina Justitiae*). Original Writs besides, when once framed, are not at any time to be altered, except by Parliamentary authority (*b*).

Of so much weight in the English law, are the original delineations of cases we mention, that no cause is suffered to be proceeded upon, unless they first appear as legal introductors to it. However important or interesting the case, the Judge, till he sees the Writ he is used to, or at least a Writ issued from the right Manufactory, is both deaf and dumb. He is without <131> eyes to see, or ears to hear. And, when a case of a new kind

(*a*) Cunningham's Law Dictionary. See *Pleadings.* [[De Lolme cites, with some variation, Timothy Cunningham, *A New and Complete Law-Dictionary, or, General Abridgment of the Law* (1764–65), s.v. "Pleadings."]]

(*b*) Writs, legally issued, are also necessary for executing the different incidental proceedings that may take place in the course of a law suit, such as producing witnesses, &c. The names given to the different kinds of writs, are usually derived from the first Latin words by which they began when they were written in Latin, or at least from some remarkable word in them; which gives rise to expressions sufficiently uncouth and unintelligible. Thus, a *Pone,* is a writ issued to oblige a person in certain cases to give sureties (*Pone per vadium,* and *salvos plegios*). [["Take bail for the appearance (of the defendant)" and "safe surety."]] A writ of *Subpoena* is to oblige witnesses, and sometimes other classes of persons, to appear before a Court. An action of *Qui tam,* is that which is brought to sue for a proportional share of a fine established by some penal Statute, by the person who laid an information: the words in the writ being, *Qui tam pro Domino rege, quam pro seipso in hac parte sequitur,* &c. &c. [["Who sues in this behalf for our lord the king, as well as for himself, etc."]]

offers, for which there is as yet no Writ in being, should the Lord Chancellor and Masters in Chancery disagree in creating one, or prove unequal to the arduous task, the Great National Council, that is Parliament themselves, are in such emergency expresly applied to: by means of their collected wisdom, the right mystical words are brought together: the Judge is restored to the free use of his organs of hearing and of speech; and, by the creation of a new *Writ*, a new province is added to the Empire of the Courts of Law.

In fine, those precious Writs, those valuable Briefs (*Brevia*) as they are also called by way of eminence, which are the elixir and quintessence of the Law, have been committed to the special care of Officers appointed for that purpose, whose offices derive their names from those peculiar instruments they respectively use for the preservation of the deposit with which they are intrusted; the one being called the office of the *Hamper,* and the other, of the *Small bag* (*a*).

To say the truth, however, the creating of a new Writ, upon any new given case, is mat-<132>ter of more difficulty than the generality of Readers are aware of. The very importance which is thought to be in those professional forms of words, renders them really important. As every thing without them is illegal in a Court of Common Law, so with them every thing becomes legal, that is to say, they empower the Court legally to determine upon every kind of suit to which they are made to serve as introductors. The creating of a new Writ, therefore, amounts in its consequences to the framing of a new law, and a law of a general nature too: now, the creating of such a law, on the first appearance of a new case, which law is afterwards to be applied to all such cases as may be similar to the first, is really matter

(*a*) *Hanaperium & Parva baga;* the Hanaper Office, and the Petty-bag Office: the above two Latin words, it is not improper to observe, do not occur in Tully's works. To the care of the Petty-bag office those writs are trusted in which the King's business is concerned; and to the Hanaper office, those which relate to the Subject. [[As De Lolme correctly explains, the Hanaper Office and the Petty-bag Office were the names of the offices that kept records of the common law writs issued by the Court of Chancery. Though the offices were given Latin names, the terms "do not occur in Tully's [Cicero's] works"; that is, the offices were unknown to Roman law.]]

of difficulty; especially, when men are as yet in the dark as to the best kind of provision to be made for the case in question, or even when it is not perhaps yet known whether it be proper to make any provision at all. The framing of a new Writ under such circumstances, is a measure on which Lawyers or Judges will not very willingly either venture of themselves, or apply to the Legislature for that purpose. <133>

Owing to the above mentioned real difficulty in creating new Writs on the one hand, and to the absolute necessity of such Writs in the Courts of Common Law on the other, many new species of claims and cases (the arising of which is from time to time the unavoidable consequences of the progress of trade and civilization) are left unprovided for, and remain like so many vacant spaces in the Law, or rather, like so many inaccessible spots, which the laws in being cannot reach: now, this is a great imperfection in the distribution of Justice, which should be open to every individual, and provide remedies for every kind of claim which Men may set up against one another.

To remedy the above inconvenience, or rather in some degree to palliate it, law fictions have been resorted to, in the English law, by which Writs, being warped from their actual meaning, are made to extend to cases to which they in no shape belong.

Law fictions of the kind we mention were not unknown to the old Roman Jurisconsults; and as an instance of their ingenuity in that respect, may be mentioned that kind of action, in which a Daughter was called a Son (*a*). Several in-<134>stances might also be quoted of the fictitious use of Writs in the English Courts of Common Law. A very remarkable ex-

---

(*a*) From the above instance it might be concluded that the Roman Jurisconsults were possessed of still greater power than the English Parliament; for it is a fundamental principle with the English Lawyers, that Parliament can do every thing, *except* making a Woman a Man, or a Man a Woman. [[By "Roman Jurisconsults," De Lolme likely refers to the several praetorian edicts to which he returns in book 1, chapter 11, pp. 106–108; these edicts relaxed the rules of exclusively patriarchal succession to enable inheritance to pass through female descendants. In his reference to "the English lawyers," he likely refers to the constitutional claim, as articulated by Blackstone, that in the exercise of its legislative sovereignty, Parliament "can, in short, do any thing that is not naturally impossible." See Blackstone, *Commentaries on the Laws of England,* 1:156.]]

pedient of that sort occurs in the method generally used to sue for the
payment of certain kinds of debt, before the Court of Common Pleas,
such, if I am not mistaken, as a salary for work done, indemnity for fulfilling
orders received, &c. The Writ issued in those cases, is grounded on the
supposition, that the person sued has trespassed on the ground of the Plaintiff, and broken by force of arms through his fences and inclosures; and
under this predicament the Defendant is brought before the Court: this
Writ, which has been that which Lawyers have found of most convenient
use, to introduce before a Court of Common Law the kinds of claim we
mention, is called in technical language a *Clausum fregit.*[13]—In order to
bring a person before the Court of King's Bench, to answer demands of
much the same nature with those above, a Writ, called a *Latitat,*[14] is issued,
in which it is taken for granted that the Defendant insidiously conceals
himself, and is lurking in <135> some County, different from that in which
the Court is sitting; the expressions used in the Writ being, that "he runs
up and down and secretes himself"; though no such fact is seriously meant
to be advanced either by the Attorney or the Party.

The same principle of strict adherence to certain forms long since established, has also caused Lawyers to introduce into their proceedings, fictitious names of persons who are supposed to discharge the office of sureties; and in certain cases, it seems, the name of a fictitious person is
introduced in a Writ along with that of the principal Defendant, as being
joined in a common cause with him. Another instance of the same high
regard of Lawyers, and Judges too, for certain old forms, which makes them
more unwilling to depart from such forms than from the truth itself of
facts, occurs in the above mentioned expedient used to bring ordinary

13. "Breaking his enclosure." "Trespass" came to cover a large and varied group of
writs used to redress injuries to property and to persons. Trespass *clausum fregit* originally
handled cases involving illegal entry on privately owned land.

14. "Conceals himself." The writ of *latitat* brought a suit before the Court of King's
Bench by ordering a sheriff to arrest an allegedly recalcitrant defendant for a fictitious
trespass committed in the county of Middlesex, where the court enjoyed original jurisdiction. The fiction was developed in the sixteenth century and dramatically increased
the business of the King's Bench at the expense of the Court of Common Pleas.

causes before the Court of Exchequer, in order to be tried there at Common Law; which is, by making a declaration that the Plaintiff is a King's debtor, though neither the Court, nor the Plaintiff's Attorney, lay any serious stress on the assertion (*a*). <136>

(*a*) Another instance of the strict adherence of the English Lawyers to their old established forms in preference even to the truth of facts, occurs in the manner of executing the very Act mentioned in this Chapter, passed in the reign of George I. for preventing personal Arrest for debts under forty shillings. [[See above, p. 92, note 5.]] If the defendant, after being personally served with a copy of the process, does not appear on the appointed days, the method is to suppose that he has actually made his appearance, and the cause is proceeded upon according to this supposition: fictitious names of bails are also resorted to.

The inhabitants of Bengal, and other East-India provinces, have been prodigiously surprised, it is said, at the refinements, fictions, and intricacy of the English law, in regard to civil matters, which was introduced among them a few years ago; and it is certainly not to be doubted that they may have been astonished. [[De Lolme refers to the Regulating Act of 1773, which introduced a new administrative structure and court system for the East India Company's rule in Bengal and other territories. The legislation did not directly transfer English law to British India but created the institutional structure that made possible the introduction of English legal forms and procedures.]]

∞ CHAPTER XI[1] ∞

The Subject continued. The Courts of Equity.

However, there are limits to the law fictions and subtilties we mention; and the remedies of the Law cannot by their means be extended to all possible cases that arise, unless too many absurdities are suffered to be accumulated; nay, there have been instances in which the improper application of Writs, in the Courts of Law, has been checked by authority. In order therefore to remedy the inconveniences we mention, that is, in order to extend the administration of distributive Justice to all possible cases, by freeing it from the professional difficulties that have gradually grown up <137> in its way, a new kind of Courts has been instituted in England, called *Courts of Equity.*

The generality of people, misled by this word *Equity,* have conceived false notions of the office of the Courts we mention; and it seems to be generally thought that the Judges who sit in them, are only to follow the rules of natural Equity; by which People appear to understand, that in a Court of Equity, the Judge may follow the dictates of his own private feelings, and ground his decisions as he thinks proper, on the peculiar circumstances and situation of those persons who make their appearance before him. Nay, Doctor Johnson, in his abridged Dictionary, gives the following definition of the power of the Court of Chancery, considered as a Court of Equity: "The Chancellor hath power to moderate and temper the written law, and subjecteth himself only to the law of nature and conscience": for which definition Dean Swift, and Cowell, who was a Lawyer, are quoted

---

1. This chapter first appeared in the 1781 edition.

104

as authorities.[2] Other instances might be produced of Lawyers who have been inaccurate in their definitions of the true office of the Judges of Equity. And the above named Doctor himself is on no subject a despicable authority.

Certainly the power of the Judges of Equity cannot be to alter, by their own private power, the Written Law, that is, Acts of Parlia-<138>ment, and thus to controul the Legislature. Their office only consists, as will be proved in the sequel, in providing remedies for those cases for which the public good requires that remedies should be provided, and in regard to which the Courts of Common Law, shackled by their original forms and institutions, cannot procure any;—or in other words—the Courts of Equity have a power to administer Justice to individuals, unrestrained, not by the Law, but by the professional law difficulties which Lawyers have from time to time contrived in the Courts of Common Law, and to which the Judges of those Courts have given their sanction.

An office of the kind here mentioned, was soon found necessary in Rome, for reasons of the same nature with those above delineated. For, it is remarkable enough, that the Body of English Lawyers, by refusing admittance to the Code of Roman Laws, as it existed in the latter times of the Empire, have only subjected themselves to the same difficulties under which the old Roman Jurisconsults laboured, during the time they were raising the structure of those same Laws. And it may also be observed, that the English Lawyers or Judges have fallen upon much the same expedients as those which the Roman Jurisconsults and Praetors had adopted.

This office of a Judge of *Equity*, was in <139> time assumed by the Praetor in Rome, in addition to the judicial power he before possessed (*a*).[3] At the beginning of the year for which he had been elected, the Praetor made

---

(*a*) The Praetor thus possessed two distinct branches of judicial authority, in the same manner as the Court of Exchequer does in England, which occasionally sits as a Court of Common Law, and a Court of Equity.

2. Samuel Johnson, *A Dictionary of the English Language* (1755). De Lolme cites one of Johnson's definitions for *chancellor*, not his definition for *chancery*.

3. De Lolme argues for the parallel between the English "Judge of Equity" and the Roman praetor by emphasizing the function of each official in providing new legal remedies to supplement and thereby modify existing law. The account obscures many key institutional differences, particularly the manner in which the praetor did not actually decide cases but rather authorized which cases would be tried before another legal official.

a declaration of those remedies for new difficult cases, which he had determined to afford during the time of his Magistracy; in the choice of which
he was no doubt directed, either by his own observations, while out of
office, on the propriety of such remedies, or by the suggestions of experienced Lawyers on the subject. This Declaration (*Edictum*) the Praetor produced *in albo,* as the expression was. Modern Civilians have made many
conjectures on the real meaning of the above words; one of their suppositions, which is as likely to be true as any other, is, that the Praetor's *Edictum,* or heads of new law remedies, were written on a whitened wall, by
the side of his Tribunal.

Among the provisions made by the Roman Praetors in their capacity of
Judges of Equity, may be mentioned those which they introduced in favour
of emancipated Sons, and of Relations by the Women's side (*Cognati*), in
regard to the right of inheriting. Emancipated Sons were <140> supposed,
by the Laws of the Twelve Tables, to have ceased to be the children of their
Father, and as a consequence, a legal claim was denied them on the paternal
inheritance: Relations by the Women's side were taken no notice of, in that
article of the same laws which treated of the right of succession, mention
being only made of relations by the Men's side (*Agnati*). The former, the
Praetor admitted, by the Edict *Unde Liberi,* to share their Father's (or
Grandfather's) inheritance along with their brothers; and the latter he put
in possession of the patrimony of a kinsman deceased, by means of the
Edict *Unde Cognati,* when there were no relations by the Men's side. These
two kinds of inheritance were not however called *haereditas,* but only *bonorum possessio;* these words being very accurately distinguished, though the
effect was in the issue exactly the same (*a*).[4] <141>

4. De Lolme refers to praetorian edicts that permitted patterns of inheritance to descendants such as daughters or emancipated sons, who were otherwise excluded from
succession under Roman civil law. *Bonorum possessio* denoted the form of title by which
an individual who was not an heir under the civil law held an estate.

(*a*) As the power of Fathers, at Rome, was unbounded, and lasted as long as their
life, the emancipating of Sons was a case that occurred frequently enough, either for the
security, or satisfaction, of those who engaged in any undertaking with them. The power
of Fathers had been carried so far by the laws of Romulus, confirmed afterwards by those
of the Twelve Tables, that they might sell their Sons for slaves as often as three times, if,
after a first or second sale, they happened to acquire their liberty: it was only after being
sold for the third time, and then becoming again free, that Sons could be entirely released

In the same manner, the Laws of the Twelve Tables had provided relief only for cases of theft; and no mention was made in them of cases of goods taken away by force (a deed which was not looked upon in so odious a light at Rome as theft, which was considered as the peculiar guilt of slaves). In process of time the Praetor promised relief to such persons as might have their goods taken from them by open force, and gave them an action for the recovery of four times the value, against those who had committed the fact with an evil intention. *Si cui dolo malo bona rapta esse dicentur, ei in quadruplum* JUDICIUM DABO.[5]

Again, neither the Law of the Twelve Tables, nor the Laws made afterwards in the Assemblies of the People, had provided remedies <142> except for very few cases of fraud. Here the Praetor likewise interfered in his capacity of Judge of Equity, though so very late as the times of Cicero; and promised relief to defrauded persons, in those cases in which the Laws in being afforded no action. *Quae dolo malo facta esse dicentur, si de his rebus alia actio non erit, & justa causa esse videbitur,* JUDICIUM DABO (*a*).[6] By

---

from the paternal authority. On this law-doctrine was founded the peculiar formality and method of emancipating Sons. A pair of scales, and some copper coin were first brought; without the presence of these ingredients the whole business would have been void: and the Father then made a formal sale of his son to a person appointed to buy him, who was immediately to free, or *manumit* him: these sales and manumissions were repeated three times. Five witnesses were to be present, besides a Man to hold the scales (*Libripens*), and another (*Antestatus*) occasionally to remind the witnesses to be attentive to the business before them.

(*a*) At the same time that the Praetor proffered a new Edict, he also made public those peculiar formulae by which the execution of the same was afterwards to be required from him. The name of that Praetor who first produced the Edict above mentioned, was Aquilius, as we are informed by Cicero, in that elegant story well known to Scholars, in which he relates the kind of fraud that was put upon Canius, a Roman Knight, when he purchased a pleasure-house and gardens, near Syracuse, in Sicily. This account Cicero concludes with observing that Canius was left without remedy, "as Aquilius, his Colleague and friend, had not yet published his formulae concerning fraud." *Quid enim faceret? nondum enim Aquilius, Collega & familiaris meus, protulerat de dolo malo formulas.* Off. III. 14. [[De Lolme translates and quotes Cicero's *De officiis* (Of duties), book 3, chapter 14.]]

5. "If it shall be shown that goods have been forcibly taken from anyone with an evil intention, I will grant him a trial at law, with power to sue for fourfold damages."

6. "Whatever shall be shown to have been done with an evil intention, I will grant a trial at law to the injured party, provided there is no other legal process applicable to such matters, and the cause shall appear to be just."

Edicts of the same nature, Praetors in process of time gave relief in certain cases to married Women, and likewise to Minors (*Minoribus* xxv *annis succurrit Praetor,* &c. (*a*). <143>

The Courts of Equity established in England, have in like manner provided remedies for a very great number of cases, or species of demand, for which the Courts of Common Law, cramped by their forms and peculiar law tenets, can afford none. Thus, the Courts of Equity may, in certain cases, give actions for and against infants, notwithstanding their minority—and for and against married Women, notwithstanding their coverture. Married Women may even in certain cases, sue their husbands before a Court of Equity. Executors may be made to pay interest for money that lies long in their hands. Courts of Equity may appoint Commissioners to hear the evidence of absent witnesses. When other proofs fail, they may impose an oath on either of the Parties; or, in <144> the like case of a failure of proofs, they may compel a trader to produce his books of trade. They may also confirm a title to land, though one has lost his writings, &c. &c.

The power of the Courts of Equity in England, of which the Court of Chancery is the principal one, no doubt owes its origin to the power possessed by this latter, both of creating, and issuing Writs. When new complicated cases offered, for which a new kind of Writ was wanted, the Judges of Chancery, finding that it was necessary that justice should be done, and at the same time being unwilling to make general and perpetual provisions

(*a*) The Law Collection, or System, that was formed by the series of Edicts published at different times by Praetors, was called *Ius Praetorium,* and also *Ius Honorarium* (*not strictly binding*). The laws of the Twelve Tables, together with all such other Laws as had at any time been passed in the Assembly of the People, were called by way of eminence, *Ius Civile.* The distinction was exactly of the same nature as that which takes place in England, between the Common and Statute Laws, and the law or practice of the Courts of Equity. The two branches of the Praetor's judicial office were very accurately distinguished; and there was, besides, this capital difference between the remedies or actions which he gave in his capacity of Judge of Civil Law, and those in his capacity of Judge of Equity, that the former, being grounded on the *Ius Civile,* were perpetual; the latter must be preferred within the year, and were accordingly called *Actiones annuae,* or *Actiones praetoriae;* in the same manner as the former were called *Actiones civiles,* or *Actiones perpetuae.* [[As the praetor served in office for one year, the validity of his edict was likewise limited to one year. The development of the *jus honorarium,* however, was a product of the cumulative process by which praetors both maintained earlier edicts (*edictum tralaticium*) and introduced new ones (*edictum perpetuum*). De Lolme returns to and clarifies this point below, p. III, note a.]]

on the cases before them by creating new Writs, commanded the appearance of both Parties, in order to procure as complete information as possible in regard to the circumstances attending the case; and then they gave a decree upon the same by way of experiment.

To beginnings and circumstances like these the English Courts of Equity, it is not to be doubted, owe their present existence. In our days, when such strict notions are entertained concerning the power of Magistrates and Judges, it can scarcely be supposed that those Courts, however useful, could gain admittance. Nor indeed, even in the times when they were instituted, were their proceedings <145> free from opposition; and afterwards, so late as the reign of Queen Elizabeth, it was adjudged in the case of *Colleston and Gardner,* that the killing of a Sequestrator from the Court of Chancery, in the discharge of his business, was no murder; which judgement could only be awarded on the ground that the Sequestrator's commission, and consequently the power of his Employers, was illegal (*a*).[7] However, the authority of the Courts of Equity has in process of time become settled; one of the constituent branches of the Legislature even receives at present appeals from the decrees passed in those Courts; and I have no doubt that several Acts of the whole Legislature might be produced, in which the office of the Courts of Equity is openly acknowledged.

The kind of process that has in time been established in the Court of Chancery, is as follows. After a petition is received by the Court, the person sued is served with a writ of *Subpoena,* <146> to command his appearance.

(*a*) When Sir Edward Coke was Lord Chief Justice of the King's Bench, and Lord Ellesmere Lord Chancellor, during the reign of James I. a very serious quarrel also took place between the Courts of Law, and those of Equity, which is mentioned in the fourth Chapter of the third Book of Judge Blackstone's Commentaries; a Work in which more might have been said on the subject of the Courts of Equity. [[Blackstone's account of the famous 1616 conflict between Coke and Ellesmere appeared in *Commentaries on the Laws of England,* 3:53–54.]]

7. De Lolme's account in the text requires some clarification and correction. The law case to which he refers, *Colston* (or *Coulston*) *v. Gardner,* was decided in the Court of Chancery in 1680. The incident to which he refers—the killing of a legal officer ("Sequestrator") of the Court of Chancery—was not the subject of this case. Rather, the incident was mentioned by Heneage Finch, the Lord Chancellor Nottingham, in his 1680 decree. Nottingham, however, dated the incident to the reign of James I and not to the prior reign of Queen Elizabeth. See *Cases Argued and Decreed in the High Court of Chancery,* 3 vols. (London, 1730), 2:45.

If he does not appear, an attachment is issued against him; and if a *non inventus* is returned, that is, if he is not to be found, a proclamation goes forth against him; then a commission of rebellion is issued for apprehending him, and bringing him to the Fleet prison. If the person sued stands farther in contempt, a Serjeant at arms is to be sent out to take him; and if he cannot be taken, a sequestration of his land may be obtained till he appears. Such is the power which the Court of Chancery, as a Court of Equity, hath gradually acquired to compel appearance before it. In regard to the execution of the Decrees it gives, it seems that Court has not been quite so successful; at least, those Law-writers whose Works I have had an opportunity to see, hold it as a maxim, that the Court of Chancery cannot bind the estate, but only the person; and as a consequence, a person who refuses to submit to its decree, is only to be confined to the Fleet prison (*a*).[8] <147>

On this occasion I shall observe, that the authority of the Lord Chancellor, in England, in his capacity of a Judge of Equity, is much more narrowly limited than that which the Praetors in Rome had been able to assume. The Roman Praetors, we are to remark, united in themselves the double office of deciding cases according to the Civil Law (*Ius civile*), and to the Praetorian Law, or Law of Equity; nor did there exist any other Court besides their own, that might serve as a check upon them: hence it happened that their proceedings in the career of Equity, were very arbitrary indeed.

(*a*) The Court of Chancery was very likely the first instituted of the two Courts of Equity: as it was the Highest Court in the Kingdom, it was best able to begin the establishment of an office, or power, which naturally gave rise at first to so many objections. The Court of Exchequer, we may suppose, only followed the example of the Court of Chancery: in order the better to secure the new power it assumed, it even found it necessary to bring out the whole strength it could muster; and both the Treasurer and the Chancellor of the Exchequer sit (or are supposed to sit) in the Court of Exchequer, when it is formed as a Court of Equity. [[The Chancery and the Exchequer served as important administrative units of medieval royal government and finance. Chancery was additionally functioning as a court of equity directly under the authority of the Lord Chancellor by the early fifteenth century. The equity practice of the Exchequer was operating by the mid–sixteenth century, though its major growth occurred after 1580.]]

8. Fleet prison was one of several London jails of medieval origin that housed debtors as well as those confined by the Court of Chancery. De Lolme exaggerates the extent to which the modern Chancery was constrained to confine only the person and not the estate of an individual found guilty of contempt.

In the first place, they did not use to make it any very strict rule to adhere to the tenor of their own Edicts, during the whole year which their office lasted; and they assumed a power of altering them as they thought proper. To remedy so capital a defect in the distribution of Justice, a law was passed so late as the year of Rome 687 (not long before Tully's time) which was called *Lex Cornelia,* from the name of C. Cornelius, a Tribune of the People, who propounded it under the Consulship of C. Piso, and Man. Glabrio.[9] By this law it was enacted, <148> that Praetors should in future constantly decree according to their own Edicts, without altering any thing in them during the whole year of their Praetorship. Some modern Civilians produce a certain Senatusconsult to the same effect, which, they say, had been passed a hundred years before; while others are of opinion that the same is not genuine: however, supposing it to be really so, the passing of the law we mention, shews that it had not been so well attended to as it ought to have been.

Though the above mentioned arbitrary proceedings of Praetors were put a stop to, they still retained another privilege, equally hurtful; which was, that every new Praetor, on his coming into office, had it in his power to retain only what part he pleased of the Edicts of his predecessors, and to reject the remainder: from which it followed that the Praetorian Laws or Edicts, though provided for so great a number of important cases, were really in force for only one year, the time of the duration of a Praetor's office (*a*). Nor was a re-<149>gulation made to remedy this capital defect in the Roman Jurisprudence, before the time of the Emperor Hadrian; which is another remarkable proof of the very great slowness with which useful public regulations take place in every Nation. Under the reign of the Emperor we mention, the most useful Edicts of former Praetors were by his order collected, or rather compiled into one general Edict, which was

---

(*a*) Those Edicts of their predecessors in office, which the new Praetors thought proper to retain, were called *Edicta Tralatitia;* those which they themselves published (as also the alterations they made in former ones) were called *Edicta Nova.* From the above mentioned power exercised by every new Praetor in turn, their Edicts were sometimes distinguished by the appellation of *Leges annuae,* annual laws. See Orat. in Ver. 1. 42. [[De Lolme cites Marcus Tullius Cicero, *Verrine Orations, Second Part of the Speech Against Gaius Verres,* book 1, chapter 42 (section 109).]]

9. De Lolme refers to the *Lex Cornelia de Edictus* (67 B.C.E.), which ordered the praetors to administer justice according to the terms of the perpetual edicts.

thenceforwards to be observed by all civil Judges in their decisions, and was accordingly called the perpetual Edict (*perpetuum Edictum*). This Edict, though now lost, soon grew into great repute; all the Jurisconsults of those days vied with each other in writing commentaries upon it; and the Emperor himself thought it so glorious an act of his reign, to have caused the same to be framed, that he considered himself on that account as being another Numa (*a*).[10] <150>

But the Courts of Equity in England, notwithstanding the extensive jurisdiction they have been able in process of time to assume, never superseded the other Courts of law. These Courts still continue to exist in the same manner as formerly, and have proved a lasting check on the innovations, and in general the proceedings, of the Courts of Equity. And here we may remark the singular, and at the same time effectual, means of balancing each other's influence, reciprocally possessed by the Courts of the two different species. By means of its exclusive privilege both of creating and issuing writs, the Court of Chancery has been able to hinder the Courts of Common Law from arrogating to themselves the cognizance of those new cases which were not provided for by any law in being, and thus dangerously uniting in themselves the power of Judges of Equity with that of Judges of Common Law. On the other hand, the Courts of <151> Common Law are alone invested with the power of punishing (or allowing damages for) those cases of violence by which the proceedings of the Courts of Equity might be opposed; and by that means they have been able to obstruct the enterprizes of the latter, and prevent their effecting in themselves the

(*a*) Several other more extensive law compilations were framed after the perpetual Edict we mention; there having been a kind of emulation between the Roman Emperors, in regard to the improvement of the Law. At last, under the reign of Justinian, that celebrated Compilation was published, called the Code of Justinian, which, under different titles, comprises the Roman Laws, the Edicts of the Praetors, together with the *rescripts* of the Emperors; and an equal sanction was given to the whole. This was an event of much the same nature as that which will take place in England, whenever a coalition shall be effected between the Courts of Common Law, and those of Equity, and both shall thenceforwards be bound alike to frame their Judgments from the whole mass of decided cases and precedents then existing, at least of such as it will be possible to bring consistently together into one compilation.

10. Numa Pompilius was the early Roman king and lawgiver traditionally credited as the author of Rome's pagan religion. Numa ruled from 715 B.C.E. to 673 B.C.E., some eight hundred years before the reign of Emperor Hadrian, 117–138 C.E.

like dangerous union of the two offices of Judges of Common Law, and of Equity.

Owing to the situation of the English Courts of Equity, with respect to the Courts of Common Law, those Courts have really been kept within limits that may be called exactly defined, if the nature of their functions be considered. In the first place, they can neither touch Acts of Parliament, nor the established practice of the other Courts, much less reverse the judgments already passed in these latter, as the Roman Praetors sometimes used to do in regard to the decisions of their predecessors in office, and sometimes also in regard to their own. The Courts of Equity are even restrained from taking cognizance of any case for which the other Courts can possibly afford remedies. Nay, so strenuously have the Courts of Common Law defended the verge of their frontier, that they have prevented the Courts of Equity from using in their proceedings the <152> mode of Trial by a Jury; so that, when in a case already begun to be taken cognizance of by the Court of Chancery, the Parties happen to join issue on any particular fact (the truth or falsehood of which a Jury is to determine), the Court of Chancery is obliged to deliver up the cause to the Court of King's Bench, there to be finally decided (*a*). In fine, the example of the regularity of the proceedings, practised in the Courts of Common Law, has been communicated to the Courts of Equity; and Rolls or Records are carefully kept of the pleadings, determinations, and acts of those Courts, to serve as rules for future decisions (*b*).

So far therefore from having it in his power *"to temper and moderate,"* (that is, *to alter*) the Written Law or Statutes, a Judge of Equity we find, cannot alter the Unwritten Law, that is to say, the established practice of the other Courts, and the judgments grounded thereupon,—nor even can he meddle with those cases for which either the Written or Unwritten Law have already made general provisions, and <153> of which there is a possibility for the ordinary Courts of Law to take cognizance.

From all the above observations it follows, that, of the Courts of Equity

(*a*) See Cunningham's and Jacob's Law Dictionaries, *passim*. [[For Jacob and Cunningham, respectively, see above, book 1, chapter 10, p. 98, note a, and p. 99, note a.]]

(*b*) The Master of the Rolls is the Keeper of those records, as the title of this office expresses. His office in the Court of Chancery is of great importance, as he can hear and determine causes in the absence of the Lord Chancellor.

as established in England, the following definition may be given, which is, that they are a kind of *inferior experimental* Legislature, continually employed in finding out and providing law remedies for those new species of cases for which neither the Courts of Common Law, nor the Legislature, have as yet found it convenient or practicable to establish any. In doing which, they are to forbear to interfere with such cases as they find already in general provided for. A Judge of Equity is also to adhere in his decisions, to the system of decrees formerly passed in his own Court, regular records of which are kept for that purpose.

From this latter circumstance it again follows, that a Judge of Equity, by the very exercise he makes of his power, is continually abridging the arbitrary part of it; as every new case he determines, every precedent he establishes, becomes a land-mark or boundary which both he and his successors in office are afterwards expected to regard.

Here it may be added as a conclusion, that appeals from the Decrees passed in the Courts of Equity are carried to the House of <154> Peers; which bare circumstance might suggest that a Judge of Equity is subjected to certain positive rules, besides those *"of nature and conscience only"*; an appeal being naturally grounded on a supposition that some rules of that kind were neglected.

The above discussion on the English Law, has proved much longer than I intended at first; so much as to have swelled, I find, into two new additional Chapters. However, I confess I have been under the greater temptation to treat at some length the subject of the Courts of Equity, as I have found the error (which may be called a constitutional one) concerning the arbitrary office of those Courts, to be countenanced by the apparent authority of Lawyers, and of Men of abilities, at the same time that I have not seen in any book any attempt made professedly to confute the same, nor indeed to point out the nature and true office of the Courts of Equity.

Of Criminal Justice.

We are now to treat of an article, which, though it does not in England, and indeed should not in any State, make part of the powers which are properly Constitutional, <155> that is, of the reciprocal rights by means of which the Powers that concur to form the Government constantly balance each other, yet essentially interests the security of individuals, and, in the issue, the Constitution itself; I mean to speak of Criminal Justice. But, previous to an exposition of the laws of England on this head, it is necessary to desire the Reader's attention to certain considerations.

When a Nation entrusts the power of the State to a certain number of persons, or to one, it is with a view to two points: the one, to repel more effectually foreign attacks; the other, to maintain domestic tranquillity.

To accomplish the former point, each individual surrenders a share of his property, and sometimes, to a certain degree, even of his liberty. But, though the power of those who are the Heads of the State may thereby be rendered very considerable, yet it cannot be said, that liberty is, after all, in any high degree endangered, because, should ever the Executive Power turn against the Nation a strength which ought to be employed solely for its defence, this Nation, if it were really free, by which I mean, unrestrained by political prejudices, would be at no loss for providing the means of its security. <156>

In regard to the latter object, that is, the maintenance of domestic tranquillity, every individual must, exclusive of new renunciations of his natural liberty, moreover surrender, which is a matter of far more dangerous consequence, a part of his personal security.

The Legislative power, being, from the nature of human affairs, placed in the alternative, either of exposing individuals to dangers which it is at the same time able extremely to diminish, or of delivering up the State to the boundless calamities of violence and anarchy, finds itself compelled to reduce all its members within reach of the arm of the public Power, and, by withdrawing in such cases the benefit of the Social strength, to leave them exposed, bare, and defenceless, to the exertion of the comparatively immense power of the Executors of the laws.

Nor is this all; for, instead of that powerful re-action which the public authority ought in the former case to experience, here it must find none; and the law is obliged to proscribe even the attempt of resistance. It is therefore in regulating so dangerous a power, and in guarding lest it should deviate from the real end of its institution, that legislation ought to exhaust all its efforts. <157>

But here it is of great importance to observe, that the more powers a Nation has reserved to itself, and the more it limits the authority of the Executors of the laws, the more industriously ought its precautions to be multiplied.

In a State where, from a series of events, the will of the Prince has at length attained to hold the place of law, he spreads an universal oppression, arbitrary and unresisted; even complaint is dumb; and the individual, undistinguishable by him, finds a kind of safety in his own insignificance. With respect to the few who surround him, as they are at the same time the instruments of his greatness, they have nothing to dread but momentary caprices; a danger against which, if there prevails a certain general mildness of manners, they are in a great measure secured.

But in a State where the Ministers of the laws meet with obstacles at every step, even their strongest passions are continually put in motion; and that portion of public authority, deposited with them to be the instrument of national tranquillity, easily becomes a most formidable weapon.

Let us begin with the most favourable supposition, and imagine a Prince whose intentions are in every case thoroughly upright,—let us even suppose that he never lends an ear to the <158> suggestions of those whose interest it is to deceive him: nevertheless, he will be subject to error: and this error, which, I will farther allow, solely proceeds from his attachment to the public welfare, yet may very possibly happen to prompt him to act as if his views were directly opposite.

When opportunities shall offer (and many such will occur) of procuring a public advantage by overleaping restraints, confident in the uprightness of his intentions, and being naturally not very earnest to discover the distant evil consequences of actions in which, from his very virtue, he feels a kind of complacency, he will not perceive, that, in aiming at a momentary advantage, he strikes at the laws themselves on which the safety of the Nation rests, and that those acts, so laudable when we only consider the motive of them, make a breach at which tyranny will one day enter.

Yet farther, he will not even understand the complaints that will be made against him. To insist upon them will appear to him to the last degree injurious: pride, when perhaps he is least aware of it, will enter the lists; what he began with calmness, he will prosecute with warmth; and if the laws shall not have taken every possible precaution, he may think he is acting a very honest part, while he treats as <159> enemies of the State, Men whose only crime will be that of being more sagacious than himself, or of being in a better situation for judging of the results of measures.

But it were mightily to exalt human nature, to think that this case of a Prince who never aims at augmenting his power, may in any shape be expected frequently to occur. Experience, on the contrary, evinces that the happiest dispositions are not proof against the allurements of power, which has no charms but as it leads on to new advances: authority endures not the very idea of restraint; nor does it cease to struggle till it has beaten down every boundary.

Openly to level every barrier, at once to assume the absolute Master, are, as we said before, fruitless tasks. But it is here to be remembered, that those powers of the People which are reserved as a check upon the Sovereign, can only be effectual so far as they are brought into action by private individuals. Sometimes a Citizen, by the force and perseverance of his complaints, opens the eyes of the Nation; at other times, some member of the Legislature proposes a law for the removal of some public abuse: these, therefore, will be the persons against whom the Prince will direct all his efforts (*a*). <160>

And he will the more assuredly do so, as, from the error so usual among

(*a*) By the word Prince, I mean those who, under whatever appellation and in whatever Government it may be, are at the head of public affairs.

Men in power, he will think that the opposition he meets with, however general, wholly depends on the activity of but one or two leaders; and amidst the calculations he will make, both of the supposed smallness of the obstacle which offers to his view, and of the decisive consequence of the single blow he thinks he needs to strike, he will be urged on by the despair of ambition on the point of being baffled, and by the most violent of all hatreds, that which was preceded by contempt.

In that case which I am still considering, of a really free Nation, the Sovereign must be very careful that military violence do not make the smallest part of his plan: a breach of the social compact like this, added to the horror of the expedient, would infallibly endanger his whole authority. But, on the other hand, as he has resolved to succeed, he will in defect of other resources, try the utmost extent of the legal powers which the Constitution has intrusted with him; and if the laws have not in a manner provided for every possible case, he will avail himself of the imperfect precautions themselves that have been taken, as a cover to his tyrannical proceedings; he <161> will pursue steadily his particular object, while his professions breathe nothing but the general welfare, and destroy the assertors of the laws, under the very shelter of the forms contrived for their security (a).

This is not all; independently of the immediate mischief he may do, if the Legislature do not interpose in time, the blows will reach the Constitution itself; and the consternation becoming general amongst the People, each individual will find himself enslaved in a State which yet may still exhibit all the common appearances of liberty.

Not only, therefore, the safety of the individual, but that of the Nation itself, requires the utmost precautions in the establishment of that necessary, but formidable, prerogative of dispensing punishments. The first to

---

(a) If there were any person who charged me with calumniating human Nature, for it is her alone I am accusing here, I would desire him to cast his eyes on the History of a Lewis XI.—of a *Richelieu,* and, above all, on that of England before the Revolution: he would see the arts and activity of Government increase, in proportion as it gradually lost its means of oppression. [[De Lolme's examples—the government of France under King Louis XI (1461–83) and under Cardinal Richelieu's leadership (1624–42), and the government of England before 1688—illustrate the general tendency of sovereigns to expand and consolidate political power beyond established legal boundaries.]]

be taken, even without which it is impossible to avoid the dangers above suggested, is, that it never be left at the disposal, nor, if it be possible, exposed to the influence, of the Man who is the depositary of the public power. <162>

The next indispensable precaution is, that neither shall this power be vested in the legislative Body; and this precaution, so necessary alike under every mode of Government, becomes doubly so, when only a small part of the Nation has a share in the legislative power.

If the judicial authority were lodged in the legislative part of the People, not only the great inconvenience must ensue of its thus becoming independent, but also that worst of evils, the suppression of the sole circumstance that can well identify this part of the Nation with the whole, which is, a common subjection to the rules which they themselves prescribe. The legislative Body, which could not, without ruin to itself, establish, openly and by direct laws, distinctions in favour of its Members, would introduce them by its judgments; and the People, in electing Representatives, would give themselves Masters.

The judicial power ought therefore absolutely to reside in a subordinate and dependent body; dependent, not in its particular acts, with regard to which it ought to be a sanctuary, but in its rules and in its forms, which the legislative authority must prescribe. How is this body to be composed? In this respect farther precautions must be taken.

In a State where the Prince is absolute <163> Master, numerous Bodies of Judges are most convenient, inasmuch as they restrain, in a considerable degree, that respect of Persons which is one inevitable attendant on that mode of Government. Besides, those bodies, whatever their outward privileges may be, being at bottom in a state of great weakness, have no other means of acquiring the respect of the people than their integrity, and their constancy in observing certain rules and forms: nay, these circumstances united, in some degree over-awe the Sovereign himself, and discourage the thoughts he might entertain of making them the tools of his caprices (*a*).

(*a*) The above observations are in a great measure meant to allude to the French *Parlemens,* and particularly that of Paris, which forms such a considerable Body as to have been once summoned as a fourth Order to the General Estates of the kingdom.

But, in an effectually limited Monarchy, that is, where the Prince is understood to be, and in fact is, subject to the laws, numerous <164> Bodies of Judicature would be repugnant to the spirit of the Constitution, which requires, that all powers in the State should be as much confined as the end of their institution can allow; not to add, that in the vicissitudes incident to such a State, they might exert a very dangerous influence.

Besides, that awe which is naturally inspired by such Bodies, and is so useful when it is necessary to strengthen the feebleness of the laws, would not only be superfluous in a State where the whole power of the Nation is on their side, but would moreover have the mischievous tendency to introduce another sort of fear than that which Men must be taught to entertain. Those mighty Tribunals, I am willing to suppose, would preserve, in all situations of affairs, that integrity which distinguishes them in States of a different Constitution; they would never inquire after the influence, still less the political sentiments, of those whose fate they <165> were called to decide; but these advantages not being founded in the necessity of things, and the power of such Judges seeming to exempt them from being so very virtuous, Men would be in danger of taking up the fatal opinion, that the simple exact observance of the laws is not the only task of prudence: the Citizen called upon to defend, in the sphere where fortune has placed him, his own rights, and those of the Nation itself, would dread the consequence of even a lawful conduct, and though encouraged by the law, might desert himself when he came to behold its Ministers.

In the assembly of those who sit as his Judges, the Citizen might possibly

---

The weight of that body, increased by the circumstance of the Members holding their places for life, has in general been attended with the advantage just mentioned, of placing them above being over-awed by private individuals in the administration either of civil or criminal Justice; it has even rendered them so difficult to be managed by the Court, that the Ministers have been at times obliged to appoint particular Judges, or *Commissaries,* to try such Men as they had resolved to ruin.

These, however, are only local advantages, and relative to the nature of the French Government, which is an uncontrouled Monarchy, with considerable remains of Aristocracy. But in a free State, such a powerful Body of Men, vested with the power of deciding on the life, honour, and property, of the Citizens, would, as will be presently shewn, be productive of very dangerous political consequences; and the more so, if such Judges had, as is the case all over the world, except here, the power of deciding upon the matter of law, and the matter of fact.

descry no enemies: but neither would he see any Man whom a similiarity of circumstances might engage to take a concern in his fate: and their rank, especially when joined with their numbers, would appear to him, to lift them above that which over-awes injustice, where the law has been unable to secure any other check, I mean the reproaches of the Public.

And these his fears would be considerably heightened, if, by the admission of the Jurisprudence received among certain Nations, he beheld those Tribunals, already so formidable, <166> wrap themselves up in mystery, and be made, as it were, inaccessible (*a*).

He could not think, without dismay, of those vast prisons within which he is one day perhaps to be immured—of those proceedings, unknown to him, through which he is to pass—of that total seclusion from the society of other Men—nor of those long and secret examinations, in which, abandoned wholly to himself, he will have nothing but a passive defence to oppose to the artfully varied questions of Men whose intentions he shall at

(*a*) An allusion is made here to the secrecy with which the proceedings, in the administration of criminal Justice, are to be carried on, according to the rules of the civil law, which in that respect are adopted over all Europe. As soon as the prisoner is committed, he is debarred of the sight of every body, till he has gone through his several examinations. One or two Judges are appointed to examine him, with a Clerk to take his answers in writing; and he stands alone before them in some private room in the prison. The witnesses are to be examined apart, and he is not admitted to see them till their evidence is closed: they are then *confronted* together before all the Judges, to the end that the witnesses may see if the prisoner is really the Man they meant in giving their respective evidences, and that the prisoner may object to such of them as he shall think proper. This done, the depositions of those witnesses who are adjudged upon trial to be exceptionable, are set aside: the depositions of the others are to be laid before the Judges, as well as the answers of the prisoner, who has been previously called upon to confirm or deny them in their presence; and a copy of the whole is delivered to him, that he may, with the assistance of a Counsel, which is now granted him, prepare for his justification. The judges are, as has been said before, to decide both upon the matter of law and the matter of fact, as well as upon all incidents that may arise during the course of the proceedings, such as admitting witnesses to be heard in behalf of the prisoner, &c.

This mode of criminal Judicature may be useful as to the bare discovering of truth, a thing which I do not propose to discuss here; but, at the same time, a prisoner is so completely delivered up into the hands of the Judges, who even can detain him almost at pleasure by multiplying or delaying his examinations, that, whenever it is adopted, Men are almost as much afraid of being accused, as of being guilty, and especially grow very cautious how they interfere in public matters. We shall see presently how the Trial by Jury, peculiar to the English Nation, is admirably adapted to the nature of a free State.

least <167> mistrust, and in which, his spirits broken down by solitude, shall receive no support, either from the counsels of his friends, or the looks of those who shall offer up vows for his deliverance.

The security of the individual, and the consciousness of that security, being then equally essential to the enjoyment of liberty, and necessary for the preservation of it, these two points must never be left out of sight, in the establishment of a judicial power; and I conceive that they necessarily lead to the following maxims. <168>

In the first place I shall remind the reader of what has been laid down above, that the judicial authority ought never to reside in an independent Body; still less in him who is already the trustee of the executive power.

Secondly, the party accused ought to be provided with every possible means of defence. Above all things, the whole proceedings ought to be public. The Courts, and their different forms, must be such as to inspire respect, but never terror; and the cases ought to be so accurately ascertained, the limits so clearly marked, as that neither the executive power, nor the Judges, may ever hope to transgress them with impunity.

In fine, since we must absolutely pay a price for the advantage of living in society, not only by relinquishing some share of our natural liberty (a surrender which, in a wisely framed Government, a wise Man will make without reluctance) but even also by resigning part of even our personal security, in a word, since all judicial power is an evil, though a necessary one, no care should be omitted to reduce as far as possible the dangers of it.

And as there is however a period at which the prudence of Man must stop, at which the safety of the individual must be given up, <169> and the law is to resign him over to the judgment of a few persons, that is, to speak plainly, to a decision in some sense arbitrary, it is necessary that this law should narrow as far as possible this sphere of peril, and so order matters, that when the subject shall happen to be summoned to the decision of his fate by the fallible conscience of a few of his fellow-creatures, he may always find in them advocates, and never adversaries.

The Subject continued.

After having offered to the reader, in the preceding Chapter, such general considerations as I thought necessary, in order to convey a juster idea of the spirit of the criminal Judicature in England, and of the advantages peculiar to it, I now proceed to exhibit the particulars.

When a person is charged with a crime, the Magistrate, who is called in England *a Justice of the Peace,* issues a warrant to apprehend him; but this warrant can be no more than an order for bringing the party before him: he must then hear him, and take down in writ-<170>ing his answers, together with the different informations. If it appears on this examination, either that the crime laid to the charge of the person who is brought before the Justice, was not committed, or that there is no just ground to suspect him of it, he must be set absolutely at liberty: if the contrary results from the examination, the party accused must give bail for his appearance to answer to the charge; unless in capital cases, for then he must, for safer custody, be really committed to prison, in order to take his trial at the next Sessions.

But this precaution of requiring the examination of an accused person, previous to his imprisonment, is not the only care which the law has taken in his behalf; it has farther ordained that the accusation against him should be again discussed, before he can be exposed to the danger of a trial. At every session the Sheriff appoints what is called the *Grand Jury.* This Assembly must be composed of more than twelve Men, and less than twenty-four; and is always formed out of the most considerable persons in the County. Its function is to examine the evidence that has been given in support of every charge: if twelve of those persons do not concur in <171> the opinion that an accusation is well grounded, the party is immediately discharged; if, on the contrary, twelve of the grand Jury find the proofs sufficient, the prisoner is said to be indicted, and is detained in order to go through the remaining proceedings.

On the day appointed for his Trial, the prisoner is brought to the bar of the Court, where the Judge, after causing the bill of indictment to be read in his presence, must ask him how he would be tried: to which the prisoner answers, *by God and my Country;* by which he is understood to claim to be tried by a Jury, and to have all the judicial means of defence to which the law intitles him. The Sheriff then appoints what is called the Petty Jury: this must be composed of twelve Men, chosen out of the county where the crime was committed, and possessed of a landed income of ten pounds by the year; their declaration finally decides on the truth or falshood of the accusation.

As the fate of the prisoner thus entirely depends on the Men who compose this Jury, Justice requires that he should have a share in the choice of them; and this he has through the extensive right which the law has granted him, of challenging, or objecting to, such of them as he may think exceptionable.[1] <172>

These challenges are of two kinds. The first, which is called the challenge to the *array,* has for its object to have the whole pannel set aside: it is proposed by the prisoner when he thinks that the Sheriff who formed the pannel is not indifferent in the cause; for instance, if he thinks he has an interest in the prosecution, that he is related to the prosecutor, or in general to the party who pretends to be injured.

The second kind of challenges are called, to the Polls (*in capita*): they are exceptions proposed against the Jurors, severally, and are reduced to four heads by Sir Edward Coke.[2] That which he calls *propter honoris res-*

---

1. As De Lolme noted previously, in chapter 9, p. 81, note a, the right of the accused to challenge potential jurors was rarely utilized in practice. His account here of the rights enjoyed by those facing trial for criminal offences reports more accurately the formal legal protections than the routine practices of trial and conviction.

2. See Edward Coke, *First Part of the Institutes of the Laws of England,* 156. (The "First Part" of Coke's *Institutes* is the same work also commonly referred to as *Coke upon Littleton.*) For Coke's *Institutes,* see above, book 1, chapter 9, p. 85, note 8.

pectum,[3] may be proposed against a Lord impannelled on a jury; or he might challenge himself. That *propter defectum*[4] takes place when a Juror is legally incapable of serving that office, as, if he was an alien; if he had not an estate sufficient to qualify him, &c. That *propter delictum*[5] has for its object to set aside any Juror convicted of such crime or misdemeanor as renders him infamous, as felony, perjury, &c. That *propter affectum*[6] is proposed against a Juror who has an interest in the conviction of the prisoner: he, for instance, who has an action depending between him and the prisoner; he who is of kin to the prosecutor, or <173> his counsel, attorney, or of the same society or corporation with him, &c. (*a*).

In fine, in order to relieve even the imagination of the prisoner, the law allows him, independently of the several challenges above mentioned, to challenge peremptorily, that is to say, without shewing any cause, twenty Jurors successively (*b*).

When at length the Jury is formed, and they have taken their oath, the indictment is opened, and the prosecutor produces the proofs of his accusation. But, unlike to the rules of the Civil Law, the witnesses deliver their evidence in the presence of the prisoner: the latter may put questions to them; he may also produce witnesses in his behalf, and have them examined upon oath. Lastly, he is allowed to have a Counsel to assist him, not only in the discussion of any point of law which may be complicated with the fact, but also in the investigation of the fact itself, and <174>

(*a*) When the prisoner is an alien, one half of the Jurors must also be aliens; a Jury thus formed is called a Jury *de medietate linguae.* [[Literally "of mixed language." This jury comprised an equal number of natives and foreigners.]]

(*b*) When these several challenges reduce too much the number of Jurors on the pannel, which is forty-eight, new ones are named on a writ of the Judge, who are named the *Tales,* from those words of the writ, *decem* or *octo tales.* [["Ten or eight of such kind."]]

3. "From respect to his dignity."
4. "Because of incapacity."
5. "Because of delinquency."
6. "Because of interest."

who points out to him the questions he ought to ask, or even asks them for him (*a*).

Such are the precautions which the law has devised for cases of common prosecutions; but in those for High Treason, and for misprision of treason, that is to say, for a conspiracy against the life of the King, or against the State, and for a concealment of it (*b*), accusations which suppose a heat of party and powerful accusers, the law has provided for the accused party farther safe-guards.

First, no person can be questioned for any treason, except a direct attempt on the life of the King, after three years elapsed since the offence. 2°. The accused party may, independently of his other legal grounds of challenging, *peremptorily* challenge thirty-five Jurors. 3°. He may have two Counsel to assist him through the whole course of the proceedings. 4°. That his witnesses may not be kept away, the Judges must grant him the same compulsive process to bring them in, which they issue to compel the evidences against him. 5°. A copy of his indictment must be delivered <175> to him ten days at least before the trial, in presence of two witnesses, and at the expence of five shillings; which copy must contain all the facts laid to his charge, the names, professions, and abodes, of the Jurors who are to be on the pannel, and of all the witnesses who are intended to be produced against him (*c*).

When, either in cases of high treason, or of inferior crimes, the prosecutor and the prisoner have closed their evidence, and the witnesses have answered to the respective questions both of the Bench, and of the Jurors,

(*a*) This last article however is not established by law, except in cases of treason; it is done only through custom and the indulgence of the Judges. [[According to the strict rules of common law, defendants in trials for capital crimes (in contrast to civil suits) were not allowed legal counsel, and the judge was responsible for advising the accused. However, by De Lolme's time the practice developed of allowing the accused to receive occasional advice from counsel on questions of law. The right to a full defense by counsel in cases of high treason was established by statute in 1696.]]

(*b*) The penalty of a misprision of treason is, the forfeiture of all goods, and imprisonment for life.

(*c*) Stat. 7 Will. III. c. 3. and 7 Ann. c. 21. The latter was to be in force only after the death of the late Pretender. [[De Lolme refers to legislation enacted in 1696 and 1709. The "late Pretender" is James Francis Edward Stuart, who died in 1766 and was the heir of the deposed James II.]]

one of the Judges makes a speech, in which he sums up the facts which have been advanced on both sides. He points out to the Jury what more precisely constitutes the hinge of the question before them; and he gives them his opinion, both with regard to the evidences that have been given, and to the point of law which is to guide them in their decision. This done, the Jury withdraw into an adjoining room, where they must remain without eating and drinking, and without fire, till they have agreed unanimously among themselves, unless the Court give a permission to the contrary. Their decla-<176>ration or verdict (*veredictum*) must (unless they choose to give a special verdict) pronounce expressly, either that the prisoner is guilty, or that he is not guilty, of the fact laid to his charge. Lastly, the fundamental maxim of this mode of proceeding, is, that the Jury must be unanimous.

And as the main object of the institution of the Trial by a Jury, is to guard accused persons against all decisions whatsoever by Men invested with any permanent official authority (*a*), it is not only a settled principle that the opinion which the Judge delivers has no weight but such as the Jury choose to give it, but their verdict must besides comprehend the whole matter in trial, and decide as well upon the fact, as upon the point of law that may arise out of it: in other words, they must pronounce both on the commission of a certain fact, and on the reason which makes such fact to be contrary to law (*b*). <177>

(*a*) "Laws," as *Junius* says extremely well, "are intended, not to trust to what Men will do, but to guard against what they may do." [["Junius" was the pseudonymous author of a famous and frequently reprinted series of political letters attacking government ministers and policy that appeared in London's the *Public Advertiser* between 1769 and 1772. De Lolme cites, with slight variation, a passage from the letter of July 29, 1769, which Junius addressed to William Blackstone.]]

(*b*) Unless they choose to give a *special* verdict.—"When the Jury," says Coke, "doubt of the law, and intend to do that which is just, they find the *special* matter, and the entry is, *Et super totâ materiâ petunt discretionem Justiciariorum.*" Inst. iv. p. 41. [["On the whole matter they desire the opinion of the judges." In a "special verdict" in a criminal trial, the jury determined the facts of the case but left to the court the question of law, such as (for example) whether a particular homicide constituted murder or manslaughter. De Lolme cites Edward Coke's discussion of "special verdicts" in *Institutes of the Laws of England*, part 4, p. 41. (The "Fourth Part" of Coke's Institutes was published posthumously in 1644.)]]—These words of Coke, we may observe, confirm beyond a doubt the power of the Jury to determine on the whole matter in trial: a power which in all

This is even so essential a point, that a bill of indictment must expressly
be grounded upon those two objects. Thus, an indictment for treason must
charge, that the alledged facts were committed with a treasonable intent
(*proditoriè*). An indictment for murder must express, that the fact has been
committed with *malice prepense,* or aforethought. An indictment for rob-
bery must charge, that the things were taken with an intention to rob, (*an-
imo furandi*), &c. &c. (*a*).

Juries are even so uncontrolable in their verdict, so apprehensive has the
Constitution been lest precautions to restrain them in the exercise of their
function, however specious in the beginning, might in the issue be converted <178> to the very destruction of the ends of that institution, that it
is a repeated principle that a Juror, in delivering his opinion, is to have no
other rule but his opinion itself,—that is to say, no other rule than the belief
which results to his mind from the facts alledged on both sides, from their
probability, from the credibility of the witnesses, and even from all such
circumstances as he may have a private knowledge of. Lord Chief Justice

---

constitutional views is necessary; and the more so, since a prisoner cannot in England
challenge the Judge, as he can under the Civil Law, and for the same causes as he can a
witness.

(*a*) The principle that a Jury is to decide both on the fact and the *criminality* of it,
is so well understood, that if a verdict were so framed as only to have for its object the
bare existence of the fact laid to the charge of the prisoner, no punishment could be
awarded by the Judge in consequence of it. Thus, in the prosecution of Woodfall, for
printing Junius's letter to the King, the Jury brought in the following verdict, *guilty of
printing and publishing, only;* the consequence of which was the discharge of the prisoner.
[[De Lolme refers to the 1770 trial in the Court of King's Bench of the printer Henry
Woodfall, who was prosecuted for seditious libel for the publication of Junius's "Letter
to the King" of December 19, 1769, which attacked government policy on the American
colonies. The jury's verdict—"guilty of printing and publishing only"—defied the instruction given by the presiding judge, Chief Justice Lord Mansfield, who maintained
that the judges would decide the legal question of whether Junius's letter constituted a
seditious libel and sought to restrict the jury to the factual question of whether or not
Woodfall was the letter's publisher. The law remained more controversial and unsettled
than De Lolme's account indicates. The matter was not fully resolved until the 1792
enactment of Fox's libel law, which gave the jury the authority to determine the general
legal issue.]]

Hale expresses himself on this subject, in the following terms, in his History of the Common Law of England, chap. 12. § 11.[7]

"In this recess of the Jury, they are to consider their evidence, to weigh the credibility of the witnesses, and the force and efficacy of their testimonies; wherein (as I before said) they are not precisely bound to the rules of the Civil Law, viz. to have two witnesses to prove every fact, unless it be in cases of treason, nor to reject one witness because he is single, or always to believe two witnesses, if the probability of the fact does upon other circumstances reasonably encounter them; for the Trial is not here simply by witnesses, but *by Jury:* nay, it may so fall out, that a Jury upon their own knowledge may know a <179> thing to be false that a witness swore to be true, or may know a witness to be incompetent or incredible, though nothing be objected against him—and may give their verdict accordingly" (*a*).

If the verdict pronounces *not guilty,* the prisoner is set at liberty, and cannot, on any pretence, be tried again for the same offence. If the verdict declares him *guilty,* then, and not till then, the Judge enters upon his function as a Judge, and pronounces the punishment which the law appoints (*b*). But, even in this case, he is not to judge according to his own <180> discretion only; he must strictly adhere to the letter of the law; no constructive extension can be admitted; and however criminal a fact might in itself be, it would pass unpunished if it were found not to be positively

---

(*a*) The same principles and forms are observed in civil matters; only peremptory challenges are not allowed.

(*b*) When the party accused is one of the Lords temporal, he likewise enjoys the universal privilege of being judged by his Peers; though the Trial then differs in several respects. In the first place, as to the number of the Jurors: all the Peers are to perform the function of such, and they must be summoned at least twenty days beforehand. II. When the Trial takes place during the session, it is said to be in the *High Court of Parliament;* and the Peers officiate at once as Jurors and Judges: when the Parliament is not sitting, the Trial is said to be in the Court of the *High Steward of England;* an office which is not usually in being, but is revived on those occasions; and the High Steward performs the office of Judge. III. In either of these cases, unanimity is not required; and the majority, which must consist of twelve persons at least, is to decide.

7. De Lolme quotes Hale in support of the early doctrine (later described as the "self-informing jury") that the evidence considered by a jury in deciding its verdict was not limited to the evidence presented at trial. For Hale, see above, book 1, chapter 2, p. 38, note 3.

comprehended in some one of the cases provided for by the law. The evil that may arise from the impunity of a crime, that is, an evil which a new law may instantly stop, has not by the English laws been considered as of magnitude sufficient to be put in comparison with the danger of breaking through a barrier on which so mightily depends the safety of the individual (*a*).

To all these precautions taken by the law for the safety of the Subject, one circumstance must be added, which indeed would alone justify the partiality of the English Lawyers to their laws in preference to the Civil Law,—I mean the absolute rejection they have made of <181> torture (*b*). Without repeating here what has been said on this subject by the admirable Author of the Treatise on *Crimes and Punishments,*[8] I shall only observe, that the torture, in itself so horrible an expedient, would, more especially in a free State, be attended with the most fatal consequences. It was absolutely necessary to preclude, by rejecting it, all attempts to make the pursuit of guilt an instrument of vengeance against the innocent. Even the convicted criminal must be spared, and a practice at all rates exploded, which

(*a*) I shall give here an instance of the scruple with which the English Judges proceed upon occasions of this kind. Sir *Henry Ferrers* having been arrested by virtue of a warrant, in which he was termed a *Knight,* though he was a Baronet, Nightingale his servant took his part, and killed the Officer; but it was decided, that as the Warrant "was an ill Warrant, the killing an Officer in executing that Warrant, cannot be murder, because no good Warrant: wherefore he was found not guilty of the murder and manslaughter."—See Croke's Rep. P. III. p. 371. [[De Lolme refers to the 1635 "Sir Henry Ferrer's Case" heard by the Court of King's Bench and reported in *Reports of Sir George Croke, Knight,* ed. and trans. Harbottle Grimstone (1657–61), 3:371.]]

(*b*) Coke says (Inst. III. p. 35.) that when John Holland, Duke of Exeter, and William de la Poole, Duke of Suffolk, renewed, under Henry VI. the attempts made to introduce the Civil Law, they exhibited the torture as a *beginning thereof.* The instrument was called the Duke of Exeter's daughter. [[De Lolme cites Edward Coke's discussion in *Institutes of the Laws of England,* part 3, p. 35. (The "Third Part" of Coke's *Institutes* was published posthumously in 1644.) Coke reports these developments to have occurred in the years 1448–50.]]

8. Chapter 16 of Cesare Beccaria's 1764 *Dei delitti e delle pene* (On crimes and punishments) contained a comprehensive condemnation of the practice of judicial torture to secure criminal confessions.

might so easily be made an instrument of endless vexation and persecution (*a*). <182>

For the farther prevention of abuses, it is an invariable usage, that the Trial be public. The prisoner neither makes his appearance, nor pleads, but in places where every body may have free entrance; and the witnesses when they give their evidence, the Judge when he delivers his opinion, the Jury when they give their verdict, are all under the public eye. Lastly, the Judge cannot change either the place or the kind of punishment ordered by the law; and a Sheriff who should take away the life of a Man in a manner different from that which the law prescribes, would be prosecuted as guilty of murder (*b*).

In a word, the Constitution of England being a free Constitution, demanded from that circumstance alone (as I should already have but too often repeated, if so fundamental a truth could be too often urged) extraordinary precautions to guard against the dangers which unavoidably attend the Power of inflicting punishments; and it is particularly when considered in this light, that the Trial by Jury proves an admirable institution. <183>

By means of it, the Judicial Authority is not only placed out of the hands of the Man who is vested with the Executive Authority—it is even out of the hands of the Judge himself. Not only, the person who is trusted with the public power cannot exert it, till he has as it were received the permission to that purpose, of those who are set apart to administer the laws; but these

---

(*a*) Judge Foster relates, from Whitlock, that the Bishop of London having said to Felton, who had assassinated the Duke of Buckingham, "If you will not confess, you *must go to the Rack*"; the Man replied, "If it must be so, I know not who I may accuse in the extremity of the torture; Bishop Laud perhaps, or any Lord at this Board."

"Sound sense, (adds Foster) in the mouth of an Enthusiast and a Ruffian!"

Laud having proposed the Rack, the matter was shortly debated at the Board, and it ended in a reference to the Judges, who unanimously resolved that the Rack could not be legally used. [[De Lolme refers to the 1628 trial of John Felton, as reported in Michael Foster, *Report of some proceedings on the Commission of Oyer and Terminer and gaol delivery . . . to which are added discourses upon a few branches of the Crown Law* (1762), 244 and 244n.]]

(*b*) And if any other person but the Sheriff, even the Judge himself, were to cause death to be inflicted upon a Man, though convicted, it would be deemed homicide. See Blackstone, book iv. ch. 14. [[Blackstone's statement, part of his general treatment of homicide, appeared in *Commentaries on the Laws of England,* 4:179.]]

latter are also restrained in a manner exactly alike, and cannot make the law speak, but when, in their turn, they have likewise received permission.

And those persons to whom the law has thus exclusively delegated the prerogative of deciding that a punishment is to be inflicted,—those Men without whose declaration the Executive and the Judicial Powers are both thus bound down to inaction, do not form among themselves a permanent Body, who may have had time to study how their power can serve to promote their private views or interest: they are Men selected at once from among the people, who perhaps never were before called to the exercise of such a function, nor foresee that they ever shall be called to it again.

As the extensive right of challenging, effectually baffles, on the one hand, the secret prac-<184>tices of such as, in the face of so many discouragements, might still endeavour to make the Judicial Power subservient to their own views, and on the other excludes all personal resentments, the sole affection which remains to influence the integrity of those who alone are intitled to put the public power into action, during the short period of their authority, is, that their own fate as subjects, is essentially connected with that of the Man whose doom they are going to decide.

In fine, such is the happy nature of this institution, that the Judicial Power, a power so formidable in itself, which is to dispose without finding any resistance, of the property, honour, and life of individuals, and which, whatever precautions may be taken to restrain it, must in a great degree remain arbitrary, may be said in England, to exist,—to accomplish every intended end,—and to be in the hands of nobody (*a*).

In all these observations on the advantages <185> of the English criminal laws, I have only considered it as connected with the Constitution, which is a free one; and it is in this view alone that I have compared it with the Jurisprudence received in other States. Yet, abstractedly from the weighty constitutional considerations which I have suggested, I think there are still other interesting grounds of pre-eminence on the side of the laws of England.

(*a*) The consequence of this Institution is, that no Man in England ever meets the Man of whom he may say, "That Man has a power to decide on my death or life." If we could for a moment forget the advantages of that Institution, we ought at least to admire the ingenuity of it.

In the first place, they do not permit that a Man should be made to run the risque of a trial, but upon the declaration of twelve persons at least (*the Grand Jury*). Whether he be in prison, or on his Trial, they never for an instant refuse free access to those who have either advice, or comfort, to give him: they even allow him to summon all who may have any thing to say in his favour. And lastly, what is of very great importance, the witnesses against him must deliver their testimony in his presence; he may cross examine them, and, by one unexpected question, confound a whole system of calumny: indulgences these, all denied by the laws of other Countries.

Hence, though an accused person may be exposed to have his fate decided by persons (*the Petty Jury*) who possess not, perhaps, all <186> that sagacity which in some delicate cases it is particularly advantageous to meet with in a Judge, yet this inconvenience is amply compensated by the extensive means of defence with which the law, as we have seen, has provided him. If a Juryman does not possess that expertness which is the result of long practice, yet neither does he bring to judgement that hardness of heart which is, more or less also, the consequence of it: and bearing about him the principles, let me say, the unimpaired instinct of humanity, he trembles while he exercises the awful office to which he finds himself called, and in doubtful cases always decides for mercy.

It is to be farther observed, that in the usual course of things, Juries pay great regard to the opinions delivered by the Judges: that in those cases where they are clear as to the fact, yet find themselves perplexed with regard to the degree of guilt connected with it, they leave it, as has been said before, to be ascertained by the discretion of the Judge, by returning what is called a *Special Verdict:* that, whenever circumstances seem to alleviate the guilt of a person, against whom nevertheless the proof has been positive, they temper their verdict by recommending him to the mercy of the King; which seldom fails to produce <187> at least a mitigation of the punishment: that, though a Man, once acquitted, can never under any pretence whatsoever be again brought into peril for the same offence, yet a new Trial would be granted, if he had been found guilty upon proofs strongly suspected of being false (Blackst. b. iv. c. 27).[9] Lastly, what distinguishes the laws of

9. De Lolme cites Blackstone's "Of Trial and Conviction" in *Commentaries on the*

England from those of other Countries in a very honourable manner, is, that as the torture is unknown to them, so neither do they know any more grievous punishment than the simple deprivation of life.[10]

All these circumstances have combined to introduce such a mildness into the exercise of criminal Justice, that the trial by Jury is that point of their liberty to which the people of England are most thoroughly and universally wedded; and the only complaint I have ever heard uttered against it, has been by Men who, more sensible of the necessity of public order than alive to the feelings of humanity, think that too many offenders escape with impunity. <188>

Laws of England, book 4, chapter 27. English law, as De Lolme reports, was purposefully asymmetric in treating an acquittal as final but in allowing a new trial in cases of conviction where there was strong reason to believe that the jury had reached a verdict contrary to the evidence.

10. English law, in fact, allowed for several forms of aggravated capital punishment, such as burning, disemboweling, and quartering in cases of high treason, or drawing and hanging or drawing and burning in cases of petit treason.

CHAPTER XIV

The Subject concluded.—
Laws relative to Imprisonment.

But what completes that sense of independence which the laws of England procure to every individual (a sense which is the noblest advantage attending liberty) is the greatness of their precautions upon the delicate point of Imprisonment.

In the first place, by allowing in most cases, of enlargement upon bail, and by prescribing, on that article, express rules for the Judges to follow, they have removed all pretexts which circumstances might afford of depriving a man of his liberty.

But it is against the Executive Power that the Legislature has, above all, directed its efforts: nor has it been but by slow degrees that it has been enabled to wrest from it a branch of power which enabled it to deprive the people of their Leaders, as well as to intimidate those who might be tempted to <189> assume the function; and which, having thus all the efficacy of more odious means without the dangers of them, was perhaps the most formidable weapon with which it might attack public liberty.

The methods originally pointed out by the laws of England for the enlargement of a person unjustly imprisoned, were the writs of *mainprize,* *de odio & atiâ,* and *de homine replegiando.*[1] Those writs, which could not be denied, were an order to the Sheriff of the County in which a person was confined, to inquire into the causes of his confinement; and, according

---

1. "Of hatred and ill will" and "of redemption of the man."

to the circumstances of his case, either to discharge him completely, or upon bail.

But the most useful method, and which even, by being most general and certain, has tacitly abolished all the others, is the writ of *Habeas Corpus,* so called because it begins with the words *Habeas corpus ad subjiciendum.*[2] This writ, being a writ of high prerogative, must issue from the Court of King's Bench: its effects extend equally to every County; and the King by it requires, or is understood to require, the person who holds one of his subjects in custody, to carry him before the Judge, with the date of the confinement, <190> and the cause of it, in order to discharge him, or continue to detain him, according as the Judge shall decree.

But this writ, which might be a resource in cases of violent imprisonment effected by individuals, or granted at their request, was but a feeble one, or rather was no resource at all, against the prerogative of the Prince, especially under the reigns of the Tudors, and in the beginning of that of the Stuarts. And even in the first years of Charles the First, the Judges of the King's Bench, who in consequence of the spirit of the times, and of their holding their places *durante bene placito,* were constantly devoted to the Court, declared, "that they could not, upon a *habeas corpus,* either bail or deliver a prisoner, though committed without any cause assigned, in case he was committed by the special command of the King, or by the Lords of the Privy Council."[3]

Those principles and the mode of procedure which resulted from them, drew the attention of Parliament; and in the Act called the Petition of Right,[4] passed in the third year of the reign of Charles the First, it was enacted, that no person should be kept <191> in custody, in consequence of such imprisonments.

2. "You shall cause the body to be brought before."

3. De Lolme quotes the sense but not the exact words of Chief Justice Nicholas Hyde's statement in the famous 1627 Five Knights' Case, where five gentlemen sued out a writ of habeas corpus in King's Bench following their imprisonment for failing to comply with the crown's Forced Loan of 1626. The failure of the legal proceeding, as De Lolme reports, helped stimulate the parliamentary initiative in the 1628 Petition of Right; see above book 1, chapter 3, p. 49, note 3.

4. See above, book 1, chapter 7, p. 70, note 3.

But the Judges knew how to evade the intention of this Act: they indeed did not refuse to discharge a Man imprisoned without a cause; but they used so much delay in the examination of the causes, that they obtained the full effect of an open denial of Justice.

The Legislature again interposed, and in the Act passed in the sixteenth year of the reign of Charles the First, the same in which the Star-Chamber was suppressed, it was enacted that "if any person be committed by the King himself in person, or by his Privy Council, or by any of the Members thereof, he shall have granted unto him, without any delay upon any pretence whatsoever, a writ of *Habeas Corpus;* and that the Judge shall thereupon, within three Court days after the return is made, examine and determine the legality of such imprisonment."[5]

This Act seemed to preclude every possibility of future evasion: yet it was evaded still; and, by the connivance of the Judges, the person who detained the prisoner could without danger, wait for a second, and a third writ, called an *Alias* and a *Pluries,* before he produced him.[6] <192>

All these different artifices gave at length birth to the famous Act of *Habeas Corpus,* passed in the thirtieth year of the reign of Charles the Second, which is considered in England as a second Great Charter,[7] and has finally suppressed all the resources of oppression (*a*).

The principle articles of this Act are, to fix the different terms allowed for bringing a prisoner: those terms are proportioned to the distance; and none can in any case exceed twenty days.

2. That the Officer and Keeper neglecting to make due returns, or not delivering to the prisoner, or his agent, within six hours after demand, a copy of the warrant of commitment, or shifting the custody of the prisoner from one to another, without sufficient reason or authority (specified in the

(*a*) The real title of this Act is, *An Act for better securing the Subject, and for prevention of imprisonment beyond the Seas.*

5. The statute "for regulating the Privy Council and for taking away the court commonly called the Star Chamber" was enacted in 1641.

6. The two writs directed a sheriff to produce a defendant who had not been located on the basis of an earlier writ.

7. That is, a second "Magna Carta." The Habeas Corpus Amendment Act was enacted in 1679.

act), shall for the first offence forfeit one hundred pounds, and for the second two hundred, to the party grieved, and be disabled to hold his office. <193>

3. No person, once delivered by *Habeas Corpus,* shall be recommitted for the same offence, on penalty of five hundred pounds.

4. Every person committed for treason or felony, shall, if he require it in the first week of the next term, or the first day of the next session, be indicted in that term or session, or else admitted to bail, unless the King's witnesses cannot be produced at that time: and if not indicted and tried in the second term or session, he shall be discharged of his imprisonment for such imputed offence.

5. Any of the twelve Judges, or the Lord Chancellor, who shall deny a writ of *Habeas Corpus,* on sight of the warrant, or on oath that the same is refused, shall forfeit severally to the party grieved five hundred pounds.

6. No inhabitant of England (except persons contracting, or convicts praying to be transported) shall be sent prisoner to Scotland, Ireland, Jersey, Guernsey, or any place beyond the Seas, within or without the King's dominions,—on pain, that the party committing, his advisers, aiders, and assistants, shall forfeit to the party grieved a sum not less than five hundred pounds, to be recovered with treble costs,—shall be disabled to bear any <194> office of trust or profit,—shall incur the penalties of a *praemunire* (*a*), and be incapable of the King's pardon. <195>

(*a*) The Statutes of *praemunire,* thus called from the writ for their execution, which begins with the words *praemunire* (for *praemonere*) *facias,* were originally designed to oppose the usurpations of the Popes. The first was passed under the reign of Edward the First, and has been followed by several others, which even before the Reformation, established such effectual provisions as to draw upon one of them the epithet of *Execrabile Statutum.* The offences against which those Statutes were framed, were likewise distinguished by the appellation of *praemunire;* and under that word were included in general all attempts to promote the Pope's authority at the expence of the King's. The punishment decreed for such cases, was also called a *praemunire:* it has since been extended again to several other kinds of offence, and amounts to "the imprisonment for life, and forfeiture of all goods and rents of lands during life." See Blackstone's Com. book iv. ch. 8. [[De Lolme draws selectively on Blackstone's chapter-length "Of Praemunire" in *Commentaries on the Laws of England,* 4:102–18. "Praemunire facias" is "You shall cause to be forewarned." "Execrabile Statutum" is "the execrable statute."]]

BOOK II

Some Advantages peculiar
to the English Constitution.
1. The Unity of the Executive Power.

We have seen in former Chapters, the resources allotted to the different parts of the English Government for balancing each other, and how their reciprocal actions and reactions produce the freedom of the Constitution, which is no more than an equilibrium between the ruling Powers of the State. I now propose to shew that the particular nature and functions of these same constituent parts of the Government, which give it so different an appearance from that of other free States, are moreover attended with peculiar and very great advantages, which have not hitherto been suffi-ciently observed. <196>

The first peculiarity of the English Government, as a free Government, is its having a King,—its having thrown into one place the whole mass, if I may use the expression, of the Executive Power, and having invariably and for ever fixed it there. By this very circumstance also has the *depositum* of it been rendered sacred and inexpugnable;—by making one great, very great Man, in the State, has an effectual check been put to the pretensions of those who otherwise would strive to become such, and disorders have been prevented, which, in all Republics, ever brought on the ruin of liberty, and before it was lost, obstructed the enjoyment of it.

If we cast our eyes on all the States that ever were free, we shall see that the People ever turning their jealousy, as it was natural, against the Executive Power, but never thinking of the means of limiting it that has so happily taken place in England (a), never employed any other expedient besides the obvious one, of trusting that Power to Magistrates whom they appointed annually; which <197> was in great measure the same as keeping the management of it to themselves. Whence it resulted that the People, who, whatever may be the frame of the Government, always possess, after all, the reality of power, thus uniting in themselves with this reality of power the actual exercise of it, in form as well as in fact, constituted the whole State. In order therefore legally to disturb the whole State, nothing more was requisite than to put in motion a certain number of individuals.

In a State which is small and poor, an arrangement of this kind is not attended with any great inconveniences, as every individual is taken up with the care of providing for his subsistence, as great objects of ambition are wanting, and as evils cannot, in such a State, ever become much complicated. In a State that strives for aggrandisement, the difficulties and danger attending the pursuit of such a plan, inspire a general spirit of caution, and every individual makes a sober use of his rights as a Citizen.

But when, at length, those exterior motives come to cease, and the passions, and even the virtues, which they excited, thus become reduced to a state of inaction, the People <198> turn their eyes back towards the interior of the Republic, and every individual, in seeking then to concern himself in all affairs, seeks for new objects that may restore him to that state of exertion which habit, he finds, has rendered necessary to him, and to exercise a share of power which, small as it is, yet flatters his vanity.

As the preceding events must needs have given an influence to a certain number of Citizens, they avail themselves of the general disposition of the people, to promote their private views: the legislative power is thenceforth continually in motion; and as it is badly informed and falsely directed, almost every exertion of it is attended with some injury either to the Laws, or the State.

This is not all; as those who compose the general Assemblies cannot, in

(a) The rendering that power dependent on the People for its supplies.—See on this subject Chapter vi. Book I.

consequence of their numbers, entertain any hopes of gratifying their own private ambition, or in general their own private passions, they at least seek to gratify their political caprices, and they accumulate the honours and dignities of the State on some favourite whom the public voice happens to raise at that time.

But, as in such a State there can be, from the irregularity of the determinations of the <199> People, no such thing as a settled course of measures, it happens that Men never can exactly tell the present state of public affairs. The power thus given away is already grown very great, before those by whom it was given so much as suspect it; and he himself who enjoys that power, does not know its full extent: but then, on the first opportunity that offers, he suddenly pierces through the cloud which hid the summit from him, and at once seats himself upon it. The People, on the other hand, no sooner recover sight of him, than they see their Favourite now become their Master, and discover the evil, only to find that it is past remedy.

As this power, thus surreptitiously acquired, is destitute of the support both of the law and of the ancient course of things, and is even but indifferently respected by those who have subjected themselves to it, it cannot be maintained but by abusing it. The People at length succeed in forming somewhere a centre of union; they agree in the choice of a Leader; this Leader in his turn rises; in his turn also he betrays his engagements; power produces its wonted effects; and the Protector becomes a Tyrant. <200>

This is not all; the same causes which have given a Master to the State, give it two, give it three. All those rival powers endeavour to swallow up each other; the State becomes a scene of endless quarrels and broils, and is in a continual convulsion.

If amidst such disorders the People retained their freedom, the evil must indeed be very great, to take away all the advantages of it; but they are slaves, and yet have not what in other Countries makes amends for political servitude, I mean tranquillity.

In order to prove all these things, if proofs were deemed necessary, I would only refer the reader to what every one knows of Pisistratus and Megacles, of Marius and Sylla, of Caesar and Pompey.[1] However, I cannot

---

1. De Lolme invokes famous examples from antiquity of paired political leaders, first allies and then rivals, who undermined republican systems by exercising autocratic

avoid translating a part of the speech which a Citizen of Florence addressed once to the Senate: the reader will find in it a kind of abridged story of all Republics; at least of those which, by the share allowed to the People in the Government, deserved that name, and which, besides, have attained a certain degree of extent and power.

"And that nothing human may be perpetual and stable, it is the will of Heaven <201> that in all States whatsoever, there should arise certain destructive families, who are the bane and ruin of them. Of this our own Republic affords as many and more deplorable examples than any other, as it owes its misfortunes not only to one, but to several such families. We had at first the *Buondelmonti* and *Huberti*. We had afterwards the *Donati* and the *Cerchi;* and at present, (shameful and ridiculous conduct!) we are waging war among ourselves for the *Ricci* and the *Albizzi*.

"When in former times the Ghibelins were suppressed, every one expected that the Guelfs, being then satisfied, would have chosen to live in tranquillity; yet, but a little time had elapsed, when they again divided themselves into the factions of the *Whites* and the *Blacks*. When the Whites were suppressed, new parties arose, and new troubles followed. Sometimes battles were fought in favour of the Exiles; and at other times, quarrels broke out between the Nobility and the People. And, as if resolved to give away to others what we ourselves neither could, nor would, peaceably enjoy, we committed the care of our liberty <202> sometimes to King Robert, and at other times to his brother, and at length to the Duke of Athens; never settling nor resting in any kind of Government, as not knowing either how to enjoy liberty, or support servitude" (*a*).

The English Constitution has prevented the possibility of misfortunes

---

power: Meglaces and Pisastratus, tyrants of Athens, in the mid-sixth century B.C.E.; Gaius Marius and Lucius Cornelius Sulla (or Sylla), popular generals who served as consuls and tyrants of Rome in the early first century B.C.E.; and Julius Caesar and Gnaeus Pompeius Magnus (Pompey the Great), Roman generals who opposed each other in the civil war of 49–45 B.C.E. that preceded Caesar's final consolidation of power over the Roman Senate.

(*a*) See the History of Florence, by Machiavel, lib. iii. [[De Lolme quotes the discussion in book 3, chapter 5, of Machiavelli's 1525 *History of Florence,* which treated at length the destructive power of factions to undermine republican liberty and the public good. De Lolme earlier referred to this material in book 1, chapter 8, p. 78.]]

of this kind. Not only by diminishing the power, or rather the *actual exercise* of the power, of the People (*a*), and making them share in the Legislature only by their Representatives, the irresistible violence has been avoided of those numerous and general Assemblies, which, on whatever side they throw their weight, bear down every thing. Besides, as the power of the People, when they have any kind of power, and know how to use it, is at all times really formidable, the Constitution has set a counterpoise to it; and the Royal authority is this counterpoise. <203>

In order to render it equal to such a task, the Constitution has, in the first place, conferred on the King, as we have seen before, the exclusive prerogative of calling and dismissing the legislative Bodies, and of putting a negative on their resolutions.

Secondly, it has also placed on the side of the King the whole Executive Power in the Nation.

Lastly, in order to effect still nearer an equilibrium, the Constitution has invested the Man whom it has made the sole Head of the State, with all the personal privileges, all the pomp, all the majesty, of which human dignities are capable. In the language of the law, the King is Sovereign Lord, and the People are his subjects;—he is universal proprietor of the whole Kingdom;—he bestows all the dignities and places;—and he is not to be addressed but with the expressions and outward ceremony of almost Eastern humility. Besides, his person is sacred and inviolable; and any attempt whatsoever against it, is, in the eye of the law, a crime equal to that of an attack against the whole State.

In a word, since, to have too exactly completed the equilibrium between the power <204> of the People, and that of the Crown, would have been to sacrifice the end to the means, that is, to have endangered liberty with a view to strengthen the Government, the deficiency which ought to remain on the side of the Crown, has at least been in appearance made up, by conferring on the King all that sort of strength that may result from the opinion and reverence of the people; and amidst the agitations which are the unavoidable attendants of liberty, the Royal power, like an anchor that

(*a*) We shall see in the sequel, that this diminution of the exercise of the power of the People has been attended with a great increase of their liberty.

resists both by its weight and the depth of its hold, insures a salutary stead-iness to the vessel of the State.

The greatness of the prerogative of the King, by its thus procuring a great degree of stability to the State in general, has much lessened the pos-sibility of the evils we have above described; it has even, we may say, totally prevented them, by rendering it impossible for any Citizen even to rise to any dangerous greatness.

And to begin with an advantage by which the people easily suffer them-selves to be influenced, I mean that of birth, it is impossible for it to produce in England effects in any degree dangerous: for though there are <205> Lords who, besides their wealth, may also boast of an illustrious descent, yet that advantage, being exposed to a continual comparison with the splen-dor of the Throne, dwindles almost to nothing; and in the gradation uni-versally received of dignities and titles, that of Sovereign Prince and King places him who is invested with it, out of all degree of proportion.

The ceremonial of the Court of England is even formed upon that prin-ciple. Those persons who are related to the King, have the title of Princes of the blood, and, in that quality, an indisputed pre-eminence over all other persons (*a*). Nay, the first Men in the Nation think it an honourable dis-tinction to themselves to hold the different menial offices, or titles, in his Houshold. If we therefore were to set aside the extensive and real power of the King, as well as the numerous means he possesses of gratifying the am-bition and hopes of individuals, and were to consider only the Majesty of his title, and that kind of strength founded on public opinion, which results from <206> it, we should find that advantage so considerable, that to at-tempt to enter into a competition with it, with the bare advantage of high birth, which itself has no other foundation than public opinion, and that too in a very subordinate degree, would be an attempt completely extravagant.

If this difference is so great as to be thoroughly submitted to, even by those persons whose situation might incline them to disown it, much more

(*a*) This, by Stat. of the 31st of Hen. VIII. extends to the sons, grandsons, brothers, uncles, and nephews, of the reigning King. [[The 1539 legislation, "for the precedence of the lords in the Parliament chamber," specified the order of precedence for royal officials and blood relations who sat in the House of Lords.]]

does it influence the minds of the people. And if, notwithstanding the value which every Englishman ought to set upon himself as a Man, and a free Man, there were any whose eyes were so very tender as to be dazzled by the appearance and the arms of a Lord, they would be totally blinded when they came to turn them towards the Royal Majesty.

The only Man therefore, who, to those who are unacquainted with the Constitution of England, might at first sight appear in a condition to put the Government in danger, would be a Man who, by the greatness of his abilities and public services, might have acquired in a high degree the love of the people, and obtained a great influence in the House of Commons.

But how great soever this enthusiasm of the public may be, barren applause is the only <207> fruit which the Man whom they favour can expect from it. He can hope neither for a Dictatorship, nor a Consulship, nor in general for any power under the shelter of which he may at once safely unmask that ambition with which we might suppose him to be actuated,— or, if we suppose him to have been hitherto free from any, grow insensibly corrupt. The only door which the Constitution leaves open to his ambition, of whatever kind it may be, is a place in the administration, during the pleasure of the King. If, by the continuance of his services, and the preservation of his influence, he becomes able to aim still higher, the only door which again opens to him, is that of the House of Lords.

But this advance of the favourite of the people towards the establishment of his greatness, is at the same time a great step towards the loss of that power which might render him formidable.

In the first place, the People seeing that he is become much less dependent on their favour, begin, from that very moment, to lessen their attachment to him. Seeing him moreover distinguished by privileges which are the object of their jealousy, I mean their political jealousy, and member of a body <208> whose interests are frequently opposite to their's, they immediately conclude that this great and new dignity cannot have been acquired but through a secret agreement to betray them. Their favourite, thus suddenly transformed, is going, they make no doubt, to adopt a conduct entirely opposite to that which has till then been the cause of his advancement and high reputation, and, in the compass of a few hours, completely renounce those principles which he has so long and so loudly professed. In this certainly the People are mistaken; but yet neither would they be wrong, if they feared that a zeal hitherto so warm, so constant, I will even add, so sincere, when it concurred with their Favourite's private interest, would, by being thenceforth often in opposition to it, become gradually much abated.

Nor is this all; the favourite of the people does not even find in his new acquired dignity, all the increase of greatness and eclat that might at first be imagined.

Hitherto he was, it is true, only a private individual; but then he was the object in which the whole Nation interested themselves; his actions and words were set forth in the public prints; and he every where met with applause and acclamation. <209>

All these tokens of public favour are, I know, sometimes acquired very lightly; but they never last long, whatever people may say, unless real services are performed; now, the title of Benefactor to the Nation, when deserved, and universally bestowed, is certainly a very handsome title, and which does no-wise require the assistance of outward pomp to set it off. Besides, though he was only a Member of the inferior body of the Legislature, we must observe, he was the first; and the word *first* is always a word of very great moment.

But now that he is made Lord, all his greatness, which hitherto was indeterminate, becomes defined. By granting him privileges established and fixed by known laws, that uncertainty is taken from his lustre which is of so much importance in those things which depend on imagination; and his value is lowered, just because it is ascertained.

Besides, he is a Lord; but then there are several Men who possess but small abilities and few estimable qualifications, who also are Lords; his lot is, nevertheless, to be seated among them; the law places him exactly on the same level with them; and all that is real in his greatness, is thus lost in a croud of dignities, hereditary and conventional. <210>

Nor are these the only losses which the favourite of the People is to suffer. Independently of those great changes which he descries at a distance, he feels around him alterations no less visible, and still more painful.

Seated formerly in the Assembly of the Representatives of the People, his talents and continual success had soon raised him above the level of his fellow Members; and, being carried on by the vivacity and warmth of the

public favour, those who might have been tempted to set up as his competitors, were reduced to silence, or even became his supporters.

Admitted now into an Assembly of persons invested with a perpetual
and hereditary title, he finds Men hitherto his superiors,—Men who see
with a jealous eye the shining talents of the *homo novus*,[2] and who are firmly
resolved, that after having been the leading Man in the House of Commons, he shall not be the first in their's.

In a word, the success of the favourite of the People was brilliant, and
even formidable; but the Constitution, in the very reward it prepares for
him, makes him find a kind of Ostracism. His advances were sudden, and
his course rapid; he was, if you please, like a torrent ready to bear down
every thing before <211> it, but this torrent is compelled, by the general
arrangement of things, finally to throw itself into a vast reservoir, where it
mingles, and loses its force and direction.

I know it may be said, that, in order to avoid the fatal step which is to
deprive him of so many advantages, the favourite of the People ought to
refuse the new dignity which is offered to him, and wait for more important
successes from his eloquence in the House of Commons, and his influence
over the People.

But those who give him this counsel, have not sufficiently examined it.
Without doubt there are Men in England, who in their present pursuit of
a project which they think essential to the public good, would be capable
of refusing for a while a dignity which would deprive their virtue of opportunities of exerting itself, or might more or less endanger it: but woe to
him who should persist in such a refusal, with any pernicious design! and
who, in a Government where liberty is established on so solid and extensive
a basis, should endeavour to make the People believe that their fate depends
on the persevering virtue of a single Citizen. His ambitious views being at
last discovered (nor could it be long before they were so), his obstinate
resolu-<212>lution to move out of the ordinary course of things, would
indicate aims, on his part, of such an extraordinary nature, that all Men
whatever, who have any regard for their Country, would instantly rise up

2. "New man."

from all parts to oppose him, and he must fall, overwhelmed with so much ridicule, that it would be better for him to fall from the Tarpeian rock (*a*).[3]

In fine, even though we were to suppose that the new Lord might, after his exaltation, have preserved all his interest with the People, or, what would be no less difficult, that any Lord whatever could, by dint of his wealth and high birth, rival the splendor of the Crown itself, all these advantages, how great soever we may suppose them, as they <213> would not of themselves be able to confer on him the least executive authority, must for ever remain mere showy unsubstantial advantages. Finding all the active powers in the State concentered in that very seat of power which we suppose him inclined to attack, and there secured by formidable provisions, his influence must always evaporate in ineffectual words; and after having advanced himself, as we suppose, to the very foot of the Throne, finding no branch of independent power which he might appropriate to himself, and thus at last give a reality to his political importance, he would soon see it, however great it might have at first appeared, decline and die away.

God forbid, however, that I should mean that the People of England are so fatally tied down to inaction, by the nature of their Government, that they cannot, in times of oppression, find means of appointing a Leader. No; I only meant to say that the laws of England open no door to those accumulations of power, which have been the ruin of so many Republics; that they offer to the ambitious no possible means of taking advantage of the inadvertence, or even the gratitude, of the People, to make

(*a*) The Reader will perhaps object, that no Man in England can possibly entertain such views as those I have suggested here: this is precisely what I intended to prove. The essential advantage of the English Government above all those that have been called *free*, and which in many respects were but apparently so, is, that no person in England can entertain so much as a thought of his ever rising to the level of the Power charged with the execution of the Laws. All Men in the State, whatever may be their rank, wealth, or influence, are thoroughly convinced that they must in reality as well as in name, continue to be *Subjects;* and are thus compelled really to love, to defend, and to promote, those laws which secure the liberty of the Subject. This latter observation will be again introduced in the sequel.

3. The Tarpeian Rock, an elevated cliff overlooking the Roman Forum, was used during the Roman Republic as the execution site for traitors, who were thrown to their death from it.

themselves their Tyrants; and that the public power, of which the King has been made <214> the exclusive depositary, must remain unshaken in his hands, so long as things continue to keep in the legal order; which, it may be observed, is a strong inducement to him constantly to endeavour to maintain them in it (*a*). <215>

(*a*) There are several events, in the English History, which put in a very strong light this idea of the stability which the power of the Crown gives to the State.

One, is the facility with which the great Duke of Marlborough, and his party at home, were removed from their several employments. Hannibal, in circumstances nearly similar, had continued the war against the will of the Senate of Carthage: Caesar had done the same in Gaul; and when at last he was expressly required to deliver up his commission, he marched his army to Rome, and established a military despotism. But the Duke, though surrounded, as well as the above named Generals, by a victorious army, and by Allies in conjunction with whom he had carried on such a successful war, did not even hesitate to surrender his commission. [[The British general John Churchill, the Duke of Marlborough, became a national hero through a series of important victories over the French during the War of the Spanish Succession (1704–11). Notwithstanding his popularity and military successes, a change of government ministry led to his abrupt dismissal from office in 1711.]] He knew that all his soldiers were inseparably prepossessed in favour of that Power against which he must have revolted: he knew that the same prepossessions were deeply rooted in the minds of the whole Nation, and that every thing among them concurred to support the same Power: he knew that the very nature of the claims he must have set up, would instantly have made all his Officers and Captains turn themselves against him, and, in short, that in an enterprize of that nature, the arm of the sea he had to repass, was the smallest of the obstacles he would have to encounter.

The other event I shall mention here, is that of the Revolution of 1689. If the long established power of the Crown had not beforehand prevented the people from accustoming themselves to fix their eyes on some particular Citizens, and in general had not prevented all Men in the State from attaining any too considerable degree of power and greatness, the expulsion of James II. might have been followed by events similar to those which took place at Rome after the death of Caesar.

The Subject concluded.—The Executive Power is more easily confined when it is ONE.

Another great advantage, and which one would not at first expect, in this *unity* of the public power in England,—in this union, and, if I may so express myself, in this coacervation, of all the branches of the Executive authority, is the greater facility it affords of restraining it.

In those States where the execution of the laws is intrusted to several different hands, and to each with different titles and prerogatives, such division, and the changeableness of measures which must be the consequence of it, constantly hide the true cause of the evils of the State: in the endless fluctuation of things, no political principles have time to fix among the People: and public mis-<216>fortunes happen, without ever leaving behind them any useful lesson.

At sometimes military Tribunes, and at others, Consuls, bear an absolute sway;—sometimes Patricians usurp every thing, and at other times, those who are called Nobles (*a*);—sometimes the People are oppressed by De-

(*a*) The capacity of being admitted to all places of public trust, at length gained by the Plebeians, having rendered useless the old distinction between them and the Patricians, a coalition was then effected between the great Plebeians, or Commoners, who got into these places, and the ancient Patricians: hence a new Class of Men arose, who were called *Nobiles* and *Nobilitas*. These are the words by which Livy, after that period, constantly distinguishes those Men and families who were at the head of the State. [[Titus Livius (Livy) (59 B.C.E.–17 C.E.), whose classic history of the early Roman Republic, *Ab urbe condita* (From the founding of the city) served for De Lolme, as for many early modern writers, as a major source of information and insight concerning republican political systems as well as Roman history. The political effects of the competition be-

cemvirs, and at others by Dictators.[1]

Tyranny, in such States, does not always beat down the fences that are set around it; but it leaps over them. When men think it confined to one place, it starts up again in another;—it mocks the efforts of the People, not because it is invincible, but because it is unknown;—seized by the arm of a Hercules, it escapes with the changes of a Proteus.[2]

But the indivisibility of the Public power in England has constantly kept the views and efforts of the People directed to one and the same object; and the permanence of that power <217> has also given a permanence and a regularity to the precautions they have taken to restrain it.

Constantly turned towards that ancient fortress, the Royal power, they have made it, for seven centuries, the object of their fear; with a watchful jealousy they have considered all its parts—they have observed all its outlets—they have even pierced the earth to explore its secret avenues, and subterraneous works.

United in their views by the greatness of the danger, they regularly formed their attacks. They established their works, first at a distance; then

———

tween Rome's patrician and plebeian ranks formed one of Livy's central themes, examined at length in books 3–4 and 6–7.]]

1. De Lolme invokes several institutions of republican Rome to which he refers routinely in later discussion. Two consuls were elected annually by a citizen assembly (*comitia centuriata*) and served as the chief civil and military magistrates. In later political theory, the office was commonly treated as a monarchic element of Rome's constitution. Military tribunes were appointed for each of Rome's military legions and exercised general command of the army. (De Lolme elsewhere refers to the office of plebeian tribunes [*tribuni plebis*], who protected the property and interests of Rome's plebeian citizens and had authority to veto any act or decree of the Senate or other magistrates.) The nobles (*nobiles*) were an elite group of plebeian families whose descendants came to dominate important political offices including, especially, the office of consul. Decemvirs occupied the ten-person board (*decemvirate*) of the mid-fifth century B.C.E., which produced and authorized the law of the Twelve Tables. During their period in office, the other established Roman magistracies were suspended. Dictators were Roman magistrates who were invested with extraordinary powers and appointed in times of emergency to command the army or perform other specific tasks. The authority of the dictator was limited to a brief period of time and (in theory) ended with the emergency that led to the appointment.

2. In Greek mythology, Proteus was a sea god who could change form at will. Two of his sons, Polygonos and Telegonos, were killed by Hercules.

brought them successively nearer; and, in short, raised none but what served afterwards as a foundation or defence to others.

After the great Charter was established, forty successive confirmations strengthened it. The Act called *the Petition of Right,* and that passed in the sixteenth year of Charles the First, then followed: some years after, the *Habeas Corpus* Act was established; and the Bill of Rights made at length its appearance.[3] In fine, whatever the circumstances may have been, they always had, in their efforts, that inestimable advantage of knowing with certainty the general seat of the evils they had to defend themselves against; and each calamity, each <218> particular eruption, by pointing out some weak place, has ever gained a new bulwark to public Liberty.

To say all in three words; the Executive power in England is formidable, but then it is for ever the same; its resources are vast, but their nature is at length known; it has been made the indivisible and inalienable attribute of one person alone, but then all other persons, of whatever rank or degree, become really interested to restrain it within its proper bounds (*a*).

(*a*) This last advantage of the greatness and indivisibility of the Executive power, viz. the obligation it lays upon the greatest Men in the State, sincerely to unite in a common cause with the people, will be more amply discussed hereafter, when a more particular comparison between the English Government and the Republican form, shall be offered to the Reader.

3. De Lolme refers to parliamentary measures adopted in 1215 (Magna Carta), 1628 (Petition of Right), 1679 (Habeas Corpus Act), and 1688/89 (Bill of Rights), whose significance he discussed above, book 1, especially chapters 2–3.

CHAPTER III

A second Peculiarity.—The Division
of the Legislative Power.

The second peculiarity which England, as an undivided State and a free State, exhibits in its Constitution, is the division of its Legislature. But, in order to make the <219> reader more sensible of the advantages of this division, it is necessary to desire him to attend to the following considerations.

It is, without doubt, absolutely necessary, for securing the Constitution of a State, to restrain the Executive power; but it is still more necessary to restrain the Legislative. What the former can only do by successive steps (I mean subvert the laws) and through a longer or shorter train of enterprizes, the latter does in a moment. As its bare will can give being to the laws; so its bare will can also annihilate them: and, if I may be permitted the expression,—the Legislative power can change the Constitution, as God created the light.

In order therefore to insure stability to the Constitution of a State, it is indispensably necessary to restrain the Legislative authority. But here we must observe a difference between the Legislative and Executive powers. The latter may be confined, and even is the more easily so, when undivided: the Legislative, on the contrary, in order to its being restrained, should absolutely be divided. For, whatever laws it may make to restrain itself, they never can be, relatively to it, any thing more than simple resolutions: as those bars which it might erect to stop its own motions, <220> must then be within it, and rest upon it, they can be no bars. In a word, the same kind of impossibility is found, to fix the Legislative power, when it is *one,* which Archimedes objected against his moving the Earth (*a*).

Nor does such a division of the Legislature only render it possible for it to be restrained, since each of those parts into which it is divided, can then serve as a bar to the motions of the others; but it even makes it to be actually so restrained. If it has been divided into only two parts, it is probable that they will not in all cases unite, either for *doing,* or *undoing:*—if it has been divided into three parts, the chance that no changes will be made, is thereby greatly increased.

Nay more; as a kind of point of honour will naturally take place between these different parts of the Legislature, they will therefore be led to offer to each other only such propositions as will at least be plausible; and all very prejudicial changes will thus be prevented, as it were, before their birth.

If the Legislative and Executive powers differ so greatly with regard to the necessity of their being divided, in order to their being restrained, they differ no less with regard to the other consequences arising from such division. <221>

The division of the Executive power necessarily introduces actual oppositions, even violent ones, between the different parts into which it has been divided; and that part which in the issue succeeds so far as to absorb, and unite in itself, all the others, immediately sets itself above the laws. But those oppositions which take place, and which the public good requires should take place, between the different parts of the Legislature, are never any thing more than oppositions between contrary opinions and intentions; all is transacted in the regions of the understanding; and the only contention that arises is wholly carried on with those inoffensive weapons, assents and dissents, *ayes* and *noes.*

Besides, when one of these parts of the Legislature is so successful as to engage the others to adopt its proposition, the result is, that a law takes place which has in it a great probability of being good: when it happens to

(*a*) He wanted a spot whereupon to fix his instruments. [[There are several classical sources for the statement attributed to the mathematician of Syracuse, Archimedes (ca. 287–212 B.C.E.), that he could transport the earth if only he could find a fixed point to locate his instruments. Descartes invoked the statement in his 1641 *Meditations on First Philosophy,* meditation II.1.]]

be defeated, and sees its proposition rejected, the worst that can result from it is, that a law is not made at that time; and the loss which the State suffers thereby, reaches no farther than the temporary setting aside of some more or less useful speculation. <222>

In a word, the result of a division of the Executive power, is either a more or less speedy establishment of *the right of the strongest,* or a continued state of war (*a*):—that of a division of the Legislative power, is either truth, or general tranquillity.

The following maxim will therefore be admitted. That the laws of a State may be permanent, it is requisite that the Legislative power should be divided:—that they may have weight, and continue in force, it is necessary that the Executive power should be *one.*

If the reader conceived any doubt as to the truth of the above observations, he need only cast his eyes on the history of the proceedings of the English Legislature down to our times, to find a proof of them. He would be surprised to see how little variation there has been in the political laws of this Country, especially during the last hundred years, though, it is most important to observe, the Legislature has been as it were in a continual <223> state of action, and, no dispassionate Man will deny, has generally promoted the public good. Nay, if we except the Act passed under William III. by which it had been enacted that Parliaments should sit no longer than three years, and which was repealed by a subsequent Act, under George I. which allowed them to sit for seven years, we shall not find that any law, which may really be called Constitutional, and which has been enacted since the Restoration, has been changed afterwards.[1]

(*a*) Every one knows the frequent hostilities that took place between the Roman Senate and the Tribunes. In Sweden there have been continual contentions between the King and the Senate, in which they have overpowered each other by turns. And in England, when the Executive power became double, by the King allowing the Parliament to have a perpetual and independent existence, a civil war almost immediately followed. [[De Lolme cites examples of unstable competition between political institutions that shared executive powers. In the case of England, he connects the outbreak of the Civil War in 1642 with the enactment of the 1641 Triennial Act, which curtailed the crown's control over the summoning and dissolution of Parliament.]]

1. The 1694 Triennial Act limited the duration of a parliament to three years before

Now, if we compare this steadiness of the English Government with the continual subversions of the Constitutional laws of some ancient Republics, with the imprudence of some of the laws passed in their assemblies (*a*), and with the still greater inconsiderateness with which they sometimes repealed the most salutary regulations, as it were the day after they had been enacted,—if we call to mind the extraordinary means to which the Legislature of those Republics, at times sensible how its very power was prejudicial to itself and to the State, was obliged to have recourse, in <224> order, if possible, to tie its own hands (*b*), we shall remain convinced of the great advantages which attend the constitution of the English Legislature (*c*).

Nor is this division of the English Legislature accompanied (which is indeed a very fortunate circumstance) by any actual division of the Nation: each constituent part of it possesses strength sufficient to insure respect to its resolutions, yet no real division has been made of the forces of the State. Only, a greater proportional share of all those distinctions which are calculated to gain the reverence of the People, has been allotted to those parts of the Legislature which could not possess their <225> confidence, in so

---

holding new parliamentary elections. The 1716 Septennial Act extended this maximum to seven years.

(*a*) The Athenians, among other laws, had enacted one to forbid applying a certain part of the public revenues to any other use than the expences of the Theatres and public Shews. [[De Lolme likely refers to the law, as described by Montesquieu, "to punish by death anyone who might propose that the silver destined for the theaters be converted to the uses of war." See *The Spirit of the Laws,* book 3, chapter 3, note 6.]]

(*b*) In some ancient Republics, when the Legislature wished to render a certain law permanent, and at the same time mistrusted their own future wisdom, they added a clause to it, which made it death to propose the revocation of it. Those who afterwards thought such revocation necessary to the public welfare, relying on the mercy of the People, appeared in the public Assembly with a halter about their necks. [[The Greek orator Demosthenes (384–322 B.C.E.), in his speech "Against Timocrates," refers to the practice of the Locrian lawmakers who wore ropes around their necks when they repealed previous legislation.]]

(*c*) We shall perhaps have occasion to observe, hereafter, that the true cause of the equability of the operations of the English Legislature, is the opposition that happily takes places between the different views and interests of the several bodies that compose it: a consideration this, without which all political inquiries are no more than airy speculations, and is the only one that can lead to useful practical conclusions.

high a degree as the others; and the inequalities in point of real strength between them, have been made up by the magic of dignity.

Thus, the King, who alone forms one part of the Legislature, has on his side the majesty of the kingly title: the two Houses are, in appearance, no more than Councils entirely dependent on him; they are bound to follow his person; they only meet, as it seems, to advise him; and never address him but in the most solemn and respectful manner.

As the Nobles, who form the second order of the Legislature, bear, in point both of real weight and numbers, no proportion to the body of the People (*a*), they have received <226> as a compensation, the advantage of personal honours, and of an hereditary title.

Besides, the established ceremonial gives to their Assembly a great pre-eminence over that of the Representatives of the People. They are the *upper* House, and the others are the *lower* House. They are in a more special manner considered as the King's Council, and it is in the place where they assemble that his Throne is placed.

When the King comes to the Parliament, the Commons are sent for, and make their appearance at the bar of the House of Lords. It is moreover before the Lords, as before their Judges, that the Commons bring their impeachments. When, after passing a bill in their own House, they send it to the Lords to desire their concurrence, they always order a number of their own Members to accompany it (*b*); whereas the Lords send down

(*a*) It is for want of having duly considered this subject, that Mr. Rousseau exclaims, somewhere, against those who, when they speak of General Estates of France, "dare to call the people, the *third* Estate." At Rome, where all the order we mention was inverted,—where the *fasces* were laid down at the feet of the People,—and where the Tribunes, whose function, like that of the King of England, was to oppose the establishment of new laws, were only a subordinate kind of Magistracy, many disorders followed. In Sweden, and in Scotland (before the union), faults of another kind prevailed: in the former kingdom, for instance, an overgrown body of two thousand Nobles frequently over-ruled both King and People. [[De Lolme likely refers to Jean-Jacques Rousseau's passing comment on the third estate in book 3, chapter 15, of the 1762 *Du contrat social* (The social contract). In Rome, the *fasces* (literally, "bundle")—a tied bundle of wooden rods surrounding an axe—was an ancient symbol of political authority. For tribunes *(tribuni plebis),* see above, book 2, chapter 2, p. 151, note 1.]]

(*b*) The Speaker of the House of Lords must come down from his woolpack to receive the bills which the Members of the Commons bring to their House.

their bills to them, only by some of the Assistants of their House (*a*). When the nature of the <227> alterations which one of the two Houses desires to make in a bill sent to it by the other, renders a conference between them necessary, the Deputies of the Commons to the Committee which is then formed of Members of both Houses, are to remain uncovered. Lastly, those bills which (in whichever of the two Houses they have originated) have been agreed to by both, must be deposited in the House of Lords; there to remain till the Royal pleasure is signified.

Besides, the Lords are Members of the Legislature by virtue of a right inherent in their persons, and they are supposed to sit in Parliament on their own account, and for the support of their own interests.[2] In consequence of this they have the privilege of giving their votes by *proxies* (*b*); and, when any of them dissent from the resolutions of their House, they may enter a protest against them, containing the reasons of their particular opinion. In a word, as this part of the Legislature is destined frequently to balance the power of the People, what it could not receive in real strength, it has received in outward splendor and great-<228>ness; so that, when it cannot resist by its weight, it overawes by its apparent magnitude.

In fine, as these various prerogatives by which the component parts of the Legislature are thus made to balance each other, are all intimately connected with the fortune of State, and flourish and decay according to the vicissitudes of public prosperity or adversity, it thence follows, that, though differences of opinions may at some times take place between those parts, there can scarcely arise any, when the general welfare is really in question. And when, to resolve the doubts that may arise in political speculations of this kind, we cast our eyes on the debates of the two Houses for a long

(*a*) The twelve Judges and the Masters in Chancery. There is also a ceremonial established with regard to the manner, and marks of respect, with which those two of them, who are sent with a bill to the Commons, are to deliver it.

(*b*) The Commons have not that privilege, because they are themselves *proxies* for the People.—See Coke's Inst. iv. p. 41. [[Edward Coke, *Institutes of the Laws of England*, pt. 4, p. 12. (De Lolme's note mistakes the page.)]]

2. This applies to the English peers, but not to the sixteen Scottish peers who served in the House of Lords as representatives under the terms of the 1707 Act of Union.

succession of years, and see the nature of the laws which have been proposed, of those which have passed, and of those which have been rejected,
as well as of the arguments that have been urged on both sides, we shall
remain convinced of the goodness of the principles on which the English
Legislature is formed. <229>

A third Advantage peculiar to the English Government. The Business of proposing Laws, lodged in the Hands of the People.

A third circumstance which I propose to show to be peculiar to the English Government, is the manner in which the respective offices of the three component parts of the Legislature have been divided, and allotted to each of them.

If the Reader will be pleased to observe, he will find that in most of the ancient free States, the share of the People in the business of Legislation, was to approve, or reject, the propositions which were made to them, and to give the final sanction to the laws. The function of those Persons, or in general those Bodies, who were intrusted with the Executive power, was to prepare and frame the Laws, and then to propose them to the People: and in a word, they possessed that branch of the Legislative power which may be called the *initiative*, that is, the prerogative of putting that power in action (*a*). <230>

(*a*) This power of previously considering and approving such laws as were afterwards to be propounded to the People, was, in the first times of the Roman Republic, constantly exercised by the Senate: laws were made, *Populi jussu, ex auctoritate Senatûs.* Even in cases of elections, the previous approbation and *auctoritas* of the Senate, with regard to those persons who were offered to the suffrages of the People, was required. *Tum enim non gerebat is magistratum qui ceperat, si Patres auctores non erant facti.* Cic. pro Plancio, 3. [[De Lolme cites Cicero's 54 B.C.E. speech, *Pro Plancio* (On behalf of Plancius). The quoted passages read: "In accordance with the decree of the Senate and the will of the people" and "For in the old days, the man who had been elected to an office did not enter upon it if the patricians withheld their assent."]]

This *initiative,* or exclusive right of proposing, in Legislative assemblies, attributed to the Magistrates, is indeed very useful, and perhaps even necessary, in States of a republican form, for giving a permanence to the laws, as well as for preventing the disorders and struggles for power which have been mentioned before; but upon examination we shall find that this expedient is attended with inconveniences of little less magnitude than the evils it is meant to remedy. <231>

These Magistrates, or Bodies, at first indeed apply frequently to the Legislature for a grant of such branches of power as they dare not of themselves assume, or for the removal of such obstacles to their growing authority as they do not yet think it safe for them peremptorily to set aside. But when their authority has at length gained a sufficient degree of extent and stability, as farther manifestations of the will of the Legislature could then only create obstructions to the exercise of their power, they begin to consider the Legislature as an enemy whom they must take great care never to rouse. They consequently convene the Assembly of the People as seldom as they can. When they do it, they carefully avoid proposing any thing favourable to public liberty. Soon they even entirely cease to convene the Assembly at all; and the People, after thus losing the power of legally asserting their rights, are exposed to that which is the highest degree of political ruin, the loss of even the remembrance of them; unless some indirect

---

At Venice the Senate also exercises powers of the same kind, with regard to the *Grand Council* or Assembly of the Nobles. In the Canton of Bern, all propositions must be discussed in the *Little* Council, which is composed of twenty-seven Members, before they are laid before the Council of the *Two hundred,* in whom resides the sovereignty of the whole Canton. And in Geneva, the law is, "that nothing shall be treated in the *General Council,* or Assembly of the Citizens, which has not been previously treated and approved in the Council of the *Two hundred;* and that nothing shall be treated in the *Two hundred,* which has not been previously treated and approved in the Council of the *Twenty-five.*" [[Geneva's General Council (*Conseil General*), an institution dating from the medieval period, was an assembly comprising the entire Genevan citizenry. During the course of the sixteenth century, its power was eclipsed by the small Council of the Twenty-Five (or *Petit Conseil* [Little Council]). The Council of the Twenty-Five also dominated the Council of the Two Hundred, a political body introduced in the early sixteenth century. In De Lolme's own era, opposition to the political power of Geneva's ruling families typically took the form of demands for the restoration of the authority of the General Council. See De Lolme's further discussion below, book 2, chapter 5, pp. 174–75, note a, and the editorial introduction, pp. x–xi.]]

means are found, by which they may from time to time give life to their
dormant privileges; means which may be found, and succeed pretty well in
small States, where provisions can more easily be made to answer their in-
<232>tended ends, but in States of considerable extent, have always been
found, in the event, to give rise to disorders of the same kind with those
which were at first intended to be prevented.

But as the capital principle of the English Constitution totally differs
from that which forms the basis of Republican Governments, so is it capable of procuring to the People advantages that are found to be unattainable in the latter. It is the People in England, or at least those who represent
them, who possess the *initiative* in Legislation, that is to say, who perform
the office of framing laws, and proposing them. And among the many circumstances in the English Government, which would appear entirely new
to the Politicians of antiquity, that of seeing the person intrusted with the
Executive power bear that share in Legislation which they looked upon as
being necessarily the lot of the People, and the People that which they
thought the indispensable office of its Magistrates, would not certainly be
the least occasion of their surprize.

I foresee that it will be objected, that, as the King of England has the
power of dissolving, and even of not calling Parliaments, he is hereby possessed of a prerogative which <233> in fact is the same with that which I
have just now represented as being so dangerous.

To this I answer, that all circumstances ought to be combined together.
Doubtless, if the Crown had been under no kind of dependence whatever
on the people, it would long since have freed itself from the obligation of
calling their Representatives together; and the British Parliament, like the
National Assemblies of several other Kingdoms, would most likely have no
existence now, except in History.

But, as we have above seen, the necessities of the State, and the wants
of the Sovereign himself, put him under a necessity of having frequently
recourse to his Parliament; and then the difference may be seen between
the prerogative of not calling an Assembly, when powerful causes nevertheless render such a measure necessary, and the exclusive right, when an
Assembly is convened, of *proposing* laws to it.

In the latter case, though a Prince, let us even suppose, in order to save appearances, might condescend to mention any thing besides his own wants, it would be at most to propose the giving up of some branch of his prerogative upon which he set no value, or to reform such abuses as his inclination does not lead him to imitate; but he would be very <234> careful not to touch any points which might materially affect his authority.

Besides, as all his concessions would be made, or appear to be made, of his own motion, and would in some measure seem to spring from the activity of his zeal for the public welfare, all that he might offer, though in fact ever so inconsiderable, would be represented by him as grants of the most important nature, and for which he expects the highest gratitude. Lastly, it would also be his province to make restrictions and exceptions to laws thus proposed by himself; he would also be the person who were to chuse the words to express them, and it would not be reasonable to expect that he would give himself any great trouble to avoid all ambiguity (*a*). <235>

But the Parliament of England is not, as we said before, bound down to wait passively and in silence for such laws as the Executive power may condescend to propose to them. At the opening of every Session, they of themselves take into their hands the great book of the State; they open all the pages, and examine every article.

When they have discovered abuses, they proceed to enquire into their causes:—when these abuses arise from an open disregard of the laws, they endeavour to strengthen them; when they proceed from their insufficiency, they remedy the evil by additional provisions (*b*). <236>

(*a*) In the beginning of the existence of the House of Commons, bills were presented to the King under the form of *Petitions.* Those to which the King assented, were registered among the rolls of Parliament, with his answer to them; and at the end of each Parliament, the Judges formed them into Statutes. Several abuses having crept into that method of proceeding, it was ordained that the Judges should in future make the Statute before the end of every Session. Lastly, as even that became, in process of time, insufficient, the present method of framing bills was established; that is to say, both houses now frame the Statutes in the very form and words in which they are to stand when they have received the Royal assent. [[De Lolme's periodization of English legislative practice summarizes the fuller account set out by Matthew Hale in his *History of the Common Law of England,* chapter 1.]]

(*b*) No popular Assembly ever enjoyed the privilege of starting, canvassing, and pro-

Nor do they proceed with less regularity and freedom, in regard to that important object, subsidies. They are to be the sole Judges of the quantity of them, as well as of the ways and means of raising them; and they need not come to any resolution with regard to them, till they see the safety of the Subject completely provided for. In a word, the making of laws, is not, in such an arrangement of things, a *gratuitous* contract, in which the People are to take just what is given them, and as it is given them:—it is a contract in which they *buy* and *pay,* and in which they themselves settle the different conditions, and furnish the words to express them.

The English Parliament have given a still greater extent to their advantages on so important a subject. They have not only secured to themselves a right of proposing laws and remedies, but they have also prevailed <237> on the Executive power to renounce all claim to do the same.[1] It is even a constant rule that neither the King, nor his Privy Council, can make any amendments to the bills preferred by the two Houses; but the King is merely to accept or reject them: a provision this, which, if we pay a little attention

---

posing new matter, to such a degree as the English Commons. In France, when their General Estates were allowed to sit, their *remonstrances* were little regarded, and the particular Estates of the Provinces dare now hardly present any. In Sweden, the Power of proposing new subjects was lodged in an Assembly called the *Secret Committee,* composed of Nobles, and a few of the Clergy; and is now possessed by the King. In Scotland, until the *Union,* all propositions to be laid before the Parliament, were to be framed by the persons called the *Lords of the Articles.* In regard to Ireland, all bills must be prepared by the King in his Privy Council, and are to be laid before the Parliament by the Lord Lieutenant, for their assent or dissent: only, they are allowed to discuss, among them, what they call *Heads of a bill,* which the Lord Lieutenant is desired afterwards to transmit to the King, who selects out of them what clauses he thinks proper, or sets the whole aside; and is not expected to give at any time, any precise answer to them. And in republican Governments, Magistrates are never at rest till they have entirely secured to themselves the important privilege of *proposing;* nor does this follow merely from their ambition; it is also the consequence of the situation they are in, from the principles of that mode of Government.

1. De Lolme's language here is potentially misleading. The described distribution of legislative functions between Parliament and crown emerged as a matter of developed constitutional convention. At no specific point did the king formally "renounce" the authority to propose legislation, just as the crown's failure after 1708 to exercise its legislative veto never involved a formal renunciation of the veto power.

to the subject, we shall find to have been also necessary for completely securing the freedom and regularity of the parliamentary deliberations (*a*).

I indeed confess that it seems very natural, in the modelling of a State,
to intrust this very important office of framing laws, to those persons who
may be supposed to have <238> before acquired experience and wisdom,
in the management of public affairs. But events have unfortunately demonstrated, that public employments and power improve the understanding
of Men in a less degree than they pervert their views; and it has been found
in the issue, that the effect of a regulation which, at first sight, seems so
perfectly consonant with prudence, is to confine the People to a mere passive and defensive share in Legislation, and to deliver them up to the continual enterprizes of those who, at the same time that they are under the
greatest temptations to deceive them, possess the most powerful means of
effecting it.

If we cast our eyes on the History of the ancient Governments, in those
times when the persons entrusted with the Executive power were still in a
state of dependence on the Legislature, and consequently frequently
obliged to have recourse to it, we shall see almost continual instances of
selfish and insidious laws proposed by them to the Assemblies of the people.

And those Men in whose wisdom the law had at first placed so much
confidence, became, in the issue, so lost to all sense of shame and duty, that
when arguments were found to be no longer sufficient, they had <239>
recourse to force; the legislative Assemblies became so many fields of battle,
and their power, a real calamity.

I know very well, however, that there are other important circumstances

---

(*a*) The King indeed at times sends messages to either House; and nobody, I think,
can wish that no means of intercourse should exist between him and his Parliament. But
these messages are always expressed in very general words; they are only made to desire
the House to take certain subjects into their consideration; no particular articles or clauses
are expressed; the Commons are not to declare, at any settled time, any solemn acceptation or rejection of the proposition made by the King; and, in short, the House follows
the same mode of proceeding, with respect to such messages, as they usually do in regard
to petitions presented by private individuals. Some member makes a motion upon the
subject expressed in the King's message; a bill is framed in the usual way; it may be dropt
at every stage of it; and it is never the proposal of the Crown, but the motions of some
of their own Members, which the House discuss, and finally accept or reject.

besides those I have just mentioned, which would prevent disorders of this kind from taking place in England (*a*). But, on the other hand, let us call to mind that the person who, in England, is invested with the Executive authority, unites in himself the whole public power and majesty. Let us represent to ourselves the great and sole Magistrate of the Nation, pressing the acceptance of those laws which he had proposed, with a vehemence suited to the usual importance of his designs, with the warmth of Monarchical pride, which must meet with no refusal, and exerting for that purpose all his immense resources.

It was therefore a matter of indispensable necessity, that things should be settled in England in the manner they are. As the moving springs of the Executive power are, in the hands of the King a kind of sacred <240> *depositum,* so are those of the Legislative power, in the hands of the two Houses. The King must abstain from touching them, in the same manner as all the subjects of the kingdom are bound to submit to his prerogatives. When he sits in Parliament, he has left, we may say, his executive power without doors, and can only assent, or dissent. If the Crown had been allowed to take an active part in the business of making laws, it would soon have rendered useless the other branches of the Legislature.

(*a*) I particularly mean here, the circumstance of the People having entirely delegated their power to their Representatives: the consequences of which Institution will be discussed in the next Chapter.

CHAPTER V

In which an Inquiry is made, whether it would be an Advantage to public Liberty, that the Laws should be enacted by the Votes of the People at large.

But it will be said, whatever may be the wisdom of the English Laws, how great soever their precautions may be with regard to the safety of the individual, the People, as they do not themselves expressly enact them, cannot be looked upon as a free People. The Author of the *Social Contract* carries this opi-<241>nion even farther; he says, that, "though the people of England think they are free, they are much mistaken; they are so only during the election of Members for Parliament: as soon as these are elected, the People are slaves—they are nothing" (*a*).

Before I answer this objection, I shall observe that the word *Liberty* is one of those which have been most misunderstood or misapplied.

Thus, at Rome, where that class of Citizens who were really Masters of the State, were sensible that a lawful regular authority, once trusted to a single Ruler, would put an end to their tyranny, they taught the People to believe, that, provided those who exercised a military power over them, and overwhelmed them with insults, went by the names of *Consules, Dictatores, Patricii, Nobiles,*[1] in a word, by any other appellation than that horrid one

---

(*a*) See M. Rousseau's Social Contract, chap. xv. [[De Lolme provides an incomplete reference to Rousseau's famous dismissal of English political freedom; see *The Social Contract,* book 3, chapter 15.]]

1. "Consuls, dictators, patricians, nobles." Patricians comprised a privileged class of Roman citizens who monopolized many important religious and civic offices during the period of Rome's early development. For the other institutions, see above, book 2, chapter 2, p. 151, note 1.

167

of *Rex,* they were free, and that such a valuable situation must be preserved at the price of every calamity.

In the same manner, certain Writers of the present age, misled by their inconsiderate admiration of the Governments of ancient <242> times, and perhaps also by a desire of presenting lively contrasts to what they call the degenerate manners of our modern times, have cried up the governments of Sparta and Rome, as the only ones fit for us to imitate.[2] In their opinions, the only proper employment of a free Citizen is, *to be either incessantly assembled in the forum,* or *preparing for war.—Being valiant, inured to hardships, inflamed with an ardent love of one's Country,* which is, after all, nothing more than an ardent desire of injuring all Mankind for the sake of that Society of which we are Members—*and with an ardent love of glory,* which is likewise nothing more than an ardent desire of committing slaughter, in order to make afterwards a boast of it, have appeared to these Writers to be the only social qualifications worthy of our esteem, and of the encouragement of law-givers (*a*). And while, in order to support such opinions, they have used a profusion of exaggerated expressions without any distinct meaning, and perpetually repeated, though without defining them, the words *dastardliness, corruption, greatness of* <243> *soul,* and *virtue,* they have never once thought of telling us the only thing that was worth our knowing, which is, whether men were happy under those Governments which they so much exhorted us to imitate.

Nor, while they thus misapprehended the only rational design of civil Societies, have they better understood the true end of the particular institutions by which they were to be regulated. They were satisfied when they saw the few who really governed every thing in the State, at times perform the illusory ceremony of assembling the body of the People, that they might appear to consult them: and the mere giving of votes, under any disadvantage in the manner of giving them, and how much soever the law

(*a*) I have used all the above expressions in the same sense in which they were used in the ancient Commonwealths, and still are by most of the Writers who describe their Governments.

2. Although Rousseau served as a special target in De Lolme's criticism of those theorists who equated liberty with popular legislative bodies, he here makes clear that his comments were designed to address the larger body of early modern republican theorists.

might afterwards be neglected that was thus pretended to have been made in common, has appeared to them to be Liberty.

But those Writers are in the right: a Man who contributes by his vote to the passing of a law, has himself made the law; in obeying it, he obeys himself,—he therefore is free. A play on words, and nothing more. The individual who has voted in a popular legislative Assembly, has not <244> made the law that has passed in it; he has only contributed, or seemed to contribute, towards enacting it, for his thousandth, or even ten thousandth share: he has had no opportunity of making his objections to the proposed law, or of canvassing it, or of proposing restrictions to it, and he has only been allowed to express his assent, or dissent. When a law is passed agreeably to his vote, it is not as a consequence of this his vote that his will happens to take place; it is because a number of other Men have accidentally thrown themselves on the same side with him:—when a law contrary to his intentions is enacted, he must nevertheless submit to it.

This is not all; for though we should suppose that to give a vote is the essential constituent of liberty, yet, such liberty could only be said to last for a single moment, after which it becomes necessary to trust entirely to the discretion of other persons, that is, according to this doctrine, to be no longer free. It becomes necessary, for instance, for the Citizen who has given his vote, to rely on the honesty of those who collect the suffrages; and more than once have false declarations been made of them. <245>

The Citizen must also trust to other persons for the execution of those things which have been resolved upon in common: and when the assembly shall have separated, and he shall find himself alone, in the presence of the Men who are invested with the public power, of the Consuls, for instance, or of the Dictator, he will have but little security for the continuance of his liberty, if he has only that of having contributed by his suffrage towards enacting a law which they are determined to neglect.

What then is Liberty? Liberty, I would answer, so far as it is possible for it to exist in a Society of Beings whose interests are almost perpetually opposed to each other, consists in this, that, *every Man, while he respects the persons of others, and allows them quietly to enjoy the produce of their industry, be certain himself likewise to enjoy the produce of his own industry, and that his person be also secure.* But to contribute by one's suffrage to procure these advantages to the Community,—to have a share in establishing that order, that general arrangement of things, by means of which an individual, lost as it were in the croud, is effectually protected,—to lay down the rules to be observed by those <246> who, being invested with a considerable power, are charged with the defence of individuals, and provide that they should never transgress them,—these are functions, are acts of Government, but not constituent parts of Liberty.

To express the whole in two words: To concur by one's suffrage in enacting laws, is to enjoy a share, whatever it may be, of Power: to live in a state where the laws are equal for all, and sure to be executed (whatever may be the means by which these advantages are attained) is to be free.

Be it so; we grant that to give one's suffrage is not liberty itself, but only a means of procuring it, and a means too which may degenerate to mere form; we grant also, that it is possible that other expedients might be found for that purpose, and that, for a Man to decide that a State with whose Government and interior administration he is unacquainted, is a State in which the People *are slaves, are nothing,* merely because the *Comitia* of ancient Rome are no longer to be met with in it, is a somewhat precipitate decision.[3] But still we must continue to think, that liberty would be much more complete, if the People at large were expressly called upon to <247> give their opinion concerning the particular provisions by which it is to be secured, and that the English laws, for instance, if they were made by the suffrages of all, would be wiser, more equitable, and, above all, more likely to be executed. To this objection, which is certainly specious, I shall endeavour to give an answer.

If, in the first formation of a civil Society, the only care to be taken was that of establishing, once for all, the several duties which every individual owes to others, and to the State,—if those who are intrusted with the care of procuring the performance of these duties, had neither any ambition, nor any other private passions, which such employment might put in motion, and furnish the means of gratifying; in a word, if looking upon their function as a mere task of duty, they were never tempted to deviate from

3. The Roman Republic contained several assemblies, or *comitia,* each of which had legislative power: the *comitia centuriata* and the *comitia tributa* (both comprising the entire body of citizens) and the *concilium plebis* (comprising only plebeians).

the intentions of those who had appointed them, I confess that in such a case, there might be no inconvenience in allowing every individual to have a share in the government of the community of which he is a member; or rather I ought to say, in such a Society, and among such Beings, there would be no occasion for any Government. <248>

But experience teaches us that many more precautions, indeed, are necessary to oblige Men to be just towards each other: nay, the very first expedients that may be expected to conduce to such an end, supply the most fruitful source of the evils which are proposed to be prevented. Those laws which were intended to be equal for all, are soon warped to the private convenience of those who have been made the administrators of them:— instituted at first for the protection of all, they soon are made only to defend the usurpations of a few; and as the People continue to respect them, while those to whose guardianship they were intrusted make little account of them, they at length have no other effect than that of supplying the want of real strength in those few who have contrived to place themselves at the head of the community, and of rendering regular and free from danger the tyranny of the smaller number over the greater.

To remedy, therefore, evils which thus have a tendency to result from the very nature of things,—to oblige those who are in a manner Masters of the law, to conform themselves to it,—to render ineffectual the silent, powerful, and ever active conspiracy of those who govern, requires a degree of knowledge <249> and a spirit of perseverance, which are not to be expected from the multitude.

The greater part of those who compose this multitude, taken up with the care of providing for their subsistence, have neither sufficient leisure, nor even, in consequence of their more imperfect education, the degree of information requisite for functions of this kind. Nature, besides, who is sparing of her gifts, has bestowed upon only a few Men an understanding capable of the complicated researches of Legislation; and, as a sick Man trusts to his Physician, a Client to his Lawyer, so the greater number of the Citizens must trust to those who have more abilities than themselves for the execution of things which, at the same time that they so materially concern them, require so many qualifications to perform them with any degree of sufficiency.

To these considerations, of themselves so material, another must be added, which is if possible of still greater weight. This is, that the multitude, in consequence of their very being a multitude, are incapable of coming to any mature resolution.

Those who compose a popular Assembly are not actuated, in the course of their de-<250>liberations, by any clear and precise view of any present or positive personal interest. As they see themselves lost as it were in the croud of those who are called upon to exercise the same function with themselves,—as they know that their individual votes will make no change in the public resolution, and that, to whatever side they may incline, the general result will nevertheless be the same, they do not undertake to en-quire how far the things proposed to them agree with the whole of the laws already in being, or with the present circumstances of the State, because Men will not enter upon a laborious task, when they know that it can scarcely answer any purpose.

It is, however, with dispositions of this kind, and each relying on all, that the Assembly of the People meets. But as very few among them have previously considered the subjects on which they are called upon to deter-mine, very few carry along with them any opinion or inclination, or at least any inclination of their own, and to which they are resolved to adhere. As however it is necessary at last to come to some resolution, the major part of them are determined by reasons which they would blush to pay any regard to, on much less se-<251>rious occasions. An unusual sight, a change of the ordinary place of the Assembly, a sudden disturbance, a rumour, are, amidst the general want of a spirit of decision, the *sufficiens ratio*[4] of the determination of the greatest part (*a*); and from this assemblage of separate wills, thus formed hastily and without reflection, a general will results, which is also void of reflection.

If, amidst these disadvantages, the Assembly were left to themselves, and no body had an interest to lead them into error, the evil, though very great, would not however be extreme, because such an assembly never being called

(*a*) Every one knows of how much importance it was in the Roman Commonwealth, to assemble the People, in one place rather than another. In order to change entirely the nature of their resolutions, it was often sufficient to hide from them, or let them see, the Capitol.

4. "Sufficient reason."

upon but to determine upon an affirmative or negative, that is, never having but two cases to choose between, there would be an equal chance for their choosing either; and it might be hoped that at every other turn they would take the right side.

But the combination of those who share either in the actual exercise of the public Power, <252> or in its advantages, do not thus allow themselves to sit down in inaction. They wake, while the People sleep. Entirely taken up with the thoughts of their own power, they live but to increase it. Deeply versed in the management of public business, they see at once all the possible consequences of measures. And as they have the exclusive direction of the springs of Government, they give rise, at their pleasure, to every incident that may influence the minds of a multitude who are not on their guard, and who wait for some event or other that may finally determine them.

It is they who convene the Assembly, and dissolve it; it is they who offer propositions, and make speeches to it. Ever active in turning to their advantage every circumstance that happens, they equally avail themselves of the tractableness of the People during public calamities, and its heedlessness in times of prosperity. When things take a different turn from what they expected, they dismiss the Assembly. By presenting to it many propositions at once, and which are to be voted upon in the lump, they hide what is destined to promote their own private views, or give a colour to it, by joining it with things which they know will take hold of the minds <253> of the People (*a*). By presenting in their speeches, arguments, and facts,

---

(*a*) It was thus the Senate, at Rome, assumed to itself the power of laying taxes. They promised, in the time of the war against the Veientes, to give pay to such Citizens as would inlist; and to that end they established a tribute. The people, solely taken up with the idea of not going to war at their own expence, were transported with so much joy, that they crouded at the door of the Senate, and laying hold of the hands of the Senators, called them their Fathers—*Nihil unquam acceptum à plebe tanto gaudio traditur: concursum itaque Curiam esse, prehensatasque exeuntium manus, Patres vere appellatos, &c.* See Tit. Liv. book iv. [[De Lolme cites Titus Livius (Livy), *Ab Urbe Condita*, book 4.60.1– 2. The full passage reads: "Nothing, it is said, was ever welcomed by the plebs with such rejoicing. Crowds gathered at the Curia and men grasped the hands of the senators as they came out saying that they were rightly called Fathers, and confessing that they had brought it to pass that no one, so long as he retained a particle of strength, would grudge his life's blood to so generous a country."]]

which Men have no time to examine, they lead the People into gross, and
yet decisive errors; and the commonplaces of rhetoric, supported by their
personal influence, ever enable them to draw to their side the majority of
votes.

On the other hand, the few (for there are, after all, some) who, having
meditated on the proposed question, see the consequences of the decisive
step which is just going to be taken, being lost in the croud, cannot make
their feeble voices to be heard in the midst of the universal noise and confusion. They have it no more in their power to stop the general motion,
than a Man in the midst of an army on a march, has it in his power to
avoid marching. In the mean time, the People are giving their suffrages; a
majority <254> appears in favour of the proposal; it is finally proclaimed
as the general will of all; and it is at bottom nothing more than the effect
of the artifices of a few designing Men, who are exulting among themselves
(*a*) <255>

(*a*) I might confirm all these things by numberless instances from ancient History;
but, if I may be allowed, in this case, to draw examples from my own Country, & *celebrare
domestica facta* [["And to record events familiar to me."]], I shall relate facts which will
be no less to the purpose. In Geneva, in the year 1707, a law was enacted, that a General
Assembly of the People should be held every five years, to treat of the affairs of the
Republic; but the Magistrates, who dreaded those Assemblies, soon obtained from the
Citizens themselves the repeal of the law; and the first resolution of the People, in the
first of these periodical Assemblies (in the year 1712) was to abolish them for ever. The
profound secrecy with which the Magistrates prepared their proposal to the Citizens on
that subject, and the sudden manner in which the latter, when assembled, were acquainted with it, and made to give their votes upon it, have indeed accounted but imperfectly for this strange determination of the People; and the consternation which seized
the whole Assembly when the result of the suffrages was proclaimed, has confirmed many
in the opinion that some unfair means had been used. The whole transaction has been
kept secret to this day; but the common opinion on this subject, which has been adopted
by M. Rousseau in his *Lettres de la Montagne,* is this: the Magistrates, it is said, had
privately instructed the Secretaries in whose *ears* the Citizens were to *whisper* their suffrages: when a Citizen said, *approbation,* he was understood to approve the proposal of
the Magistrates; when he said, *rejection,* he was understood to reject the *periodical Assemblies.* [[De Lolme refers to Jean-Jacques Rousseau's 1764 *Lettres de la montagne* (*Letters
from the mountain*), which analyzed and attacked the same political developments in
Geneva treated by De Lolme here, by which the Council of the Twenty-Five frustrated
the 1707 effort to restore the political capacity of the General Assembly. For these institutions, see above, book 2, chapter 4, pp. 160–61, note a.]]

In the year 1738, the Citizens enacted at once into laws a small Code of forty-four
Articles, by one single line of which they bound themselves for ever to elect the four

In a word, those who are acquainted with Republican Governments, and, in general, who know the manner in which business is transacted in numerous Assemblies, will not scruple to affirm, that the few who are united together, who take an active part in public affairs, and whose station makes them con-<256>spicuous, have such an advantage over the many who turn their eyes towards them, and are without union among themselves, that, even with a middling degree of skill, they can at all times direct, at their pleasure, the general resolutions;—that, as a consequence of the very nature of things, there is no proposal, however absurd, to which a numerous assembly of Men may not, at one time or other, be brought to assent;—and that laws would be wiser, and more likely to procure the advantage of all, if they were to be made by drawing lots, or casting dice, than by the suffrages of a multitude.

Syndics (the Chiefs of the Council of the Twenty-five) out of the Members of the same Council; whereas they were before free in their choice. They at that time suffered also the word *approved* to be slipped into the law mentioned in the Note (*a*) p. 229 [[pp. 160–61]], which was transcribed from a former Code; the consequence of which was to render the Magistrates absolute masters of the Legislature.

The Citizens had thus been successively stripped of all their *political* rights, and had little more left to them than the pleasure of being called a *Sovereign Assembly,* when they met (which idea, it must be confessed, preserved among them a spirit of resistance which it would have been dangerous for the Magistrates to provoke too far), and the power of at least *refusing* to elect the four *Syndics.* Upon this privilege the Citizens have, a few years ago, (A. 1765. to 1768.) made their last stand: and a singular conjunction of circumstances having happened at the same time, to raise and preserve among them, during three years, an uncommon spirit of union and perseverance, they have in the issue succeeded in a great measure to repair the injuries which they had been made to do to themselves, for these last two hundred years and more. (*A total change has since that time been effected by foreign forces, in the Government of the Republic* (A. 1782) *upon which this is not a proper place to make any observation.*) [[The 1738 legislation, *Règlement de l'Ilustre médiation pour la pacification des troubles de la République de Genève* (*Settlement of the illustrious mediation for the pacification of the Republic of Geneva,* or, more commonly, "Act of Mediation"), which had resulted from the political mediation of France, authorized the General Assembly to debate and vote on proposals for new laws and new taxes, though principal political authority remained with the Council of the Twenty-Five. The 1738 settlement was effectively challenged in the years 1763–70 by the party of reform. In his closing parenthetical comment, added to the 1784 edition, De Lolme refers to the events of 1782, when a league of neighboring powers, led by France, used military intervention to suppress the popular interest in Geneva.]]

CHAPTER VI

Advantages that accrue to the People from appointing Representatives.

How then shall the People remedy the disadvantages that necessarily attend their situation? How shall they resist the phalanx of those who have engrossed to themselves all the honours, dignities, and power, in the State?

It will be by employing for their defence the same means by which their adversaries carry on their attacks: it will be by using the same weapons as they do, the same order, the same kind of discipline. <257>

They are a small number, and consequently easily united;—a small number must therefore be opposed to them, that a like union may also be obtained. It is because they are a small number, that they can deliberate on every occurrence, and never come to any resolutions but such as are maturely weighed—it is because they are few, that they can have forms which continually serve them for general standards to resort to, approved maxims to which they invariably adhere, and plans which they never lose sight of:—here therefore, I repeat it, oppose to them a small number, and you will obtain the like advantages.

Besides, those who govern, as a farther consequence of their being few, have a more considerable share, consequently feel a deeper concern in the success, whatever it may be, of their enterprizes. As they usually profess a contempt for their adversaries, and are at all times acting an offensive part against them, they impose on themselves an obligation of conquering. They, in short, who are all alive from the most powerful incentives, and aim at gaining new advantages, have to do with a multitude, who, wanting only to preserve what they already possess, are unavoidably liable to long intervals of inactivity and <258> supineness. But the People, by appointing Representatives, immediately gain to their cause that advantageous activity which they before stood in need of, to put them on a par with their adversaries; and those passions become excited in their defenders, by which they themselves cannot possibly be actuated.

Exclusively charged with the care of public liberty, the Representatives of the People will be animated by a sense of the greatness of the concerns with which they are intrusted. Distinguished from the bulk of the Nation, and forming among themselves a separate Assembly, they will assert the rights of which they have been made the Guardians, with all that warmth which the *esprit de corps* is used to inspire (*a*). Placed on an elevated theatre, they will endeavour to render themselves still more conspicuous; and the arts and ambitious activity of those who govern, will now be encountered by the vivacity and perseverance of opponents actuated by the love of glory. <259>

Lastly, as the Representatives of the People will naturally be selected from among those Citizens who are most favoured by fortune, and will have consequently much to preserve, they will, even in the midst of quiet times, keep a watchful eye on the motions of Power. As the advantages they possess, will naturally create a kind of rivalship between them and those who govern, the jealousy which they will conceive against the latter, will give them an exquisite degree of sensibility on every increase of their authority. Like those delicate instruments which discover the operations of Nature, while they are yet imperceptible to our senses, they will warn the People of those things which of themselves they never see but when it is too late; and their greater proportional share, whether of real riches, or of those which lie in the opinions of Men, will make them, if I may so express myself, the barometers that will discover, in its first beginning, every tendency to a change in the Constitution (*b*). <260>

(*a*) If it had not been for an incentive of this kind, the English Commons would not have vindicated their right of taxation with so much vigilance as they have done, against all enterprizes, often perhaps involuntary, of the Lords.

(*b*) All the above reasoning essentially requires that the Representatives of the People should be united in interest with the People. We shall soon see that this union really obtains in the English Constitution, and may be called the master-piece of it. [[See below, book 2, chapters 8 and 10.]]

CHAPTER VII

The Subject continued—The Advantages that accrue
to the People from their appointing Representatives,
are very inconsiderable, unless they also entirely
trust their Legislative Authority to them.

The observations made in the preceding Chapter are so obvious, that the
People themselves, in popular Governments, have always been sensible of
the truth of them, and never thought it possible to remedy, by themselves
alone, the disadvantages necessarily attending their situation. Whenever the
oppressions of their Rulers have forced them to resort to some uncommon
exertion of their legal powers, they have immediately put themselves under
the direction of those few Men who had been instrumental in informing
and encouraging them; and when the nature of the circumstances has required any degree of firmness and perseverance in their conduct, they have
never been able to attain the ends they proposed to themselves, except by
means of the most implicit deference to those Leaders whom they had thus
appointed. <261>

But as these Leaders, thus hastily chosen, are easily intimidated by the
continual display which is made before them of the terrors of Power, as
that unlimited confidence which the People now repose in them, only takes
place when public liberty is in the utmost danger, and cannot be kept up
otherwise than by an extraordinary conjunction of circumstances, and in
which those who govern seldom suffer themselves to be caught more than
once, the People have constantly sought to avail themselves of the short
intervals of superiority which the chance of events had given them, for
rendering durable those advantages which they knew would, of themselves,

be but transitory, and for getting some persons appointed, whose peculiar office it may be to protect them, and whom the Constitution shall thence-forwards recognize. Thus it was that the People of Lacedaemon obtained their Ephori, and the People of Rome their Tribunes.[1]

We grant this, will it be said; but the Roman People never allowed their Tribunes *to conclude any thing definitively;* they, on the contrary, reserved to themselves the right of *ratifying (a)* any resolutions the latter should take. This, I answer, was the very circum-<262>stance that rendered the insti-tution of Tribunes totally ineffectual in the event. The People thus wanting to interfere with their own opinions, in the resolutions of those on whom they had, in their wisdom, determined entirely to rely, and endeavouring to settle with an hundred thousand votes, things which would have been settled equally well by the votes of their advisers, defeated in the issue every beneficial end of their former provisions; and while they meant to preserve an appearance of their sovereignty, (a chimerical appearance, since it was under the direction of others that they intended to vote) they fell back into all those inconveniences which we have before mentioned.

The Senators, the Consuls, the Dictators, and the other great Men in the Republic, whom the People were prudent enough to fear, and simple enough to believe, continued still to mix with them, and play off their political artifices. They continued to make speeches to them (*b*), and still

(*a*) See Rousseau's Social Contract. [[For Rousseau's statement concerning the Ro-man tribunes, see *The Social Contract,* book 3, chapter 15.]]

(*b*) Valerius Maximus relates that the Tribunes of the People having offered to pro-pose some regulations in regard to the price of corn, in a time of great scarcity, Scipio Nasica over-ruled the Assembly merely by saying, "Silence Romans; I know better than you what is expedient for the Republic. Which words were no sooner heard by the People, than they shewed by a silence full of veneration, that they were more affected by his authority, than by the necessity of providing for their own subsistence."—*Tacete, quaeso, Quirites. Plus enim ego quam vos quid reipublicae expediat intelligo. Quâ voce audîtâ, omnes pleno venerationis silentio, majorem ejus autoritatis quam alimentorum suorum curam ege-runt.* [[De Lolme cites and translates Valerius Maximus (ca. 20 B.C.E.–50 C.E.), *Factorum ac dictorum memorabilium libri IX* (Nine books of memorable deeds and sayings), book 3, chapter 7, section 3.]]

1. The ephori of the ancient republic of Sparta (or "Lacedaemon") were five mag-istrates elected annually by the popular assembly. Like the tribunes of republican Rome, the ephori functioned to protect the interests and liberties of the populace against the power of the Spartan kings and wealthier citizens.

availed them-<263>selves of their privilege of changing at their pleasure the place and form of the public meetings. When they did not find it possible by such means to direct the resolutions of the Assemblies, they pretended that the omens were not favourable, and under this pretext, or others of the same kind, they dissolved them (*a*). And the Tribunes, when they had succeeded so far as to effect an union among themselves, thus were obliged to submit to the pungent mortification of seeing those projects which they had pursued with infinite labour, and even through the greatest dangers, irrecoverably defeated by the most despicable artifices.

When, at other times, they saw that a confederacy was carrying on with uncommon warmth against them, and despaired of suc-<264>ceeding by employing expedients of the above kind, or were afraid of diminishing their efficacy by a too frequent use of them, they betook themselves to other stratagems. They then conferred on the Consuls, by the means of a short form of words for the occasion (*b*) an absolute power over the lives of the Citizens, or even appointed a Dictator. The People, at the sight of the State masquerade which was displayed before them, were sure to sink into a state of consternation; and the Tribunes, however clearly they might see through the artifice, also trembled in their turn, when they thus beheld themselves left without defenders (*c*).

At other times, they brought false accusations against the Tribunes before

(*a*) *Quid enim majus est, si de jure Augurum quaerimus*, says Tully, who himself was an Augur, and a Senator into the bargain, *quam posse a summis imperiis & summis potestatibus Comitatus & Concilia, vel instituta dimittere, vel habita rescindere! Quid gravius, quam rem susceptam dirimi, si unus Augur* ALIUM (id est, alium diem) *dixerit!*—See De Legib. lib. ii. § 12. [[De Lolme quotes Marcus Tullius Cicero, *De legibus*, book 2, 12. The quoted passage reads: "For if we consider their legal rights, what power is greater than that of adjourning assemblies and meetings convened by the highest officials, with or without imperium, or that of declaring null and void the acts of assemblies presided over by such officials? What is of graver import than the abandonment of any business already begun, if a single augur says, 'on another day'?"]]

(*b*) *Videat Consul ne quid detrimenti Respublica capiat.* [["Let the consul take heed that the Republic receive no injury."]]

(*c*) "The Tribunes of the People," says Livy, who was a great admirer of the Aristocratical power, "and the People themselves, durst neither lift up their eyes, nor even mutter, in the presence of the Dictator." *Nec adversus Dictatoriam vim, aut Tribuni plebis, aut ipsa Plebs, attollere oculos, aut hiscere, audebant*—See Tit. Liv. lib. vi. § 16. [[Titus Livius (Livy), *Ab urbe condita*, book 6, 16.3–4.]]

the Assembly itself; or, by privately slandering them with the People, they totally deprived them of their confidence. It was through artifices of this kind, that the People were brought to behold, without concern, the murder of Tiberius <265> Gracchus, the only Roman that was really virtuous,— the only one who truly loved the People. It was also in the same manner that Caius, who was not deterred by his brother's fate from pursuing the same plan of conduct, was in the end so entirely forsaken by the People, that nobody could be found among them who would even lend him a horse to fly from the fury of the Nobles; and he was at last compelled to lay violent hands upon himself, while he invoked the wrath of the Gods on his inconstant fellow-citizens.[2]

At other times, they raised divisions among the People. Formidable combinations broke out, on a sudden, on the eve of important transactions; and all moderate Men avoided attending Assemblies, where they saw that all was to be tumult and confusion.

In fine, that nothing might be wanting to the insolence with which they treated the Assemblies of the People, they sometimes falsified the declarations of the number of the votes; they even once went so far as to carry off the urns into which the Citizens were to throw their suffrages (*a*). <266>

(*a*) The reader with respect to all the above observations, may see Plutarch's Lives, particularly the Lives of the two Gracchi. [[Plutarch (ca. 46–ca. 120 C.E.) was the Greek essayist and moral philosopher whose *Parallel Lives* contained paired biographies of Greek and Roman leaders. His *Lives* of the brothers Tiberius and Caius Gracchus described in detail the incidents and political abuses discussed by De Lolme in this chapter.]] I must add, that I have avoided drawing any instance from those Assemblies in which one half of the people were made to arm themselves against the other. I have here only alluded to those times which immediately either preceded or followed the third Punic war, that is, of those which are commonly called the *best period* of the Republic. [[The Third (and final) Punic War was fought between Rome and Carthage from 149 to 146 B.C.E.]]

2. Tiberius Gracchus (163–133 B.C.E.) and his younger brother, Caius (154–121 B.C.E.), were members of a politically important Roman family. Both served as Roman tribunes, in which capacity they promoted measures in support of the plebeian citizens and earned the fierce opposition of leading patrician families. Tiberius was killed near the Roman Forum in an armed confrontation with his political adversaries. Caius's death, by suicide, followed a failed attempt to defeat his political opponents in the Senate.

The Subject concluded.—Effects that have resulted, in the English Government, from the People's Power being completely delegated to their Representatives.

But when the People have entirely trusted their power to a moderate number of persons, affairs immediately take a widely different turn. Those who govern are from that moment obliged to leave off all those stratagems which had hitherto ensured their success. Instead of those Assemblies which they affected to despise, and were perpetually comparing to storms, or to the current of the *Euripus* (*a*), <267> and in regard to which they accordingly thought themselves at liberty to pass over the rules of Justice, they now find that they have to deal with Men who are their equals in point of education and knowledge, and their inferiors only in point of rank and form. They, in consequence, soon find it necessary to adopt quite different methods; and, above all, become very careful not to talk to them any more about the

---

(*a*) Tully makes no end of his similes on this subject. *Quod enim fretum, quem Euripum, tot motus, tantas & tam varias habere putatis agitationes fluctuum, quantas perturbationes & quantos aestus habet ratio Comitiorum?* See Orat. pro Muraenâ. [["Euripus" referred to the channel of water that separated Boeotia, on the Attic shore, from the island of Euboea. De Lolme quotes Marcus Tullius Cicero, *Pro Muraenâ* (On behalf of Muraenâ). The passage reads: "Can you think of any strait, any channel, that has the currents and variety of rough patches and changes of tide strong enough to match the upsets of the ebb and flow that accompany the working of elections?"]]—*Concio,* says he in another place, *quae ex imperitissimis constat, &c.* De Amicitiâ, § 25. [[Marcus Tullius Cicero, *De amicitiâ* (On friendship), 25. The full passage reads: "A public assembly, though composed of very ignorant men, can, nevertheless, usually see the difference between a demagogue—that is, a smooth-tongued, shallow citizen—and one who has stability, sincerity, and weight."]]

sacred chickens, the *white* or *black* days, and the Sibylline books.[1]—As they see their new adversaries expect to have a proper regard paid to them, that single circumstance inspires them with it:—as they see them act in a regular manner, observe constant rules, in a word proceed with *form,* they come to look upon them with respect, from the very same reason which makes them themselves to be reverenced by the People.

The Representatives of the People, on the other hand, do not fail soon to procure for themselves every advantage that may enable them effectually to use the powers with which they have been intrusted, and to adopt every rule of proceeding that may make their resolutions to be truly the result of reflection and deliberation. Thus it was that the Representatives of the English Nation, soon after their <268> first establishment, became formed into a separate Assembly: they afterwards obtained the liberty of appointing a President:—soon after, they insisted upon their being consulted on the last form of the Acts to which they had given rise:—lastly, they insisted on thenceforth framing them themselves.

In order to prevent any possibility of surprize in the course of their proceedings, it is a settled rule with them, that every proposition, or bill, must be read three times, at different prefixed days, before it can receive a final sanction: and before each reading of the bill, as well as at its first introduction, an express resolution must be taken to continue it under consideration. If the bill be rejected, in any one of those several operations, it must be dropped, and cannot be proposed again during the same Session (*a*). <269>

(*a*) It is moreover a settled rule in the House of Commons, that no Member is to speak more than once in the same day. When the number and nature of the clauses of a Bill require that it should be discussed in a freer manner, a Committee is appointed for that purpose, who are to make their report afterwards to the House. When the subject is of importance, this Committee is formed of the whole House, which still continues to sit in the same place, but in a less solemn manner, and under another President, who is called the Chairman of the Committee. In order to form the House again, the mace is replaced on the Table, and the Speaker goes again into his chair.

1. De Lolme refers to several techniques used by Rome's governors to decide public matters in a manner that avoided reasoned explanations or regular procedures. Rome's armies consulted the feeding habits of "sacred chickens" and other birds to divine their fortunes in future battles. "*White* or *black* days" is an apparent reference to days on which

The Commons have been, above all, jealous of the freedom of speech in their assembly. They have expressly stipulated, as we have above mentioned, that none of their words or speeches should be questioned in any place out of their House. In fine, in order to keep their deliberations free from every kind of influence, they have denied their President the right to give his vote, or even his opinion:—they moreover have settled it as a rule, not only that the King could not send to them any express proposals about laws, or other subjects, but even that his name should never be mentioned in the deliberations (*a*).

But that circumstance which, of all others, constitutes the superior excellence of a Government in which the People act only through their Representatives, that is, by means of an assembly formed of a moderate number of persons, and in which it is possible for every Member to propose new subjects, and to argue and to canvass the questions that arise, is that <270> such a Constitution is the only one that is capable of the immense advantage, and of which I do not know if I have been able to convey an adequate idea to the reader when I mentioned it before (*b*), I mean that of putting into the hands of the People the moving springs of the Legislative authority.

In a Constitution where the People at large exercise the function of enacting the Laws, as it is only to those persons towards whom the Citizens are accustomed to turn their eyes, that is to the very Men who govern, that the Assembly have either time or inclination to listen, they acquire, at length, as has constantly been the case in all Republics, the exclusive right of proposing, if they please, when they please, in what manner they please. A prerogative this, of such extent, that it would suffice to put an assembly formed of Men of the greatest parts, at the mercy of a few dunces, and renders completely illusory the boasted power of the People. Nay more, as

---

public records, such as the praetor's edicts, were or were not publicly displayed on the "alba" or white tablets. The "Sibylline books" were collections of Greek oracular prophesies which, according to legend, were acquired for Rome by Tarquin II, who ruled as king from 535 B.C.E. to 510 B.C.E., and were later consulted in times of grave crisis.

(*a*) If any person were to mention in his speech, what the King *wishes should be, would be glad to see,* &c. he would be immediately *called to order,* for attempting to *influence the debate.*

(*b*) See chap. iv. of this Book.

this prerogative is thus placed in the very hands of the adversaries of the People, it forces the People to remain exposed to their attacks, in a condition perpetually passive, <271> and takes from them the only legal means by which they might effectually oppose their usurpations.

To express the whole in a few words. A *representative* Constitution places the remedy in the hands of those who feel the disorder; but a *popular* Constitution places the remedy in the hands of those who cause it; and it is necessarily productive, in the event, of the misfortune—of the political calamity, of trusting the care and the means of repressing the invasions of power, to the Men who have the enjoyment of power.

CHAPTER IX

A farther Disadvantage of Republican
Governments.—The People are necessarily
betrayed by those in whom they trust.

However, those general assemblies of a People who were made to determine
upon things which they neither understood nor examined,—that general
confusion in which the Ambitious could at all times hide their artifices, and
carry on their schemes with safety, were not the only evils attending the
ancient Commonwealths. There was a more secret <272> defect, and a
defect that struck immediately at the very vitals of it, inherent in that kind
of Government.

It was impossible for the People ever to have faithful defenders. Neither
those whom they had expresly chosen, nor those whom some personal advantages enabled to govern the Assemblies (for the only use, I must repeat
it, which the People ever make of their power, is either to give it away, or
allow it to be taken from them) could possibly be united to them by any
common feeling of the same concerns. As their influence put them, in a
great measure, upon a level with those who were invested with the executive
authority, they cared little to restrain oppressions out of the reach of which
they saw themselves placed. Nay, they feared they should thereby lessen a
power which they knew was one day to be their own; if they had not even
already an actual share in it (*a*).

(*a*) How could it be expected that Men who entertained views of being Praetors,
would endeavour to restrain the power of the Praetors,—that Men who aimed at being
one day Consuls, would wish to limit the power of the Consuls,—that Men whom their

Thus, at Rome, the only end which the Tribunes ever pursued with any degree of sin-<273>cerity and perseverance, was to procure to the People, that is to themselves, an admission to all the different dignities in the Republic. After having obtained that a law should be enacted for admitting Plebeians to the Consulship, they procured for them the liberty of intermarrying with the Patricians. They afterwards rendered them admissible to the Dictatorship, to the office of military Tribune, to the Censorship: in a word, the only use they made of the power of the People, was to increase privileges which they called the privileges of all, though they and their friends alone were ever likely to have the enjoyment of them.[1]

But we do not find that they ever employed the power of the People in things really beneficial to the People. We do not find that they ever set bounds to the terrible power of its Magistrates, that they ever repressed that class of Citizens who knew how to make their crimes pass uncensured,— in a word that they ever endeavoured, on the one hand to regulate, and on the other to strengthen, the judicial power; precautions these, without which men might struggle to the end of time, and never attain true liberty (*a*). <274>

And indeed the judicial power, that sure *criterion* of the goodness of a Government, was always, at Rome, a mere instrument of tyranny. The Consuls were at all times invested with an absolute power over the lives of the Citizens. The Dictators possessed the same right: so did the Praetors, the Tribunes of the People, the judicial Commissioners named by the Senate, and so, of course, did the Senate itself; and the fact of the three hundred and seventy deserters whom it commanded to be thrown down at one time, as Livy relates, from the Tarpeian rock, sufficiently shews that it well knew how to exert its power upon occasion.[2]

---

influence among the People made sure of getting into the Senate, would seriously endeavour to confine the authority of the Senate?

(*a*) Without such precautions, laws must always be as Pope expresses it,

Still for the strong too weak, the weak too strong.

[[De Lolme quotes Alexander Pope's 1733 *An Essay on Man,* epistle 3, line 194.]]

1. De Lolme here returns to and expands upon a theme he first introduced in book 2, chapter 2; see p. 150, note a.

2. For Tarpeian Rock, see book 2, chapter 1, p. 148, note 3.

It even may be said, that, at Rome, the power of life and death, or rather
the right of killing, was annexed to every kind of authority whatever, even
to that which results from mere influence, or wealth; and the only consequence of the murder of the Gracchi, which was accompanied by the
slaughter of three hundred, and afterwards of four thousand unarmed Citizens, whom the Nobles *knocked on the head,* was to engage the Senate to
erect a Temple to *Concord.* [3] The *Lex Porcia de tergo civium,* [4] which has been
so much celebrated, was attended with no other effect but that of more
completely securing against the danger of a retaliation, such Consuls, Praetors, Quaestors, &c. <275> as, like Verres, [5] caused the inferior Citizens of
Rome to be scourged with rods, and put to death upon crosses, through
mere caprice and cruelty (*a*).

In fine, nothing can more completely shew to what degree the Tribunes
had forsaken the interests of the People, whom they were appointed to
defend, than the fact of their having allowed the Senate to invest itself with
the power of taxation: they even suffered it to assume to itself the power,

(*a*) If we turn our eyes to Lacedaemon, we shall see, from several instances of the
justice of the Ephori, that matters were little better ordered there, in regard to the administration of public justice. [[The ephori of Sparta (or "Lacedaemon") are described
above, book 2, chapter 7, p. 179, note 1.]] And in Athens itself, which is the only one of
the ancient Commonwealths in which the people seem to have enjoyed any degree of
real liberty, we see the Magistrates proceed nearly in the same manner as they now do
among the Turks: and I think no other proof needs to be given than the story of that
Barber in the Piraeus, who having spread about the Town the news of the overthrow of
the Athenians in Sicily, which he had heard from a stranger who had stopped at his shop,
was put to the torture, by the command of the Archons, because he could not tell the
name of his author.—See *Plut. Life of Nicias.* [[Plutarch's "Life of Nicias" described the
career of the Athenian politician and military commander Nicias (d. 414 B.C.E.). For
Plutarch's *Lives,* see above, book 2, chapter 7, p. 181, note a.]]

3. The deaths of the Gracchi are described above, book 2, chapter 7, p. 181, note 2.

4. The *Lex Porcia* (195 B.C.E.), secured by Marcus Porcius Cato, prohibited the punishment of Roman citizens by beating with rods (*de tergo civium,* on the back of citizens).

5. Gaius Verres (ca. 120–43 B.C.) was a Roman magistrate and governor of Sicily, prosecuted by Cicero in 70 B.C.E., whose rule became notorious for political abuse and personal corruption.

not only of dispensing with the laws, but also of abrogating them (*a*). <276> In a word, as the necessary consequence of the *communicability* of power, a circumstance essentially inherent in the republican form of government, it is impossible for it ever to be restrained within certain rules. Those who are in a condition to control it, from that very circumstance, become its defenders. Though they may have risen, as we may suppose, from the humblest stations, and such as seemed totally to preclude them from all ambitious views, they have no sooner reached a certain degree of eminence, than they begin to aim higher. Their endeavours had at first no other object, as they professed, and perhaps with sincerity, than to see the laws impartially executed: their only view now is to set themselves above them; and seeing themselves raised to the level of a class of Men who pos-<277>sess all the power, and enjoy all the advantages, in the State, they make haste to associate themselves with them (*b*).

(*a*) There are frequent instances of the Consuls taking away from the Capitol the tables of the laws passed under their predecessors. Nor was this, as we might at first be tempted to believe, an act of violence which success alone could justify; it was a consequence of the acknowledged power enjoyed by the Senate, *cujus erat gravissimum judicium de jure legum* [["whose was the most solemn right of decision on the laws"]], as we may see in several places in Tully. Nay, the Augurs themselves, as Tully informs us, enjoyed the same privilege. "If laws have not been laid before the people, in the legal form, they (the Augurs) may set them aside; as was done with respect to the *Lex Tetia*, by the decree of the College, and to the *leges Liviae*, by the advice of Philip, who was Consul and Augur." *Legem si non jure rogata est, tollere possunt; ut Tetiam, decreto Collegii, ut Livias, consilio Philippi, Consulis & Auguris*—See De Legib. lib. ii. § 12. [[De Lolme quotes and translates Cicero, *De legibus,* 2.12.]]

(*b*) Which always proves an easy thing. It is in Commonwealths the particular care of that class of Men who are at the head of the State, to keep a watchful eye over the People, in order to draw over to their own party any Man who happens to acquire a considerable influence among them; and this they are (and indeed must be) the more attentive to do, in proportion as the nature of the Government is more democratical.

The Constitution of Rome had even made express provisions on that subject. Not only the Censors could at once remove any Citizen into what Tribe they pleased, and even into the Senate, and we may easily believe that they made a political use of this privilege; but it was moreover a settled rule, that all persons who had been promoted to any public office by the People, such as the Consulship, the Edileship, or Tribuneship, became *ipso facto,* members of the Senate.—See Middleton's *Dissertation on the Roman Senate.* [[De Lolme cites, but mistakenly titles, Conyers Middleton's 1747 *A Treatise on the Roman Senate.*]]

Personal power and independence on the laws, being, in such States, the immediate consequence of the favour of the People, they are under an unavoidable necessity of being betrayed. Corrupting, as it were, every thing they touch, they cannot show a preference to a Man, but they thereby attack his virtue; they cannot raise him, without immediately losing him and weakening their own cause; <278> nay, they inspire him with views directly opposite to their own, and send him to join and increase the number of their enemies.

Thus, at Rome, after the feeble barrier which excluded the People from offices of power and dignity had been thrown down, the great Plebeians, whom the votes of the People began to raise to those offices, were immediately received into the Senate, as has been just now observed. From that period, their families began to form, in conjunction with the ancient Patrician families, a new combination or political association of persons (a); and as this combination was formed of no particular class of Citizens, but of all those in general who had influence enough to gain admittance into it, a single overgrown head was now to be seen in the Republic, which, consisting of all those who had either wealth or power of any kind, and disposing at will of the laws and the power of the People (b) soon lost all regard to moderation and decency.[6] <279>

Every Constitution, therefore, whatever may be its form, which does not provide for inconveniences of the kind here mentioned, is a Constitution essentially imperfect. It is in Man himself that the source of the evils to be remedied, lies; general precautions therefore can alone prevent them. If it be a fatal error entirely to rely on the justice and equity of those who govern, it is an error no less dangerous to imagine, that, while virtue and moderation

(a) Called *Nobiles* and *Nobilitas.*
(b) It was, in several respects, a misfortune for the People of Rome, whatever may have been said to the contrary by the Writers on this subject, that the distinction between the Patricians and the Plebeians was ever abolished; though, to say the truth, this was an event which could not be prevented.
6. De Lolme here returns to a theme initially considered in book 2, chapter 2, concerning the abuses which occurred when members of Rome's plebeian ranks came to acquire political offices from which they were originally excluded; see book 2, chapter 2, p. 150, note a.

are the constant companions of those who oppose the abuses of Power, all ambition, all thirst after dominion, have retired to the other party.

Though wise Men sometimes may, led astray by the power of names and the heat of political contentions, lose sight of what ought to be their real aim, they nevertheless know that it is not against the *Appii,* the *Coruncanii,* the *Cethegi,*[7] but against all those who can influence the execution of the laws, that precautions ought to be taken,—that it is not the Consul, the Praetor, the Archon, the Minister, the King, whom we ought to dread, nor the Tribune or the Representative of the People, on whom we ought implicitly to rely; but that all those persons, without distinction, ought to be the objects of our jealousy, who, <280> by any methods, and under any names whatsoever, have acquired the means or turning against each individual the collective strength of all, and have so ordered things around themselves, that whoever attempts to resist them, is sure to find himself engaged alone against a thousand.

7. De Lolme refers to the names of plebeian families whose members attained high public office in the Republic.

CHAPTER X

Fundamental difference between the English Government, and the Governments just described.— In England all Executive Authority is placed out of the hands of those in whom the People trust. Usefulness of the Power of the Crown.

In what manner then, has the English Constitution contrived to find a remedy for evils which, from the very nature of Men and things, seem to be irremediable? How has it found means to oblige those persons to whom the People have given up their power, to make them effectual and lasting returns of gratitude? those who enjoy an exclusive authority, to seek the advantage of all?—those who make the laws, to make only equitable ones?—It has been by subjecting them themselves to those laws, and for that purpose excluding them from all share in the execution of them. <281>

Thus, the Parliament can establish as numerous a standing army as it pleases; but immediately another Power comes forward, which takes the absolute command of it, which fills all the posts in it, and directs its motions at its pleasure. The Parliament may lay new taxes; but immediately another Power seizes upon the produce of them, and alone enjoys the advantages and glory arising from the disposal of it. The Parliament may even, if you please, repeal the laws on which the safety of the Subject is grounded; but it is not their own caprices and arbitrary humours, it is the caprice and passions of other Men, which they will have gratified, when they shall thus have overthrown the columns of public liberty.

And the English Constitution has not only excluded from any share in the Execution of the laws, those in whom the People trust for the enacting

192

of them, but it has also taken from them what would have had the same pernicious influence on their deliberations—the hope of ever invading that executive authority, and transfering it to themselves.

This authority has been made in England one single, indivisible prerogative; it has been made for ever the unalienable attribute of one <282> person, marked out and ascertained beforehand by solemn laws and long established custom; and all the active forces in the State have been left at his disposal.

In order to secure this prerogative still farther against all possibility of invasions from individuals, it has been heightened and strengthened by every thing that can attract and fix the attention and reverence of the people. The power of conferring, and withdrawing, places and employments has also been added to it, and ambition itself has thus been interested in its defence, and service.

A share in the Legislative power has also been given to the Man to whom this prerogative has been delegated: a passive share indeed, and the only one that can, with safety to the State, be trusted to him, but by means of which he is enabled to defeat every attempt against his constitutional authority.

Lastly, he is the only self-existing and permanent Power in the State. The Generals, the Ministers of State, are so only by the continuance of his pleasure. He would even dismiss the Parliament themselves, if ever he saw them begin to entertain dangerous designs; and he needs only say one word to disperse <283> every power in the State that may threaten his authority. Formidable prerogatives these; but with regard to which we shall be inclined to lay aside our apprehensions, if we reflect, on the one hand, on the great privileges of the People by which they have been counterbalanced, and on the other, on the happy consequences that result from their being thus united together.

From this unity, and, if I may so express myself, this total sequestration of the Executive authority, this advantageous consequence in the first place follows, which has been mentioned in a preceding Chapter, that the attention of the whole Nation is directed to one and the same object. The People, besides, enjoy this most essential advantage, which they would vainly endeavour to obtain under the government of many,—they can give their confidence, without giving power over themselves, and against themselves; they can appoint Trustees, and yet not give themselves Masters.

Those Men to whom the People have delegated the power of framing the Laws, are thereby made sure to feel the whole pressure of them. They can increase the prerogatives <284> of the executive authority, but they cannot invest themselves with it:—they have it not in their power to command its motions, they only can unbind its hands.

They are made to derive their importance, nay they are indebted for their existence, to the need in which that Power stands of their assistance; and they know that they would no sooner have abused the trust of the People, and completed the treacherous work, than they would see themselves dissolved, spurned, like instruments now spent, and become useless.

This same disposition of things also prevents in England, that essential defect, inherent in the Government of many, which has been described in the preceding Chapter.

In that sort of Government, the cause of the People, as has been observed, is continually deserted and betrayed. The arbitrary prerogatives of the governing Powers are at all times either openly or secretly favoured, not only by those in whose possession they are, not only by those who have good reason to hope that they shall at some future time share in the exercise of them, but also by the whole croud of those Men who, in consequence of the natural disposition of Mankind to over-<285>rate their own advantages, fondly imagine, either that they shall one day enjoy some branch of this governing authority, or that they are even already, in some way or other, associated to it.

But as this authority has been made, in England, the indivisible, unalienable attribute of one alone, all other persons in the State are, *ipso facto,* interested to confine it within its due bounds. Liberty is thus made the common cause of all: the laws that secure it are supported by Men of every rank and order; and the Habeas Corpus Act,[1] for instance, is as zealously defended by the first Nobleman in the Kingdom, as by the meanest Subject.

Even the Minister himself, in consequence of this *inalienability* of the

---

1. For the importance of the writ of Habeas Corpus and of the 1679 Habeas Corpus Amendment Act, see De Lolme's discussion above, book 1, chapter 14.

executive authority, is equally interested with his fellow-citizens to maintain the laws on which public liberty is founded. He knows, in the midst of his schemes for enjoying or retaining his authority, that a Court-intrigue, or a caprice, may at every instant confound him with the multitude, and the rancour of a successor long kept out, send him to linger in the same jail which his temporary passions might tempt him to prepare for others. <286>

In consequence of this disposition of things, great Men, therefore, are made to join in a common cause with the People, for restraining the excesses of the governing Power; and, which is no less essential to the public welfare, they are also, from this same cause, compelled to restrain the excess of their own private power or influence, and a general spirit of justice beomes thus diffused through all parts of the State.

The wealthy Commoner, the Representative of the People, the potent Peer, always having before their eyes the view of a formidable Power, of a Power from the attempts of which they have only the shield of the laws to protect them, and which would, in the issue, retaliate an hundred fold upon them their acts of violence, are compelled, both to wish only for equitable laws, and to observe them with scrupulous exactness.

Let then the People dread (it is necessary to the preservation of their liberty), but let them never entirely cease to love, the Throne, that sole and indivisible seat of all the active powers in the State.

Let them know, it is that, which, by lending an immense strength to the arm of Justice, has enabled her to bring to account as <287> well the most powerful, as the meanest offender,—which has suppressed, and if I may so express myself, weeded out all those tyrannies, sometimes confederated with, and sometimes adverse to, each other, which incessantly tend to grow up in the middle of civil societies, and are the more terrible in proportion as they feel themselves to be less firmly established.

Let them know, it is that, which, by making all honours and places depend on the will of one Man, has confined within private walls those projects the pursuit of which, in former times, shook the foundations of whole States,—has changed into intrigues the conflicts, the outrages of ambition,—and that those contentions which, in the present times, afford them only matter of amusement, are the Volcanos which set in flames the ancient Commonwealths.

It is that, which, leaving to the rich no other security for his palace than that which the peasant has for his cottage, has united his cause to that of this latter, the cause of the powerful to that of the helpless, the cause of the Man of extensive influence and connections, to that of him who is without friends.

It is the Throne above all, it is this jealous Power, which makes the People sure that its <288> Representatives never will be any thing more than its Representatives: at the same time it is the ever subsisting Carthage which vouches to it for the duration of their virtue.[2]

2. De Lolme's reference to the English constitution's "ever subsisting Carthage" was likely offered as a rejoinder to Montesquieu's more sober judgment that since "all human things have an end," England eventually would "lose its liberty; it will perish. Rome, Lacedaemonia, and Carthage have surely perished." See *The Spirit of the Laws,* book 11, chapter 6. De Lolme cites and discusses this passage, below, in book 2, chapter 18, p. 304.

The Powers which the People themselves exercise.— The Election of Members of Parliament.

The English Constitution having essentially connected the fate of the Men to whom the People trust their power, with that of the People themselves, really seems, by that caution alone, to have procured the latter a complete security.

However, as the vicissitude of human affairs may, in process of time, realize events which at first had appeared most improbable, it might happen that the Ministers of the Executive power, notwithstanding the interest they themselves have in the preservation of public liberty, and in spite of the precautions expressly taken in order to prevent the effect of their influence, should, at length employ such efficacious means of corruption as might bring about a surrender of some of the laws upon <289> which this public liberty is founded. And though we should suppose that such a danger would really be chimerical, it might at least happen, that, conniving at a vicious administration, and being over liberal of the produce of the labours of the People, the Representatives of the People might make them suffer many of the evils which attend worse forms of Government.

Lastly, as their duty does not consist only in preserving their constituents against the calamities of an arbitrary Government, but moreover in procuring them the best administration possible, it might happen that they would manifest, in this respect, an indifference which would, in its consequences, amount to a real calamity.

It was therefore necessary that the Constitution should furnish a remedy for all the above cases; now, it is in the right of electing Members of Parliament, that this remedy lies.

When the time is come at which the commission which the People had given to their delegates expires, they again assemble in their several Towns or Counties: on these occasions they have it in their power to elect again those <290> of their Representatives whose former conduct they approve, and to reject those who have contributed to give rise to their complaints. A simple remedy this, and which only requiring in its application, a knowledge of matters of fact, is entirely within the reach of the abilities of the People; but a remedy, at the same time, which is the most effectual that could be applied: for, as the evils complained of, arise merely from the peculiar dispositions of a certain number of individuals, to set aside those individuals, is to pluck up the evil by the roots.

But I perceive, that, in order to make the reader sensible of the advantages that may accrue to the People of England, from their right of election, there is another of their rights, of which it is absolutely necessary that I should first give an account. <291>

The Subject continued.—Liberty of the Press.

As the evils that may be complained of in a State do not always arise merely from the defect of the laws, but also from the non-execution of them, and this non-execution of such a kind, that it is often impossible to subject it to any express punishment, or even to ascertain it by any previous definition, Men, in several States, have been led to seek for an expedient that might supply the unavoidable deficiency of legislative provisions, and begin to operate, as it were, from the point at which the latter begin to fail: I mean here to speak of the Censorial power; a power which may produce excellent effects, but the exercise of which (contrary to that of the legislative power) must be left to the People themselves.

As the proposed end of Legislation is not, according to what has been above observed, to have the particular intentions of individuals, upon every case, known and complied with, but solely to have what is most conducive to the public good on the occasions that arise, found out, and established, it is not an essential <292> requisite in legislative operations, that every individual should be called upon to deliver his opinion; and since this expedient, which at first sight appears so natural, of seeking out by the advice of all that which concerns all, is found liable, when carried into practice, to the greatest inconveniences, we must not hesitate to lay it aside entirely. But as it is the opinion of individuals alone, which constitutes the check of a censorial power, this power cannot possibly produce its intended effect any farther than this public opinion is made known and declared: the sentiments of the People are the only thing in question here: therefore it is necessary that the People should speak for themselves, and manifest those sentiments. A particular Court of Censure therefore essentially frustrates its intended purpose; it is attended, besides, with very great inconveniences.

As the use of such a Court is to determine upon those cases which lie out of the reach of the laws, it cannot be tied down to any precise regulations. As a farther consequence of the arbitrary nature of its functions, it cannot even be subjected to any constitutional check; and it continually presents to the eye the view of a power entirely arbitrary, and which in its different exertions may affect <293> in the most cruel manner, the peace and happiness of individuals. It is attended, besides, with this very pernicious consequence, that, by dictating to the people their judgments of Men or measures, it takes from them that freedom of thinking, which is the noblest privilege, as well as the firmest support of Liberty (a).

We may therefore look upon it as a farther proof of the soundness of the principles <294> on which the English constitution is founded, that it

(a) M. de Montesquieu, and M. Rousseau, and indeed all the Writers on this subject I have met with, bestow vast encomiums on the Censorial Tribunal that had been instituted at Rome [[Montesquieu discussed Rome's constitution and tribunes at many points in his 1734 *Considerations on the Causes of the Greatness and Decline of the Romans* and *The Spirit of the Laws*. De Lolme here may recall the passage in *Spirit of the Laws*, book 4, chapter 11, where Montesquieu endorsed Cicero's judgment that "the establishment of tribunes in Rome saved the republic." Rousseau's most sustained discussion of Rome's tribunes—the substance of which was more qualified than De Lolme's note suggests—appeared in *The Social Contract*, book 4, chapter 5, "Of the Tribunate."]];— they have not been aware that this power of Censure, lodged in the hands of peculiar Magistrates, with other discretionary powers annexed to it, was no other than a piece of State-craft, like those described in the preceding Chapters, and had been contrived by the Senate as an additional means of securing its authority.—Sir Thomas More has also adopted similar opinions on the subject; and he is so far from allowing the people to canvass the actions of their Rulers, that in his System of Polity, which he calls *An Account of Utopia* (the happy Region,—εὖ and τόπος) he makes it death for individuals to talk about the conduct of Government. [[De Lolme likely refers to the rule in Utopia, which was governed by an elected prince and elected senate: "It is a capital offence to make plans about public business outside the senate or the popular assembly." See Thomas More, *Utopia*, ed. George M. Logan, Robert M. Adams, and Clarence H. Miller (Cambridge: Cambridge University Press, 1995), 123.]]

    I feel a kind of pleasure, I must confess, to observe on this occasion, that though I have been called by some an advocate for Power, I have carried my ideas of Liberty farther than many Writers who have mentioned that word with much enthusiasm.

has allotted to the People themselves the province of openly canvassing and arraigning the conduct of those who are invested with any branch of public authority; and that it has thus delivered into the hands of the People at large, the exercise of the censorial power. Every subject in England has not only a right to present petitions to the King, or to the Houses of Parliament, but he has a right also to lay his complaints and observations before the Public, by means of an open press. A formidable right this, to those who rule mankind; and which, continually dispelling the cloud of majesty by which they are surrounded, brings them to a level with the rest of the people, and strikes at the very being of their authority.

And indeed this privilege is that which has been obtained by the English Nation, with the greatest difficulty, and latest in point of time, at the expence of the Executive power. Freedom was in every other respect already established, when the English were still, with regard to the public expression of their sentiments, under restraints that may be called despotic. History abounds with instances of the severity of the Court of Star-Chamber, <295> against those who presumed to write on political subjects. It had fixed the number of printers and printing-presses, and appointed a *Licenser,* without whose approbation no book could be published. Besides, as this Tribunal decided matters by its own single authority, without the intervention of a Jury, it was always ready to find those persons guilty, whom the Court was pleased to look upon as such; nor was it indeed without ground that Chief Justice Coke, whose notions of liberty were somewhat tainted with the prejudices of the times in which he lived, concluded the elogiums he has bestowed on this Court, with saying, that "the right institution and orders thereof being observed, it doth keep all England in quiet."[1]

After the Court of Star-Chamber had been abolished, the Long Parliament, whose conduct and assumed power were little better qualified to bear a scrutiny, revived the regulations against the freedom of the press. Charles the Second, and after him James the Second, procured farther renewals of them. These latter acts having expired in the year 1692, were at this aera,

---

1. Edward Coke, *Institutes of the Laws of England,* part 4 (1644), p. 64.

although posterior to the Revolution, continued for two years longer;
<296> so that it was not till the year 1694, that, in consequence of the
Parliament's refusal to continue the prohibitions any longer, the freedom
of the press (a privilege which the Executive power could not, it seemed,
prevail upon itself to yield up to the people) was finally established.[2]

In what does then this liberty of the press precisely consist? Is it a liberty
left to every one to publish any thing that comes into his head? to calum-
niate, to blacken, whomsoever he pleases? No; the same laws that protect
the person and the property of the individual, do also protect his reputation; and they decree against libels, when really so, punishments of much
the same kind as are established in other Countries. But, on the other hand,
they do not allow, as in other States, that a Man should be deemed guilty
of a crime for merely publishing something in print; and they appoint a
punishment only against him who has printed things that are in their nature
criminal, and who is declared guilty of so doing by twelve of his equals,
appointed to determine upon his case, with the precautions we have before
described.

The liberty of the press, as established in England, consists therefore, to
define it more <297> precisely, in this, That neither the Courts of Justice,
nor any other Judges whatever, are authorised to take any notice of writings
intended for the press, but are confined to those which are actually printed,
and must, in these cases, proceed by the Trial by Jury.

It is even this latter circumstance which more particularly constitutes the
freedom of the press. If the Magistrates, though confined in their proceedings to cases of criminal publications, were to be the sole Judges of the
criminal nature of the things published, it might easily happen that, with
regard to a point which, like this, so highly excites the jealousy of the governing Powers, they would exert themselves with so much spirit and per-

2. Although the Licensing Act regulating publication was not renewed after 1695,
Parliament continued to consider proposed legislation to regulate the press over the next
decade. As De Lolme goes on to explain, the failure to renew the Licensing Acts brought
to an end the system of prepublication censorship of the press. Thereafter, the content
of newspaper and other writing was generally regulated by the law of blasphemy and
libel.

severance, that they might, at length, succeed in completely striking off all the heads of the hydra.

But whether the authority of the Judges be exerted at the motion of a private individual, or whether it be at the instance of the Government itself, their sole office is to declare the punishment established by the law:—it is to the Jury alone that it belongs to determine on the matter of law, as well as on the matter of fact; that is, to determine, not only whether the writing which is the subject of the <298> charge has really been composed by the Man charged with having done it, and whether it be really meant of the person named in the indictment,—but also, whether its contents are criminal.[3]

And though the law in England does not allow a Man, prosecuted for having published a libel, to offer to support by evidence the truth of the facts contained in it, (a mode of proceeding which would be attended with very mischievous consequences, and is every where prohibited), yet (*a*) as the indictment is to express that the facts are *false, malicious,* &c. and the Jury, at the same time, are sole masters of their verdict, that is, may ground it upon what considerations they please, it is very probable that they would acquit the accused party, if the facts asserted in the writing before them, were matter of undoubted truth, and of a general evil tendency. They, at least, would certainly have it their power.

And this would still more likely be the case if the conduct of the Government itself was arraigned; because, besides this conviction <299> which we suppose in the Jury, of the certainty of the facts, they would also be influenced by their sense of a principle generally admitted in England, and which, in a late celebrated cause, has been strongly insisted upon, viz. That, "though to speak ill of individuals was deserving of reprehension, yet the

(*a*) In actions for damages between individuals, the case, if I mistake not, is different, and the defendant is allowed to produce evidence of the facts asserted by him. [[In the case of a civil suit between private parties, the defendant would enter a plea of justification and could defeat the accusation by establishing the truth of the statement alleged to be libelous.]]

3. As in his previous treatment of this point in book 1, chapter 13, p. 128, note a, De Lolme treats as legally settled the still strongly contested issue of the jury's authority to determine the question in law of what constituted criminal libel.

public acts of Government ought to lie open to public examination, and that it was a service done to the State, to canvass them freely" (*a*).

And indeed this extreme security with which every man in England is enabled to communicate his sentiments to the Public, and the general concern which matters relative to the Government are always sure to create, has wonderfully multiplied all kinds of public papers. Besides those which, being published at the end of every year, month, or week, present to the reader a recapitulation of every thing interesting that may have been done or said during their respective periods, there are several others, which making their appearance every day, or every other day, communicate to the public the several measures taken by <300> the Government, as well as the different causes of any importance, whether civil or criminal, that occur in the Courts of Justice, and sketches from the speeches either of the Advocates or the Judges, concerned in the management and decision of them. During the time the Parliament continues sitting, the votes or resolutions of the House of Commons, are daily published by authority; and the most interesting speeches in both Houses, are taken down in short-hand, and communicated to the Public, in print.[4]

Lastly, the private anecdotes in the Metropolis, and the Country, concur also towards filling the collection; and as the several public papers circulate, or are transcribed into others, in the different Country Towns, and even find their way into the villages, where every Man, down to the labourer, peruses them with a sort of eagerness, every individual thus becomes acquainted with the State of the Nation, from one end to the other; and by

---

(*a*) See Serjeant Glynn's Speech for Woodfall in the prosecution against the latter, by the Attorney-General, for publishing Junius's letter to the King. [[De Lolme quotes the sense but not the exact words of Serjeant John Glynn's arguments in defense of Henry Woodfall during his 1770 trial for seditious libel for the publication of Junius's "Letter to the King," which appeared in the *Public Advertiser* on December 19, 1769. De Lolme earlier discussed the episode in book 1, chapter 13, p. 128, note a.]]

4. The votes and resolutions of the House of Commons were printed in the London *Gazette,* which was "published by authority" and carried government information and official notices. Newspaper reports of speeches and debates within the House of Commons, however, were traditionally prohibited as a matter of well-settled parliamentary privilege. After 1771, the Commons ceased to enforce this privilege, and detailed accounts of parliamentary deliberations became a staple of England's periodical press.

these means the general intercourse is such, that the three Kingdoms seem as if they were one single Town.

And it is this public notoriety of all things, that constitutes the supplemental power, or check, which, we have above said, is so useful to remedy the unavoidable insufficiency <301> of the laws, and keep within their respective bounds all those persons who enjoy any share of public authority.

As they are thereby made sensible that all their actions are exposed to public view, they dare not venture upon those acts of partiality, those secret connivances at the iniquities of particular persons, or those vexatious practices, which the Man in office is but too apt to be guilty of, when, exercising his office at a distance from the public eye, and as it were in a corner, he is satisfied that provided he be cautious, he may dispense with being just. Whatever may be the kind of abuse in which persons in power may, in such a state of things, be tempted to indulge themselves, they are convinced that their irregularities will be immediately divulged. The Juryman, for example, knows that his verdict, the Judge, that his direction to the Jury, will presently be laid before the Public: and there is no Man in office, but who thus finds himself compelled, in almost every instance, to choose between his duty, and the surrender of all his former reputation.

It will, I am aware, be thought that I speak in too high terms, of the effects produced by the public news-papers. I indeed confess <302> that all the pieces contained in them are not patterns of good reasoning, or of the truest Attic wit; but, on the other hand, it scarcely ever happens that a subject in which the laws, or in general the public welfare, are really concerned, fails to call forth some able writer, who, under some form or other, communicates to the public his observations and complaints. I shall add here, that, though an upright Man labouring for a while under a strong popular prejudice, may, supported by the consciousness of his innocence, endure with patience the severest imputations, the guilty Man, hearing nothing in the reproaches of the public but what he knows to be true, and already upbraids himself with, is very far from enjoying any such comfort; and that, when a man's own conscience takes part against him, the most despicable weapon is sufficient to wound him to the quick (*a*). <303>

(*a*) I shall take this occasion to observe, that the liberty of the press is so far from

Even those persons whose greatness seems most to set them above the reach of public censure, are not those who least feel its effects. They have need of the suffrages of that vulgar whom they affect to despise, and who are, after all, the dispensers of that glory, which is the real object of their ambitious cares. Though all have not so much sincerity as Alexander, they have equal reason to exclaim, *O People! what toils do we not undergo, in order to gain your applause!*

I confess that in a State where the People dare not speak their sentiments, but with a view to please the ears of their rulers, it is possible that either the Prince, or those to whom he has trusted his authority, may sometimes mistake the nature of the public sentiments, or that, for want of that affection of which they are denied all public marks, they may rest contented with inspiring terror, and make themselves amends in beholding the overawed multitude smother their complaints. <304>

But when the laws give a full scope to the People for the expression of their sentiments, those who govern cannot conceal from themselves the disagreeable truths which resound from all sides. They are obliged to put up even with ridicule; and the coarsest jests are not always those which give them the least uneasiness. Like the lion in the fable, they must bear the blows of those enemies whom they despise the most; and they are, at length, stopped short in their career, and compelled to give up those unjust pursuits which they find to draw upon them, instead of that admiration which is the proposed end and reward of their labours, nothing but mortification and disgust.

In short, whoever considers what it is that constitutes the moving principle of what we call great affairs, and the invincible sensibility of Man to the opinion of his fellow-creatures, will not hesitate to affirm that, if it were

---

being injurious to the reputation of individuals, (as some persons have complained) that it is, on the contrary, its surest guard. When there exists no means of communication with the Public, every one is exposed, without defence, to the secret shafts of malignity and envy. The Man in office loses his reputation, the Merchant his credit, the private individual his character, without so much as knowing, either who are his enemies, or which way they carry on their attacks. But when there exists a free press, an innocent Man immediately brings the matter into open day, and crushes his adversaries, at once, by a public challenge to lay before the public the grounds of their several imputations.

possible for the liberty of the press to exist in a despotic government, and (what is not less difficult) for it to exist without changing the constitution, this liberty of the press would alone form a counterpoise to the power of the Prince. If, for example, in an empire of the East, a sanctuary could be found, which, ren-<305>dered respectable by the ancient religion of the people, might ensure safety to those who should bring thither their observations of any kind, and that from thence printed papers should issue, which, under a certain seal, might be equally respected, and which in their daily appearance should examine and freely discuss the conduct of the Cadis, the Bashaws, the Vizir, the Divan, and the Sultan himself,—that would introduce immediately some degree of liberty.

〰 CHAPTER XIII 〰

The Subject continued.

Another effect, and a very considerable one, of the liberty of the press, is, that it enables the People effectually to exert those means which the Constitution has bestowed on them, of influencing the motions of the Government.

It has been observed in a former place, how it came to be a matter of impossibility for any large number of men, when obliged to act in a body, and upon the spot, to take any well-weighed resolution. But this inconvenience, which is the inevitable consequence of their <306> situation, does in no wise argue a personal inferiority in them, with respect to the few who, from some accidental advantages, are enabled to influence their determinations. It is not Fortune, it is Nature, that has made the essential differences between Men: and whatever appellation a small number of persons who speak without sufficient reflection, may affix to the general body of their fellow-creatures, the whole difference between the Statesman, and many a Man from among what they call the dregs of the People, often lies in the rough outside of the latter; a disguise which may fall off on the first opportunity; and more than once has it happened, that from the middle of a multitude in appearance contemptible, there have been seen to rise at once Viriatuses, or Spartacuses.[1]

---

1. De Lolme cites two figures of humble origin who led famous campaigns against Rome's armies. Viriatus (or Viriathus) (ca. 180–139 B.C.E.), a shepherd from the region of Lusitania in Iberia, led a successful resistance to Roman rule in Iberia during the period 147–139 B.C.E. He was finally defeated when the Roman general Servilius Caepio orchestrated his murder by bribing his servants. Spartacus (ca. 109–71 B.C.E.), a slave and

Time, and a more favourable situation (to repeat it once more) are therefore the only things wanting to the People; and the freedom of the press
affords the remedy to these disadvantages. Through its assistance every individual may, at his leisure and in retirement, inform himself of every thing
that relates to the questions on which he is to take a resolution. Through
its assistance, a whole Nation as it were holds a Council, and deliberates;
slowly indeed (for a Nation cannot be informed like <307> an assembly of
Judges), but after a regular manner, and with certainty. Through its assistance, all matters of fact are, at length, made clear; and, through the conflict
of the different answers and replies, nothing at last remains, but the sound
part of the arguments (*a*). <308>

---

gladiator from Thrace, commanded a major slave revolt in the years 73–71 B.C.E. He died
in battle against Roman forces led by Marcus Licinius Crassus.

(*a*) This right of publicly discussing political Subjects, is alone a great advantage to
a People who enjoy it; and if the Citizens of Geneva, for instance, have preserved their
liberty better than the people have been able to do in the other Commonwealths of
Switzerland, it is, I think, owing to the extensive right they possess of making public
remonstrances to their Magistrates. To these remonstrances the Magistrates, for instance
the Council of *Twenty-five,* to which they are usually made, are obliged to give an answer.
If this answer does not satisfy the remonstrating Citizens, they take time, perhaps two
or three weeks, to make a reply to it, which must also be answered; and the number of
Citizens who go up with each new remonstrance increases, according as they are thought
to have reason on their side. Thus, the remonstrances which were made some years ago,
on account of the sentence against the celebrated M. Rousseau, and were delivered at
first by only forty Citizens, were afterwards often accompanied by about nine hundred.—This circumstance, together which the ceremony with which those remonstrances (or *Representations,* as they more commonly call them) are delivered, has rendered them a great check on the conduct of the Magistrates: they even have been still
more useful to the Citizens of Geneva, as a preventative than as a remedy; and nothing
is more likely to deter the Magistrates from taking a step of any kind than the thought
that it will give rise to a *Representation.* [[In 1762, Geneva's Council of the Twenty-Five
(or *Petit Conseil*) condemned the publication and sale of Rousseau's *The Social Contract*
and *Emile,* and resolved that their author was to be arrested should he return to his native
Geneva. "Representations" was the term given to the petitions Genevan citizens addressed to the government. The 1762 condemnation of Rousseau's writings helped stimulate the publication of a large number of petitions and pamphlets, including De
Lolme's own contributions, that unsuccessfully challenged the legitimacy of the action.
For De Lolme's earlier discussion of Genevan politics, see above, book 2, chapter 4,
pp. 160–61, note a; book 2, chapter 5, pp. 174–75, note a; and the editorial introduction,
pp. x–xii.]]

Hence, though all good Men may not think themselves obliged to concur implicitly in the tumultuary resolutions of a People whom their Orators
take pains to agitate, yet, on the other hand, when this same People, left to
itself, perseveres in opinions which have for a long time been discussed in
public writings, and from which (it is essential to add) all errors concerning
facts have been removed, such perseverance is certainly a very respectable
decision; and then it is, though only then, that we may with safety say,—
"the voice of the People is the voice of God."[2]

How, therefore, can the people of England *act,* when, having formed
opinions which may really be called their own, they think they have just
cause to complain against the Administration? It is, as has been said above,
by means of the right they have of electing their Representatives; and the
same method of general intercourse that has informed them with regard
to the objects of their complaints, will likewise enable them to apply the
remedy to them.

Through this means they are acquainted with the nature of the subjects
that have been deliberated upon in the Assembly of their Re-<309>pre-
sentatives;—they are informed by whom the different motions were
made,—by whom they were supported; and the manner in which the suffrages are delivered, is such, that they always can know the names of those
who have voted constantly for the advancement of pernicious measures.

And the People not only know the particular dispositions of every Member of the House of Commons; but the general notoriety of all things gives
them also a knowledge of the political sentiments of a great number of
those whom their situation in life renders fit to fill a place in that House.
And availing themselves of the several vacancies that happen, and still more
of the opportunity of a general election, they purify either successively, or
at once, the Legislative Assembly; and thus, without any commotion or
danger to the State, they effect a material reformation in the views of the
Government.

I am aware that some persons will doubt these patriotic and systematic
views which I am here attributing to the People of England, and will object
to me the disorders that sometimes happen at Elections. But this reproach

2. De Lolme offers the English translation of the familiar Latin aphorism *"vox populi,*
vox dei."

<310> which, by the way, comes with but little propriety from Writers who would have the People transact every thing in their own persons, this reproach, I say, though true to a certain degree, is not however so much so as it is thought by certain persons who have taken only a superficial survey of the state of things.

Without doubt, in a Constitution in which all important causes of uneasiness are so effectually prevented, it is impossible but that the People will have long intervals of inattention. Being then called upon, on a sudden, from this state of inactivity, to elect Representatives, they have not examined, beforehand, the merits of those who ask them their votes; and the latter have not had, amidst the general tranquillity, any opportunity to make themselves known to them.

The Elector, persuaded, at the same time, that the person whom he will elect, will be equally interested with himself in the support of public liberty, does not enter into laborious disquisitions, and from which he sees he may exempt himself. Obliged, however, to give the preference to somebody, he forms his choice on motives which would not be excusable, if it were not that some motives are <311> necessary to make a choice, and that, at this instant, he is not influenced by any other: and indeed it must be confessed, that, in the ordinary course of things, and with Electors of a certain rank in life, that Candidate who gives the best entertainment, has a great chance to get the better of his competitors.

But if the measures of Government, and the reception of those measures in Parliament, by means of a too complying House of Commons, should ever be such as to spread a serious alarm among the People, the same causes which have concurred to establish public liberty, would, no doubt operate again, and likewise concur in its support. A general combination would then be formed, both of those Members of Parliament who have remained true to the public cause, and of persons of every order among the People. Public meetings, in such circumstances, would be appointed, general subscriptions would be entered into, to support the expences whatever they might be, of such a necessary opposition; and all private and unworthy purposes being suppressed by the sense of the National danger, the choice of the electors would then be wholly determined by the consider-<312>ation of the public spirit of the Candidates, and the tokens given by them of such spirit.

Thus were those Parliaments formed, which suppressed arbitrary taxes and imprisonments. Thus was it, that, under Charles the Second, the People, when recovered from that enthusiasm of affection with which they received a King so long persecuted, at last returned to him no Parliaments but such as were composed of a majority of Men attached to public liberty. Thus it was, that, persevering in a conduct which the circumstances of the times rendered necessary, the People baffled the arts of the Government; and Charles dissolved three successive Parliaments, without any other effect but that of having those same Men rechosen, and set again in opposition to him, of whom he hoped he had rid himself for ever.[3]

Nor was James the Second happier in his attempts than Charles had been. This Prince soon experienced that his Parliament was actuated by the same spirit as those which had opposed the designs of his late brother; and having suffered himself to be led into measures of violence, instead of being better taught by the discovery he made of the real sentiments of the People, his reign was terminated <313> by that catastrophe with which every one is acquainted.[4]

Indeed, if we combine the right enjoyed by the People of England, of electing their Representatives, with the whole of the English Government, we shall become continually more and more sensible of the excellent effects that may result from that right. All Men in the State are, as has been before observed, really interested in the support of public liberty;—nothing but temporary motives, and such as are quite peculiar to themselves, can possibly induce the Members of any House of Commons to connive at measures destructive of this liberty: the People, therefore, under such circumstances, need only change these Members in order effectually to reform the conduct of that House: and it may fairly be pronounced beforehand, that

3. De Lolme first discussed the constitutional significance of the reigns of Charles II and James II above, book 1, chapter 3. The last three Parliaments of Charles II, also known as the "Exclusion Parliaments" on the basis of the abortive efforts to exclude the future James II from the throne, met successively and briefly in the years 1679–81. The first of these Parliaments passed the 1679 Habeas Corpus Amendment Act, discussed and celebrated by De Lolme above, book 1, chapter 14. Charles II was forced to dissolve each of these Parliaments to prevent the passage of measures in opposition to royal policy.

4. The famous "catastrophe" was the Glorious Revolution of 1688, when the crown was transferred from James II to Queen Mary and King William III.

a House of Commons, composed of a new set of persons, will from this bare circumstance, be in the interests of the People.

Hence, though the complaints of the People do not always meet with a speedy and immediate redress (a celerity which would be the symptom of a fatal unsteadiness in the Constitution, and would sooner or later bring on its ruin) yet, when we attentively consider <314> the nature and the resources of this Constitution, we shall not think it too bold an assertion to say, that it is impossible but that complaints in which the People persevere, that is, to repeat it once more, well-grounded complaints, will sooner or later be redressed.

Right of Resistance.

But all those privileges of the People, considered in themselves, are but feeble defences against the real strength of those who govern. All those provisions, all those reciprocal Rights, necessarily suppose that things remain in their legal and settled course: what would then be the resource of the People, if ever the Prince, suddenly freeing himself from all restraint, and throwing himself as it were out of the Constitution, should no longer respect either the person or the property of the subject, and either should make no account of his conventions with his Parliament, or attempt to force it implicitly to submit to his will?—It would be resistance. <315>

Without entering here into the discussion of a doctrine which would lead us to enquire into the first principles of Civil Government, consequently engage us in a long disquisition, and with regard to which, besides, persons free from prejudices agree pretty much in their opinions, I shall only observe here (and it will be sufficient for my purpose) that the question has been decided in favour of this doctrine by the Laws of England, and that resistance is looked upon by them as the ultimate and lawful resource against the violences of Power.

It was resistance that gave birth to the Great Charter, that lasting foundation of English Liberty; and the excesses of a Power established by force, were also restrained by force (*a*). <316> It has been by the same means that,

---

(*a*) Lord Lyttelton says extremely well in his Persian Letters, "If the privileges of the People of England be concessions from the Crown, is not the power of the Crown itself, a concession from the People?" It might be said with equal truth, and somewhat more in point to the subject of this Chapter,—If the privileges of the People be an encroach-

at different times, the People have procured the confirmation of the same Charter. Lastly, it has also been the resistance to a King who made no account of his own engagements, that has, in the issue, placed on the Throne the family which is now in possession of it.

This is not all; this resource which, till then, had only been an act of force, opposed to other acts of force, was, at that aera, expresly recognized by the Law itself. The Lords and Commons, solemnly assembled, declared, that "King James the Second, having endeavoured to subvert the Constitution of the Kingdom, by breaking the original contract between King and People, and having violated the fundamental laws, and withdrawn himself, had abdicated the Government; and that the Throne was thereby vacant" (a).[1]

And lest those principles to which the Revolution thus gave a sanction, should, in process of time, become mere *arcana* of State, exclusively appropriated, and only known, to a certain class of Subjects, the same Act, we have just mentioned, expresly insured to in-<317>dividuals the right of publicly preferring complaints against the abuses of Government, and moreover, of being provided with arms for their own defence. Judge Blackstone expresses himself in the following terms, in his Commentaries on the Laws of England. (B. I. Ch. i.)

"And lastly, to vindicate those rights, when actually violated or attacked, the subjects of England are entitled, in the first place, to the regular administration and free course of justice in the Courts of law; next, to the right of petitioning the King and Parliament for redress of grievances; and, lastly, to the right of having and using arms for self-preservation and defence."[2]

Lastly, this right of opposing violence, in whatever shape, and from

---

ment on the power of Kings, the power itself of Kings was at first an encroachment (no matter whether effected by surprize) on the natural liberty of the people. [[George Lord Lyttleton, *Letters from a Persian in England to His Friend at Ispahan* (1735), letter 59.]]

(a) The Bill of Rights has since given a new sanction to all these principles.

1. De Lolme quotes from the "Declaration of the Lords Spiritual and Temporal, and Commons," issued on February 13, 1688/89. The Parliamentary Bill of Rights, enacted soon afterward, contained a slightly altered formulation of this claim.

2. William Blackstone, *Commentaries on the Laws of England,* 1:140.

whatever quarter, it may come, is so generally acknowledged, that the Courts of law have sometimes grounded their judgments upon it. I shall relate on this head a fact which is somewhat remarkable.

A Constable, being out of his precinct, arrested a woman whose name was *Anne Dekins;* one *Tooly* took her part, and in the heat of the fray, killed the assistant of the Constable. <318>

Being prosecuted for murder, he alleged, in his defence, that the illegality of the imprisonment was a sufficient provocation to make the homicide *excusable,* and intitle him to the benefit of Clergy. The Jury having settled the matter of fact, left the *criminality* of it to be decided by the Judge, by returning a *special verdict.* The cause was adjourned to the King's Bench, and thence again to Serjeants Inn, for the opinion of the twelve Judges. Here follows the opinion delivered by Chief Justice Holt, in giving judgment.

"If one be imprisoned upon an unlawful authority, it is a sufficient provocation to all people, out of compassion, much more so when it is done under colour of justice; and when the liberty of the subject is invaded, it is a provocation to all the subjects of England. A Man ought to be concerned for *Magna Charta* and the laws; and if any one against law imprison a Man, he is an offender against Magna Charta." After some debate, occasioned chiefly by Tooly's appearing not to have known that the Constable was out of his precinct, seven of the Judges were of opinion that the prisoner <319> was guilty of Manslaughter, and he was admitted to the benefit of Clergy (*a*).

But it is with respect to this right of an ultimate resistance, that the advantage of a free press appears in a most conspicuous light. As the most important rights of the People, without the prospect of a resistance which overawes those who should attempt to violate them, are little more than

(*a*) See Reports of Cases argued, debated, and adjudged in *Banco Reginae,* in the time of the late Queen Anne. [[De Lolme cites, with deletions and slight variations, Chief Justice Sir John Holt's comments in the 1709 case of *R. v. Tooley, Arch and Lawson.* "Benefit of clergy"—a medieval privilege that originally enabled members of the clergy who had been convicted in the royal courts to receive lesser punishment from the ecclesiastical courts—in the eighteenth century typically functioned to mutate a capital felony into a noncapital offense.]]

mere shadows,—so this right of *resisting*, itself, is but vain, when there exists no means of effecting a general union between the different parts of the People.

Private individuals, unknown to each other, are forced to bear in silence injuries in which they do not see other people take a concern. Left to their own individual strength, they tremble before the formidable and ever-ready power of those who govern; and as these latter well know, nay, are apt to over-rate the advantages of their own situation, they think they may venture upon any thing.

But when they see that all their actions are exposed to public view,— that in consequence of the celerity with which all things <320> become communicated, the whole Nation forms, as it were, one continued *irritable* body, no part of which can be touched without exciting an universal *tremor,* they become sensible that the cause of each individual is really the cause of all, and that to attack the lowest among the People, is to attack the whole People.

Here also we must remark the error of those who, as they make the liberty of the people to consist in their power, so make their power consist in their action.

When the People are often called to act in their own persons, it is impossible for them to acquire any exact knowledge of the state of things. The event of one day effaces the notions which they had begun to adopt on the preceding day; and amidst the continual change of things, no settled principle, and above all no plans of union, have time to be established among them.—You wish to have the People love and defend their laws and liberty; leave them, therefore, the necessary time to know what laws and liberty are, and to agree in their opinion concerning them;—you wish an union, a *coalition,* which cannot be obtained but by a slow and peaceable *process,* forbear therefore continually to shake the vessel. <321>

Nay farther, it is a contradiction, that the People should *act,* and at the same time retain any real power. Have they, for instance, been forced by the weight of public oppression to throw off the restraints of the law, from which they no longer received protection, they presently find themselves suddenly become subject to the command of a few Leaders, who are the more absolute in proportion as the nature of their power is less clearly ascertained: nay, perhaps they must even submit to the toils of war, and to military discipline.

If it be in the common and legal course of things that the People are called to move, each individual is obliged, for the success of the measures in which he is then made to take a concern, to join himself to some party; nor can this party be without a Head. The Citizens thus grow divided among themselves, and contract the pernicious habit of submitting to Leaders. They are, at length, no more than the clients of a certain number of Patrons; and the latter soon becoming able to command the arms of the Citizens in the same manner as they at first governed their votes, make little account of a People with one part of which they know how to curb the other. <322>

But when the moving springs of Government are placed entirely out of the body of the People, their action is thereby disengaged from all that could render it complicated, or hide it from the eye. As the People thenceforward consider things speculatively, and are, if I may be allowed the expression, only spectators of the game, they acquire just notions of things; and as these notions, amidst the general quiet, get ground and spread themselves far and wide, they at length entertain, on the subject of their liberty, but one opinion.

Forming thus, as it were, one body, the People, at every instant, has it in its power to strike the decisive blow which is to level every thing. Like those mechanical powers the greatest efficiency of which exists at the instant which precedes their entering into action, it has an immense force, just because it does not yet exert any; and in this state of stillness, but of attention, consists its true *momentum.*[3]

With regard to those who (whether from personal privileges, or by virtue of a commission from the People) are intrusted with the active part of Government, as they, in the mean while, see themselves exposed to <323> public view, and observed as from a distance by Men free from the spirit of party, and who place in them but a conditional trust, they are afraid of exciting a commotion which, though it might not prove the destruction of all power, yet would surely and immediately be the destruction of their

3. "Movement" or "power" (figurative).

own. And if we might suppose that, through an extraordinary conjunction of circumstances, they should resolve among themselves upon the sacrifice of those laws on which public liberty is founded, they would no sooner lift up their eyes towards that extensive Assembly which views them with a watchful attention, than they would find their public virtue return upon them, and would make haste to resume that plan of conduct out of the limits of which they can expect nothing but ruin and perdition.

In short, as the body of the People cannot act without either subjecting themselves to some Power, or effecting a general destruction, the only share they can have in a Government with advantage to themselves, is not to interfere, but to influence,—to be able to act, and not to act.

The Power of the People is not when they strike, but when they keep in awe: it is <324> when they can overthrow every thing, that they never need to move; and Manlius included all in four words, when he said to the People of Rome, *Ostendite bellum, pacem habebitis.*[4]

4. "Make but a show of war, and you shall have peace." De Lolme quotes the statement attributed to the Roman consul Marcus Manlius Capitolinus, who was credited with saving Rome from attack by the Gauls in 390 B.C.E. and who later led a rebellion of plebeian debtors against their patrician creditors. (Livy gives a slightly different version of the statement in *Ab urbe condita,* book 6, chapter 18.7.)

CHAPTER XV[1]

Proofs drawn from Facts, of the Truth of the Principles laid down in the present Work.—1. The peculiar Manner in which Revolutions have always been concluded in England.

It may not be sufficient to have proved by arguments the advantages of the English Constitution: it will perhaps be asked, whether the effects correspond to the theory? To this question (which I confess is extremely proper) my answer is ready; it is the same which was once made, I believe, by a Lacedemonian, *Come and see.*

If we peruse the English History, we shall be particularly struck with one circumstance to be observed in it, and which distinguishes most advantageously the English Government from all other free governments; I mean the <325> manner in which Revolutions and public commotions have always been terminated in England.

If we read with some attention the History of other free States, we shall see that the public dissensions that have taken place in them, have constantly been terminated by settlements in which the interests only of a *few* were really provided for; while the grievances of the *many* were hardly, if at all, attended to. In England the very reverse has happened, and we find Revolutions always to have been terminated by extensive and accurate provisions for securing the general liberty.

The History of the ancient Grecian Commonwealths, but above all of

---

1. This chapter first appeared in the original English-language edition of 1775.

220

the Roman Republic, of which more complete accounts have been left us, afford striking proof of the former part of this observation. What was, for instance, the consequence of that great Revolution by which the Kings were driven from Rome, and in which the Senate and Patricians acted as the advisers and leaders of the People? The consequence was, as we find in Dionysius of Halicarnassus,[2] and Livy, that the Senators immediately assumed all those powers, lately so much complained of by themselves, which the Kings <326> had exercised. The execution of their future decrees was intrusted to two Magistrates taken from their own body, and entirely dependent on them, whom they called *Consuls,* and who were made to bear about them all the ensigns of power which had formerly attended the Kings. Only, care was taken that the axes and *fasces,*[3] the symbols of the power of life and death over the Citizens, which the Senate now claimed to itself, should not be carried before both Consuls at once, but only before one at a time, for fear, says Livy, of doubling the terror of the People (*a*).

Nor was this all: the Senators drew over to their party those Men who had the most interest at that time among the People, and admitted them as Members into their own body (*b*); which indeed was a precaution they could not prudently avoid taking. But the interests of the great Men in the Republic being thus provided for, the Revolution ended. The new Senators, as well as the old, took care not to lessen, by making provisions for the <327> liberty of the People, a power which was now become their own.

(*a*) "Omnia jura (*Regum*) omnia insignia, primi Consules tenuere; id modò cautum eft ne si ambo fasces haberent, duplicatus terror videretur. *Tit. Liv.* lib. ii. § 1. [[Titus Livius (Livy) *Ab urbe condita,* book 2, chapter 18. De Lolme's English text provides an approximate translation of the passage quoted in his note.]]

(*b*) These new Senators were called *conscripti:* hence the name of *Patres Conscripti,* afterwards indiscriminately given to the whole Senate.— *Tit. Liv.* ibid. [[The *patres conscripti,* who started to be made senators at the time of the expulsion of the Tarquin kings in 510 B.C.E., were not members of the patrician class that composed the original Roman senate. The term *conscripti* was used to distinguish these senators from the patricians (*patricii*). See Titus Livius (Livy), *Ab urbe condita,* book 2, chapter 1.10–11.]]

2. Greek historian and rhetorician of the late first century B.C.E., whose *Antiquitates Romanae* charted the history of Rome from its mythic beginnings to the period of the First Punic War in 264–241 B.C.E.

3. On the "axes and fasces," see above, book 2, chapter 3, p. 157, note a.

Nay, they presently stretched this power beyond its former tone; and the punishments which the Consul inflicted in a military manner on a number of those who still adhered to the former mode of Government, and even upon his own children, taught the People what they had to expect for the future, if they presumed to oppose the power of those whom they had thus unwarily made their Masters.

Among the oppressive laws, or usages, which the Senate, after the expulsion of the Kings, had permitted to continue, those which were most complained of by the People, were those by which those Citizens who could not pay their debts with the interest (which at Rome was enormous) at the appointed time, became slaves to their Creditors, and were delivered over to them bound with cords: hence the word *Nexi*,[4] by which that kind of Slaves were denominated. The cruelties exercised by Creditors on those unfortunate Men, whom the private calamities caused by the frequent wars in which Rome was engaged, rendered very numerous, at last roused the body of the People: they abandoned both the City, and their inhuman fellow-citizens, and retreated to the other side of the River *Anio*. <328>

But this second Revolution, like the former, only procured the advancement of particular persons. A new office was created, called the Tribune-ship. Those whom the People had placed at their head when they left the City, were raised to it. Their duty, it was agreed, was for the future to protect the Citizens; and they were invested with a certain number of prerogatives for that purpose. This Institution, it must however be confessed, would have, in the issue, proved very beneficial to the People, at least for a long course of time, if certain precautions had been taken with respect to it, which would have much lessened the future personal importance of the new Tribunes (*a*): but these precautions the latter did not think proper to suggest; and in regard to those abuses themselves which had at

---

(*a*) Their number, which was only Ten, ought to have been much greater; and they never ought to have accepted the power left to each of them, of stopping by his single opposition the proceedings of all the rest. [[On the Roman tribunes, see above, book 2, chapter 2, p. 151, note 1; book 2, chapter 3, p. 157, note a; book 2, chapter 12, p. 200, note a.]]

4. "Bonds." The term applied to persons delivered bound to their creditors, for default of payment, *until satisfaction was made*.

first given rise to the complaints of the People, no farther mention was made of them (*a*).

As the Senate and Patricians, in the early ages of the Commonwealth, kept closely united together, the Tribunes, for all their personal <329> privileges, were not able, however, during the first times after their creation, to gain an admittance either to the Consulship, or into the Senate, and thereby to separate their condition any farther from that of the People. This situation of their's, in which it was to be wished they might always have been kept, produced at first excellent effects, and caused their conduct to answer in a great measure the expectations of the People. The Tribunes complained loudly of the exorbitancy of the powers possessed by the Senate and Consuls; and here we must observe, that the power exercised by these latter over the lives of the Citizens, had never been yet subjected (which will probably surprise the Reader), to any known laws, though sixty years had already elapsed since the expulsion of the Kings. The Tribunes therefore insisted, that laws should be made in that respect, which the Consuls should thenceforwards be bound to follow; and that they should no longer be left, in the exercise of their power over the lives of the Citizens, to their own caprice and wantonness (*b*). <330>

Equitable as these demands were, the Senate and Patricians opposed them with great warmth, and either by naming Dictators, or calling in the assistance of the Priests, or other means, they defeated for nine years together, all the endeavours of the Tribunes. However, as the latter were at that time in earnest, the Senate was at length obliged to comply; and the *Lex Terentilla* was passed, by which it was enacted that a general Code of Laws should be made.[5]

(*a*) A number of seditions were afterwards raised upon the same account.

(*b*) "Quod Populus in se jus dederit, eo Consulem usurum; non ipsos libidinem ac licentiam suam pro lege habituros."—*Tit. Liv.* lib. iii. § 9. [[Titus Livius (Livy), *Ab urbe condita,* book 3, chapter 9.5. The quoted passage reads: "Such authority over them as the people had granted the consuls, they should enjoy. But they should not make a law of their own whims and caprices."]]

5. De Lolme refers to legislation proposed in 462 B.C.E. by Gaius Terentilius Harsa that "five men be appointed to write down laws on the powers of consuls." According to Livy's account, the proposed law was not adopted; see Titus Livius (Livy), *Ab urbe condita,* book 3, chapter 9.

These beginnings seemed to promise great success to the cause of the People. But, unfortunately for them, the Senate found means to have it agreed, that the office of Tribune should be set aside during the whole time that the Code should be framing. They moreover obtained, that the ten Men, called Decemvirs, to whom the charge of composing this Code was to be given, should be taken from the body of the Patricians.[6] The same causes, therefore, produced again the same effects; and the power of the Senate and Consul was left in the new Code, or laws of the Twelve Tables, as undefined as before. As to the laws above mentioned, concerning debtors, which never had ceased to be bitterly complained of by the People, and in regard to which some satisfaction ought in com-<331>mon justice, to have been given them, they were confirmed, and a new terror added to them from the manner in which they were worded.

The true motive of the Senate, when they thus trusted the framing of the new laws to a new kind of Magistrates, called Decemvirs, was that, by suspending the ancient office of Consul, they might have a fair pretence for suspending also the office of Tribune, and thereby rid themselves of the People, during the time that the important business of framing the Code should be carrying on: they even, in order the better to secure that point, placed the whole power in the Republic, in the hands of these new Magistrates. But the Senate and Patricians experienced then, in their turn, the danger of entrusting Men with an uncontrolled authority. As they themselves had formerly betrayed the trust which the People had placed in them, so did the Decemvirs, on this occasion, likewise deceive them. They retained, by their own private authority, the unlimited power that had been conferred on them, and at last exercised it on the Patricians as well as the Plebeians. Both parties therefore united against them, and the Decemvirs were expelled from the City. <332>

The former dignities of the Republic were restored, and with them the office of Tribune. Those from among the People who had been most instrumental in destroying the power of the Decemvirs, were, as it was nat-

6. The decemvirs began work in 451 B.C.E. on a summation of basic legal rules and procedure that eventually resulted in the Twelve Tables. As De Lolme reports, while the decemvirs held office, other Roman magistracies—such as the office of consul and tribune—were suspended.

ural, raised to the Tribuneship; and they entered upon their offices possessed of a prodigious degree of popularity. The Senate and the Patricians
were, at the same time, sunk extremely low in consequence of the long
tyranny which had just expired; and those two circumstances united, afforded the Tribunes but too easy an opportunity of making the present
Revolution end as the former ones had done, and converting it to the advancement of their own power. They got new personal privileges to be
added to those which they already possessed, and moreover procured a law
to be enacted, by which it was ordained, that the resolutions taken by the
Comitia Tributa[7] (an Assembly in which the Tribunes were admitted to
propose new laws) should be binding upon the whole Commonwealth:—
by which they at once raised to themselves an *imperium in imperio,*[8] and
acquired, as Livy expresses it, a most active weapon (*a*). <333>

From that time great commotions arose in the Republic, which, like all
those before them, ended in promoting the power of a *few.*—Proposals for
easing the People of their debts, for dividing with some equality amongst
the Citizens the lands which were taken from the enemy, and for lowering
the rate of the interest of money, were frequently made by the Tribunes.
And indeed all these were excellent regulations to propose; but, unfortunately for the People, the proposals of them were only pretences made use
of by the Tribunes for promoting schemes of a fatal though somewhat remote, tendency, to public liberty. Their real aims were at the Consulship,
the Praetorship, the Priesthood, and other offices of Executive power,
which they were intended to control, and not to share. To these views they
constantly made the cause of the People subservient:—I shall relate among
other instances, the manner in which they procured to themselves an admittance to the office of Consul.

Having during several years, seized every opportunity of making
speeches to the People on that subject, and even excited seditions in order
to overcome the opposition of the Senate, they at last availed themselves
of the <334> circumstance of an *interregnum* (a time, during which there

(*a*) *Acerrimum telum.* [[Titus Livius (Livy), *Ab urbe condita,* book 3, chapter 55.5.]]
7. See above, book 2, chapter 5, p. 170, note 3.
8. "A power within a power."

happened to be no other Magistrates in the Republic besides themselves) and proposed to the Tribes, whom they had assembled, to enact the three following laws:—the first for settling the rate of interest of money; the second for ordaining that no Citizen should be possessed of more than five hundred acres of land; and the third, for providing that one of the two Consuls should be taken from the body of the Plebeians. But on this occasion it evidently appeared, says Livy, which of the laws in agitation were most agreeable to the People, and which, to those who proposed them; for the Tribes accepted the laws concerning the interest of money, and the lands; but as to that concerning the Plebeian Consulship, they rejected it: and both the former articles would from that moment have been settled, if the Tribunes had not declared, that the Tribes were called upon, either to accept, or reject, all their three proposals at once (*a*). <335> Great commotions ensued thereupon, for a whole year; but at last the Tribunes, by their perseverance in insisting that the Tribes should vote on their three *rogations,* jointly, obtained their ends, and overcame both the opposition of the Senate, and the reluctance of the People.

In the same manner did the Tribunes get themselves made capable of filling all other places of executive power, and public trust, in the Republic. But when all their views of that kind were accomplished, the Republic did not for all this enjoy more quiet, nor was the interest of the People better attended to, than before. New struggles then arose for actual admission to those places; for procuring them to relations, or friends; for governments of provinces, and commands of armies. A few Tribunes, indeed, did at times apply themselves seriously, out of real virtue and love of their duty, to remedy the grievances of the People; but both their fellow Tribunes, as we may see in History, and the whole body of those Men upon whom the People had, at different times, bestowed Consulships, Aedileships, Censorships, and other dignities without number, united together with the

(*a*) "Ab Tribunis, velut per interregnum, concilio Plebis habito, apparuit quae ex promulgatis Plebi, quae latoribus, gratiora essent; nam de foenore atque agro rogationes jubebant, de plebeio Consulatu antiquabant (*antiquis stabant*): & perfecta utraque res esset, ni Tribuni se in omnia simul consulere Plebem dixissent."—*Tit. Liv.* lib. vi. § 39. [[Titus Livius (Livy), *Ab urbe condita,* book 6, chapter 39.1–3. De Lolme's text provides an approximate translation of the passage quoted in his note.]]

utmost ve-<336>hemence against them; and the real Patriots, such as Tiberius Gracchus, Caius Gracchus, and Fulvius, constantly perished in the
attempt.[9]

I have been somewhat explicit on the effects produced by the different
Revolutions that have happened in the Roman Republic, because its History is much known to us, and we have either in Dionysius of Halicarnassus, or Livy, considerable monuments of the more ancient part of it.
But the History of the Grecian Commonwealths would also have supplied
us with a number of facts to the same purpose. That Revolution, for instance, by which the *Pisistratidae* were driven out of Athens—that by which
the *Four hundred,* and afterwards the *Thirty,* were established, as well as
that by which the latter were in their turn expelled, all ended in securing
the power of *a few.*—The Republic of Syracuse, that of Corcyra, of which
Thucydides has left us a pretty full account, and that of Florence, of which
Machiavel has written the History, also present us a series of public commotions ended by treaties, in which, as in the Roman Republic, the grievances of the People, though ever so loudly complained of in the beginning
by those who acted as their defenders, were, <337> in the issue, most care-
lessly attended to, or even totally disregarded (*a*).[10]

But if we turn our eyes towards the English History, scenes of a quite
different kind will offer to our view; and we shall find, on the contrary, that
Revolutions in England have always been terminated by making such pro-

(*a*) The Revolutions which have formerly happened in France, have all ended like
those above mentioned: of this a remarkable instance may be seen in the note (*a*) p. 29,
30. of this Work. The same facts are also to be observed in the History of Spain, Denmark, Sweden, Scotland, &c.; but I have avoided mentioning States of a Monarchical
form, till some observations are made, which the Reader will find in the XVIth Chapter.
[[See above, book 1, chapter 2, p. 37, note a; and below, book 2, chapter 17.]]

9. For Tiberius Gracchus and Caius Gracchus, see above, book 2, chapter 7, p. 181,
note 2. Marcus Fulvius Flaccus was an ally of Caius Gracchus, with whom he served as
tribune in 122 B.C.E. He was murdered by his political opponents in 121 B.C.E.

10. In giving examples of ancient and early modern republics in which the interests
of the populace were neglected by the political elites, De Lolme refers to Thucydides'
(ca. 460 B.C.E.–ca. 400 B.C.E.) *History of the Peloponnesian War* and to Machiavelli's 1525
History of Florence, as well as to the previously cited writings of Livy and Dionysius of
Halicarnassus.

visions, and only such, as all orders of the People were really and indiscriminately to enjoy.[11]

Most extraordinary facts, these! and which, from all the other circumstances that accompanied them, we see, all along, to have been owing to the impossibility (a point that has been so much insisted upon in former Chapters) in which those who possessed the confidence of the People, were, of transferring to themselves any branch of the Executive authority, and thus separating their own condition from that of the rest of the People. <338>

Without mentioning the compacts which were made with the first Kings of the Norman line, let us only cast our eyes on *Magna Charta,* which is still the foundation of English liberty. A number of circumstances which have been described in the former part of this work, concurred at that time to strengthen the Regal power to such a degree that no Men in the State could entertain a hope of succeeding in any other design than that of setting bounds to it. How great was the union which thence arose among all orders of the People!—what extent, what caution, do we see in the provisions made by the Great Charter! All the objects for which men naturally wish to live in a state of Society, were settled in its thirty-eight Articles. The judicial authority was regulated. The person and property of the individual were secured. The safety of the Merchant and stranger was provided for. The higher class of Citizens gave up a number of oppressive privileges which they had long since accustomed themselves to look upon as their undoubted rights (*a*). Nay, the imple-<339>ments of tillage of the *Bondman,* or Slave, were also secured to him; and for the first time perhaps in the annals of the World, a civil war was terminated by making stipulations in favour of those unfortunate Men to whom the avarice and lust of dominion inherent in human Nature, continued, over the greatest part of the Earth, to deny the common rights of Mankind.

Under Henry the Third great disturbances arose; and they were all ter-

---

(*a*) All possessors of lands took the engagement to establish in behalf of their Tenants and Vassals (*erga suos*) the same liberties which they demanded from the King.—*Mag. Char.* cap. xxxviii. [[Magna Carta, chap. 38. See above, book 1, chapter 2, pp. 35–37.]]

11. De Lolme, here and in the paragraphs which complete the chapter, returns to the English constitutional history he set out more fully in book 1, chapters 1–3.

minated by solemn confirmations given to the Great Charter. Under Edward I. Edward II. Edward III. and Richard II. those who were intrusted with the care of the interests of the People, lost no opportunity that offered, of strengthening still farther that foundation of public liberty, of taking all such precautions as might render the Great Charter still more effectual in the event.—They had not ceased to be convinced that their cause was the same with that of all the rest of the People.

Henry of Lancaster having laid claim to the Crown, the Commons received the law from the victorious party. They settled the Crown upon Henry, by the name of Henry the Fourth; and added to the Act of Settlement, provisions which the Reader may see in <340> the second Volume of the *Parliamentary History* of England. Struck with the wisdom of the conditions demanded by the Commons, the Authors of the Book just mentioned, observe (perhaps with some simplicity) that the Commons of England *were no fools at that time.* They ought rather to have said,—The Commons of England were happy enough to form among themselves an Assembly in which every one could propose what matters he pleased, and freely discuss them;—they had no possibility left of converting either these advantages, or in general the confidence which the People had placed in them, to any private views of their own: they, therefore, without loss of time endeavoured to stipulate useful conditions with that Power by which they saw themselves at every instant exposed to be dissolved and dispersed, and applied their industry to insure the safety of the whole People, as it was the only means they had of procuring their own.

In the long contentions which took place between the Houses of York and Lancaster, the Commons remained spectators of disorders which, in those times, it was not in their power to prevent: they successively acknowledged the title of the victorious parties; but <341> whether under Edward the Fourth, under Richard the Third, or Henry the Seventh, by whom those quarrels were terminated, they continually availed themselves of the importance of the services which they were able to perform to the new established Sovereign, for obtaining effectual conditions in favour of the whole body of the People.

At the accession of James the First, which as it placed a new Family on the Throne of England, may be considered as a kind of Revolution, no demands were made by the Men who were at the head of the Nation, but in favour of general liberty.

After the accession of Charles the First, discontents of a very serious nature began to take place, and they were terminated in the first instance, by the Act called the *Petition of Right,* which is still looked upon as a most precise and accurate delineation of the rights of the People (*a*). <342>

At the Restoration of Charles the Second, the Constitution being re-established upon its former principles, the former consequences produced by it, began again to take place; and we see at that aera, and indeed during the whole course of that Reign, a continued series of precautions taken for securing the general liberty.

Lastly, the great event which took place in the year 1689, affords a striking confirmation of the truth of the observation made in this Chapter. At this aera the political wonder again appeared—of a Revolution terminated by a series of public Acts in which no interests but those of the People at large were considered and provided for;—no clause, even the most indirect, was inserted, either to gratify the present ambition, or favour the future views, of those who were personally concerned in bringing those Acts to a conclusion. Indeed, if any thing is capable of conveying to us an adequate idea of the soundness, as well as peculiarity, of the principles on which the English Government is founded, <343> it is the attentive perusal of the System of public Compacts to which the Revolution of the year 1689 gave rise,— of the Bill of Rights with all its different clauses, and of the several Acts which under two subsequent Reigns, till the accession of the House of Hanover, were made in order to strengthen it.

(*a*) The disorders which took place in the latter part of the reign of that Prince, seem indeed to contain a complete contradiction of the assertion which is the subject of the present Chapter; but they, at the same time, are a no less convincing confirmation of the truth of the principles laid down in the course of this whole Work. The above mentioned disorders took rise from that day in which Charles the First gave up the power of dissolving his Parliament; that is, from the day in which the Members of that Assembly acquired an independent, personal, permanent authority, which they soon began to turn against the People who had raised them to it. [[See De Lolme's previous discussion of this episode in book 2, chapter 3, p. 155, note a.]]

Second Difference—The Manner after which the Laws for the Liberty of the Subject are executed in England.

The second difference I mean to speak of, between the English Government and that of other free States, concerns the important object of the execution of the Laws. On this article, also, we shall find the advantage to lie on the side of the English Government; and, if we make a comparison between the History of those States and that of England, it will lead us to the following <344> observation, viz. that, though in other free States the laws concerning the liberty of the Citizens were imperfect, yet the execution of them was still more defective. In England, on the contrary, the laws for the security of the Subject, are not only very extensive in their provisions, but the manner in which they are executed, carries these advantages still farther; and English Subjects enjoy no less liberty from the spirit both of justice and mildness, by which all branches of the Government are influenced, than from the accuracy of the laws themselves.

The Roman Commonwealth will here again supply us with examples to prove the former part of the above assertion. When I said, in the foregoing Chapter, that, in times of public commotion, no provisions were made for the body of the People, I meant no provisions that were likely to prove effectual in the event. When the People were roused to a certain degree, or when their concurrence was necessary to carry into effect certain resolutions, or measures, that were particularly interesting to the Men in power,

---

1. This chapter first appeared in the original English-language edition of 1775.

the latter could not, with any prudence, openly profess a contempt for the
<345> political wishes of the People; and some declarations expressed in
general words, in favour of public liberty, were indeed added to the laws
that were enacted on those occasions. But these declarations, and the principles which they tended to establish, were afterwards even openly disregarded in practice.

Thus, when the People were made to vote, about a year after the expulsion of the Kings, that the Regal Government never should be again
established in Rome, and that those who should endeavour to restore it,
should be devoted to the Gods, an article was added which, in general
terms, confirmed to the Citizens the right they had before enjoyed under
the Kings, of appealing to the People from the sentences of death passed
upon them. No punishment (which will surprise the Reader) was decreed
against those who should violate this law; and indeed the Consuls, as we
may see in Dionysius of Halicarnassus and Livy,[2] concerned themselves but
little about the appeals of the Citizens, and in the more than military exercise of their functions, continued to sport with rights which they ought
to have respected, however imperfectly and loosely they had been secured.
<346>

An article to the same purport with the above, was afterwards also added
to the laws of the Twelve Tables; but the Decemvirs,[3] to whom the execution of those laws was at first committed, behaved exactly in the same
manner, and even worse than the Consuls had done before them; and after
they were expelled (a) the Magistrates who succeeded them, appear to have
been as little tender of the lives of the Citizens. I shall, among many in-

(a) At the time of the expulsion of the Decemvirs, a law was also enacted, that no
Magistrate should be created from whom no appeal could be made to the People (Mag-
istratus sine provocatione. Tit. Liv. book iii. § 55.) [["A magistrate without appeal." See
Titus Livius (Livy), Ab urbe condita, book 3, chapter 55.5. The decemvirs were expelled
from Rome in 449 B.C.E.]] by which the people expressly meant to abolish the Dictatorship: but, from the fact that will just now be related, and which happened about ten
years afterwards, we shall see that this law was not better observed than the former ones
had been.

2. For Livy see above, book 2, chapter 2, p. 150, note a; for Dionysius see book 2,
chapter 15, p. 221, note 2.

3. See above, book 2, chapter 15, pp. 224, note 6.

stances, relate one which will shew upon what slight grounds the Citizens were exposed to have their lives taken away.—Spurius Maelius being accused of endeavouring to make himself King, was summoned by the Master of the Horse, to appear before the Dictator, in order to clear himself of this somewhat extraordinary imputation. Spurius took refuge among the People; the Master of the Horse pursued him, and killed him on the spot. The multitude <347> having thereupon expressed a great indignation, the Dictator had them called to his Tribunal, and declared that Spurius had been lawfully put to death, even though he might be innocent of the crime laid to his charge, for having refused to appear before the Dictator, when summoned to do so by the Master of the Horse (*a*).

About one hundred and forty years after the times we mention, the law concerning the appeals to the People, was enacted for the third time. But we do not see that it was better observed afterwards than it had been before: we find it frequently violated, since that period, by the different Magistrates of the Republic, and the Senate itself, notwithstanding this same law, at times made formidable examples of the Citizens. Of this we have an instance in the three hundred soldiers who had pillaged the Town of Rhegium. The Senate, of its own authority, ordered them all to be put to death. In vain did the Tribune Flaccus remonstrate against so severe an <348> exertion of public justice on Roman Citizens; the Senate, says Valerius Maximus, nevertheless persisted in its resolution (*b*).

(*a*) "Tumultuantem deinde multitudinem, incerta existimatione facti, ad concionem vocari jussit, & *Maelium jure caesum* pronunciavit, *etiamsi regni crimine insons fuerit, qui vocatus à Magistro equitum, ad Dictatorem non venisset.* Tit. Liv. lib. iv. § 15. [[Titus Livius (Livy), *Ab urbe condita,* book 4, chapter 15.1. De Lolme's text provides an approximate translation of the passage cited in his note.]]

(*b*) Val. Max. book ii. c. 7. [[Valerius Maximus, *Factorum ac dictorum memorabilium libri IX,* book 2, chapter 7, section 15t. For Valerius Maximus, see above, book 2, chapter 7, p. 179, note b.]] This Author does not mention the precise number of those who were put to death on this occasion; he only says that they were executed fifty at a time, in different successive days; but other Authors make the number of them amount to four thousand. Livy speaks of a whole Legion.—*Legio Campana quae Rhegium occupaverat, obsessa, deditione factâ, securi percussa est.*—Tit. Liv. lib. xv. *Epit.* [["The Campanian legion, which had forcibly taken possession of Rhegium, besieged there, lay down their arms, and are punished with death." In modern editions of Livy's *Ab urbe condita,* an account of the incident (but not the precise sentence quoted by De Lolme) appears in

All these laws for securing the lives of the Citizens, had hitherto been enacted without any mention being made of a punishment against those who should violate them. At last the celebrated *Lex Porcia* was passed, which subjected to banishment those who should cause a Roman Citizen to be scourged and put to death. From a number of instances posterior to this law, it appears that it was not better observed than those before it had been: Caius Gracchus, therefore, caused the *Lex Sempronia* to be enacted, by which a new sanction was given to it.[4] But this second law did not secure his own life, and that of his friends, better than the *Lex Porcia* had done that of his brother, and those who had sup-<349>ported him: indeed, all the events which took place about those times, rendered it manifest that the evil was such as was beyond the power of any laws to cure.—I shall here mention a fact which affords a remarkable instance of the wantonness with which the Roman Magistrates had accustomed themselves to take away the lives of the Citizens. A Citizen, named Memmius, having put up for the Consulship, and publicly canvassing for the same, in opposition to a Man whom the Tribune Saturninus supported, the latter caused him to be apprehended, and made him expire under blows in the public Forum. The Tribune even carried his insolence so far, as Cicero informs us, as to give to this act of cruelty, transacted in the presence of the whole People assembled, the outward form of a lawful act of public Justice (*a*). <350>

---

the summary to book 12.]]—I have here followed Polybius, who says that only three hundred were taken and brought to Rome. [[De Lolme refers to Polybius (ca. 203–ca. 120 B.C.E.), the Greek historian whose *Historiae* (Histories) covered the history of Rome from 220 to 146 B.C.E. Polybius's account appears in book 1, chapter 7.]]

4. For *Lex Porcia,* see above, book 2, chapter 9, p. 188, note 4. The *Lex Sempronia de Provocatione* (123 B.C.E.) strengthened the rules that granted Roman citizens the right to appeal before a popular assembly the criminal convictions and punishments imposed by a magistrate, including capital sentences.

(*a*) The fatal forms of words (*cruciatús carmina*) used by the Roman Magistrates when they ordered a Man to be put to death, resounded (says Tully in his speech for *Rabirius*) in the Assembly of the People, in which the Censors had forbidden the common Executioner ever to appear. *I Lictor, colliga manus. Caput obnubito. Arbori infelici suspendito.* [[De Lolme quotes from the oration of Marcus Tullius Cicero, *Pro Rabirio perduellionis reo.* The passage reads: "Lictor, go bind his hands. Veil his head. Hang him from the tree of shame."]]—Memmius being a considerable Citizen, as we may conclude from his canvassing with success for the Consulship, all the great Men in the Republic

Nor were the Roman Magistrates satisfied with committing acts of injustice in their political capacity, and for the support of the power of that Body of which they made a part. Avarice and private rapine were at last added to political ambition. The Provinces were first oppressed and plundered. The calamity, in process of time, reached Italy itself, and the centre of the Republic; till at last the *Lex Calpurnia de repetundis* was enacted to put a stop to it. By this law an action was given to the Citizens and Allies for the recovery of the money extorted from them by Magistrates, or Men in power; and the *Lex Junia* afterwards added the penalty of banishment to the obligation of making restitution.[5]

But here another kind of disorder arose. The Judges proved as corrupt, as the Magistrates had been oppressive. They equally betrayed, in their own province, the cause of the Republic with which they had been intrusted; and rather chose to share in the plunder of the Consuls, the Praetors, and the <351> Proconsuls, than put the laws in force against them.

New expedients were, therefore, resorted to, in order to remedy this new evil. Laws were made for judging and punishing the Judges themselves; and above all, continual changes were made in the manner of composing their Assemblies. But the malady lay too deep for common legal provisions to remedy. The guilty Judges employed the same resources in order to avoid conviction, as the guilty Magistrates had done; and those continual changes at which we are amazed, were made in the constitution of the judiciary Bodies (*a*), instead of obviating the cor-<352>ruption of the Judges, only

---

took the alarm at the atrocious action of the Tribune: the Senate, the next day, issued out its solemn mandate, or form of words, to the Consuls, *to provide that the Republic should receive no detriment;* and the Tribune was killed in a pitched battle that was fought at the foot of the Capitol. [[The killing of Gaius Memmius occurred in 99 B.C.E.]]

5. *Lex Calpurnia de repetundis* was adopted in 149 B.C.E. De Lolme's reference to the Lex Junia appears somewhat confused. The *Lex Junia* of 59 B.C.E. reformed the Lex Calpurnia de repetundis by extending its application to additional groups of magistrates. An earlier Lex Junia of 126 B.C.E. established the punishment of banishment, but for a different set of offenses.

(*a*) The Judges (over the Assembly of whom the Praetor usually presided) were taken from the body of the Senate, till some years after the last Punic War; when the *Lex Sempronia,* proposed by Caius S. Gracchus, enacted that they should in future be taken from the Equestrian Order. The Consul Caepio procured afterwards a law to be enacted,

transferred to other Men the profit arising from becoming guilty of it. It was grown to be a general complaint, so early as the times of the Gracchi, that no Man who had money to give, could be brought to punishment (*a*). Cicero says that in his time, the same opinion was become settled and universally received (*b*); and his Speeches are full of his lamentations on what he calls the *levity*, and the *infamy*, of the public Judgments.

Nor was the impunity of corrupt Judges, the only evil under which the Republic laboured. Commotions of the whole Empire at last took place. The horrid vexations, and afterwards the acquittal, of Aquilius, Proconsul of Syria, and of some others who had been guilty of the same crimes, drove the Provinces of Asia to desperation: and then it was that that terrible war of Mithri-<353>dates arose, which was ushered in by the death of eighty thousand Romans, massacred in one day, in all the Cities of Asia (*c*).[6]

The Laws and public Judgments not only thus failed of the end for which they had been established: they even became, at length, new means of oppression added to those which already existed. Citizens possessed of

---

by which the Judges were to be taken from both orders, equally. The *Lex Servilia* soon after put the Equestrian Order again in possession of the *Judgments;* and after some years, the *Lex Livia* restored them entirely to the Senate.—The *Lex Plautia* enacted afterwards, that the Judges should be taken from the three Orders; the Senatorian, Equestrian, and Plebeian. The *Lex Cornelia,* framed by the Dictator Sylla, enacted again that the Judges should be entirely taken from the body of the Senate. The *Lex Aurelia* ordered anew, that they should be taken from the three Orders. Pompey made afterwards a change in their number, which he fixed at seventy-five, and in the manner of electing them. And lastly, Caesar entirely restored the Judgments to the Order of the Senate. [[De Lolme's survey of the changing composition of the Roman judiciary covers over seventy years of development, from the passage of the Lex Sempronia Judiciaria in 122 B.C.E. to the adoption of Julius Caesar's *Lex Judiciaria* in 46 B.C.E.]]

(*a*) App. de Bell. Civ. [[De Lolme refers to the work of the Roman historian Appian of Alexandria (ca. 95–ca. 165 C.E.), part of whose *Roman History* was devoted to the civil wars *(De bello civile).*]]

(*b*) Act. in Verr. i. § 1. [[De Lolme cites Marcus Tullius Cicero, *Verrine Orations, First Part of the Speech Against Gaius Verres at the First Hearing,* 1.1. De Lolme previously treated the abuses of power in Rome exemplified in the case of Gaius Verres; see above, book 2, chapter 9, p. 188, note 5.]]

(*c*) Appian.

6. Mithridates VI of Pontus (132–63 B.C.E.) fought a series of wars against Rome in the years 88–84 B.C.E., 83–81 B.C.E., and 75–65 B.C.E. The massacre of Roman citizens in Anatolia led to the outbreak of the first war.

wealth, persons obnoxious to particular Bodies, or the few Magistrates who attempted to stem the torrent of the general corruption, were accused and condemned; while Piso, of whom Cicero in his speech against him relates facts which make the Reader shudder with horror, and Verres, who had been guilty of enormities of the same kind, escaped unpunished.[7]

Hence a war arose still more formidable than the former, and the dangers of which we wonder that Rome was able to surmount. The greatest part of the Italians revolted at once, exasperated by the tyranny of the public Judgments; and we find in Cicero, who informs us of the cause of this revolt, which was called the *Social war,* a very expressive account both of the unfortunate condition of <354> the Republic, and of the perversion that had been made of the methods taken to remedy it. "—An hundred and ten years are not yet elapsed (says he) since the law for the recovery of money extorted by Magistrates was first propounded by the Tribune Calpurnius Piso. A number of other laws to the same effect, continually more and more severe, have followed: but so many persons have been accused, so many condemned, so formidable a war has been excited in Italy by the terror of the public Judgments, and when the laws and Judgments have been suspended, such an oppression and plunder of our Allies have prevailed, that we may truly say that it is not by our own strength, but by the weakness of others, that we continue to exist" (*a*).

I have entered into these particulars with regard to the Roman Commonwealth, because the facts on which they are grounded, are remarkable of themselves, and yet no just conclusion could be drawn from them, unless a series of them were presented to the Reader. Nor are we to account for these facts, by the luxury which prevailed in the latter ages of the Republic, by the corruption of <355> the manners of the Citizens, their degeneracy from their ancient principles, and such like loose general phrases, which

---

(*a*) See Cic. de Off. lib. ii. § 75. [[Cicero, *De officiis,* book 2, section 75. Cicero, at the start of the quotation, refers to the adoption of the Lex Calpurnia in 149 B.C.E.]]

7. The abuses committed by Lucius Calpurnius Piso Caesoninus in his administration of Macedonia, 57–55 B.C.E., were condemned by Cicero in two speeches to the Roman Senate, *De provinciis consularibus* and *In Pisonem.*

may perhaps be useful to express the manner itself in which the evil became manifested, but by no means set forth the causes of it.

The above disorders arose from the very nature of the Government of the Republic,—of a Government in which the Executive and Supreme Power being made to centre in the Body of those in whom the People had once placed their confidence, there remained no other effectual Power in the State that might render it necessary for them to keep within the bounds of justice and decency. And in the mean time, as the People, who were intended as a check over that Body, continually gave a share in this Executive authority to those whom they intrusted with the care of their interests, they increased the evils they complained of, as it were at every attempt they made to remedy them, and instead of raising up Opponents to those who were become the enemies of their liberty, as it was their intention to do, they continually supplied them with new Associates. <356>

From this situation of affairs, flowed as an unavoidable consequence, that continual desertion of the cause of the People, which, even in time of Revolutions, when the passions of the People themselves were roused, and they were in a great degree united, manifested itself in so remarkable a manner. We may trace the symptoms of the great political defect here mentioned, in the earliest ages of the Commonwealth, as well as in the last stage of its duration. In Rome, while small and poor, it rendered vain whatever rights or power the People possessed, and blasted all their endeavours to defend their liberty, in the same manner as, in the more splendid ages of the Commonwealth, it rendered the most salutary regulations utterly fruitless, and even instrumental to the ambition and avarice of a few. The prodigious fortune of the Republic, in short, did not create the disorder, it only gave full scope to it.

But if we turn our view towards the History of the English Nation, we shall see how, from a Government in which the above defects did not exist, different consequences have followed:—how cordially all ranks of Men have always united together to lay under proper re-<357>straints this Executive power, which they knew could never be their own. In times of public Revolutions, the greatest care, as we have before observed, was taken to ascertain the limits of that Power; and after peace had been restored to the State, those who remained at the head of the Nation, continued to manifest an unwearied jealousy in maintaining those advantages which the united efforts of all had obtained.

Thus it was made one of the Articles of Magna Charta,[8] that the Executive Power should not touch the person of the Subject but in consequence of a judgment passed upon him by his peers; and so great was afterwards the general union in maintaining this law, that the *Trial by Jury*, that admirable mode of proceeding which so effectually secures the Subject against all the attempts of Power, even (which seemed so difficult to obtain) against such as might be made under the sanction of the Judicial authority, hath been preserved to this day. It has even been preserved in all its original purity, though the same has been successively suffered to decay, and then to be lost, in the other Countries of Europe, where it had been formerly <358> known (*a*). Nay, though this privilege of being tried by one's peers, was at first a privilege of Conquerors and Masters, exclusively appropriated to those parts of Nations which had originally invaded and subdued the rest by arms, it has in England been successively extended to every Order of the People.

(*a*) The Trial by Jury was in use among the Normans long before they came over to England; but it is now utterly lost in that Province: it even began very early to degenerate there from its first institution: we see in Hale's History of the *Common Law* of England, that the unanimity among Jurymen was not required in Normandy for making a verdict, a good verdict; but when Jurymen dissented, a number of them was taken out, and others added in their stead, till an unanimity was procured.—In Sweden, where, according to the opinion of the Learned in that Country, the *Trial by Jury* had its first origin, only some forms of that Institution are now preserved in the lower Courts in the Country, where sets of Jurymen are established for life, and have a salary accordingly. See *Robinson's State of Sweden.*—And in Scotland, the vicinity of England has not been able to preserve to the Trial by Jury its genuine ancient form: the unanimity among Jurymen is not required, as I have been told, to form a Verdict; but the majority is decisive. [[Hale's account of the Norman practice concerning jury voting appeared in chapter 6 of his *History of the Common Law of England.* De Lolme's source concerning juries in Sweden is John Robinson's 1694 *An account of Sweden; together with an extract of the history of that kingdom.* He correctly reports that juries in Scotland, which were used only in cases involving the most serious forms of criminal offense, were not required to reach unanimous verdicts.]]

8. Magna Carta, chapter 29.

And not only the person, but also the property, of the individual, has been secured against all arbitrary attempts from the Executive power, and the latter has been success-<359>ively restrained from touching any part of the property of the Subject, even under pretence of the necessities of the State, any otherwise than by the free grant of the Representatives of the People. Nay, so true and persevering has been the zeal of these Representatives, in asserting on that account the interests of the Nation, from which they could not separate their own, that this privilege of taxing themselves, which was in the beginning grounded on a most precarious tenure, and only a mode of governing adopted by the Sovereign for the sake of his own convenience, has become, in time, a settled right of the People, which the Sovereign has found it at length necessarily solemnly and repeatedly to acknowledge.

Nay more, the Representatives of the People have applied this right of *Taxation* to a still nobler use than the mere preservation of property; they have in process of time, succeeded in converting it into a regular and constitutional means of influencing the motions of the Executive Power. By means of this Right, they have gained the advantage of being constantly called to concur in the measures of the Sovereign,—of having the greatest <360> attention shewn by him to their requests, as well as the highest regard paid to any engagements that he enters into with them. Thus has it become at last the peculiar happiness of English Subjects, to whatever other People either ancient or modern we compare them, to enjoy a share in the Government of their Country, by electing Representatives, who, by reason of the peculiar circumstances in which they are placed, and of the extensive rights they possess, are both *willing* faithfully to serve those who have appointed them, and *able* to do so.

And indeed the Commons have not rested satisfied with establishing, once for all, the provisions for the liberty of the People which have been just mentioned: they have afterwards made the preservation of them, the first object of their care (*a*), and taken every opportunity of giving them new vigour and life. <361>

(*a*) The first operation of the Commons, at the beginning of a Session, is to appoint four grand Committees. The one is a Committee of Religion, another of Courts of

Thus, under Charles the First, when attacks of a most alarming nature were made on the privilege of the People to grant free supplies to the Crown, the Commons vindicated, without loss of time, that great right of the Nation, which is the Constitutional bulwark of all others, and hastened to oppugn, in their beginning, every precedent of a practice that must in the end have produced the ruin of public liberty.

They even extended their care to abuses of every kind. The judicial authority, for instance, which the Executive Power had imperceptibly assumed to itself, both with respect to the person and property of the individual, was abrogated by the Act which abolished the Court of Star Chamber; and the Crown was thus brought back to its true Constitutional office, viz. the countenancing, and supporting with its strength, the execution of the Laws.[9]

The subsequent endeavours of the Legislature have carried even to a still greater extent the above privileges of the People. They have moreover succeeded in restraining the Crown from any attempt to seize and confine, even for the shortest time, the person of the Subject, unless it be in the cases ascertained by the Law, of which the Judges of it are to decide. <362>

Nor has this extensive unexampled freedom at the expence of the Executive Power, been made, as we might be inclinable to think, the exclusive appropriated privilege of the great and powerful. It is to be enjoyed alike by all ranks of Subjects. Nay, it was the injury done to a common Citizen that gave existence to the Act which has completed the security of this interesting branch of public liberty.— *The oppression of an obscure individual,* says Judge Blackstone, *gave rise to the famous Habeas Corpus Act:* Junius has quoted this observation of the Judge; and the same is well worth repeating a third time, for the just idea it conveys of that readiness of all Orders of

---

Justice, another of Trade, and another of Grievances: they are to be standing Committees during the whole Session.

9. De Lolme discussed these episodes, including the 1641 statute abolishing the Star Chamber, in book 1, chapter 3, pp. 47–50.

Men, to unite in defence of common liberty, which is a characteristic circumstance in the English Government (*a*).[10]

And this general union in favour of public liberty, has not been confined to the framing <363> of laws for its security: it has operated with no less vigour in bringing to punishment such as have ventured to infringe them; and the Sovereign has constantly found it necessary to give up the violators of those laws, even when his own Servants, to the Justice of their Country.

Thus we find, so early as the reign of Edward the First, Judges who were convicted of having committed exactions in the exercise of their offices, to have been condemned by a sentence of Parliament (*b*). From the immense fines which were laid upon them, and which it seems they were in a condition to pay, we may indeed conclude that, in those early ages of the Constitution, the remedy was applied rather late to the disorder; but yet it was at last applied.

Under Richard the Second, examples of the same kind were renewed. Michael de la Pole, Earl of Suffolk, who had been Lord Chancellor of the kingdom, the Duke of Ireland, and the Archbishop of York, having <364> abused their power by carrying on designs that were subversive of public liberty, were declared guilty of High-treason; and a number of Judges who,

---

(*a*) The individual here alluded to was one Francis Jenks, who having made a motion at Guildhall, in the year 1676, to petition the King for a new Parliament, was examined before the Privy Council, and afterwards committed to the Gate-house, where he was kept about two months, through the delays made by the several Judges to whom he applied, in granting him a *Habeas Corpus.*—See the *State Trials,* vol. vii. anno 1676. [[Francis Jenks (or Jenkes) was held by order of the Privy Council from June 29 to August 18, 1676, notwithstanding repeated legal efforts to secure his release. De Lolme refers to the report of his case in *A Collection of State-Trials and Proceedings upon High-Treason and other Crimes and Misdemeanours . . . ,* 8 vols. (London, 1730–35), 7:468–76.]]

(*b*) Sir Ralph de Hengham, Chief Justice of the King's Bench, was fined 7,000 marks; Sir Thomas Wayland, Chief Justice of the Common Pleas, had his whole estate forfeited; and Sir Adam de Stratton, Chief Baron of the Exchequer, was fined 34,000 marks. [[The trials and convictions occurred in 1289, under the initiative of King Edward I, who was credited by Matthew Hale and other legal historians with major reforms of English law and justice.]]

10. Blackstone, *Commentaries on the Laws of England,* 3:135. Junius's discussion of the Habeas Corpus Act appeared in his letter of January 21, 1772, addressed to "Lord Chief Justice Mansfield." For the *Letters of Junius,* see above, book 1, chapter 13, p. 127, note a.

in their judicial capacity, had acted as their instruments, were involved in the same condemnation (*a*).

Under the reign of Henry the Eighth, Sir Thomas Empson, and Edmund Dudley, who <365> had been the promoters of the exactions committed under the preceding reign, fell victims to the zeal of the Commons for vindicating the cause of the People.[11] Under King James the First, Lord Chancellor Bacon experienced that neither his high dignity, nor great personal qualifications, could screen him from having the severest censure passed upon him, for the corrupt practices of which he had suffered himself to become guilty. And under Charles the First, the Judges having attempted to imitate the example of the Judges under Richard the Second, by delivering opinions subversive of the rights of the People, found the same spirit of watchfulness in the Commons, as had proved the ruin of the former. Lord Finch, keeper of the Great Seal, was obliged to fly beyond sea. The Judges Davenport and Crawley were imprisoned: and Judge Berkeley was seized while sitting upon the Bench, as we find in Rushworth.[12]

(*a*) The most conspicuous among these Judges were Sir Robert Belknap, and Sir Robert Tresilian, Chief Justice of the King's Bench. The latter had drawn up a string of questions calculated to confer a despotic authority on the Crown, or rather on the Ministers above named, who had found means to render themselves entire Masters of the person of the King. These questions Sir Robert Tresilian proposed to the Judges, who had been summoned for that purpose, and they gave their opinions in favour of them. One of these opinions of the Judges, among others, tended to no less than to annihilate, at one stroke, all the rights of the Commons, by taking from them that important privilege mentioned before, of starting and freely discussing whatever subjects of debate they think proper:—the Commons were to be restrained, under pain of being punished as traitors, from proceeding upon any articles besides those limited to them by the King. All those who had had a share in the above declarations of the Judges, were attainted of high-treason. Some were hanged; among them was Sir Robert Tresilian; and the others were only banished, at the intercession of the Bishops.—See the Parl. History of England, vol. i. [[The trial and conviction of Richard II's judges and ministers occurred in 1388, as part of the political contest between the crown and the supporters of the Duke of Gloucester. De Lolme refers to the account of these proceedings in *The Parliamentary or Constitutional History of England; being a faithful account of all the most remarkable transactions in Parliament . . . Collected . . . by Several Hands,* 24 vols. (London, 1751–61), 1:427–35.]]

11. Richard (not Thomas) Empson and Edmund Dudley were executed for treason in 1510 and posthumously condemned by parliamentary attainder the following year.

12. Francis Bacon was impeached on charges of bribery, to which he confessed, in

In the reign of Charles the Second, we again find fresh instances of the vigilance of the Commons. Sir William Scroggs, Lord Chief Justice of the King's-Bench, Sir Francis North, Chief Justice of the Common Pleas, Sir Thomas Jones, one of the Judges of the <366> King's-Bench, and Sir Richard Weston, one of the Barons of the Exchequer, were impeached by the Commons, for partialities shewn by them in the administration of justice; and Chief Justice Scroggs, against whom some positive charges were well proved, was removed from his employments.[13]

The several examples offered here to the Reader, have been taken from several different periods of the English History, in order to shew that neither the influence, nor the dignity, of the infractors of the laws, even when they have been the nearest Servants of the Crown, have ever been able to check the zeal of the Commons in asserting the rights of the People. Other examples might perhaps be related to the same purpose; though the whole number of those to be met with, will, upon enquiry, be found the smaller, in proportion as the danger of infringing the laws has always been indubitable.

So much regularity has even (from all the circumstances above mentioned) been introduced into the operations of the Executive Power in England,—such an exact Justice have the People been accustomed, as a consequence, to expect from that quarter, that even the Sovereign, for his having once suf-<367>fered himself personally to violate the safety of the Subject, did not escape severe censure. The attack made by order of Charles the Second, on the person of Sir John Coventry, filled the Nation with astonishment; and this violent gratification of private passion, on the part of the Sovereign (a piece of self-indulgence with regard to inferiors, which

---

1621. Sir John Finch fled to Holland following his impeachment by Parliament in 1640. The parliamentary actions against the common law judges Davenport, Crawley, and Berkeley occurred that same year and formed part of the parliamentary attack on royal ministers who supported the extension of the crown's prerogative powers. De Lolme cites John Rushworth's *Historical Collections of Private Passages of State,* which covered the period 1618–48 and originally appeared in 8 volumes from 1659 to 1701. Rushworth discussed the sentencing of Berkeley in volume 5, p. 361.

13. The House of Commons prepared articles of impeachment against the judges in 1680. The following year, Scroggs was tried but not convicted by the House of Lords, and soon after he was removed from the chief justiceship of King's Bench.

whole classes of individuals in certain Countries almost think that they have a right to) excited a general ferment. "This event (says Bishop Burnet) put the House of Commons in a furious uproar. . . . It gave great advantages to all those who opposed the Court; and the names of the *Court* and *Country* party, which till now had seemed to be forgotten, were again revived" (*a*).

There are the limitations that have been set, in the English Government, on the operations of the Executive Power: limitations to which we find nothing comparable in any other free States, ancient or modern; and which are owing, as we have seen, to that <368> very circumstance which seemed at first sight to prevent the possibility of them, I mean the greatness and unity of that Power; the effect of which has been, in the event, to unite upon the same object, the views and efforts of all Orders of the People.

From this circumstance, that is, the *unity* and peculiar stability of the Executive Power in England, another most advantageous consequence has followed, that has been before noticed, and which it is not improper to mention again here, as this Chapter is intended to confirm the principles laid down in the former ones,—I mean the unremitted continuance of the same general union among all ranks of Men, and the spirit of mutual justice which thereby continues to be diffused through all orders of Subjects.

Though surrounded by the many boundaries that have just now been described, the Crown, we must observe, has preserved its Prerogative undivided: it still possesses its whole effective strength, and is only tied by its own engagements, and the consideration of what it owes to its dearest interests.

The great, or wealthy Men in the Nation, who, assisted by the body of the People, have succeeded in reducing the exercise, of its au-<369>thority within such well defined limits, can have no expectation that it will continue

(*a*) See Burnet's History, vol. i. anno 1669.—An Act of Parliament was made on this occasion, for giving a farther extent to the provisions before made for the personal security of the Subject; which is still called the *Coventry* Act. [[Sir John Coventry, whose satiric remarks in the House of Commons angered Charles II, was attacked and injured by officers of the royal guard. The 1671 Coventry Act, enacted in response, made maiming a capital crime and specified that those who assaulted Coventry should not be eligible to receive a pardon from the crown. De Lolme's authority for this incident is *A History of My Own Time* by Gilbert Burnet (1643–1715), which was published posthumously in 1724–34.]]

to confine itself to them, any longer than they themselves continue, by the justice of their own conduct, to deserve that support of the People which alone can make them appear of consequence in the eye of the Sovereign,— no probable hopes that the Crown will continue to observe those laws by which their wealth, dignity, liberty, are protected, any longer than they themselves also continue to observe them.

Nay more, all those claims of their rights which they continue to make against the Crown, are encouragements which they give to the rest of the People to assert their own rights against them. Their constant opposition to all arbitrary proceedings of that Power, is a continual declaration they make against any acts of oppression which the superior advantages they enjoy, might entice them to commit on their inferior fellow-subjects. Nor was that severe censure, for instance, which they concurred in passing on an unguarded violent action of their Sovereign, only a restraint put on the per-sonal actions of future English Kings: no, it was a much more extensive pro-vision for the securing of <370> public liberty;—it was a solemn engagement entered into by all the powerful Men in the State to the whole body of the People, scrupulously to respect the person of the lowest among them.

And indeed the constant tenor of the conduct even of the two Houses of Parliament shews us, that the above observations are not matters of mere speculation. From the earliest times we see the Members of the House of Commons to have been very cautious not to assume any distinction that might alienate from them the affections of the rest of the People (*a*). Whenever those privileges which were necessary to them for the discharge of their trust have proved burdensome to the Community, they have re-trenched them. And those of their Members who have applied either these privileges, or in general <371> that influence which they derived from their

---

(*a*) In all cases of public offences, down to a simple breach of the peace, the Members of the House of Commons have no privilege whatever above the rest of the People: they may be committed to prison by any Justice of the peace; and are dealt with afterwards in the same manner as any other Subjects. With regard to civil matters, their only privi-lege is to be free from Arrests during the time of a Session, and forty days before, and forty days after; but they may be sued, by process against their goods, for any just debt during that time.

situation, to any oppressive purposes, they themselves have endeavoured to bring to punishment.

Thus, we see, that in the reign of James the First, Sir Giles Mompesson, a Member of the House of Commons, having been guilty of monopolies and other acts of great oppression on the People, was not only expelled, but impeached and prosecuted with the greatest warmth by the House, and finally condemned by the Lords to be publicly degraded from his rank of a Knight, held for ever an infamous person, and imprisoned during life.

In the same reign, Sir John Bennet, who was also a Member of the House of Commons, having been found to have been guilty of several corrupt practices, in his capacity of Judge of the *Prerogative* Court of Canterbury, such as taking exorbitant fees, and the like, was expelled the House, and prosecuted for these offences.[14]

In the year 1641, Mr. Henry Benson, Member for Knaresborough, having been detected in selling protections, experienced likewise the indignation of the House, and was expelled.[15] <372>

In fine, in order as it were to make it completely notorious, that neither the condition of Representative of the People, nor even any degree of influence in their House, could excuse any one of them from strictly observing the rules of justice, the Commons did on one occasion pass the most severe censure they had power to inflict, upon their Speaker himself, for having, in a single instance, attempted to convert the discharge of his duty as Speaker into a means of private emolument.—Sir John Trevor, Speaker of the House of Commons, having, in the sixth year of the reign of King William, received a thousand guineas from the City of London, "as a gratuity for the trouble he had taken with regard to the passing of the *Orphan Bill*," was voted guilty of a High crime and misdemeanour, and expelled the House. Even the inconsiderable sum of twenty guineas which Mr.

14. The parliamentary impeachments of Mompesson and Bennet both occurred in 1621 (the same year as the prosecution of Francis Bacon, discussed above, p. 243, note 12). Mompesson was charged with abuses in the conduct of his office as licenser of inns. Bennet was charged with judicial abuses in his administration of intestate estates.

15. "Protections" were legal documents shielding an individual from arrest or legal process. Benson was both expelled from the 1641 session and declared "unfit and uncapable ever to sit in Parliament."

Hungerford, another Member, had been weak enough to accept on the same score, was looked upon as deserving the notice of the House; and he was likewise expelled (*a*).[16] <373>

If we turn our view towards the House of Lords, we shall find that they have also constantly taken care that their peculiar privileges should not prove impediments to the common justice which is due to the rest of the People (*b*). They have constantly agreed to every just proposal that has been made to them on that subject by the Commons: and indeed, if we consider the numerous and oppressive privileges claimed by the *Nobles* in most other Countries, and the vehement spirit with which they are commonly asserted, we shall think it no small praise to the body of the Nobility in England (and also to the nature of that Government of which they make <374> a part) that it has been by their free consent that their privileges have been confined to what they now are; that is to say, to no more, in general, than what is necessary to the accomplishment of the end and constitutional design of that House.

In the exercise of their Judicial authority with regard to civil matters, the Lords have manifested a spirit of equity nowise inferior to that which they have shewn in their Legislative capacity. They have, in the discharge

(*a*) Other examples of the attention of the House of Commons to the conduct of their Members, might be produced, either before, or after, that which is mentioned here. The reader may, for instance, see the relation of their proceedings in the affair of the *South Sea Company* Scheme; and a few years after, in that of the *Charitable Corporation;* a fraudulent scheme particularly oppressive to the poor, for which several Members were expelled. [[The 1720 crash of shares in the South Sea Company, a financial and trading corporation licensed in 1711, caused large financial losses to many elite investors. In the subsequent public scandal and parliamentary investigation, several prominent political leaders, including company directors and others accused of accepting bribes from the company, were forced to resign their offices and expelled from the House of Commons. In 1732 three members were expelled from the House of Commons for their participation in the fraudulent scheme to divert for personal gain funds of the Charitable Corporation, which had been established "for Relief of industrious Poor."]]

(*b*) In case of a public offence, or even a simple breach of the peace, a Peer may be committed, till he finds bail, by any Justice of the peace: and Peers are to be tried by the common course of law, for all offences under felony. With regard to civil matters, they are at all times free from *arrests;* but execution may be had against their effects, in the same manner as against those of other Subjects.

16. Trevor was convicted and expelled, along with Hungerford, in 1695. The episode ended Trevor's parliamentary career, though he returned to public office in 1702 under the patronage of Queen Anne.

of that function, (which of all others is so liable to create temptations) shewn an uncorruptness really superior to what any judicial Assembly in any other Nation can boast. Nor do I think that I run any risk of being contradicted, when I say that the conduct of the House of Lords, in their civil judicial capacity, has constantly been such as has kept them above the reach of even suspicion or slander.

Even that privilege which they enjoy, of exclusively trying their own Members, in case of any accusation that may affect their life (a privilege which we might at first sight think repugnant to the idea of a regular Government, and even alarming to the rest of the People) has constantly been made use of <375> by the Lords to do justice to their fellow-subjects; and if we cast our eyes either on the collection of the *State Trials,* or on the History of England, we shall find very few examples, if any, of a Peer, really guilty of the offence laid to his charge, that has derived any advantage from his not being tried by a Jury of *Commoners.*

Nor has this just and moderate conduct of the two Houses of Parliament in the exercise of their powers (a moderation so unlike what has been related of the conduct of the powerful Men in the Roman Republic) been the only happy consequence of that salutary jealousy which those two Bodies entertain of the power of the Crown. The same motive has also engaged them to exert their utmost endeavours to put the Courts of Justice under proper restraints: a point of the highest importance to public liberty.

They have, from the earliest times, preferred complaints against the influence of the Crown over these Courts, and at last procured Laws to be enacted by which such influence has been intirely prevented: all which measures, we must observe, were at the same time strong declarations that no Subjects, however exalted their rank might be, were to think themselves exempt from submitting to the uniform course <376> of the Law, or hope to influence or over-awe it. The severe examples which they have united to make on those Judges who had rendered themselves the instruments of the passions of the Sovereign, or of the designs of the Ministers of the Crown, are also awful warnings to the Judges who have succeeded them, never to attempt to deviate in favour of any, the most powerful individuals, from that strait line of Justice which the joint Wisdom of the Legislature has once marked out to them.

This singular situation of the English Judges relatively to the three Con-

stituent Powers of the State, (and also the formidable support which they
are certain to receive from them as long as they continue to be the faithful
Ministers of Justice) has at last created such an impartiality in the distribution of public Justice in England, has introduced into the Courts of Law
the practice of such a thorough disregard of either the influence or wealth
of the contending Parties, and procured to every individual, both such an
easy access to these Courts, and such a certainty of redress, as are not to be
paralleled in any other Government.—Philip de Comines, so long as three
hundred years ago, commended in strong terms the exactness with which
Justice is done in England to <377> all ranks of Subjects (*a*); and the impartiality with which the same is administered in these days, will with still
more reason create the surprize of every Stranger who has an opportunity
of observing the customs of this Country (*b*). <378>

Indeed, to such a degree of impartiality has the administration of public
Justice been brought in England, that it is saying nothing beyond the exact
truth, to affirm that any violation of the laws, though perpetrated by Men
of the most extensive influence, nay, though committed by the special di-

(*a*) See page 36 of this Work. [[The testimony of Philippe de Comines, in fact, appears above in book 1, chapter 2, p. 37, note a, and p. 43, note a.]]

(*b*) A little after I came to England for the first time (if the Reader will give me leave
to make mention of myself in this case) an action was brought in a Court of Justice
against a Prince very nearly related to the Crown; and a Noble Lord was also, much
about that time, engaged in a law-suit for the property of some valuable lead-mines in
Yorkshire. I could not but observe that in both these cases a decision was given against
the two most powerful parties; though I wondered but little at this, because I had before
heard much of the impartiality of the law proceedings in England, and was prepared to
see instances of that kind. But what I was much surprised at, was that nobody appeared
to be in the least so, not even at the strictness with which the ordinary course of the law
had, particularly in the former case, been adhered to,—and that those proceedings which
I was disposed to consider as great instances of Justice, to the production of which some
circumstances peculiar to the times, at least some uncommon virtue or spirit on the part
of the Judges, must have more or less co-operated, were looked upon by all those whom
I heard speak about it, as being nothing more than the common and expected course of
things. This circumstance became a strong inducement to me to enquire into the nature
of a Government by which such effects were produced. [[The first law case De Lolme
mentions was the extensively publicized 1770 case of Richard Lord Grosvenor versus
Henry Frederick, Duke of Cumberland, before the Court of King's Bench, in which
the brother of King George III was found guilty of "criminal conversation" for his
adulterous relationship with Lady Grosvenor. De Lolme's second case has not been
identified.]]

rection of the very first Servants of the Crown, will be publicly and completely redressed. And the very lowest of subjects will obtain such redress, if he has but spirit enough to stand forth, and appeal to the laws of his Country.—Most extraordinary circumstances these! which those who know the difficulty that there is in establishing just laws among Mankind, and in providing afterwards for their due execution, only find credible because they are matters of fact, and can begin to account for, only when they look up to the constitution of the Government itself; that is to say, when they consider the circumstances in which the Executive Power, or the Crown, is placed in relation to the two Bodies that concur with it to form the Legislature,—the circumstances in which those two Assemblies are placed in relation to the Crown, and to each other, and the situation in which all <379> the Three find themselves with respect to the whole Body of the People (*a*). <380>

(*a*) The assertion above made with respect to the impartiality with which Justice is, in all cases, administered in England, not being of a nature to be proved by alledging single facts, I have entered into no particulars on that account. However, I have subjoined here two cases which, I think, cannot but appear remarkable to the Reader.

The first is the case of the prosecution commenced in the year 1763, by some Journeymen Printers, against the King's Messengers, for apprehending and imprisoning them for a short time, by virtue of a *General Warrant* from the Secretaries of State; and that which was afterwards carried on by another private individual, against one of the Secretaries themselves.—In these actions, all the ordinary forms of proceeding used in cases of actions between private Subjects, were strictly adhered to; and both the Secretary of State, and the Messengers, were, in the end, condemned. Yet, which it is proper the Reader should observe, from all the circumstances that accompanied this affair, it is difficult to propose a case in which Ministers could, of themselves, be under greater temptations to exert an undue influence to hinder the ordinary course of Justice. Nor were the Acts for which those Ministers were condemned, Acts of evident oppression, which nobody could be found to justify. They had done nothing but follow a practice of which they found several precedents established in their Offices; and their case, if I am well informed, was such, that most individuals, under similar circumstances, would have thought themselves authorised to have acted as they had done. [[General Warrants, effectively made illegal in a series of famous cases before the Courts of Common Pleas and King's Bench in the 1760s and condemned in a 1766 resolution of the House of Commons, were issued for the arrest of unnamed persons or for the seizure of unspecified papers. De Lolme appears to refer to the case of *Entick v. Carrington*, which was decided in the Court of Common Pleas in 1765. John Entick, a printer involved in the publication of several seditious numbers of the journal *The Monitor, or British Freeholder*, brought the case against Nathan Carrington, who had entered his home and seized his

In fine, a very remarkable circumstance in the English Government (and which alone evinces something peculiar and excellent in its Nature), is that spirit of extreme mildness with which Justice in criminal cases, is administered in England; a point with regard to which England differs from all other Countries in the World. <381>

When we consider the punishments in use in the other States in Europe, we wonder how Men can be brought to treat their fellow-creatures with so much cruelty; and the bare consideration of those punishments would sufficiently convince us (supposing we did not know the fact from other circumstances) that the Men in those States who frame the laws, and preside over their execution, have little apprehension that either they, or their friends, will ever fall victims to those laws which they thus rashly establish.

In the Roman Republic, circumstances of the same nature with those just mentioned, were also productive of the greatest defects in the kind of criminal Justice which took place in it. That class of Citizens who were at the head of the Republic, and who knew how mutually to exempt each other from the operation of any too severe laws or practice, not only allowed them-

---

property under the authority of a General Warrant. In dating the case to 1763, De Lolme may have confused this litigation with the well-known General Warrants case of that year, *Rex v. Wilkes,* which grew out of the government prosecution of John Wilkes for seditious libel in connection with his authorship and publication of issue no. 45 of the journal *North Britain.*]]

The second case I propose to relate, affords a singular instance of the confidence with which all Subjects in England claim what they think their just rights, and of the certainty with which the remedies of the law are in all cases open to them. The fact I mean, is the Arrest executed in the reign of Queen Anne, in the year 1708, on the person of the Russian Ambassador, by taking him out of his Coach for the sum of fifty pounds—And the consequences that followed this fact are still more remarkable. The Czar highly resented this affront, and demanded that the Sheriff of Middlesex, and all others concerned in the Arrest, should be punished with instant death. "But the Queen," (to the amazement of that despotic Court, says Justice Blackstone, from whom I borrow this fact) "the Queen directed the Secretary of State to inform him that she could inflict no punishment upon any, the meanest, of Her Subjects, unless warranted by the law of the land."—An act was afterwards passed to free from arrests the persons of foreign Ministers, and such of their servants as they have delivered a list of, to the Secretary of State. A copy of this Act elegantly engrossed and illuminated, continues Judge Blackstone, was sent to Moscow, and an Ambassador extraordinary commissioned to deliver it. [[Blackstone's account of this episode appears in *Commentaries on the Laws of England,* 1:246–47.]]

selves great liberties, as we have seen, in disposing of the lives of the inferior Citizens, but had also introduced into the exercise of the illegal powers they assumed to themselves in that respect, a great degree of cruelty (*a*). <382>

Nor were things more happily conducted in the Grecian Republics. From their Democratical nature, and the frequent Revolutions to which they were subject, we naturally expect to see that authority to have been used with mildness, which those who enjoyed it must have known to have been but precarious; yet, such were the effects of the violence attending those very Revolutions, that a spirit both of great irregularity and cruelty had taken place among the Greeks, in the exercise of the power of inflicting punishments. The very harsh laws of *Draco* are well known, of which it was said that they were not written with ink, but with blood.[17] The severe laws of the Twelve Tables among the Romans, were in great part brought over from Greece. And it was an opinion commonly received in Rome, that the cruelties practised by the Magistrates on the Citizens, were only imitations of the examples which the Greeks had given them (*b*). <383>

In fine, the use of Torture, that method of administering Justice in which folly may be said to be added to cruelty, had been adopted by the Greeks, in consequence of the same causes which had concurred to produce the irregularity of their criminal Justice. And the same practice continues, in these days, to prevail on the continent of Europe, in consequence of that

---

(*a*) The common manner in which the Senate ordered Citizens to be put to death, was by throwing them head-long from the top of the Tarpeian Rock. The Consuls, or other particular Magistrates, sometimes caused Citizens to expire upon a cross; or, which was a much more common case, ordered them to be beaten to death, with their heads fastened between the two branches of a fork; which they called *cervicem furcae inserere* [["to put the neck upon the fork"]].

(*b*) Caesar expressly reproaches the Greeks with this fact, in his speech in favour of the accomplices of Catiline, which Sallust has transmitted to us.—*Sed eodem illo tempore, Graeciae morem imitati,* (Majores nostri) *verberibus animadvertebant in cives, de condemnatis ultimum supplicium sumptum.* [["In that early period, and with that generous disposition, they looked toward Greece, and from that nation imported the custom of punishing some offenses by the lictor's rod, and in capital cases they pronounce judgment of death." De Lolme cites the account of the Cataline conspiracy of 63 B.C.E. *(Bellum Catilinae),* published by Gaius Sallustius Crispus (86–34 B.C.E.).]]

17. The legal compilation of Draco (ca. 621 B.C.E.), a legislator of ancient Athens, was written "with blood" on account of the notorious severity of its penal sanctions.

general arrangement of things which creates there such a carelessness about remedying the abuses of public Authority.

But the nature of that same Government which has procured to the People of England all the advantages we have before described, has, with still more reason, freed them from the most oppressive abuses which prevail in other countries.

That wantonness in disposing of the dearest rights of Mankind, those insults upon human Nature, of which the frame of the Governments established in other States, unavoidably becomes more or less productive, are entirely banished from a Nation which has the happiness of having its interests taken care of by Men who continue to be themselves ex-<384>posed to the pressure of those laws which they concur in making, and of every tyrannic practice which they suffer to be introduced,—by Men whom the advantages which they possess above the rest of the People, render only more exposed to the abuses they are appointed to prevent, only more alive to the dangers against which it is their duty to defend the Community (*a*).

Hence we see that the use of Torture has, from the earliest times, been utterly unknown in England. And all attempts to introduce it, whatever might be the power of those who made them, or the circumstances in which they renewed their endeavours, have been strenuously opposed and defeated (*b*). <385>

(*a*) Historians take notice that the Commons, in the reign of Charles II. made haste to procure the abolition of the old Statute, *De Haeretico comburendo,* (For burning Heretics) as soon as it became to be publicly known that the presumptive Heir to the Crown was a Roman Catholic. [[Parliament repealed *De Haeretico comburendo* in 1677.]] Perhaps they would not have been so diligent and earnest, if they had not been fully convinced that a Member of the House of Commons, or his friends, may be brought to trial as easily as any other individuals among the people, so long as an express and written law may be produced against them,

(*b*) The Reader may on this subject see again the Note in page 181 [[p. 130]] of this Work, where the opposition is mentioned, that was made to the Earl of Suffolk, and the Duke of Exeter, when they attempted to introduce the practice of Torture: this even was one of the causes for which the latter was afterwards impeached.—The Reader is also referred to the Note following that which has just been quoted, in which the solemn declaration is related, that was given by the Judges against the practice of Torture, in the case of Felton, who had assassinated the Duke of Buckingham. [[See above, book 1, chapter 13, p. 130, note b, and p. 131, note a.]]

From the same cause also arose that remarkable forbearance of the English Laws, to use any cruel severity in the punishments which experience shewed it was necessary for the preservation of Society to establish: and the utmost vengeance of those laws, even against the most enormous Offenders, never extends beyond the simple deprivation of life (*a*).[18]

Nay, so anxious has the English Legislature been to establish mercy, even to convicted Offenders, as a fundamental principle of the Government of England, that they made <386> it an express article of that great public Compact which was framed at the important aera of the Revolution, that "no cruel and unusual punishments should be used" (*b*).—They even endeavoured, by adding a clause for that purpose to the Oath which Kings were thenceforward to take at their Coronation, as it were to render it an everlasting obligation of English Kings, to make Justice to be "executed with mercy" (*c*).[19] <387>

(*a*) A very singular instance occurs in the History of the year 1605, of the care of the English Legislature not to suffer precedents of cruel practices to be introduced. During the time that those concerned in the Gun-powder plot were under sentence of death; a motion was made in the House of Commons to petition the King, that the execution might be staid, in order to consider of some extraordinary punishment to be inflicted upon them: but this motion was rejected. A proposal of the same kind was also made in the House of Lords, where it was dropped.—See the Parliamentary History of England, vol. v. anno 1605. [[De Lolme refers to parliamentary discussions reported in *Parliamentary or Constitutional History of England,* 5:143–45.]]

(*b*) See the Bill of Rights, Art. x.—"Excessive bail ought not to be required, nor excessive fines imposed; nor cruel and unusual punishments inflicted." [[On the 1688/ 89 Bill of Rights, see above, book 1, chapter 3, p. 53, note a.]]

(*c*) Those same dispositions of the English Legislature, which have led them to take such precautions in favour even of convicted offenders, have still more engaged them to make provisions in favour of such persons as are only suspected and accused of having committed offences of any kind. Hence the zeal with which they have availed themselves of every important occasion, such for instance as that of the Revolution, to procure new confirmations to be given to the institution of the Trial by Jury, to the laws on imprisonments, and in general to that system of criminal Jurisprudence of which a description has been given in the first part of this Work, to which I refer the Reader. [[See above, book 1, chapters 12–14.]]

18. De Lolme here exaggerates the mildness of England's legal sanctions; see above, book 1, chapter 13, p. 134, note 10.

19. De Lolme quotes, with slight alteration, the 1689 "Act for Establishing the Coronation Oath." The clause and phrase did not, in fact, constitute one of the several changes to the Coronation Oath introduced by the statute.

A more inward View of the English Government than has hitherto been offered to the Reader in the course of this Work.—Very essential differences between the English Monarchy, as a Monarchy, and all those with which we are acquainted.

The Doctrine constantly maintained in this Work, and which has, I think, been sufficiently supported by facts and comparisons drawn from the History of other Countries, is, that the remarkable liberty enjoyed by the English Nation, is essentially owing to the impossibility under which their Leaders, or in general all Men of power among them, are placed, of invading and transferring to themselves any branch of the Governing Executive authority; which authority is exclusively vested, and firmly secured, in the Crown. Hence the anxious care with which those Men continue to watch the exercise of that authority. Hence their perseverance in observing every kind of engagement which themselves may have entered into with the rest of the People.

But here a consideration of a most important kind presents itself.— How comes the <388> Crown in England, thus constantly to preserve to itself (as we see it does) the Executive authority in the State, and moreover to preserve it so completely as to inspire the great Men in the Nation with that conduct so advantageous to public Liberty, which has just been mentioned? All these are effects which we do not find, upon examination,

1. This chapter first appeared in the original English-language edition of 1775 and was considerably expanded in the 1784 edition.

that the power of *Crowns* has hitherto been able to produce in other Countries.

In all States of a Monarchical form, we indeed see that those Men whom their rank and wealth, or their personal power of any kind, have raised above the rest of the people, have formed combinations among themselves to oppose the power of the Monarch. But their views, we must observe, in forming these combinations, were not by any means to set general and impartial limitations on the Sovereign authority. They endeavoured to render themselves entirely independent of that authority; or even utterly to annihilate it, according to circumstances.

Thus we see that in all the States of ancient Greece, the Kings were at last destroyed and exterminated. The same event happened in Italy, where in remote times there existed for a while several kingdoms, as we learn both from the ancient Historians, and the <389> Poets. And in Rome, we even know the manner and circumstances in which such a revolution was brought about.

In more modern times, we see the numerous Monarchical Sovereignties which had been raised in Italy on the ruins of the Roman Empire, to have been successively destroyed by powerful factions; and events of much the same nature have at different times taken place in the Kingdoms established in the other parts of Europe.

In Sweden, Denmark, and Poland, for instance, we find that the *Nobles* have commonly reduced their Sovereigns to the condition of simple Presidents over their Assemblies,—of mere ostensible Heads of the Government.

In Germany, and in France, Countries where the Monarchs being possessed of considerable demesnes, were better able to maintain their independence than the Princes just mentioned, the Nobles waged war against them, sometimes singly, and sometimes jointly; and events similar to these have successively happened in Scotland, Spain, and the modern Kingdoms of Italy.

In fine, it has only been by means of standing armed forces that the Sovereigns of most of the <390> Kingdoms we have mentioned, have been able in a course of time to assert the prerogatives of their Crown. And it is only by continuing to keep up such forces, that, like the Eastern Monarchs, and indeed like all the Monarchs that ever existed, they continue to be able to support their authority.

How therefore can the Crown of England, without the assistance of any armed force, maintain, as it does, its numerous prerogatives? How can it, under such circumstances, preserve to itself the whole Executive power in the State? For here we must observe, the Crown in England does not derive any support from what regular forces it has at its disposal; and if we doubted this fact, we need only look to the astonishing subordination in which the military is kept to the civil power, to become convinced that an English King is not indebted to his army for the preservation of his authority (*a*).

If we could suppose that the armies of the Kings of Spain or of France, for instance, were, through some very extraordinary circumstance, all to vanish in one night, the power of those Sovereigns, we must not doubt, would, ere six months, be reduced to a mere shadow. <391> They would immediately behold their prerogatives, however formidable they may be at present, invaded and dismembered (*b*): and supposing that regular Governments continued to exist, they would be reduced to have little more influence in them, than the Doges of Venice, or of Genoa, possess in the Governments of those Republics (*c*).

How, therefore, to repeat the question once more, which is one of the most interesting that can occur in politics, how can the Crown in England, without the assistance of any armed force, avoid those dangers to which all other Sovereigns are exposed?

(*a*) Henry VIII. the most absolute Prince, perhaps, who ever sat upon a Throne, kept no standing army. [[The absence of a large standing army in England was conventionally associated with the preservation of English liberty. Given its increasing involvement in Continental and overseas wars throughout the period after 1688, England in fact regularly maintained a large land force. However, the parliamentary legislation which funded the army and provided for its military discipline through the Mutiny Act was enacted and renewed on a temporary basis, usually for the period of one year.]]

(*b*) As was the case in the several Kingdoms into which the Spanish Monarchy was formerly divided; and, in not very remote times, in France itself.

(*c*) Or than the Kings of Sweden were allowed to enjoy, before the last Revolution in that Country. [[De Lolme refers to the political events in Sweden in 1772, when the new king, Gustavus III, successfully restored much of the monarchic power that had been surrendered in the constitutional settlement of 1720; see below, pp. 264–65 and p. 265, note 7. The doges of Venice and of Genoa served as the chief magistrates in a system where political power was principally held by an oligarchy of leading families.]]

How can it, without any such force, accomplish even incomparably greater works than those Sovereigns, with their powerful armies, are, we find, in a condition to perform?—How can it bear that universal effort (unknown in other Monarchies) which, we have seen, is continually and openly exerted against it? How can it even continue to resist it so powerfully as to preclude all individuals whatever, from ever entertaining any views besides <392> those of setting just and *general* limitations to the exercise of its authority? How can it enforce the laws upon all Subjects, indiscriminately, without injury or danger to itself? How can it, in fine, impress the minds of all the great Men in the State with so lasting a jealousy of its power, as to necessitate them, even in the exercise of their undoubted rights and privileges, to continue to court and deserve the affection of the rest of the People?

Those great Men, I shall answer, who even in quiet times prove so formidable to other Monarchs, are in England divided into two Assemblies; and such, it is necessary to add, are the principles upon which this division is made, that from it results, as a necessary consequence, the solidity and indivisibility of the power of the Crown (*a*).

The Reader may perceive that I have led him, in the course of this Work, much beyond the line within which Writers on the subject of Government have confined themselves, or rather, that I have followed a track entirely different from that which those Writers have pursued. But as the observation just made on the stability of the power of the Crown in England, and the cause of it, is new in its <393> kind, so do the principles from which its truth is to be demonstrated, totally differ from what is commonly looked upon as the foundation of the science of Politics. To lay these principles here before the Reader, in a manner completely satisfactory to him, would lead us into philosophical discussions on what really constitutes the basis of Governments and Power amongst Mankind, both extremely long, and in a great measure foreign to the subject of this book. I shall therefore content myself with proving the above observations by facts; which is more,

---

(*a*) I have not flattered myself, in writing this Chapter that it would be perfectly understood, nor is it designed for the generality of readers.

after all, than political Writers usually undertake to do with regard to their speculations.

As I chiefly proposed to shew how the extensive liberty the English enjoy, is the result of the peculiar frame of their Government, and occasionally to compare the same with the Republican form, I even had at first intended to confine myself to that circumstance, which both constitutes the essential difference between those two forms of Government, and is the immediate cause of English liberty; I mean the having placed all the executive authority in the State out of the hands of those in whom the People trust. With regard to the remote cause of that same liberty, that is to say, the stability of the power of the Crown, <394> this singular solidity without the assistance of any armed force, by which this executive authority is so secured, I should perhaps have been silent, had I not found it absolutely necessary to mention the fact in this place, in order to obviate the objections which the more reflecting part of Readers might otherwise have made, both to several of the observations before offered to them, and to a few others which are soon to follow.

Besides, I shall confess here, I have been several times under apprehensions, in the course of this Work, lest the generality of Readers, misled by the similarity of names, should put too extensive a construction upon what I said with regard to the usefulness of the power of the Crown in England;—lest they should think, for instance, that I attributed the superior advantages of the English mode of Government over the Republican form, merely to its approaching nearer to the nature of the Monarchies established in the other parts of Europe, and that I looked upon every kind of Monarchy, as being in itself preferable to a Republican Government: an opinion, which I do not by any means or in any degree entertain; I have too much affection, or if you please, prepossession, in favour of that form of Government under which I was born; and as I am sensible of its defects, so do I <395> know how to set a value upon the advantages by which it compensates for them.

I therefore have, as it were, made haste to avail myself of the first opportunity of explaining my meaning on this subject,—of indicating that the power of the Crown in England stands upon foundations entirely different from those on which the same Power rests in other Countries,—and of engaging the Reader to observe (which for the present will suffice) that as the English Monarchy differs in its nature and main foundations, from every other, so all that is said here of its advantages, is peculiar and confined to it.

But, to come to the proofs (derived from facts) of the solidity accruing to the power of the Crown in England, from the *co-existence* of the two Assemblies which concur to form the English Parliament, I shall first point out to the Reader several open acts of these two Houses, by which they have by turns effectually defeated the attacks of each other upon its prerogative.

Without looking farther back for examples than the reign of Charles the Second, we see that the House of Commons had, in that reign, begun to adopt the method of adding (or tacking, as it is commonly expressed) <396> such bills as they wanted more particularly to have passed, to their money bills. This forcible use they made of their undoubted privilege of granting money, if suffered to have grown into common practice, would have totally destroyed the aequilibrium that ought to subsist between them and the Crown. But the Lords took upon themselves the task of maintaining that aequilibrium: they complained with great warmth of the several precedents that were made by the Commons, of the practice we mention: they insisted that Bills should be framed *"in the old and decent way of Parliament"*; and at last have made it a standing order of their House, to reject, upon the sight of them, all bills that are tacked to money bills.[2]

Again, about the thirty-first year of the same reign, a strong party prevailed in the House of Commons; and their efforts were not entirely confined, if we may credit the Historians of those times, to serving their Constituents faithfully, and providing for the welfare of the State. Among other bills which they proposed in their House, they carried one to exclude from the Crown the immediate Heir to it; an affair this, of a very high nature, and with regard to which it may well be questioned whether the legislative Assem-<397>blies have a right to form a resolution, without the express and declared concurrence of the body of the People. But both the Crown

---

2. See De Lolme's earlier reference to these conflicts and to the Lords' order concerning "tacking" bills, at book 1, chapter 6, p. 66, note a.

and the Nation were delivered from the danger of establishing such a precedent, by the interposition of the Lords, who threw out the bill on the first reading.[3]

In the reign of King William the Third, a few years after the Revolution, attacks were made upon the Crown from another quarter. A strong party was formed in the House of Lords; and, as we may see in Bishop Burnet's History of his Own Times, they entertained very deep designs. One of their views, among others, was to abridge the prerogative of the Crown of calling Parliaments, and judging of the proper times of doing it (*a*). They accordingly framed and carried in their House a bill for ascertaining the sitting of <398> Parliament every year: but the bill, after it had passed in their House, was rejected by the Commons (*b*).

Again, we find, a little after the accession of King George the First, an attempt was also made by a party in the House of Lords, to wrest from the Crown a prerogative which is one of its finest flowers; and is, besides, the only check it has on the dangerous views which that House (which may stop both money bills and all other bills) might be brought to entertain; I mean the right of adding new members to it, and judging of the times when it may be necessary to do so. A bill was accordingly presented, and carried, in the House of Lords, for limiting the members of that House to a fixed number, beyond which it should not be increased; but after great

---

(*a*) They, besides, proposed to have all money bills stopped in their House, till they had procured the right of taxing, themselves, their own estates; and to have a Committee of Lords, and a certain number of the Commons, appointed to confer together concerning the State of the Nation; "which Committee (says Bishop Burnet) would soon have grown to have been a Council of State, that would have brought all affairs under their inspection, and never had been proposed but when the Nation was ready to break into civil wars."—See Burnet's History, anno 1693. [[De Lolme refers to a variety of measures proposed in the years immediately following the 1688 Glorious Revolution, and often initiated by Whig leaders in the House of Lords, that would have further strengthened the political independence of Parliament by constraining the prerogatives of the crown. For Burnet's *History*, see above, book 2, chapter 16, p. 245, note a.]]

(*b*) Nov. 28, 1693.

3. Exclusion bills, designed to exclude from the royal succession the Catholic heir, James, Duke of York (later James II), were passed by the House of Commons in 1679, 1680, and 1681. The legislation of 1680 was rejected by the House of Lords. The two other bills failed because of the dissolution of Parliament.

pains taken to insure the success of this bill, it was at last rejected by the House of Commons.[4]

In fine, the several attempts which a majority in the House of Commons have in their turn made to restrain, farther than it now is, the influence of the Crown arising from the distribution of preferments and other advantages, have been checked by the House of <399> Lords; and all place-bills have, from the beginning of this Century, constantly miscarried in that House.[5]

Nor have these two powerful Assemblies only succeeded in thus warding off the open attacks of each other, on the power of the Crown. Their co-existence, and the principles upon which they are severally framed, have been productive of another effect much more extensive, though at first less attended to, I mean the preventing even the making of such attacks; and in times too, when the Crown was of itself incapable of defending its authority: the views of each of these two Houses, destroying, upon these occasions, the opposite views of the other, like those positive and negative equal quantities (if I may be allowed the comparison) which destroy each other on the opposite sides of an equation.

Of this we have several remarkable examples; as for instance, when the Sovereign has been a minor. If we examine the History of other Nations, especially before the invention of standing armies, we shall find that the event we mention never failed to be attended with open invasions of the Royal authority, or even sometimes with complete and settled divisions of it. In England, on the contrary, whether we look at the reign of Richard II. or that of Henry VI. or of Edward VI. we shall see that the Royal authority has been quietly exer-<400>cised by the Councils that were ap-

4. The unsuccessful legislation was introduced in 1719. George I's predecessor, Queen Anne, in 1711 created twelve new peers in order to ensure majority support in the House of Lords for the government peace policy that led to the 1713 Treaty of Utrecht.

5. "Place bills" were designed to secure the independence of the House of Commons by disqualifying any member who held a profitable office (or "place") under crown appointment. De Lolme's discussion is slightly misleading. Opposition by the House of Lords prevented the passage of several place bills in the period 1710–15, but a limited measure was enacted in 1716.

pointed to assist those Princes; and when they came of age, the same has
been delivered over to them undiminished.

But nothing so remarkable can be alledged on this subject, as the manner
in which these two Houses have acted upon those occasions when the
Crown being without any present possessor, they had it in their power, both
to settle it on what Person they pleased, and to divide and distribute its
effectual prerogatives, in what manner, and to what set of Men, they might
think proper. Circumstances like those we mention, have never failed in
other Kingdoms, to bring on a division of the effectual authority of the
Crown, or even of the State itself. In Sweden, for instance, (to speak of
that kingdom which has borne the greatest outward resemblance to that of
England) when Queen Christina was put under a necessity of abdicating
the Crown, and it was transferred to the Prince who stood next to her in
the line of Succession, the Executive authority in the State was immediately
divided, and either distributed among the Nobles, or assigned to the Senate,
into which the Nobles alone could be admitted; and the new King was only
to be a President over it.[6] <401>

After the death of Charles the Twelfth, who died without male heirs, the
disposal of the Crown (the power of which Charles the Eleventh had found
means to render again absolute) returned to the States, and was settled on
the Princess Ulrica, and the Prince her Husband. But the Senate, at the
same time it thus settled the possession of the Crown, again assumed to
itself the effectual authority which had formerly belonged to it. The privilege of assembling the States was vested in that Body. They also secured to
themselves the power of making war and peace, and treaties with foreign
powers,—the disposal of places,—the command of the army and of the
fleet,—and the administration of the public revenue. Their number was
to consist of sixteen Members. The majority of votes was to be decisive
upon every occasion. The only privilege of the new King, was to have his
vote reckoned for two: and if at any time he should refuse to attend their

6. Maria Christina Alexandra became queen of Sweden in 1632. She was forced to
abdicate in 1654 in favor of her cousin Charles Gustavus.

meetings, the business was nevertheless to be done as effectually and definitively without him (*a*).[7] <402>

But in England, the revolution of the year 1689 was terminated in a
manner totally dif-<403>ferent. Those who at that interesting epoch had
the guardianship of the Crown,—those in whose hands it lay *vacant*, did
not manifest so much as a thought to split and parcel out its prerogative.

(*a*) The Senate had procured a Seal to be made, to be affixed to their official resolutions, in case the King should refuse to lend his own. The reader will find a few more
particulars concerning the former government of Sweden, in the nineteenth Chapter.

Regulations of a similar nature had been made in Denmark, and continued to subsist,
with some variations, till the Revolution which in the last Century, placed the whole
power in the State, into the hands of the Crown, without controul. The different Kingdoms into which Spain was formerly divided, were governed in much the same manner.

And in Scotland, that Seat of anarchy and aristocratical feuds, all the great offices in
the State were not only taken from the Crown; but they were moreover made hereditary
in the principal families of the Body of the Nobles:—such were the offices of High
Admiral, High Stewart, High Constable, Great Chamberlain, and Justice General; this
latter office implied powers analogous to those of the Lord Chancellor, and the Lord
Chief Justice of the King's Bench, united.

The King's minority, or personal weakness, or in general the difficulties in which the
State might be involved, were circumstances of which the Scotch Leaders never failed
to avail themselves for invading the governing authority: a remarkable instance of the
claims they were used to set forth on those occasions, occurs in a Bill that was framed in
the year 1703, for settling the Sucession to the Crown, after the demise of the Queen,
under the title of *An Act for the Security of the Kingdom.*

The Scotch Parliament was to sit by its own authority, every year, on the first day of
November, and adjourn themselves as they should think proper.

The King was to give his assent to all laws agreed to, and offered by, the Estates; or
commission proper officers for doing the same.

A Committee of one and thirty Members, chosen by the Parliament, were to be called
the King's Council, and govern during the recess, being accountable to the Parliament.

The King not to make any foreign Treaty without the consent of Parliament.

All places and offices, both civil and military, and all pensions formerly given by the
King, shall ever after be given by Parliament. See *Parliamentary Debates.* A. 1703. [[In
treating the case of Denmark, De Lolme refers to the "revolution" that secured royal
absolutism in the period 1660–65. The Scottish legislation of 1703, designed to ensure
a Scottish heir to the Scottish throne following the death of Queen Anne, formed part
of the political maneuvering between Scotland and England that preceded the 1707 Act
of Union.]]

7. Sweden's Charles XII died without a direct male heir in 1718. A new constitutional
order, which sharply reduced the power of the crown in favor of the Council of Estates,
was consolidated in 1720.

They tendered it to a single indivisible possessor, impelled as it were by some secret power that was, unseen, operating upon them, without any salvo, without any article, to establish the greatness of themselves, or of their families. It is true, those prerogatives destructive of public liberty which the late King had assumed, were retrenched from the Crown; and thus far the two Houses agreed. But as to any attempt to transfer to other hands any part of the authority of the Crown, no proposal was even made about it. Those branches of prerogative which were taken from the kingly office, were annihilated and made to cease to exist in the State; and all the Executive authority that was thought necessary to be continued in the Government, was, as before, left undivided in the Crown. <404>

In the very same manner was the whole authority of the Crown transferred afterwards to the Princess who succeeded King William the Third, and who had no other claim to it but what was conferred on her by the Parliament. And in the same manner again was it settled, a long time beforehand, on the Princes of Hanover who have since succeeded her (a).[8]

Nay, one more extraordinary fact, and to which I desire the Reader to

(a) It may not be improper to observe here, as a farther proof of the indivisibility of the power of the Crown (which has been above said to result from the peculiar frame of the English Government) that no part of the Executive authority of the King is vested in his Privy Council, as we have seen it was in the Senate of Sweden: the whole business centers in the Sovereign; the votes of the Members are not even counted, if I am well informed: and in fact the constant style of the Law, is the King *in* Council, and not the King *and* Council. A proviso is indeed sometimes added to some Bills, that certain acts mentioned in them are to be transacted by the King in Council: but this is only a precaution taken in the view that the most important affairs of a great Nation may be transacted with proper solemnity, and to prevent, for instance, all objections that might, in process of time, be drawn from the uncertainty whether the King has assented, or not, to certain particular transactions. The King names the Members of the Privy Council; or excludes them, by causing their names to be struck out of the Book. [[A Royal Council—or more commonly, Privy Council—was a regular institution of royal government from the medieval period. The size and membership of the council was generally under the discretion of the crown. By the time of De Lolme's writing, the council's most important government functions had been replaced by the smaller committee of royal ministers and advisors referred to as the cabinet.]]

8. The 1688/89 Bill of Rights settled the crown on Anne of Denmark (the future Queen Anne) in the absence of a biological heir of William and Mary. The 1701 Act of Settlement settled the crown on the House of Hanover in the absence of a biological heir of Queen Anne.

give attention—<405>Notwithstanding all the Revolutions we mention, and although Parliament hath sat every year since the beginning of this century, and though they have constantly enjoyed the most unlimited freedom both as to the subjects and the manner of their deliberations, and numberless proposals have in consequence been made,—yet, such has been the efficiency of each House, in destroying, preventing, or qualifying, the views of the other, that the Crown has not been obliged during all that time to make use, even once, of its negative voice; and the last Bill rejected by a King of England, has been that rejected by King William the Third in the year 1692 for Triennial Parliaments (*a*).[9]

There is another instance yet more remarkable of this forbearing conduct of the Parliament in regard to the Crown, to whatever open or latent cause it may be owing, and how little their *esprit de corps* in reality leads them, amidst the apparent heat sometimes of their struggles, to invade its governing executive authority; I mean, the facility with which they have been prevailed upon to give up any essential branch of that authority, even after a <406> conjunction of preceding circumstances had caused them to be actually in possession of it; a case this, however, that has not frequently happened in the English History. After the Restoration of Charles the Second, for instance, we find the Parliament to have of their own accord passed an Act, in the first year that followed that event, by which they annihilated, at one stroke, both the independent legislative authority, and all claims to such authority, which they had assumed during the preceding disturbances:—By the Stat. 13 Car. II. c. 1. it was forbidden, under the penalty of a *praemunire* (see p. 194)[10] to affirm that either of the two Houses of Parliament, or both jointly, possess, without the concurrence of the King, the Legislative authority. In the fourth year after the Restoration, another

(*a*) He assented a few years afterwards to that Bill, after several amendments had been made in it. [[William assented to the Triennial Act of 1694, which limited the time between parliamentary elections to a maximum of three years. The legislation he vetoed in 1692 restricted even further the crown's control over the timing of parliamentary sessions and elections. The final exercise of the royal legislative veto occurred in 1708, when Queen Anne vetoed a bill for a Scottish militia.]]

9. This paragraph and the succeeding discussion to the end of part 1 (p. 274) first appeared in the fourth edition of 1784.

10. See book 1, p. 138, note a.

capital branch of the governing authority of the Crown was also restored to it, without any manner of struggle:—by the Stat. 16 Car. II. c. 1. the Act was repealed by which it had been enacted, that, in case the King should neglect to call a Parliament once at least in three years, the Peers should issue the writs for an election; and that should they neglect to issue the same, the Constituents should of themselves assemble to elect a Parliament. <407>

It is here to be observed, that, in the same reign we mention, the Parliament passed the *Habeas Corpus* Act, as well as the other Acts that prepared the same, and in general shewed a jealousy in watching over the liberty of the subject, superior perhaps to what has taken place at any other period of the English History: this is another striking confirmation of what has been remarked in a preceding Chapter, concerning the manner in which public disturbances have always been terminated in England. Here we find a series of Parliaments to have been tenaciously and perseverantly jealous of those kinds of popular universal provisions, which great Men in other States ever disdained seriously to think of, or give a place to, in those treaties by which internal peace was restored to the Nation; and at the same time these Parliaments cordially and sincerely gave up those high and splendid branches of Governing authority, which the Senates or Assemblies of great Men who surrounded the Monarchs in other limited Monarchies, never ceased anxiously to strive to assume to themselves,—and which the Monarchs, after having lost them, never were able to recover but by military violence aided by surprize, or through National com-<408>motions. All these are political singularities, certainly remarkable enough. It is a circumstance in no small degree conducive to the solidity of the executive authority of the English Crown (which is the subject of this Chapter) that those persons who seem to have it in their power to wrest the same from it, are, somehow, prevented from entertaining thoughts of doing so (*a*). <409>

(*a*) I will mention another instance of this real disinterestedness of the Parliament in regard to the power of the Crown,—nay, of the strong bent that prevails in that Assembly, to make the Crown the general depository of the executive authority in the Nation; I mean to speak of the manner in which they use to provide for the execution

As another proof of the peculiar solidity of the power of the Crown, in England, may be mentioned the facility, and safety to itself and to the State, with which it has at all times been able to deprive any particular Subjects of their different offices, however overgrown, and even dangerous, their private power may seem to be. A very remarkable instance of this kind occurred when the great Duke of Marlborough was suddenly removed from all his employments: the following is the account given by Dean Swift, in his "History of the Four last Years of the Reign of Queen Anne." <410>

"So that the Queen found herself under a necessity, by removing one person from so great a trust, to get clear of all her difficulties at once: her Majesty determined upon the latter expedient, as the shorter and safer course; and during the recess at Christmas, sent the Duke a letter to tell him she had no farther occasion for his service.

"There has not perhaps in the present age been a clearer instance to shew the instability of power which is not founded on virtue; and it may be an instruction to Princes who are well in the hearts of their People, that the overgrown power of any particular person, although supported by exor-

---

of those resolutions of an active kind they may at times come to: it is always by addressing the Crown for that purpose, and desiring it to interfere with its own executive authority. Even, in regard to the printing of their Journals, the Crown is applied to by the Commons, with a promise of making good to it the necessary expences. Certainly, if there existed in that Body any latent anxiety, any real ambition (I speak here of the general tenor of their conduct) to invest themselves with the executive authority in the State, they would not give up the providing by their own authority at least for the object just mentioned: it might give them a pretence for having a set of Officers belonging to them, as well as a Treasury of their own, and in short for establishing in their favour some sort of beginning or precedent: at the same time that a wish on their part, to be the publishers of their own Journals, could not be decently opposed by the Crown, nor would be likely to be found fault with by the Public. To some readers the fact we are speaking of may appear trifling; to me it is not so: I confess I never happen to see a paragraph in the newspapers, mentioning an address to the Crown for borrowing its executive prerogative in regard to the inconsiderable object here alluded to, without pausing for half a minute on the article. Certainly there must needs exist causes of a very peculiar nature which produce in an Assembly possessed of so much weight, that remarkable freedom from any serious ambition to push their advantages farther,—which inspire it with the great political forbearance we have mentioned, with so sincere an indifference in general, in regard to arrogating to themselves any branch of the executive authority of the Crown:—they really seem as if they did not know what to do with it after having acquired it, nor of what kind of service it may be to them.

bitant wealth, can, by a little resolution, be reduced in a moment, without any dangerous consequences. This Lord, who was, beyond all comparison, the greatest subject in Christendom, found his power, credit and influence crumble away on a sudden; and, except a few friends and followers, the rest dropped off in course, &c." (B. I. near the end.)[11]

The ease with which such a Man as the Duke was suddenly removed, Dean Swift has explained by the necessary advantages of Princes who possess the affection of their People, and <411> the natural weakness of power which is not founded on virtue. However, these are very unsatisfactory explanations. The History of Europe, in former times, offers us a continued series of examples to the contrary. We see in it numberless instances of Princes incessantly engaged in resisting in the field the competition of Subjects invested with the eminent dignities of the Realm, who were not by any means superior to them in point of virtue,—or at other times, living in a continued state of vassalage under some powerful Man whom they durst not resist, and whose *power, credit, and influence* they would have found it far from possible to *reduce in a moment, or crumble on a sudden,* by the sending of a single letter, even though assisted *by a little resolution,* to use Dean Swift's expressions, and without any dangerous consequences.

Nay, certain Kings, such as Henry the Third, of France, in regard to the Duke of Guise, and James the Second, of Scotland, in regard to the two Earls of Douglas successively, had at last recourse to plot and assassination; and expedients of a similar sudden violent kind, are the settled methods adopted by the Eastern Monarchs; nor is it very sure they can always easily do otherwise (*a*). <412>

---

11. On Marlborough's removal from office in 1711, see above, book 2, chapter 1, p. 149, note a. De Lolme's source is Jonathan Swift's *History of the Last Four Years of the Queen,* which was published posthumously in 1758.

(*a*) We might also mention here the case of the Emperor Ferdinand II. and the Duke of Valstein, which seems to have at the time made a great noise in the world.—The Earls of Douglas were sometimes attended by a retinue of two thousand horse. See Dr. Robertson's History of Scotland.—The Duke of Guise was warned some hours before his death, of the danger of trusting his person into the King's presence or house; he answered, *On n' oseroit;*—They durst not.

If Mary, Queen of Scots, had possessed a power analogous to that exerted by Queen Anne, she might perhaps have avoided being driven into those instances of ill-conduct

Even in the present Monarchies of Europe, notwithstanding the awful force by which they are outwardly supported, a discarded Minister is the cause of more or less anxiety to the governing Authority; especially if, through the length of time he has been in office, he happens to have acquired a considerable degree of influence. He is generally sent and confined to one of his estates in the country, which the Crown names to him: he is not allowed to appear at Court, nor even in the Metropolis; much less is he suffered to appeal to the People in loud complaints, to make public speeches to the great Men in the State and intrigue among them, and in short to vent his resentment by those bitter, and sometimes desperate, methods, which, in the Constitution of this Country, prove in great measure harmless. <413>

But a Dissolution of the Parliament, that is, the dismission of the whole body of the great Men in the Nation, assembled in a Legislative capacity, is a circumstance, in the English Government, in a much higher degree remarkable and deserving our notice, than the depriving any single individual, however powerful, from his public employments. When we consider in what easy and complete manner such a dissolution is effected in England, we must needs become convinced that the power of the Crown bears upon foundations of very uncommon, though perhaps hidden, strength; especially, if we attend to the several facts that take place in other Countries.

In France, for example, we find the Crown, notwithstanding the immense outward force by which it is surrounded, to use the utmost caution in its proceedings towards the Parliament of Paris: an Assembly only of a judiciary nature, without any Legislative authority or avowed claim, and which, in short, is very far from having the same weight in the kingdom of

---

which were followed by such tragical consequences. [[In his note and corresponding text, De Lolme cites celebrated cases in which monarchs resorted to force and assassination to subdue powerful rivals. The Holy Roman Emperor, Ferdinand II, was held responsible for the 1634 assassination of the Duke of Wallenstein (or Valstein). The French monarch, Henry III, orchestrated the 1588 assassination of the Duke of Guise. The 1440 execution of the Earl of Douglas and his brother occurred under the minority rule of James II of Scotland. Mary Queen of Scots was charged with the 1567 death of her second husband, Henry Stuart, Lord Darnley. De Lolme's source for the reign of James II is William Robertson's 1758 *History of Scotland.*]]

France, as the English Parliament has in England. The King never repairs
to that Assembly, to signify his intentions, or hold a *Lit de Justice,* without
the most over-awing circumstances of military apparatus and preparation,
<414> constantly choosing to make his appearance among them rather as
a military General, than as a King.

And when the late King, having taken a serious alarm at the proceedings
of this Parliament, at length resolved upon their dismission, he fenced himself, as it were, with his army; and military Messengers were sent with every
circumstance of secrecy and dispatch, who, at an early part of the day and
at the same hour, surprised each Member in his own house, causing them
severally to depart for distant parts of the country which were prescribed
to them, without allowing them time to consider, much less to meet, and
hold any consultation together.[12]

But the Person who is invested with the kingly office, in England, has
need of no other weapon, no other artillery, than the Civil *Insignia* of his
dignity, to effect a dissolution of the Parliament. He steps into the middle
of them, telling them they are dissolved; and they are dissolved:—he tells
them, they are no longer a Parliament; and they are no longer so. Like
Popilius's wand (*a*), a dissolution instantly puts a stop to their warmest
debates and most vio-<415>lent proceedings. The wonderful words by
which it is expressed have no sooner met their ears, than all their legislative
faculties are benumbed: though they may still be sitting on the same
benches, they look no longer upon themselves as forming an Assembly; they
no longer consider each other in the light of Associates or of Colleagues.
As if some strange kind of weapon, or a sudden magical effort, had been
exerted in the midst of them, all the bonds of their union are cut off; and

(*a*) He who stopt the army of King Antiochus. [[According to Livy and other classical
authors, Popilius convinced Antiochus to abandon his military campaign in Egypt
against Rome's ally, Ptolemy. His "wand" was a stick he used to draw a circle in the sand
around Antiochus, ordering him to remain in the circle until he finished delivering his
message from Rome.]]

12. The "late King" is Louis XV. De Lolme refers to the events of 1771, when the king
issued *lettres de cachet* exiling magistrates who resisted the recent campaign under the
direction of Chancellor Maupeou to curb the authority of the Parlements. On the *"Lit
de Justice,"* see above, book 1, chapter 4, p. 60, note a.

they hasten away, without having so much as the thought of continuing for a single minute the duration of their Assembly (*a*). <416>

To all these observations concerning the peculiar solidity of the authority of the Crown, in England, I shall add another that is supplied by the whole series of the English History; which is, that, though bloody broils and disturbances have often taken place in England, and war often made against the King, yet, it has scarcely ever been done but by persons who positively and expressly laid claim to the Crown. Even while Cromwell contended with an armed force against Charles the First, it was, as every one knows who has read that part of the English history, in the King's own name he waged war against him. <417>

The same objection might be expressed in a more general manner and with strict truth, by saying, that no war has been waged, in England, against the governing authority, except upon national grounds; that is to say, either

(*a*) Nor has London post-horses enough to drive them far and near into the Country, in case the declaration by which the Parliament is dissolved, also mentions the calling of a new one.

A Dissolution, when proclaimed by a common Crier assisted by a few Beadles, is attended by the very same effects.

To the account of the expedient used by the late King of France, to effect the dismission of the Parliament of Paris, we may add the manner in which the Crown of Spain, in a higher degree arbitrary perhaps than that of France, undertook, some years ago, to rid itself of the religious Society of the Jesuits, whose political influence and intrigues, had grown to give it umbrage. They were seized by an armed force, at the same minute of the same day, in every Town or Borough of that extensive Monarchy where they had residence, in order to their being hurried away to ships that were waiting to carry them into another Country: the whole business being conducted with circumstances of secrecy, surprize, and of preparation, far superior to what is related of the most celebrated conspiracies mentioned in History.

The Dissolution of the Parliament which Charles the Second had called at Oxford, is an extremely curious event: a very lively account of it is to be found in Oldmixon's History of England. [[The Jesuits were forcibly expelled from Spain in April 1767 in the sudden and clandestine manner described by De Lolme. The abortive Oxford Parliament was abruptly dismissed by Charles II after sitting for one week in April 1681. De Lolme refers to the antiroyalist account in John Oldmixon's 1729 *History of England, During the Reigns of the Royal House of Stuart.*]]

If certain alterations, however imperceptible they may perhaps be, at first, to the public eye, ever take place, the period may come at which the Crown will no longer have it in its power to dissolve the Parliament; that is to say, a Dissolution will no longer be followed by the same effects that it is at present.

when the title to the Crown has been doubtful, or when general complaints, either of a political or religious kind, have arisen from every part of the Nation: as instances of such complaints may be mentioned those which gave rise to the war against King John, which ended in the passing of the Great Charter,—the civil wars in the reign of Charles the First,—and the Revolution of the year 1689. From the facts just mentioned it may also be observed as a conclusion, that the Crown cannot depend on the great security we have been describing any longer than it continues to fulfil its engagements to the Nation, and to respect those laws which form the compact between it and the People. And the imminent dangers, or at least the alarms and perplexities, in which the Kings of England have constantly involved themselves, whenever they have attempted to struggle against the general sense of the Nation, manifestly shew that all that has been above observed concerning the security and remarkable stability some how annexed to their Office, is to <418> be understood, not of the capricious power of the Man, but of the lawful authority of the Head of the State (*a*). <419>

(*a*) One more observation might be made on the subject; which is, that, when the kingly dignity has happened in England to be wrested from the possessor, through some revolution, it has been recovered, or struggled for, with more difficulty than in other Countries: in all the other Countries upon earth, a King *de jure* (by claim) possesses advantages in regard to the King in being, much superior to those of which the same circumstance may be productive in England. The power of the other Sovereigns in the World, is not so securely established as that of an English King; but then their character is more indelible; that is to say,—till their Antagonists have succeeded in cutting them off and their families, they possess in a high degree a power to renew their claims, and disturb the State. Those family pleas or claims of priority, and in general those arguments to which the bulk of Mankind have agreed to allow so much weight, cease almost entirely to be of any effect, in England, against the person actually invested with the Kingly office, as soon the constitutional parts and springs have begun to move, and in short as soon as the machine of the Government has once begun to be in full play. An universal national ferment, similar to that which produced the former disturbances, is the only time of real danger. [[De Lolme refers obliquely to the failure of the two Jacobite rebellions to restore the Stuart dynasty in 1715–16 and 1745–46.]]

The remarkable degree of internal national quiet which, for very near a century past, has followed the Revolution of the year 1689, is a remarkable proof of the truth of the observations above made; nor do I think, that, all circumstances being considered, any other Country can produce the like instance.

Second Part of the same Chapter.

There is certainly a very great degree of singularity in all the circumstances we have been describing here: those persons who are acquainted with the history of other Countries, cannot but remark with surprise, that stability of the power of the English Crown,—that mysterious solidity,—that inward binding strength with which it is able to carry on with certainty its legal operations, amidst the clamorous struggle and uproar with which it is commonly surrounded, and without the medium of any armed threatening force. To give a demonstration of the manner in which all these things are brought to bear and operated, is not, as I said before, my design to attempt here: the principles from which such demonstration is to be derived, suppose an enquiry into the nature of Man, and of human affairs, which rather belongs to Philosophy (though to a branch hitherto unexplored) than to Politics: at least such an enquiry certainly lies out of the sphere of the common Science of Politics (*a*). However, I had a very material <420> reason in introducing all the above mentioned facts concerning the peculiar stability of the governing authority in England, in that they lead to an observation of a most important political nature; which is, that this stability allows several essential branches of English liberty to take place which without it could not exist. For there is a very essential consideration to be made in every Science, though speculators are sometimes apt to lose sight of it, which is, that in order that things may have existence, they must be *possible;* in order that political regulations of any kind may obtain their effect, they must imply no direct contradiction, either open or hidden, to the nature of things, or to the other circumstances of the Government. In reasoning from this principle, we shall find that the stability of the Governing executive authority in England, and the weight it gives to the whole machine of the State, has actually enabled the English Nation, considered as a free Nation, to enjoy several advantages which would really have been totally unattainable in the other States we have mentioned in former Chap-

(*a*) It may, if the reader pleases, belong to the Science of *Metapolitics;* in the same sense as we say *Metaphysics;* that is, the Science of those things which lie beyond physical, or substantial, things. A few more words are bestowed upon the same subject, in the Advertisement, or Preface, at the head of this Work.

ters, whatever degree of public virtue we might even suppose to have belonged to those who acted in those States as the Advisers of the People,
<421> or in general who were trusted with the business of framing the
Laws (a).

One of these advantages resulting from the Solidity of the Government,
is, the extraordinary personal freedom which all ranks of individuals in
England, enjoy at the expence of the governing authority.[13] In the Roman
Commonwealth, for instance, we see the Senate to have been vested with
a number of powers totally destructive of the liberty of the Citizens; and
the continuance of these powers was, no doubt, in a great measure owing
to the treacherous remissness of those Men in whom the People trusted for
repressing them, or even to their determined resolution not to abridge those
prerogatives. Yet, if we attentively consider the constant situation of affairs
in that Republic, we shall find that, though we might suppose those persons
to have been ever so truly attached to the cause of the People, it would not
really have been possible for them to procure to the People an entire security.
The right enjoyed by the Senate, of suddenly naming a Dictator with a
power unrestrained by any law, or of investing the Consuls with an authority of much the same kind, and the power it at times assumed of making formidable examples of arbitrary Justice, were resour-<422>ces of
which the Republic could not, perhaps, with safety have been totally deprived; and though these expcdients frequently were used to destroy the
just liberty of the People, yet they were also very often the means of preserving the Commonwealth.

Upon the same principle we should possibly find that the *Ostracism,* that
arbitrary method of banishing Citizens, was a necessary resource in the
Republic of Athens. A Venetian Noble would perhaps also confess, that
however terrible the State Inquisition established in his Republic, may be

(a) I should be very well satisfied though only the more reflecting class of readers
were fully to understand the tendency of this Chapter: in the mean time it is considerably
illustrated beyond what it was in the former Editions.

13. De Lolme here and in the following paragraphs summarizes themes he explored
at length above (book 1, chapters 6–14, and book 2, chapter 16) concerning the English
government's exceptional avoidance of arbitrary acts of executive power and equally rare
fidelity to legal norms securing individual liberty.

even to the Nobles themselves, yet it would not be prudent entirely to abolish it. And we do not know but a Minister of State in France, though we might suppose him ever so virtuous and moderate a Man, would say the same with regard to the secret imprisonments, the *lettres de cachet*, and other arbitrary deviations from the settled course of law which often take place in that Kingdom, and in the other Monarchies of Europe. No doubt, if he was the Man we suppose, he would confess the expedients we mention have in numberless instances been villainously prostituted to gratify the wantonness and private revenge of Ministers, or of those who had any interest with them; but still perhaps he would continue to give it as his opinion, that the Crown, notwithstanding its apparently immense strength, cannot avoid recurring at times to expedients <423> of this kind; much less could it publicly and absolutely renounce them for ever.

It is therefore a most advantageous circumstance in the English Government, that its security renders all such expedients unnecessary, and that the Representatives of the People have not only been constantly willing to promote the public liberty, but that the general situation of affairs has also enabled them to carry their precautions so far as they have done. And indeed, when we consider what prerogatives the Crown, in England, has sincerely renounced,—that in consequence of the independence conferred on the Judges and of the method of *Trial by Jury,* it is deprived of all means of influencing the settled course of the law both in civil and criminal matters,—that it has renounced all power of seizing the property of individuals, and even of restraining in any manner whatsoever, and for the shortest time, the liberty of their persons, we do not know what we ought most to admire, whether the public virtue of those who have deprived the supreme Executive Power of all those dangerous prerogatives, or the nature of that same Power, which has enabled it to give them up without ruin to itself— whether the happy frame of the English Government, which makes those in whom the People trust, continue so faith-<424>ful in the discharge of their duty, or the solidity of that same Government, which really can afford to leave to the People so extensive a degree of freedom (*a*).

(*a*) At the times of the invasions of the Pretender, assisted by the forces of hostile Nations, the *Habeas Corpus* Act was indeed suspended (which by the bye may serve as

Again, the Liberty of the press, that great advantage enjoyed by the English Nation, does not exist in any of the other Monarchies of Europe, however well established their power may at first seem to be; and it might even be demonstrated that it cannot exist in them.[14] The most watchful eye, we see, is constantly <425> kept in those Monarchies upon every kind of publication; and a jealous attention is paid even to the loose and idle speeches of individuals. Much unnecessary trouble (we may be apt at first to think) is taken upon this subject; but yet if we consider how uniform the conduct of all those Governments is, how constant and unremitted their cares in those respects, we shall become convinced, without looking farther, that there must be some sort of necessity for their precautions.

In Republican States, for reasons which are at bottom the same as in the before mentioned Governments, the People are also kept under the greatest restraints by those who are at the head of the State. In the Roman Commonwealth, for instance, the liberty of writing was curbed by the severest laws (*a*): with regard to the freedom of speech, things were but little better, as we may conclude from several facts; and many instances may even be

---

one proof, that in proportion as a Government is any how in danger, it becomes necessary to abridge the liberty of the subject); but the executive power did not thus of itself stretch its own authority; the precaution was deliberated upon and taken by the Representatives of the People; and the detaining of Individuals in consequence of the suspension of the Act, was limited to a certain fixed time. [[The Habeas Corpus Act was temporarily suspended by Parliament in 1715 and in 1746 in response to the Jacobite invasions.]] Notwithstanding the just fears of internal and hidden enemies which the circumstances of the times might raise, the deviation from the former course of the law was carried no farther than the single point we have mentioned: Persons detained by order of the Government, were to be dealt with in the same manner as those arrested at the suit of private individuals: the proceedings against them were to be carried on no otherwise than in a public place: they were to be tried by their Peers, and have all the usual legal means of defence allowed to them, such as calling of witnesses, peremptory challenge of Juries, &c.

(*a*) The Law of the Twelve Tables had established the punishment of death against the author of a Libel: nor was it by a *Trial by Jury* that they determined what was to be called a Libel. SI QUIS CARMEN OCCENTASSIT, ACTITASSIT, CONDIDISSIT, QUOD ALTERI FLAGITIUM FAXIT, CAPITAL ESTO. [["If anyone should sing, act, or compose a song, which shall cause dishonor or disgrace to another, he shall suffer a capital penalty." For the Twelve Tables, see above, book 1, chapter 10, p. 95, and note 8.]]

14. De Lolme here and in the following paragraphs returns to themes he explored more fully above, book 2, chapters 12–13.

produced of the dread with which the private Citizens, upon <426> certain occasions, communicated their political opinions to the Consuls, or to the Senate. In the Venetian Republic, the press is most strictly watched: nay, to forbear to speak in any manner whatsoever on the conduct of the Government, is the fundamental maxim which they inculcate on the minds of the People throughout their dominions (*a*). <427>

With respect therefore to this point, it may again be looked upon as a most advantageous circumstance in the English Government, that those who have been at the head of the People, have not only been constantly disposed to procure the public liberty, but also that they have found it possible for them to do so; and that the remarkable strength and steadiness of the Government has admitted of that extensive freedom of speaking and writing which the People of England enjoy. A most advantageous privilege, this; which affording to every Man a means of laying his complaints before the Public, procures him almost a certainty of redress against any act of oppression that he may have been exposed to: and which leaving, moreover, to every Subject a right to give his opinion on all public matters, and by thus influencing the sentiments of the Nation, to influence those of the Legislature itself (which is sooner or later obliged to pay a deference to them), procures to him a sort of Legislative authority of a much more efficacious and bene-<428>ficial nature than any formal right he might enjoy

(*a*) Of this I have myself seen a proof somewhat singular, which I beg leave of the Reader to relate. Being, in the year 1768, at Bergamo, the first Town of the Venetian State, as you come into it from the State of Milan, about an hundred and twenty miles distant from Venice, I took a walk in the evening in the neighbourhood of the Town; and wanting to know the name of several places which I saw at a distance, I stopped a young Countryman to ask him information. Finding him to be a sensible young Man, I entered into some farther conversation with him; and as he had himself a great inclination to see Venice, he asked me, whether I proposed to go there? I answered, that I did: on which he immediately warned me when I was at Venice not to speak of the Prince (*del Prencipe*) an appellation assumed by the Venetian Government, in order, as I suppose, to convey to the People a greater idea of their union among themselves. As I wanted to hear him talk farther on the subject, I pretended to be entirely ignorant in that respect, and asked for what reason I must not speak of the Prince? But he, (after the manner of the common People in Italy, who, when strongly affected by any thing, rather choose to express themselves by some vehement gesture, than by words) ran the edge of his hand, with great quickness, along his neck, meaning thereby to express, that being strangled, or having one's throat cut, was the instant consequence of taking such liberty.

of voting by a mere *yea* or *nay*, upon general propositions suddenly offered to him, and which he could have neither a share in framing, nor any opportunity of objecting to, and modifying.

A privilege which, by raising in the People a continual sense of their security, and affording them undoubted proofs that the Government, whatever may be its form, is ultimately destined to insure the happiness of those who live under it, is both one of the greatest advantages of Freedom, and its surest characteristic. The kind of security as to their persons and possessions which Subjects who are totally deprived of that privilege, enjoy at particular times, under other Governments, perhaps may intitle them to look upon themselves as the well administered property of Masters who rightly understand their own interests; but it is the right of canvassing without fear the conduct of those who are placed at their head, which constitutes a free Nation (*a*). <429>

The unbounded freedom of debate possessed by the English Parliament, is also a consequence of the peculiar stability of the Government. All Sovereigns have agreed in their jealousy of Assemblies of this kind, in their dread of the privileges of Assemblies who attract in so high a degree the attention of the rest of the People, who in a course of time become connected by so many essential ties with the bulk of the Nation, and acquire so much real influence by the essential share they must needs have in the management of public affairs, and by the eminent services, in short, which they are able to perform to the Community (*b*). Hence it has happened that Monarchs, or single Rulers, in all Countries, have endeavoured to dispense with the assistance of Assemblies like those we mention, notwithstanding the capital <430> advantages they might have derived from their services towards the good government of the State; or if the circumstances of the times have rendered it expedient for them to call such Assemblies

(*a*) If we consider the great advantages to public liberty which result from the institution of the Trial by Jury, and from the Liberty of the Press, we shall find England to be in reality a more Democratical State than any other we are acquainted with. The Judicial power, and the Censorial power, are vested in the People. [[For De Lolme's fuller exposition of this point, see above, book 1, chapter 13, and book 2, chapters 12–13.]]

(*b*) And which they do actually perform, till they are able to throw off the restraints of impartiality and moderation; a thing which, being Men, they never fail to do when their influence is generally established, and proper opportunities offer. Sovereigns know these things, and dread them.

together, they have used the utmost endeavours in abridging those privileges and legislative claims which they soon found to prove so hostile to
their security: in short, they have ever found it impracticable to place any
unreserved trust in public Meetings of this kind.[15]

We may here name Cromwell, as he was supported by a numerous army,
and possessed more power than any foreign Monarch who has not been
secured by an armed force. Even after he had *purged,* by the agency of
Colonel Pride and two regiments, the Parliament that was sitting when his
power became settled, thereby thrusting out all his opponents to the
amount of about two hundred, he soon found his whole authority endangered by their proceedings, and was at last under a necessity of turning them
out in the military manner with which every one is acquainted. Finding
still a Meeting of this kind highly expedient to legalize his military authority, he called together that Assembly which was called *Barebone's* Parliament. He had himself chosen the Members <431> of this Parliament to
the number of about an hundred and twenty, and they had severally received their summons from him; yet, notwithstanding this circumstance,
and the total want of personal weight in most of the Members, he began
in a very few months, and in the midst of his powerful victorious army, to
feel a serious alarm at their proceedings; he soon heard them talk of their
own divine commission, and of the authority they had received from the
Lord; and in short, finding he could not trust them, he employed the offices
of a second Colonel, to effect their dismission. Being now dignified with
the legal appellation of *Protector,* he ventured to call a Parliament elected
by considerable parts of the people; but though the existence of this Parliament was grounded, we might say grafted, upon his own; and though
bands of Soldiers were even posted in the avenues to keep out all such
Members as refused to take certain personal engagements to him, he made
such haste in the issue, to rid himself of their presence, as to contrive a
mean quibble or device to shorten the time of their sitting by ten or twelve
days (*a*). To a fourth As-<432>sembly he again applied; but, though the

15. This paragraph and the succeeding discussion through p. 302 first appeared in the
fourth edition of 1784.
(*a*) They were to have sat five months; but Cromwell pretended that the months were
to consist of only twenty-eight days; as this was the way of reckoning time used in paying

elections had been so managed as to procure him a formal tender of the Crown during the first sitting, he put a final end to the second with resentment and precipitation (*a*).

The example of the Roman Emperors, whose power was outwardly so prodigious, may also be introduced here. They used to shew the utmost jealousy in their conduct with respect to the Roman Senate; and that Assembly which the prepossession of the People, who looked upon it as the ancient remains of the Republic, had made it expedient to continue, were not suffered to assemble but under the drawn scymitars of the Pretorian guards.

Even the Kings of France, though their authority is so unquestioned, so universally respected, as well as strongly supported, have felt frequent anxiety from the claims and proceedings of the Parliament of Paris; an Assembly <433> of so much less weight than the English Parliament. The alarm has been mentioned which the late King at last expressed concerning their measures, as well as the expedient to which he resorted, to free himself from their presence. And when the present King thought proper to call again this Parliament together, a measure highly prudent in the beginning of his reign, every jealous precaution was at the same time taken to abridge those privileges of deliberating and remonstrating upon which any distant claim to, or struggle for, a share in the Supreme authority might be grounded.[16]

It may be objected that the pride of Kings, or single Rulers, makes them

---

the army, and the fleet. [[De Lolme refers in this note to the premature dissolution of the first Parliament of the Cromwellian Protectorate in 1655. In the paragraph to which his note refers, De Lolme discusses the 1648 purge of Parliament by Colonel Pride, which removed those opposed to the trial of Charles I; the Barebones' Parliament of 1653 (named after the London radical, Praise-God Barebones); the 1653 appointment of Cromwell as Lord Protector; and the second and final meeting of the Parliament of the Protectorate in 1656–57.]]

(*a*) The history of the conduct of the deliberating and debating Assemblies we are alluding to, in regard to the Monarchs, or single Rulers, of any denomination, who summon them together, may be expressed in a very few words. If the Monarch is unarmed, they over-rule him so as almost entirely to set him aside: if his power is of a military kind, they form connections with the army.

16. De Lolme earlier in the chapter discussed Louis XV's efforts to combat the authority of the Parlements; see note 11 in this chapter. Louis XVI first summoned the Parlements within weeks of coming to the throne in 1775.

averse to the existence of Assemblies like those we mention, and despise the capital services which they might derive from them for the good government of their Kingdoms. I grant it may in some measure be so. But if we examine into the general situation of affairs in different States, and into the examples with which their History supplies us, we shall also find that the pride of those Kings agrees in the main with the interest and quiet of their Subjects, and that their preventing the Assemblies we speak of from meeting, or, when met, from assuming too large a <434> share in the management of public affairs, is in a great measure, matter of necessity.

We may therefore reckon it as a very great advantage, that, in England, no such necessity exists. Such is the frame of the Government, that the Supreme executive authority can, both give leave to assemble, and shew the most unreserved trust, when assembled, to those two Houses which concur together to form the Legislature.

These two Houses, we see, enjoy the most complete freedom in their debates, whether the subject be *grievances,* or regulations concerning government matters of any kind: no restriction whatever is laid upon them; they may start any subject they please. The Crown is not to take any notice of their deliberations: its wishes, or even its name, are not to be introduced in the debates. And in short, what makes the freedom of deliberating, exercised by the two Houses, really to be unlimited, unbounded, is the privilege, or sovereignty we may say, enjoyed by each within its own walls, in consequence of which nothing done or said in Parliament, is to be questioned in any place out of Parliament. Nor will it be pretended by those persons who are acquainted with the English History, that those privileges of Parliament we <435> mention are nominal privileges, only privileges upon paper, which the Crown has disregarded whenever it has thought proper, and to the violations of which the Parliament have used very tamely to submit. That these remarkable advantages,—that this total freedom from any compulsion or even fear, and in short this unlimited liberty of debate, so strictly claimed by the Parliament, and so scrupulously allowed by the Crown, should be exercised year after year during a long course of time, without producing the least relaxation in the execution of the laws, the smallest degree of anarchy, are certainly very singular political phenomena.

It may be said that the remarkable Solidity of the governing Executive authority, in England, operates to the advantage of the People with respect to the objects we mention, in a twofold manner. In the first place, it takes from the great Men in the Nation all serious ambition to invade this authority, thereby preventing those anarchical and more or less bloody struggles to result from their debates, which have so constantly disturbed other Countries. In the second place, it inspires those Great Men with that salutary jealousy of the same authority which leads them to frame such effectual provi-<436>sions for laying it under proper restraints. On which I shall observe, by way of a short digression, that this distinguished *stability* of the executive authority of the English Crown, affords an explanation for the peculiar manner in which public commotions have constantly been terminated in England, compared with the manner in which the same events have been concluded in other Kingdoms. When I mentioned, in a former Chapter,[17] this peculiarity in the English Government, I mean the accuracy, impartiality, and universality, of the provisions by which peace, after internal disturbances, has been restored to the Nation, I confined my comparisons to instances drawn from Republican Governments, purposely postponing to say any thing of Governments of a Monarchical form, till I had introduced the very essential observation contained in this Chapter, which is, that the power of *Crowns,* in other Monarchies, has not been able, by itself, to produce the same effects it has in England, that is, has not been able to inspire the Great Men in the State with any thing like that salutary jealousy we mention, nor of course to induce them to unite in a real common cause with the rest of the People. In other Monar-<437>chies (*a*), those Men who, during the continuation of the public disturbances, were at the head of the People, finding it in their power, in the issue, to parcel out, more or less, the Supreme governing authority, (or even the State itself) and to transfer the same to themselves, constantly did so, in the same manner, and from the very same reasons, as it constantly happened in the ancient Commonwealths; those Monarchical Governments being in real-

(*a*) I mean, before the introduction of those numerous standing armies which are now kept by all the Crowns of Europe: since that epoch, which is of no very ancient date, no Treaty has been entered into by those Crowns with any Subjects.

17. See above, book 2, chapter 15.

ity, so far as that, of a Republican nature: and the governing authority was left, at the conclusion, in the same undefined extent it had before (*a*). But in England, the great Men in the Nation finding themselves in a situation essentially different, lost no time in pursuits like those in which the great Men of other Countries used to indulge themselves on the occasion we mention. Every Member of the Legislature plainly perceived, from the general aspect of affairs <438> and his feelings, that the Supreme executive authority in the State must in the issue fall some where undivided, and continue so; and being moreover sensible, that neither personal advantages of any kind, nor the power of any faction, but the law alone, could afterwards be an effectual restraint upon its motions, they had no thought or aim left, except the framing with care those laws on which their own liberty was to continue to depend, and to restrain a power which they, somehow, judged it so impracticable to transfer to themselves or their party, or to render themselves independent of. These observations I thought necessary to be added to those in the xv. Chapter, to which I now refer the Reader.

Nor has the great freedom of canvassing political subjects we have described, been limited to the Members of the Legislature, or confined to the walls of Westminster, that is, to that exclusive spot on which the two Houses meet: the like privilege is allowed to the other orders of the People; and a full scope is given to that spirit of party, and a complete security insured to those numerous and irregular meetings, which, especially when directed to matters of government, create so much uneasiness in the Sovereigns of other Countries. <439> Individuals even may, in such meetings, take an active part for procuring the success of those public steps which they wish to see pursued: they may frame petitions to be delivered to the Crown, or to both Houses, either to procure the repeal of measures already entered upon by Government, or to prevent the passing of such as are under consideration, or to obtain the enacting of new regulations of any kind: they may severally subscribe their names to such petitions: the law sets no

---

(*a*) As a remarkable instance of such a Treaty may be mentioned that by which the War *for the Public good* was terminated in France. It is quoted in page 30 of this Work. [[See above, book 1, chapter 2, p. 37, note a.]]

restriction on their numbers; nor has it, we may say, taken any precaution to prevent even the abuse that might be made of such freedom.

That mighty political engine, the press, is also at their service: they may avail themselves of it to advertise the time and place, as well as the intent, of the meetings, and moreover to set off and inculcate the advantages of those notions which the wish is to see adopted.

Such meetings may be repeated; and every individual may deliver what opinion he pleases on the proposed subjects, though ever so directly opposite to the views or avowed designs of the Government. The Member of the Legislature may, if he chooses, have admittance among them, and again enforce those topics which have not obtained the success he expected, in <440> that House to which he belongs. The disappointed Statesman, the Minister turned out, also find the door open to them: they may bring in the whole weight of their influence and of their connections: they may exert every nerve to enlist the Assembly in the number of their supporters: they are bid to do their worst: they fly through the Country from one place of meeting to another: the clamour increases: the Constitution, one may think, is going to be shaken to its very foundations:—but these mighty struggles, by some means or other, always find a proportionate degree of re-action: new difficulties, and at last insuperable impediments, grow up in the way of those who would take advantage of the general ferment to raise themselves on the wreck of the governing Authority: a secret force exerts itself, which gradually brings things back to a state of moderation and calm; and that sea so stormy, to appearance so deeply agitated, constantly stops at certain limits which it seems as if it wanted the power to pass.

The impartiality with which justice is dealt to all orders of Men in England, is also in great measure owing to the peculiar stability of the Government: the very remarkable, high degree, to which this impartiality is carried, is <441> one of those things which, being impossible in other Countries, are possible under the Government of this Country. In the ancient Commonwealths, from the instances that have been introduced in a former place, and from others that might be quoted, it is evident that no redress was to be obtained for the acts of injustice or oppression committed by the Men possessed of influence or wealth upon the inferior Citizens. In the Monarchies of Europe, in former times, abuses of a like kind prevailed to a most enormous degree. In our days, notwithstanding the great degrees of strength acquired by the different Governments, it is matter of the utmost difficulty for subjects of the inferior classes to obtain the remedies of the law against certain individuals: in some Countries it is impossible, let the abuse be ever so flagrant; an open attempt to pursue such remedies being moreover attended with danger. Even in those Monarchies of Europe in which the Government is supported both by real strength, and by civil Institutions of a very advantageous nature, great differences prevail between individuals in regard to the facility of obtaining the remedies of the law; and to seek for redress is at best in many cases, so arduous and precarious an attempt as to take from injured individuals <442> all thoughts of encountering the difficulty. Nor are these abuses we mention, in the former or present Governments of Europe, to be attributed only to the want of resolution in the Heads of these Governments. In some Countries, the Sovereign by an open design to suppress these abuses, would have endangered at once his whole authority; and in others, he would find obstructions multiply so in his way as to compel him, and perhaps soon enough too, to drop the undertaking.—How can a Monarch make, alone, a persevering stand against the avowed expectations of all the great Men by whom he is surrounded, and against the loud claims of powerful classes of individuals? In a Commonwealth, what is a Senate to do when they find that their refusing to protect a powerful Offender of their own class, or to indulge some great Citizen with the impunity of his friends, is likely to be productive of serious divisions among themselves, or perhaps of disturbances among the People?

If we cast our eyes on the strict and universal impartiality with which justice is administered in England, we shall soon become convinced that some inward essential difference exists between the English Government, and those of other Countries, and that its power is <443> founded on causes of a distinct nature. Individuals of the most exalted rank do not entertain so much as the thought to raise the smallest direct opposition to the operation of the law. The complaint of the meanest Subject, if preferred and supported in the usual way, immediately meets with a serious regard. The Oppressor of the most extensive influence, though in the midst of a train of retainers, nay, though in the fullest flight of his career and pride, and surrounded by thousands of applauders and partisans, is stopped short at the sight of the legal paper which is delivered into his hands, and a Tip-staff is sufficient to bring him away, and produce him before the Bench.

Such is the *greatness* and uninterrupted *prevalence* of the law (*a*), such is in short the continuity of omnipotence, of resistless superiority, it exhibits, that the extent of its effects at length ceases to be a subject of observation to the Public.

Nor are great or wealthy Men to seek for redress or satisfaction of any kind, by any other means than such as are open to all: even the Sovereign has bound himself to resort to no other: and experience has shewn that he may without danger, trust the protection of his per-<444>son, and of the places of his residence, to the slow and litigious assistance of the law (*b*).

Another very great advantage attending this remarkable stability of the English Government we are describing, is, that the same is operated without the assistance of an armed standing force: the constant expedient this, of all other Governments. On this occasion I shall introduce a passage of Doctor Adam Smith (*c*), in a Work published since the present Chapter was first written, in which passage an opinion certainly erroneous is contained: the mistakes of persons of his very great abilities deserve attention. This Gentleman, struck with the necessity of a sufficient power of re-action, of a sufficient strength, on the side of Government, to resist the agitations attending on liberty, has looked round, and judged the English Government derived the singular stability it manifests from the standing force it has at its disposal: the following are his expressions. "To a Sovereign who feels himself supported, not only by <445> the natural Aristocracy of the Country, but by a well regulated standing army, the rudest, the most

---

(*a*) *Lex magna est & praevalebit.*

(*b*) I remember, during the time after my first coming to this Country, I took notice of the boards set up from place to place behind the inclosure of Richmond park, "Whoever trespasses upon this ground will be *prosecuted.*"

(*c*) An *Inquiry into the Nature and Causes of the Wealth of Nations.* Book V. Chap. I. Vol. II. p. 313, 314. [[De Lolme quotes Adam Smith's 1776 *An Inquiry into the Nature and Causes of the Wealth of Nations,* book 5, chapter 1, part 1, paragraph 41 (emphasis added by De Lolme).]]

groundless, and the most licentious remonstrances can give little disturbance. He can safely pardon or neglect them, and his consciousness of his
superiority naturally disposes him to do so. *That degree of liberty which
approaches to licentiousness, can be tolerated only in Countries where the Sovereign is secured by a well regulated standing army"* (a).

The above positions are grounded on the notion that an army places in
the hand of the Sovereign an united irresistible strength, a strength liable
to no accident, difficulties, or exceptions; a supposition this, which is not
conformable to experience. If a Sovereign was endued with a kind of extraordinary power attending on his person, at once to lay under water whole
legions of insurgents, or to repulse and sweep them away by slashes and
shocks of the electrical fluid, then indeed he might use the great forbearance
above described:—though it is not perhaps very likely he would put up
<446> with the *rude* and *groundless* remonstrances of his subjects, and with
their *licentious* freedom, yet, he might, with safety, do or not do so, at his
own choice. But an army is not that simple weapon which is here supposed.
It is formed of Officers and Soldiers who feel the same passions with the
rest of the People, the same disposition to promote their own interest and
importance, when they find out their strength, and proper opportunities
offer. What will therefore be the resource of the Sovereign, if, into that army
on the assistance of which he relies, the same party spirit creeps by which
his other Subjects are actuated? whereto will he take his refuge, if the same
political caprices, abetted by the serious ambition of a few leading Men,
the same restlessness, and at last perhaps the same disaffection, begin to
pervade the smaller kingdom of the army, by which the main Kingdom or
Nation are agitated?

The prevention of dangers like those just mentioned, constitutes the
most essential part of the precautions and state craft of Rulers, in those
Governments which are secured by standing armed forces. Mixing the
troops formed of natives with foreign auxiliaries, dispersing them in numerous bodies over the country, and continually shifting their quarters, are

(a) The Author's design in the whole passage, is to shew that standing armies, under
proper restrictions, cannot be hurtful to public liberty; and may in some cases be useful
to it, by freeing the Sovereign from any troublesome jealousy in regard to this liberty.

among <447> the methods that are used; which it does not belong to our subject to enumerate, any more than the extraordinary expedients employed by the Eastern Monarchs for the same purposes. But one caution very essential to be mentioned here, and which the Governments we allude to, never fail to take before every other, is to retrench from their unarmed Subjects, a freedom which, transmitted to the Soldiery, would be attended with so fatal consequences: hindering so bad examples from being communicated to those in whose hands their power and life are trusted, is what every notion of self-preservation suggests to them: every weapon is accordingly exerted to suppress the rising and spreading of so awful a contagion.

In general, it may be laid down as a maxim, that, where the Sovereign looks to his army for the security of his person and authority, the same military laws by which this army is kept together, must be extended over the whole Nation: not in regard to military duties and exercises; but certainly in regard to all that relates to the respect due to the Sovereign and to his orders. The martial law, concerning these tender points, must be universal. The jealous regulations concerning mutiny and contempt of orders, cannot be severely enforced on <448> that part of the Nation which secures the subjection of the rest, and enforced too through the whole scale of military subordination, from the Soldier to the Officer, up to the very Head of the military System,—while the more numerous and inferior part of the People are left to enjoy an unrestrained freedom:—that secret disposition which prompts Mankind to resist and counteract their Superiors, cannot be surrounded by such formidable checks on the one side, and be left to be indulged to a degree of licentiousness and wantonness, on the other.

In a Country where an army is kept, capable of commanding the obedience of the Nation, this army will, both imitate for themselves the licentiousness above mentioned, and check it in the People. Every Officer and Soldier, in such a Country, claim a superiority in regard to other individuals; and in proportion as their assistance is relied upon by the Government, expect a greater or less degree of submission from the rest of the People (*a*). <449>

(*a*) In the beginning of the passage which is here examined, the Author says, "Where

The same Author concludes his above quoted observations concerning the security of the <450> power of an armed Sovereign, by immediately adding: "It is in such Countries only that it is unnecessary that the Sovereign should be trusted with any discretionary power for suppressing even the wantonness of this licentious liberty."[18] The idea here expressed coinciding with those already discussed, I shall say nothing farther on the subject. My reason for introducing the above expressions, has been, that they lead me to take notice of a remarkable circumstance in the English Government. From the expressions, *it is unnecessary the Sovereign should be trusted with any discretionary power,* the Author appears to think that a Sovereign at the head of an army, and whose power is secured by this army, uses to wait to

---

the Sovereign is himself the General, and the principal Nobility and Gentry of the Country, the chief Officers of the army,—where the military force is placed under the command of those who have the greatest interest in the support of the civil authority, because they have the greatest share of that authority, a standing army can never be dangerous to liberty. On the contrary, it may in some cases be favourable to liberty, &c. &c." [[*Wealth of Nations,* book 5, chapter 1, part 1, paragraph 41.]]—In a Country so circumstanced, a standing army can never be dangerous to liberty: no, not the liberty of those principal Nobility and Gentry, especially if they have wit enough to form combinations among themselves against the Sovereign. Such an union as is here mentioned, of the civil and military powers, in the Aristocratical body of the Nation, leaves both the Sovereign and the People without resource. If the former Kings of Scotland had imagined to adopt the expedient of a standing army, and had trusted this army thus defrayed by them, to those Noblemen and Gentlemen who had rendered themselves hereditary Admirals, hereditary High Stewards, hereditary High Constables, hereditary great Chamberlains, hereditary Justices General, hereditary Sheriffs of Counties, &c. they would have but badly mended the disorders under which the Government of their Country laboured: they would only have supplied these Nobles with fresh weapons against each other, against the Sovereign, and against the People.

If those Members of the British Parliament who sometimes make the whole Nation resound with the clamour of their dissensions, had an army under their command which they might engage in the support of their pretensions, the rest of the People would not be the better for it. Happily the swords are secured, and force is removed from their Debates.

The Author we are quoting, has deemed a Government to be a simpler machine, and an army a simpler instrument, than they in reality are. Like many other persons of great abilities, while struck with a certain particular consideration, he has overlooked others no less important.

18. De Lolme quotes, with minor alteration, the concluding sentence of Smith, *Wealth of Nations,* book 5, chapter 1, part 1, paragraph 41.

set himself in motion, till he has received leave for that purpose, that is, till he has been trusted with a power for so doing. This notion in the Author we quote, is borrowed from the steady and thoroughly legal Government of this Country; but the like law doctrine, or principle, obtains under no other Government. In all Monarchies, <451> (and it is the same in Republics) the Executive power in the State is supposed to possess, originally and by itself, all manner of lawful authority: every one of its exertions is deemed to be legal; and they do not cease to be so, till they are stopped by some express and positive regulation. The Sovereign, and also the civil Magistrate, till so stopped by some positive law, may come upon the Subject when they choose; they may question any of his actions; they may construe them into unlawful acts; and inflict a penalty, as they please: in these respects they may be thought to abuse, but not to exceed, their power. The authority of the Government, in short, is supposed to be unlimited so far as there are no visible boundaries set up against it: behind and within these boundaries, lies whatever degree of liberty the Subject may possess.

In England, the very reverse obtains. It is not the authority of the Government, it is the liberty of the Subject, which is supposed to be unbounded. All the Individual's actions are supposed to be lawful, till that law is pointed out which makes them to be otherwise. The *onus probandi*[19] is here transferred from the Subject to the Prince. The Subject is not at any time to shew the grounds of his conduct. When the <452> Sovereign or Magistrate think proper to exert themselves, it is their business to find out and produce the law in their own favour, and the prohibition against the Subject (*a*). <453>

---

19. "Burden of proof."

(*a*) I shall take the liberty to mention another fact respecting myself, as it may serve to elucidate the above observations; or at least my manner of expressing them. I remember when I was beginning to pay attention to the operations of the English Government, I was under a prepossession of quite a contrary nature to that of the Gentleman whose opinions have been above discussed: I used to take it for granted that every article of liberty the Subject enjoys in this Country, was grounded upon some positive law by which this liberty was insured to him. In regard to the freedom of the press I had no doubt but it was so, and that there existed some particular law, or rather series of laws or legislative paragraphs, by which this freedom was defined and carefully secured: and as the liberty of writing happened at that time to be carried very far, and to excite a great

This kind of law principle, owing to the general spirit by which all parts of the Government are influenced, is even carried so far, that any quibble, or trifling circumstance, by which an Offender may be enabled to step aside and escape, though ever so narrowly, the reach of the law, are sufficient to screen him from punishment, let the immorality or intrinsic guilt of his conduct be ever so openly admitted (*a*).

Such a narrow circumscription of the exertions of the Government, is very extraordinary: it does not exist in any Country but this; nor <454> could it. The situation of other Governments is such that they cannot thus allow themselves to be shut out of the unbounded space unoccupied by

---

deal of attention, (the noise about the Middlesex Election had not yet subsided) I particularly wished to see those laws I supposed, not doubting but there must be something remarkable in the wording of them. I looked into those Law Books I had opportunities to come at, such as Jacob's and Cunningham's *Law Dictionaries,* Wood's *Institutes,* and Judge Blackstone's *Commentaries.* I also found means to have a sight of Comyn's *Digest of the Laws of England,* and I was again disappointed: this Author, though his Work consists of five folio Volumes, had not had, any more than the Authors just mentioned, any room to spare for the interesting law I was in search of. [[The "Middlesex Election" refers to the political controversies of 1768–70, when the House of Commons refused to seat John Wilkes, who had been elected to represent the county of Middlesex in a series of elections and special by-elections. For the publications by Blackstone, Jacob, and Cunningham, respectively, see above, book 1, chapter 4, p. 60, note 6, and chapter 10, p. 98, note a, and p. 99, note a. De Lolme refers also to Thomas Wood's 1720 *An Institute of the Laws of England* and to John Comings's *Digest of the Laws of England,* which was published posthumously in 1762–67.]] At length it occurred to me, though not immediately, that this Liberty of the press was grounded upon its not being prohibited,—that this want of prohibition was the sole, and at the same time solid, foundation of it. This led me, when I afterwards thought of writing something upon the Government of this Country, to give the definition of the freedom of the press which is contained in p. 296, 297 [[see book 2, chapter 12, p. 202]]: adding to it the important consideration of all actions respecting publications being to be decided by a Jury.

(*a*) A number of instances, some even of a ludicrous kind, might be quoted in support of the above observation. Even only a trifling flaw in the words of an Indictment, is enough to make it void. The reader is also referred to the fact mentioned in the note, p. 180 [[see book 1, chapter 13, p. 130, note a]], and to that in p. 317, 318 [[see book 2, chapter 14, p. 216]], of this Work.

I do not remember the name of that party Writer who, having published a treasonable writing in regard to which he escaped punishment, used afterwards to answer to his friends, when they reproached him with his rashness, *I knew I was writing within an inch of the gallows.* The law being both ascertained and strictly adhered to, he had been enabled to bring his words and positions so nicely within compass.

any law, in order to have their motions confined to that spot which express and previously declared provisions have chalked out. The power of these Governments being constantly attended with more or less precariousness, there must be a degree of *discretion* answerable to it (*a*).

The foundation of that law principle, or doctrine, which confines the exertion of the power of the Government to such cases only as are expressed by a law in being, was laid when the great Charter was passed: this restriction was implied in one of those general impartial articles which the Barons united with the People to obtain from the Sovereign. The Crown, at that time, derived from its foreign <455> dominions, that stability and inward strength in regard to the English Nation, which is now in a secret hidden manner annexed to the Civil branch of its Office, and which, though operating by different means, continues to maintain that kind of confederacy against it, and union between the different Orders of the People. By the article in *Magna Charta* here alluded to, the Sovereign bound itself neither to *go,* nor *send,* upon the Subject, otherwise than by the Trial of Peers, and the Law of the land (*b*). This Article was however afterwards disregarded in practice, in consequence of the lawful efficiency which the King claimed for his *Proclamations,* and especially by the institution of the Court of *Star Chamber,* which grounded its proceedings not only upon these Proclamations, but also upon the particular rules it chose to frame within itself. By the abolition of this Court (and also of the Court of High Commission) in the reign of Charles the First, the above provision of the Great Charter was put in actual force; and it has appeared by the <456> event, that the very extraordinary restriction upon the governing authority we are alluding

---

(*a*) It might perhaps also be proved, that the great lenity used in England in the administration of criminal Justice, both in regard to the mildness, and to the frequent remitting, of punishments, is essentially connected with the same circumstance of the *stability* of the Government. Experience shews that it is needless to use any great degree of harshness and severity in regard to Offenders; and the Supreme governing authority is under no necessity of shewing the subordinate Magistracies any bad example in that respect.

(*b*) . . . *Nec super eum ibimus, nec super eum mittemus, nisi per legale judicium parium vel per legem terrae.* Cap. XXIX. [[". . . nor will we pass upon him, nor condemn him, but by lawful judgment of his peers, or by the law of the land." Magna Carta, chapter 29; and see above, book 1, chapter 2, p. 36, note a.]]

to, and its execution, are no more than what the intrinsic situation of things, and the strength of the Constitution, can bear (*a*).

The law doctrine we have above described, and its being strictly regarded by the High governing authority, I take to be the most characteristic circumstance in the English Government, and the most pointed proof that can be given of the true freedom which is the consequence of its frame. The practice of the Executive authority thus to square its motions upon such laws, and such only, as are ascertained and declared beforehand, cannot be the result of that kind of stability which the Crown <457> might derive from being supported by an armed force, or as the above mentioned Author has expressed it, from the Sovereign being the General of an army: such a rule of acting is even contradictory to the office of a General: the operations of a General eminently depend for their success, on their being sudden, unforeseen, attended by surprize.

In general, that stability of the power of the English Crown we have described, cannot be the result of that kind of strength which arises from an armed force: the kind of strength which is conferred by such a weapon as an army, is too uncertain, too complicate, too liable to accidents; in a word, it falls infinitely short of that degree of steadiness which is necessary to counterbalance, and at last quiet, those extensive agitations in the People which sometimes seem to threaten the destruction of order and Government. An army, if its support be well directed, may be useful to prevent this restlessness in the People from beginning to exist; but it cannot keep it within bounds, when it has once taken place.

(*a*) The Court of Star Chamber was like a Court of Equity in regard to criminal matters: it took upon itself to decide upon those cases of offence upon which the usual Courts of Law, when uninfluenced by the Crown, refused to decide, either on account of the silence of the laws in being, or of the particular rules they had established within themselves; which is exactly the office of the Court of Chancery (and of the Exchequer) in regard to matters of property. (See back, p. 138 [[p. 105]]). [[For the court of Star Chamber, see above, book 1, chapter 3, p. 50, note a. For the equity jurisprudence of the Courts of Chancery and Exchequer, see above, book 1, chapter 11, p. 110, note a.]] The great usefulness of Courts of this kind, has caused the Courts of Equity in regard to civil matters, to be supported and continued; but experience has shewn, as is above observed, that no essential inconvenience can arise from the Subject being indulged with the very great freedom he has acquired by the total abolition of all arbitrary or provisional Courts in regard to criminal matters.

If from general arguments and considerations, we pass to particular facts, we shall actually find that the Crown, in England, does <458> not rely for its support, nor ever has relied, upon the army of which it has the command. From the earliest times, that is, long before the invention of standing armies among European Princes, the Kings of England possessed an authority certainly as full and extensive as that which they do now enjoy. After the weight they derived from their possessions beyond sea had been lost, a certain arrangement of things began to be formed at home which supplied them with a strength of another kind, though not less solid: and they began to derive from the Civil branch of their regal Office that secure power which no other Monarchs had ever possessed, except through the assistance of Legions and Praetorian guards, or of armies of Janissaries, or of Strelitzes.[20]

The Princes of the House of Tudor, to speak of a very remarkable period in the English History,[21] though they had no other visible present force than inconsiderable retinues of servants, were able to exert a power equal to that of the most absolute Monarchs who ever did reign, equal to that of the Domitians or Commoduses, or of the Amuraths or Bajazets: nay, it even was superior, if we consider the slow steadiness and outward show of legality with which it was attended throughout.[22] <459>

The stand which the Kings of the House of Stuart were able to make, though unarmed, and only supported by the civil authority of their Office, during a long course of years, against the restless spirit which began to actuate the Nation, and the vehement political and religious notions that broke out in their time, is still more remarkable than even the exorbibitant power of the Princes of the House of Tudor, during whose reign prepossessions of quite a contrary nature were universal.

The struggle opened with the reign of James the First: yet, he peaceably

20. De Lolme refers, in turn, to military forces of the Roman emperors, Ottoman sultans, and Russian czars.
21. For De Lolme's more detailed discussion of the critical constitutional developments under the Tudor and Stuart monarchs, which he summarizes in the following paragraphs, see above, book 1, chapter 3.
22. "Domitians or Commoduses" refers to Roman emperors of the first and second centuries; "Amuraths [or 'Murads'] or Bajazets [or 'Beyazids']" refers to Ottoman sultans from the fifteenth to seventeenth centuries.

weathered the beginning storm, and transmitted his authority undiminished to his Son. Charles the First was indeed at last crushed under the ruins of the Constitution; but if we consider that, after making the important national concessions contained in the *Petition of right,* he was able, single and unarmed, to maintain his ground without loss or real danger during a space of eleven years, that is, till the year 1640 and those that followed, we shall be inclined to think that, had he been better advised, he might have avoided the misfortunes that befell him at length.

Even the events of the reign of James the Second afford a proof of that solidity which is <460> annexed to the authority of the English Crown. Notwithstanding the whole Nation, not excepting the army, were in a manner unanimous against him, he was able to reign full four years, standing single against all, without meeting with any open resistance. Nor was such justifiable and necessary resistance easily brought about at length (*a*). Though it is not to be doubted that the dethroning of James the Second would have been effected in the issue, and perhaps in a very tragical manner, yet, if it had not been for the assistance of the Prince of Orange, the event would certainly have been postponed till a few years later. That authority on which James relied with so much con-<461>fidence, was not annihilated at the time it was, otherwise than by a ready and considerable armed force being brought against it from the other side of the Sea, like a solid Fortress, which, though without any visible out-works, requires, in order to be compelled to surrender, to be battered with cannon.

If we look into the manner in which this Country has been governed since the Revolution, we shall evidently see that it has not been by means

(*a*) Mr. Hume is rather too anxious in his wish to exculpate James the Second. He begins the conclusive character he gives of him, with representing him as a Prince *whom we may safely pronounce more unfortunate than criminal.* If we consider the solemn engagements entered into, not by his predecessors only, but by himself, which this Prince endeavoured to break, how cool and deliberate his attack on the liberties and religion of the People was, how unprovoked the attempt, and in short how totally destitute he was of any plea of self-defence or necessity, a plea to which most of the Princes who have been at variance with their Subjects had some sort of more or less distant claim, we shall look upon him as being perhaps the guiltiest Monarch that ever existed. [[David Hume's judgment of James II appeared in the final chapter (chap. 71) of his multivolume *The History of England,* which was first published in 1754–62.]]

of the army the Crown has under its command, that it has been able to preserve and exert its authority. It is not by means of their Soldiers that the Kings of Great Britain prevent the manner in which elections are carried on, from being hurtful to them; for, these Soldiers must move from the places of election one day before such elections are begun, and not return till one day after they are finished. It is not by means of their military force that they prevent the several kinds of civil Magistracies in the Kingdom from invading and lessening their prerogative; for this military force is not to act till called for by these latter, and under their direction. It is not by means of their army that they lead the two Branches of the Legislature into that respect of their regal authority we have before described; since each <462> of these two Branches, severally, is possessed with an annual power of disbanding this army (a).

There is another circumstance, which abstractedly of all others, makes it evident that the executive authority of the Crown is not supported by the army: I mean the very singular subjection in which the military is kept in regard to the civil power in this Country.

In a Country where the governing authority in the State is supported by the army, the military profession, who, in regard to the other professions, have on their side the advantage of present force, being now moreover countenanced by the law, immediately acquire, or rather assume, a general ascendency; and the Sovereign, far from wishing to discourage their claims, feels an inward happiness in seeing that instrument on which he rests his authority, additionally strengthened by the respect of the <463> People, and receiving a kind of legal sanction from the general outward consent.

And not only the military profession at large, but the individuals belonging to it, also claim personally a pre-eminence: chief Commanders,

(a) The generality of the People have from early times been so little accustomed to see any display of force used to influence the debates of the Parliament, that the attempt made by Charles the First to seize the *five Members,* attended by a retinue of about two hundred Servants, was the actual spark that set in a blaze the heap of combustibles which the preceding contests had accumulated. The Parliament, from that fact, took a pretence to make military preparations in their turn; and then the civil war began. [[The incident, in which the king attempted the arrest of five parliamentary opponents in the chamber of the House of Commons, occurred in January 1642.]]

Officers, Soldiers or Janissaries, all claim in their own spheres, some sort of exclusive privilege: and these privileges, whether of an honorific, or of a more substantial kind, are violently asserted, and rendered grievous to the rest of the Community, in proportion as the assistance of the military force is more evidently necessary to, and more frequently employed by, the Government. These things cannot be otherwise.

Now, if we look into the facts that take place in England, we shall find that a quite different order prevails from what is above described. All Courts of a military kind are under a constant subordination to the ordinary Courts of Law. Officers who have abused their private power, though only in regard to their own Soldiers, may be called to account before a Court of Common Law, and compelled to make proper satisfaction. Even any flagrant abuse of authority committed by Members of Courts Martial, when sitting to judge their own people, and determine upon cases of a bare mi-<464>litary kind, makes them liable to the animadversion of the civil Judge (*a*). <465>

(*a*) A great number of instances might be produced to prove the above mentioned subjection of the Civil to the Military power, I shall introduce one which is particularly remarkable: I meet with it in the periodical publications of the year 1746.

A Lieutenant of Marines, whose name was *Frye,* had been charged, while in the West Indies, with contempt of orders, for having refused, when ordered by the Captain, to assist another Lieutenant in carrying another Officer prisoner on board the Ship: the two Lieutenants wanted to have the Captain give the order in writing. For this Lieutenant *Frye* was tried at Jamaica by a Court Martial, and sentenced to fifteen years imprisonment, besides being declared incapable of serving the King. He was brought home; and his case, after being laid before the Privy Council, appearing in a justifiable light, he was released. Some time after he brought an action against Sir *Chaloner Ogle,* who had sat as President to the above Court Martial, and had a verdict in his favour for one thousand pounds damages (it was also proved that he had been kept fourteen months in the most severe confinement before he was brought to his Trial). The Judge moreover informed him that he was at liberty to bring his action against any of the Members of the said Court Martial he could meet with. The following part of the affair is still more remarkable.

Upon application made by Lieutenant *Frye,* Sir John Willes, Lord Chief Justice of the Common Pleas, issued his Writ against Admiral *Mayne,* and Captain *Rentone,* two of the persons who had sat in the above Court Martial, who happened to be at that time in England, and were Members of the Court Martial that was then sitting at Deptford, to determine on the affair between Admirals Mathews and Lestock of which Admiral *Mayne* was moreover President; and they were arrested immediately after the breaking

To the above facts concerning the pre-eminence of the Civil over the Military Power at large, it is needless to add that all offences com-<466>mitted by persons of the military profession, in regard to individuals belonging to the other classes of the People, are to be determined upon by the Civil Judge. Any use they may make of their force, unless expressly applied to, and directed by, the Civil Magistrate, let the occasion be what it may, makes them liable to be convicted of murder for any life that may have been lost. Pleading the duties or customs of their profession in extenuation of any offence, is a plea which the Judge will not so much as understand. Whenever claimed by the Civil power, they must be delivered up immediately. Nor can it, in general, be said, that the countenance shewn to the military profession by the Ruling power in the State, has constantly been such as to inspire the bulk of the People with a disposition tamely to bear their acts of oppression, or to raise in Magistrates and Juries any degree of pre-possession sufficient to lead them always to determine with partiality in their favour (*a*). <467>

---

up of the Court. The other Members resented highly what they thought the insult: they met twice on the subject; and came to certain *Resolutions,* which the Judge Advocate was directed to deliver to the Board of Admiralty, in order to their being laid before the King. In these resolutions they demanded "satisfaction for the high insult on their President, from all persons, how high soever in office, who have set on foot this arrest, or in any degree advised or promoted it:"—moreover complaining, that, by the said arrest, "the order, discipline and government of his Majesty's armies by Sea was dissolved, and the Statute 13 Car. II. made null and void."

The altercations on that account lasted some months. At length the Court Martial thought it necessary to submit; and they sent to Lord Chief Justice Willes, a letter signed by the seventeen Officers, Admirals and Commanders, who composed it, in which they acknowledged that *"the resolutions of the 16 and 21 May were unjust and unwarrantable, and do ask pardon of his Lordship, and the whole Court of Common Pleas, for the indignity offered to him and the Court."*

This letter Judge Willes read in the open Court, and directed the same to be registered in the *Remembrance* Office, "as a memorial *to the present and future ages, that whoever set themselves above the Law, will, in the end, find themselves mistaken."* The letter from the Court Martial, together with Judge Willes's acceptation, were inserted in the next Gazette, 15th November 1746. [[De Lolme correctly dates the legal contests that followed Frye's court martial. The "Statute 13 Car. II" is a reference to 1661 legislation concerning naval discipline and the punishment of offenders by courts martial.]]

(*a*) The Reader may see in the publications of the year 1770, the clamour that was raised on account of a General in the army (Gen. Gansell) having availed himself of the

The subjection of the Military to the Civil power, carried to that extent it is in England, is another characteristic and distinctive circumstance in the English Government.

It is sufficiently evident that a King does not look to his army for his support, who takes so little pains to bribe and unite it to his interest.

In general, if we consider all the different circumstances in the English Government, we shall find that the army cannot possibly procure to the Sovereign any permanent strength, any strength upon which he can rely, and from it expect the success of any future and distant measures.

The public notoriety of the Debates in Parliament, induces all individuals, Soldiers as well as others, to pay some attention to political subjects; and the liberty of speaking, printing, and intriguing, being extended to every order of the Nation by whom they are surrounded, makes them liable to imbibe every <468> notion that may be directly contrary to the views of that Power which keeps them.

The case would be still worse if the Sovereign was engaged in a contest with a very numerous part of the Nation. The general concern would increase in proportion to the vehemence of the Parliamentary Debates: Individuals, in all the different classes of the Public, would try their eloquence on the same subjects; and this eloquence would be in great measure exerted, during such interesting times, in making converts of the Soldiery: these evils the Sovereign could not obviate, nor even know, till it should be in every respect too late. A Prince engaged in the contest we suppose, would scarcely have completed his first preparations,—his project would scarcely be half ripe for execution, before his army would be taken from him. And the more powerful this army might be, the more adequate, seemingly, from its numbers, to the task it is intended for, the more open it would be to the danger we mention.

Of this, James the Second made a very remarkable experiment. He had

---

vicinity of his Soldiers to prevent certain Sheriff's Officers from executing an arrest upon his person, at Whitehall. It however appeared that the General had done nothing more than put forth a few of his Men in order to perplex and astonish the Sheriff's Officers; and in the mean time he took an opportunity for himself to slip out of the way. The violent clamour we mention, was no doubt owing to the party spirit of the time; but it nevertheless shews what the notions of the bulk of the People were on the subject.

augmented his army to the number of thirty thousand. But when the day finally came in which their support was to have been useful to him, some deserted to the enemy; others threw their arms; <469> and those who continued to stand together, shewed more inclination to be spectators of, than agents in, the contest. In short, he gave all over for lost, without making any manner of trial of their assistance (*a*). <470>

From all the facts before introduced, it is evident that the power of the Crown, in England, bears upon foundations that are quite peculiar to it, and that its security and strength are obtained by means totally different from those by which the same advantages are so incompletely procured, and so deeply paid for, in other Countries.

(*a*) The army made loud rejoicings on the day of the *acquittal of the Bishops,* even in the presence of the King, who had purposely repaired to Hounslow Heath on that day. He had not been able to bring a single regiment to declare an approbation of his measures in regard to the Test and penal Statutes. The celebrated ballad *lero lero lillibulero,* which is reported to have had such an influence on the minds of the people at that time, and of which Bishop Burnet says, *"never perhaps so slight a thing had so great an effect"* originated in the army: *"the whole army, and at last people both in City and Country, were perpetually singing it."* [[De Lolme describes incidents in the summer of 1688 which preceded James II's flight from England.]]

To a King of England engaged in a project against public liberty, a numerous army, ready formed before hand, must, in the present situation of things, prove a very great impediment: he cannot possibly give his attention to the proper management of it: the less so, as his measures for that purpose must often be contradictory to those he is to pursue with the rest of the People.

If a King of England, wishing to set aside the present Constitution, and to assimilate his power to that of the other Sovereigns of Europe, was to do me the honour to consult me as to the means of obtaining success, I would recommend to him, as his first preparatory step, and before his real project is even suspected, to disband his army, keeping only a strong guard, not exceeding twelve hundred Men. This done, he might, by means of the weight and advantages of his place, set himself about undermining such constitutional laws as he dislikes; using as much temper as he can, that he may have the more time to proceed. And when at length things should be brought to a crisis, then I would advise him to form another army, out of those friends or class of the People whom the turn and incidents of the preceding contests, will have linked and rivetted to his interest: with this army he might now take his chance: the rest would depend on his generalship: and even in a great measure on his bare reputation in that respect.

This advice to the King of England I suppose, I would however conclude with observing to him, that his situation is as advantageous, to the full, as that of any King upon earth, and upon the whole, that all the advantages that can possibly arise from the success of his plan, cannot make it worth his while to undertake it.

It is without the assistance of an armed force that the Crown, in England, is able to manifest that fearlessness of particular individuals, or whole classes of them, with which it discharges its legal functions and duties. It is without the assistance of an armed force, it is <471> able to counterbalance the extensive and unrestrained freedom of the People, it is able to exert that resisting strength which constantly keeps increasing in a superior proportion to the force by which it is opposed, that ballasting power by which, in the midst of boisterous winds and gales, it recovers and rights again the Vessel of the State (*a*).

It is from the Civil branch of its Office, the Crown derives that strength by which it subdues even the Military power, and keeps it in a state of subjection to the Laws unexampled in any other Country. It is from an happy arrangement of things, it derives that uninterrupted steadiness, that invisible solidity, which procures to the Subject both so certain a protection, and so extensive a freedom. It is from the Nation, it receives the force with which it <472> governs the Nation. Its resources are, accord, and not compulsion,—free action, and not fear,—and it continues to reign through the play, the struggle, of the voluntary passions of those who pay obedience to it (*b*).

(*a*) There is a number of circumstances in the English Government which those persons who wish for speculative meliorations, such as Parliamentary reform, or other changes of a like kind, do not perhaps think of taking into consideration. If so, they are, in their proceedings, in danger of meddling with a number of strings, the existence of which they do not suspect. While they only mean reformation and improvement, they are in danger of removing the *Talisman* on which the existence of the Fabric depends, or, like King *Nisus*'s daughter, of cutting off the fatal hair with which the fate of the City is connected. [[In Greek mythology, the daughter of Nisus of Megara cut off the king's lock of red hair, which had kept him and his city invincible.]]

(*b*) Many persons, satisfied with seeing the elevation and upper parts of a building, think it immaterial to give a look under ground, and notice the foundation. Those Readers therefore who choose, may consider the long Chapter that has just been concluded, as a kind of foreign digression, or parenthesis, in the course of the Work.

How far the examples of Nations who have lost their liberty, are applicable to England.

Every Government, those Writers observe who have treated these subjects, containing within itself the efficient cause of its ruin, a cause which is essentially connected with those very circumstances that had produced its prosperity, the advantages attending the English Government cannot therefore, according to these Writers, exempt it from that hidden defect which is secretly working its ruin; and M. de Montesquieu, giving his opinion both on the effect and the cause, says, "the English Constitution will lose its liberty, will perish: <473> Have not Rome, Lacedaemon, and Carthage, perished? It will perish when the Legislative power shall have become more corrupt than the Executive."[1]

Though I do by no means pretend that any human establishment can escape the fate to which we see every thing in Nature is subject, nor am so far prejudiced by the sense I entertain of the great advantages of the English Government, as to reckon among them that of eternity, I will however observe in general, that, as it differs by its structure and resources from all those with which History makes us acquainted, so it cannot be said to be liable to the same dangers. To judge of the one from the other, is to judge by analogy where no analogy is to be found; and my respect for the author I have quoted will not hinder me from saying, that his opinion has not the same weight with me on this occasion, that it has on many others.

---

1. De Lolme cites, with some variations, a concluding paragraph of Montesquieu's celebrated exposition of the English constitution; see *The Spirit of the Laws,* book 11, chapter 6.

Having neglected, as indeed all systematic Writers upon Politics have done, very attentively to enquire into the real foundations of Power, and of Government, among Mankind, the principles he lays down are not always so clear, or even so just, as we might <474> have expected from a Man of so true a genius. When he speaks of England, for instance, his observations are much too general: and though he had frequent opportunities of conversing with Men who had been personally concerned in the public affairs of this Country, and he had been himself an eye-witness of the operations of the English Government, yet, when he attempts to describe it, he rather tells us what he conjectured than what he saw.

The examples he quotes, and the causes of dissolution which he assigns, particularly confirm this observation. The Government of Rome, to speak of the one which, having gradually, and as it were of itself, fallen to ruin, may afford matter for exact reasoning, had no relation to that of England. The Roman People were not, in the latter ages of the Commonwealth, a People of Citizens, but of Conquerors. Rome was not a State, but the head of a State. By the immensity of its conquests, it came in time to be in a manner only an accessory part of its own Empire. Its power became so great, that, after having conferred it, it was at length no longer able to resume it: and from that moment it became itself subjected to it, from the same reason that the Provinces themselves were so. <475>

The fall of Rome, therefore, was an event peculiar to its situation; and the change of manners which accelerated this fall, had also an effect which it could not have had but in that same situation. Men who had drawn to themselves all the riches of the World, could no longer content themselves with the supper of Fabricius, and the cottage of Cincinnatus.[2] The People, who were masters of all the corn of Sicily and Africa, were no longer obliged to plunder their neighbours for their's. All possible Enemies, besides, being exterminated, Rome, whose power was military, became to be no longer an army; and that was the aera of her corruption: if, indeed, we ought to

2. Caius Fabricius Luscinus (d. 250 B.C.E.) and Lucius Quinctius Cincinnatus (b. 519 B.C.E.) were Roman generals and political leaders distinguished for their virtue and poverty.

give that name to what was the inevitable consequence of the nature of things.

In a word, Rome was destined to lose her Liberty when she lost her Empire; and she was destined to lose her Empire, whenever she should begin to enjoy it.

But England forms a Society founded upon principles absolutely different. All liberty, and power, are not accumulated as it were on one point, so as to leave, every where else, only slavery and misery, consequently only seeds of division and secret animosity. From the one end of the Island to the other <476> the same laws take place, and the same interests prevail: the whole Nation, besides, equally concurs in the formation of the Government: no part, therefore, has cause to fear that the other parts will suddenly supply the necessary forces to destroy its liberty; and the whole have, of course, no occasion for those ferocious kinds of virtue which are indispensably necessary to those who, from the situation in which they have brought themselves, are continually exposed to such dangers, and after having invaded every thing, must abstain from every thing.

The situation of the People of England, therefore, essentially differs from that of the People of Rome. The form of the English Government does not differ less from that of the Roman Republic; and the great advantages it has over the latter for preserving the liberty of the People from ruin, have been described at length in the course of this Work.

Thus, for instance, the total ruin of the Roman Republic was principally brought about by the exorbitant power to which several of its Citizens were successively enabled to rise. In the latter age of the Commonwealth, those Citizens went so far as to divide among themselves the dominions of the Republic, in much the same manner as they might have done lands <477> of their own. And to them, others in a short time succeeded, who not only did the same, but who even proceeded to that degree of tyrannical insolence, as to make cessions to each other, by express and formal compacts, of the lives of thousands of their Fellow-citizens. But the great and constant authority and weight of the Crown, in England, prevent, in their very beginning, as we have seen, all misfortunes of this kind; and the reader may recollect what has been said before on that subject.

At last the ruin of the Republic, as every one knows, was completed.

One of those powerful Citizens we mention, in process of time found means to exterminate all his competitors: he immediately assumed to himself the whole power of the State; and established for ever after an arbitrary Monarchy.[3] But such a sudden and violent establishment of a Monarchical power, with all the fatal consequences that would result from such an event, are calamities which cannot take place in England: that same kind of power we see, is already in being; it is ascertained by fixed laws, and established upon regular and well-known foundations.

Nor is there any great danger that that power may, by means of those legal prero-<478>gatives it already possesses, suddenly assume others, and at last openly make itself absolute. The important privilege of granting to the Crown its necessary supplies, we have before observed, is vested in the Nation: and how extensive soever the prerogatives of a King of England may be, it constantly lies in the power of his People either to grant, or deny him, the means of exercising them.

This right possessed by the People of England, constitutes the great difference between them, and all the other Nations that live under Monarchical Governments. It likewise gives them a great advantage over such as are formed into Republican States, and confers on them a means of influencing the conduct of the Government, not only more effectual, but also (which is more in point to the subject of this Chapter) incomparably more lasting and secure than those reserved to the People, in the States we mention.

In those States, the political rights which usually fall to the share of the People, are those of voting in general Assemblies, either when laws are to be enacted, or Magistrates to be elected. But as the advantages arising from these general rights of giving votes, <479> are never very clearly ascertained by the generality of the People, so neither are the consequences attending particular forms or modes of giving these votes, generally and completely understood. They accordingly never entertain any strong and constant preference for one method rather than another; and it hence always proves but too easy a thing in Republican States, either by insidious proposals made at particular times to the People, or by well-contrived precedents, or other

3. De Lolme refers to Julius Caesar and the establishment of the emperorship.

means, first to reduce their political privileges to mere ceremonies and forms, and at last, entirely to abolish them.

Thus, in the Roman Republic, the mode which was constantly in use for about one hundred and fifty years, of dividing the Citizens into *Centuriae* when they gave their votes, reduced the right of the greater part of them, during that time, to little more than a shadow. After the mode of dividing them by Tribes had been introduced by the Tribunes, the bulk of the Citizens indeed were not, when it was used, under so great a disadvantage as before; but yet the great privileges exercised by the Magistrates in all the public assemblies, the power they assumed of moving the Citizens out of one <480> Tribe into another, and a number of other circumstances, continued to render the rights of the Citizens more and more ineffectual; and in fact we do not find that when those rights were at last entirely taken from them, they expressed any very great degree of discontent.[4]

In Sweden (the former Government of which partook much of the Republican form)[5] the right allotted to the People in the Government, was that of sending Deputies to the General States of the Kingdom, who were to give their votes on the resolutions that were to be taken in that Assembly. But the privilege of the People of sending such Deputies was, in the first place, greatly diminished by several essential disadvantages under which these Deputies were placed with respect to the Body, or *Order,* of the Nobles. The same privilege of the People was farther lessened by their Deputies being deprived of the right of freely laying their different proposals before the States, for their assent or dissent, and attributing the exclusive right of framing such proposals, to a private Assembly which was called the *Secret Committee.* Again, the right allowed to the Order of the Nobles, of having a number of Members in this Secret Committee double to that of all the

---

4. Before the period of the Republic, the Roman people were made up of three tribes, each of which contained ten *curiae,* or courts. Under Servius Tullius, who ruled as king 578–534 B.C.E., a census was introduced, which organized the citizenry into six classes and each class into centuries (*centuriae*), or groups of a hundred. In the political assembly called *comitia centuriata,* votes were cast by hundreds; in the *comitia tributa,* votes were cast by tribes; and in the *comitia auriata,* votes were cast by whole courts.

5. De Lolme here describes the 1720 constitution of Sweden; see above, book 2, chapter 17, pp. 264–65 and p. 265, note 7.

other Or-<481>ders taken together, rendered the rights of the People still more ineffectual. At the last Revolution those rights we mention have been in a manner taken from the People; and they do not seem to have made any great efforts to preserve them (*a*).

But the situation of affairs in England is totally different from that which we have just described. The political rights of the People are inseparably connected with the right of Property—with a right which it is as difficult to invalidate by artifice, as it is dangerous to attack it by force, and which we see that the most arbitrary Kings, in the full career of their power, have never offered to violate without the greatest precautions. A King of England who would enslave his People, must begin with doing, for his first act, what all other Kings reserve for the last; and he cannot attempt to deprive his Subjects of their political privileges, without declaring war against the whole Nation at the same time, and attacking <482> every individual at once in his most permanent and best understood interest.

And that means possessed by the People of England, of influencing the conduct of the Government, is not only in a manner secure against any danger of being taken from them: it is moreover attended with another advantage of the greatest importance; which is that of conferring naturally, and as it were necessarily, on those to whom they trust the care of their interests, the great privilege we have before described, of debating among themselves whatever questions they think conducive to the good of their Constituents, and of framing whatever bills they think proper, and in what terms they choose.

This privilege of starting new subjects of deliberation, and, in short, of *propounding* in the business of legislation, which, in England, is allotted to the Representatives of the People, sets another capital difference between the English Constitution, and the government of other free States, whether limited Monarchies or Commonwealths, and prevents that which, in those States, proves a most effectual means of subverting the laws favourable to

(*a*) I might have produced examples of a number of Republican States in which the People have been brought, at one time or other, to submit to the loss of their political privileges. In the Venetian Republic, for instance, the right, now exclusively vested in a certain number of families, of enacting laws, and electing the Doge and other Magistrates, was originally vested in the whole People.

public liberty: I mean the undermining of these laws by the precedents and artful practices of those who are invested with the Executive Power in the Government. <483>

In the States we mention, the *active* share, or the business of *propounding*, in legislation, being ever alloted to those persons who are invested with the Executive authority, they not only possess a general power, by means of insidious and well timed proposals made to the People, of getting those laws repealed which set bounds to their authority; but when they do not choose openly to discover their wishes in that respect, or perhaps even fear to fail in the attempt, they have another resource, which, though slower in its operation, is not less effectual in the issue. They neglect to execute those laws which they dislike, or deny the benefit of them to the separate straggling individuals who claim them, and in short introduce practices that are directly derogatory to them. These practices in a course of time become respectable *Uses,* and at length obtain the force of *Laws.*

The People, even where they are allowed a share in legislation, being ever *passive* in the exercise of it, have no opportunities of framing new provisions by which to remove these spurious practices or regulations, and declare what the law in reality is. The only resource of the Citizens, in such a state of things, is either to be perpetually cavilling, or openly to oppose: and always exerting themselves, either too soon, or too late, they cannot come forth to defend <484> their liberty, without incurring the charge, either of disaffection, or of rebellion.

And while the whole class of Politicians, who are constantly alluding to the usual forms of limited Governments, agree in deciding that freedom, when once lost, cannot be recovered (*a*), it happens that the maxim *principiis obsta,*[6] which they look upon as the safeguard of liberty, and which they accordingly never cease to recommend, besides its requiring a degree of watchfulness incompatible with the situation of the People, is in a manner impracticable.

But the operation of preferring grievances, which in other Governments is a constant forerunner of public commotions, that of framing new law

(*a*) "Ye free Nations, remember this maxim: Freedom may be acquired, but it cannot be recovered." *Rousseau's* Social Compact, Chap. VIII. [[De Lolme quotes, with slight variation, Rousseau, *The Social Contract,* book 2, chapter 8.]]

6. "Resist innovations."

remedies, which is so jealously secured to the Ruling power in the State, are, in England, the constitutional and appropriated offices of the Representatives of the People.

How long soever the People may have remained in a state of supineness as to their most valuable interests, whatever may have been the neglect and even the errors of their Representatives, the instant the latter come either to see these errors, or to have a sense of their duty, they proceed, by means of the privilege <485> we mention, to set aside those abuses or practices which, during the preceding years, had become to hold the place of the laws. To how low soever a state public liberty may happen to be reduced, they take it where they find it, lead it back through the same path, and to the same point, from which it had been compelled to retreat; and the Ruling power, whatever its usurpations may have been, how far soever it may have overflowed its banks, is ever brought back to its old limits.

To the exertions of the privilege we mention, were owing the frequent confirmations and elucidations of the Great Charter that took place in different reigns. By means of the same privilege the Act was repealed, without public commotion, which had enacted that the King's proclamations should have the force of law: by this Act public liberty seemed to be irretrievably lost; and the Parliament who passed it, seemed to have done what the Danish Nation did about a century afterwards. The same privilege procured the peaceable abolition of the Court of Star Chamber: a Court which, though in itself illegal, had grown to be so respected through the length of time it had been suffered to exist, that it seemed to have for ever <486> fixed and rivetted the unlawful authority it conferred on the Crown. By the same means the power was set aside which the Privy Council had assumed of imprisoning the Subject without admitting to bail, and even mentioning any cause: this power was in the first instance declared illegal by the *Petition of Right;* and the attempts of both the Crown and the Judges to invalidate this declaration by introducing, or maintaining, practices that were derogatory to it, were as often obviated, in a peaceable manner, by fresh declarations, and, in the end, by the celebrated *Habeas Corpus* Act (*a*). <487>

(*a*) The case of the General Warrants may also be mentioned as an instance. The issuing of such Warrants, with the name of the persons to be arrested left blank, was a

And I shall take this opportunity to make the Reader observe, in general, how the different parts of the English Government mutually assist and support each other. It is because the whole Executive authority in the State is vested in the Crown, that the People may without danger delegate the care of their liberty to Representatives:—it is because they share in the Government only through these Representatives, that they are enabled to possess the great advantage arising from framing and proposing new laws: but for this purpose, it is again absolutely necessary that the *Crown,* that is to say, a *Veto* of extraordinary power, should exist in the State.

It is, on the other hand, because the balance of the People is placed in the right of granting to the Crown its necessary supplies, that the latter may, without danger, be intrusted with the great authority we mention; and that the right, for instance, which is vested in it of judging of the proper time for calling and dissolving Parliaments (a right absolutely necessary to its preservation) may exist without producing *ipso facto,* the ruin of public Liberty. The most singular Government upon Earth, and which has carried farthest the liberty of the in-<488>dividual, was in danger of total destruction, when Bartholomew Columbus[7] was on his

---

practice that had been followed in the Secretaries of State's office for above sixty years. In a Government differently constituted, that is, in a Government in which the Magistrates, or Executive power, should have been possessed of the *Key* of Legislation, it is difficult to say how the contest might have been terminated: these Magistrates would have been but indifferently inclined to frame and bring forth a declaration by which to abridge their assumed authority. In the Republic of Geneva, the Magistracy, instead of rescinding the judgment against M. Rousseau, of which the Citizens complained, had rather openly to avow the maxim, that standing *Uses* were valid derogations to the written Law, and ought to supersede it. This rendered the clamour more violent than before. [[See above, book 2, chapter 16, p. 251, note a, for De Lolme's previous discussion of General Warrants; and book 2, chapter 13, p. 209, note a, for his discussion of the condemnation of Rousseau by Genevan authorities. In the paragraph to which the note refers, De Lolme mentions previously treated constitutional episodes: see above, book 1, chapter 7, p. 69, note a (Statute of Proclamations); book 1, chapter 8, p. 73, note d (Star Chamber); book 1, chapter 3, pp. 49–50, and note 3 (Petition of Right); and book 1, chapter 3, p. 51, and note 5 (Habeas Corpus Act).]]

7. Christopher Columbus sent his younger brother Bartholomew (Bartolomeo) to the court of Henry VII in hopes of securing English support for the famous trans-Atlantic voyage of 1492, which eventually occurred under Spanish patronage. Bartholomew, however, never actually reached England.

passage to England, to teach Henry the Seventh the way to Mexico and Peru (*a*).

As a conclusion of this subject (which might open a field for speculations without end) I shall take notice of an advantage peculiar to the English Government, and which, more than any other we could mention, must contribute to its duration. All the political passions of Mankind, if we attend to it, are satisfied and provided for in the English Government; and whether we look at the Monarchical, or the Aristocratical, or the Democratical part of it, we find all those powers already settled in it in a regular manner, which have an unavoidable tendency to arise at one time or other, in all human Societies.

If we could for an instant suppose that the English form of Government, instead of having been the effect of a lucky concurrence of fortunate circumstances, had been established from a settled plan by a Man who had discovered, beforehand and by reasoning, all those <489> advantages resulting from it which we now perceive from experience, and had undertaken to point them out to other Men capable of judging of what he said to them, the following is, most likely, the manner in which he would have expressed himself.

"Nothing is more chimerical," he would have said, "than a state either of total equality, or total liberty, amongst Mankind. In all societies of Men, some Power will necessarily arise. This Power, after gradually becoming confined to a smaller number of persons, will, by a like necessity, at last fall into the hands of a single Leader; and these two effects (of which you may see constant examples in History) arising from the ambition of the one part of Mankind, and from the various affections and passions of the other, are absolutely unavoidable.

"Let us, therefore, admit this evil at once, since it is impossible to avoid it. Let us, of ourselves, establish a Chief among us, since we must, some time or other, submit to one: we shall by this means effectually prevent the conflicts that would arise among the competitors for that station. But let

---

(*a*) As affairs are situated in England, the dissolution of a Parliament on the part of the Crown, is no more than an appeal either to the People themselves, or to another Parliament.

us, above all, establish him single; lest, after successively raising himself on the ruins of <490> his Rivals, he should finally establish himself whether we will or not, and through a train of the most disadvantageous incidents.

"Let us even give him every thing we can possibly give without endangering our security. Let us call him our Sovereign; let us make him consider the State as being his own patrimony; let us grant him, in short, such personal privileges as none of us can ever hope to rival him in, and we shall find those things which we were at first inclined to consider as a great evil, will be in reality a source of advantages to the Community. We shall be the better able to set bounds to that Power which we shall have thus ascertained and fixed in one place. We shall have the more interested the Man whom we shall have put in possession of so many advantages, in the faithful discharge of his duty. And we shall have thus procured for each of us, a powerful protector at home, and for the whole Community, a defender against foreign enemies, superior to all possible temptation of betraying his Country.

"You may also have observed, (he would continue) that in all States, there naturally arises around the person, or persons, who are invested with the public power, a class of <491> Men, who, without having any actual share in that power, yet partake of its lustre: who, pretending to be distinguished from the rest of the Community, do, from that very circumstance, become distinguished from it: and this distinction, though only matter of opinion, and at first thus surreptitiously obtained, yet may become in time the source of very grievous effects.

"Let us therefore regulate this evil which we cannot entirely prevent. Let us establish this class of Men who would otherwise grow up among us without our knowledge, and gradually acquire the most pernicious privileges. Let us grant them distinctions that are visible and clearly ascertained: their nature will, by this means, be the better understood, and they will of course, be much less likely to become dangerous. By this means also, we shall preclude all other persons from the hopes of usurping them. As, to pretend to distinctions can thenceforward be no longer a title to obtain them, every one who shall not be expressly included in their number, must continue to confess himself one of the People; and just as we said before, let us chuse ourselves one Master that we may not have fifty, so let us again say here, let us <492> establish three hundred Lords, that we may not have ten thousand Nobles.

"Besides, our pride will better reconcile itself to a superiority which it will no longer think of disputing. Nay, as they will themselves see us to be before-hand in acknowledging it, they will think themselves under no necessity of being insolent to furnish us a proof of it. Secure as to their privileges, all violent measures on their part for maintaining, and at last perhaps extending them, will be prevented: they will never combine together with any degree of vehemence, but when they really have cause to think themselves in danger; and by having made them indisputably great Men, we shall have a chance of often seeing them behave like modest and virtuous Citizens.

"In fine, by being united in a regular Assembly, they will form an intermediate Body in the State, that is to say, a very useful part of the Government.

"It is also necessary, our Lawgiver would farther add, that We, the People, should have an influence upon the Government: it is necessary for our own security; it is no less necessary for the security of the Government itself. But experience must have taught you, at the same time, that a great <493> body of Men cannot act, without being, though they are not aware of it, the instruments of the designs of a small number of persons; and that the power of the People is never any thing but the power of a few Leaders, who (though it may be impossible to tell when, or how) have found means to secure to themselves the direction of its exercise.

"Let us, therefore, be also beforehand with this other inconvenience. Let us effect openly what would, otherwise, take place in secret. Let us intrust our power, before it be taken from us by address. Those whom we shall have expressly made the depositaries of it, being freed from any anxious care about supporting themselves, will have no object but to render it useful. They will stand in awe of us the more, because they will know that they have not imposed upon us: and instead of a small number of Leaders, who would imagine they derive their whole importance from their own dexterity, we shall have express and acknowledged Representatives, who will be accountable to us for the evils of the State.

"But above all, by forming our Government with a small number of persons, we shall <494> prevent any disorder that may take place in it, from ever becoming dangerously extensive. Nay more, we shall render it capable of inestimable combinations and resources, which would be utterly impossible in that Government of all, which never can be any thing but uproar and confusion.

"In short, by expressly divesting ourselves of a power of which we should, at best, have only an apparent enjoyment, we shall be intitled to make conditions for ourselves: we will insist that our liberty be augmented; we will, above all, reserve to ourselves the right of watching and censuring that administration which will have been established by our own consent. We shall the better see its faults, because we shall be only Spectators of it; we shall correct them the better, because we shall not have personally concurred in its operations" (a). <495>

The English Constitution being founded upon such principles as those we have just described, no true comparison can be made between it, and the Governments of any other States; and since it evidently insures, not only the liberty, but the general satisfaction in all respects, of those who are subject to it, in a much greater degree than any other Government ever did, this consideration alone affords sufficient ground to conclude, without looking farther, that it is also more likely to be preserved from ruin.

And indeed we may observe the remarkable manner in which it has been maintained in the midst of such general commotions as seemed unavoidably to prepare its destruction. It rose again, we see, after the wars between Henry the Third and his Barons; after the usurpation of Henry the Fourth; and after the long and bloody contentions between the Houses of York and Lancaster. Nay, though totally destroyed in appearance after the fall of Charles the First, and though the greatest efforts had been made to establish

---

(a) He might have added,—"As we will not seek to counteract nature, but rather to follow it, we shall be able to procure ourselves a mild Legislation. Let us not be without cause afraid of the power of one Man: we shall have no need either of a Tarpeian rock, or of a Council of *Ten*. Having expresly allowed to the People a liberty to enquire into the conduct of Government, and to endeavour to correct it, we shall need neither State-prisons, nor secret Informers." [[The Council of Ten, a major political institution of the republic of Venice in the medieval and Renaissance periods, operated in secret and exercised wide discretionary powers for preserving the security of the state.]]

another form of government in its stead, yet, no sooner was Charles the Second called over, than the Constitution was re-established upon all its ancient foundations. <496>

However, as what has not happened at one time, may happen at another, future Revolutions (events which no form of Government can totally prevent) may perhaps end in a different manner from that in which past ones have been terminated. New combinations may possibly take place among the then ruling Powers of the State, of such a nature as to prevent the Constitution, when peace shall be restored to the Nation, from settling again upon its ancient and genuine foundations; and it would certainly be a very bold assertion to decide, that both the outward form, and the true spirit of the English Government, would again be preserved from destruction, if the same dangers to which they have in former times been exposed, should again happen to take place.

Nay, such fatal changes as those we mention, may be introduced even in quiet times, or at least, by means in appearance peaceable and constitutional. Advantages, for instance, may be taken by particular factions, either of the feeble temper, or of the misconduct, of some future King. Temporary prepossessions of the People may be made use of, to make them concur in doing what will prove afterwards the ruin of their own liberty. Plans of apparent <497> improvement in the Constitution, forwarded by Men who, though with good intentions, shall proceed without a due knowledge of the true principles and foundations of Government, may produce effects quite contrary to those which were designed, and in reality prepare its ruin (*a*). The Crown, on the other hand, may, by the acquisition

(*a*) Instead of looking for the principles of Politics in their true sources, that is to say, in the nature of the affections of Mankind, and of those secret ties by which they are united together in a state of Society, Men have treated that science in the same manner as they did natural Philosophy in the times of Aristotle, continually recurring to occult causes and principles, from which no useful consequence could be drawn, Thus, in order to ground particular assertions, they have much used the word Constitution, in a personal sense, *the Constitution loves, the Constitution forbids,* and the like. At other times, they have had recourse to *Luxury,* in order to explain certain events; and at others, to a still more occult cause, which they have called *Corruption:* and abundance of comparisons drawn from the human Body, have been also used for the same purposes: continual instances of such defective arguments and considerations occur in the Works of M. *de*

of foreign dominions, acquire a fatal independency on the People: and if, without entering into any farther particulars on this subject, I were re-<498>quired to point out the principal events which would, if they were ever to happen, prove immediately the ruin of the English Government, I would say,—The English Government will be no more, either when the Crown shall become independent on the Nation for its supplies, or when the Representatives of the People shall begin to share in the Executive authority (*a*).

Montesquieu; though a man of so much genius, and from whose writings so much information is nevertheless to be derived. Nor is it only the obscurity of the writings of Politicians, and the impossibility of applying their speculative Doctrines to practical uses, which prove that some peculiar and uncommon difficulties lie in the way of the investigation of political truths; but the remarkable perplexity which Men in general, even the ablest, labour under when they attempt to descant and argue upon abstract questions in politics, also justifies this observation, and proves that the true first principles of this Science, whatever they are, lie deep both in the human feelings, and understanding.

(*a*) And if at any time, any dangerous changes were to take place in the English Constitution, the pernicious tendency of which the People were not able at first to discover, restrictions on the Liberty of the Press, and on the Power of Juries, will give them the first information.

A few additional thoughts on the attempts that
at particular times may be made to abridge the power
of the Crown, and on some of the dangers by which
such attempts may be attended.

The power of the Crown is supported by deeper, and more numerous, roots, than the generality of people are aware of, as has <499> been observed in a former Chapter; and there is no cause anxiously to fear that the wresting any capital branch of its prerogative, may be effected, in common peaceable times, by the mere theoretical speculations of Politicians. However, it is not equally impracticable that some event of the kind we mention, may be brought about through a conjunction of several circumstances. Advantage may, in the first place, be taken of the minority, or even also the inexperience or the errors, of the person invested with the kingly authority. Of this a remarkable instance happened under the reign of King George the First, while that Bill, by which the number of Peers was in future to be limited to a certain number, was under consideration in the House of Commons, to whom it had been sent from that of the Lords, where it had been passed. So unacquainted was the King at that time with his own interest, and with the constitution of that Government over which he was come to preside, that having been persuaded by that party who wished success to the Bill, that the objection made against it by the House of Commons, was only owing to an opinion they entertained of the Bill being dis-<500>agreeable to him, that he was prevailed upon to send a message to

1. This chapter first appeared in the 1781 edition.

them, to let them know that such an opinion was ill-grounded, and that should the Bill pass in their House, it would meet with his assent (*a*). Considering the prodigious importance of the consequences of such a Bill, the fact is certainly very remarkable (*b*).

With those personal disadvantages under which the Sovereign may lie for defending his authority, other causes of difficulty may concur:—such as popular discontents of long continuance in regard to certain particular abuses of influence or authority. The generality of the Public bent, at that time, both upon remedying the abuses that are complained of, and preventing the like from taking place in future, will perhaps wish to see that branch of the prerogative which gave rise to them, taken from the Crown: a general disposition to applaud such a measure, if effected, will be manifested from all quarters; and at the same time Men may not be aware that the only material consequence that may arise from depriving the Crown of that branch of power <501> which has caused the public complaints, will perhaps be the having transposed that branch of power from its former seat to another, and having trusted it to new hands, which will be still more likely to abuse it than those in which it was formerly lodged.

In general, it may be laid down as a maxim, that Power, under any form of Government, must exist, and be trusted somewhere. If the Constitution does not admit of a King, the governing authority is lodged in the hands of Magistrates. If the Government, at the same time it is a limited one, bears a Monarchical form, those shares of power that are retrenched from the King's prerogative, most likely continue to subsist, and are vested in a Senate, or Assembly of great Men under some other name of the like kind.

Thus, in the Kingdom of Sweden, which, having been a limited Monarchy, may supply examples very applicable to the Government of this Country, we find that the power of convoking the General States (or Par-

(*a*) See the Collection of *Parliamentary Debates;* I do not remember exactly what Volume. [[In a message conveyed to the House of Lords on March 2, 1719, George I reported that he was "willing that his prerogative stand not in the way" of the passage of the proposed Peerage Bill; see *A Collection of the Parliamentary Debates in England* . . . , 21 vols. (London, 1739–42), 7:113–14.]]

(*b*) This Bill has been mentioned in page 398. [[For De Lolme's fuller account of the proposed legislation and its constitutional dangers, see above, book 2, chapter 17, pp. 262–63 and p. 263, note 4.]]

liament) of that Kingdom, had been taken from the Crown; but at the same time we also find that the Swedish Senators had invested themselves with that essential branch of power which the Crown had lost.—I mean here to speak of the Govern-<502>ment of Sweden, as it stood before the last revolution.[2]

The power of the Swedish King, to confer offices and employments, had been also very much abridged. But what was wanting to the power of the King, the Senate enjoyed: it had the nomination of three persons for every vacant office, out of whom the king was to choose one.

The king of Sweden had but a limited power in regard to pardoning offenders; but the Senate likewise possessed what was wanting to that branch of his prerogative; and it appointed two persons without the consent of whom the King could not remit the punishment of any offence.

The King of England has an exclusive power in regard to foreign affairs, war, peace, treaties;—in all that relates to military affairs; he has the disposal of the existing army, of the fleet, &c. The King of Sweden had no such extensive powers; but they nevertheless existed: every thing relating to the above mentioned objects was transacted in the Assembly of the Senate; the majority decided; the King was obliged to submit to it; and his only privilege consisted in his vote being accounted two (*a*). <503>

If we pursue farther our enquiry on the subject, we shall find that the

---

(*a*) The Swedish Senate was usually composed of sixteen Members. In regard to affairs of smaller moment, they formed themselves into two divisions: in either of these when they did sit, the presence of seven Members was required for the effectual transacting of business: in affairs of importance, the assembly was formed of the whole Senate; and the presence of ten Members was required to give force to the resolutions. When the King could not, or would not, take his seat, the Senate proceeded nevertheless, and the majority continued to be equally decisive.

As the Royal Seal was necessary for putting in execution the resolutions of the Senate, King Adolphus Frederic, father to the present King, tried by refusing to lend the same, to procure that power which he had not by his suffrage, and to stop the proceedings of the Senate. Great debates, in consequence of that pretension, arose, and continued for a while; but, at last, in the year 1756, the King was over-ruled by the Senate, who ordered a seal to be made, that was named the *King's Seal,* which they affixed to their official resolutions, when the King refused to lend his own. [[Adolphus Frederick ruled as king of Sweden in 1751–71, under the limited royal authority established by the 1720 constitution. The "present king" was his son, Gustavus III.]]

2. That is, before the revolution of 1772, under the constitution of 1720. See above, book 2, chapter 17, p. 258, note c; pp. 263–65; and p. 265, note 7.

King of Sweden could not raise whom he pleased to the office of Senator, as the King of England can, in regard to the office of member of the Privy Council; but the Swedish States, in the Assembly of whom the Nobility enjoyed most capital advantages, possessed a share of the power we mention, in conjunction with the King; and in cases of vacancies in the Senate, they elected <504> three persons, out of whom the King was to return one.

The King of England may, at all times, deprive his Ministers of their employments. The King of Sweden could remove no Man from his office; but the States enjoyed the power that had been denied to the King; and they might deprive of their places both the Senators, and those persons in general who had a share in the Administration.

The King of England has the power of dissolving, or keeping assembled as long as he pleases, his Parliament. The King of Sweden had not that power; but the States might, of themselves, prolong their duration as they thought proper.

Those persons who think that the prerogative of a King cannot be too much abridged, and that Power loses all its influence on the dispositions and views of those who possess it, according to the kind of name used to express those offices by which it is conferred, may be satisfied, no doubt, to behold those branches of power that were taken from a King, distributed to several Bodies, and shared in by the Representatives of the People: but those who think that Power, when parcelled and diffused, is never so well repressed and regulated as <505> when it is confined to a sole indivisible seat, that keeps the Nation united and awake,—those who know that, names by no means altering the intrinsic nature of things, the Representatives of the People, as soon as they are vested with independent authority, become *ipso facto* its Masters,—those persons, I say, will not think it a very happy regulation in the former Constitution of Sweden, to have deprived the King of prerogatives formerly attached to his office, in order to vest the same either in a Senate, or in the Deputies of the People, and thus to have trusted with a share in the exercise of the public power, those very Men whose Constitutional office should have been to watch and restrain it.

To the indivisibility of the governing authority in England, the community of interest which takes place among all orders of Men, is owing; and from this community of interest rises as a necessary consequence, the liberty enjoyed by all ranks of subjects. This observation has been insisted upon at length in the course of this Work. The shortest reflection on the frame of the human heart, suffices to convince us of its truth, and at the same time manifests the danger that would result from making any changes in the form of the existing Go-<506>vernment by which this general community of interest might be lessened,—unless we are at the same time also determined to believe, that partial Nature forms Men in this Island, of quite other stuff than the selfish and ambitious one of which she ever made them in other Countries (*a*). <507>

(*a*) Such regulations as may capitally affect, through their consequences, the equipoise of a Government, may be brought about, even though the promoters themselves of those regulations, are not aware of their tendency. At the time the Bill was passed in the last century, by which it was enacted that the Crown should give up its prerogative of dissolving the Parliament then sitting [[De Lolme refers to the Triennial Act of 1641; see his earlier discussion at book 2, chapter 3, p. 155, note a]], the generality of People had no thought of the calamitous consequences that were to follow: very far from it. The King himself certainly felt no very great apprehension on that account; else he would not have given his assent: and the Commons themselves, it appears, had but very faint notions of the capital changes which the Bill would speedily effect in their political situation.

When the Crown of Sweden was, in the first instance, stripped of all the different prerogatives we have mentioned, it does not appear that those measures were effected by sudden, open provisions for that purpose: it is very probable they had been prepared by indirect regulations formerly made, the whole tendency of which scarcely any body perhaps could foresee at the time they were framed.

When the Bill was in agitation, that has been mentioned in page 398 [[see pp. 262–63]], and 499 [[see p. 320]], by which the House of Peers was in future to be limited to a certain number that was not to be exceeded, the great constitutional consequences of the Bill were scarcely attended to by any body. The King himself certainly saw no harm in it, since he sent an open message to promote the passing of it: a measure which I cannot say how far it was in itself regular. The Bill was, it appears, generally approved out of doors. Its fate was for a long time doubtful in the House of Commons; nor did they acquire any glory with the bulk of the People by finally rejecting it: and Judge Blackstone, as I find in his Commentaries, does not seem to have thought much of the Bill and its being rejected, as he only observes that the Commons "wished to keep the door of the House of Lords as open as possible." Yet, no Bill of greater constitutional importance was ever agitated in Parliament; since the consequences of its being passed, would have been the freeing the House of Lords, both in their Judicial and Legislative capacities, from all constitutional check whatever, either from the Crown, or the Nation. Nay, it is not to be doubted they would have acquired, in time, the right of electing their own Members: though it would be useless to point out here by what series of intermediate events the measure might have been brought about. Whether there existed any actual project of this kind, among the first framers of the Bill, does not appear: but a certain number of the Members of the House we mention, would have thought of it

But past experience does not by any means allow us to entertain so pleasing an opinion. <508> The perusal of the History of this Country will shew us, that the care of its Legislators for the welfare of the subject, always kept pace with the exigencies of their own situation. When, thro' the minority, or easy temper of the reigning Prince, or other circumstances, the dread of a superior Power began to be overlooked, the public cause was immediately deserted in a greater or less degree, and pursuit after private influence and lucrative offices took the place of patriotism. When, under the reign of Charles the First, the authority of the Crown was for a while utterly annihilated, those very Men who, till then, had talked of nothing but Magna Charta and Liberty, instantly endeavoured openly to trample both under foot.

Since the time we mention, the former Constitution of the Government having been restored, the great outlines of public liberty have indeed been warmly and seriously defended: but if any partial unjust laws or regulations have been made, especially since the Revolution of the year 1689, if any abuses injurious to particular classes of individuals have been suffered to continue (facts into the truth of which I do not propose to examine here), it will certainly be found upon enquiry, that those laws and those abuses were such as that from <509> them the Members of the Legislature well knew, that neither they, nor their friends, would ever be likely to suffer.

If through the unforeseen operation of some new regulation made to restrain the royal prerogative, or through some sudden public revolution, any particular bodies or classes of individuals were ever to acquire a personal independent share in the exercise of the governing authority, we should behold the public virtue and patriotism of the Legislators and Great Men immediately cease with its cause, and Aristocracy, as it were watchful of the opportunity, burst out at once, and spread itself over the Kingdom.

The Men who are now the Ministers, then the Partners of the Crown,

---

soon enough, if the Bill in question had been enacted into a law; and they would certainly have met with success, had they been but contented to wait, and had they taken time. Other equally important changes in the substance, and perhaps the outward form, of the Government, would have followed. [[De Lolme again returns to the 1719 legislative proposal concerning the House of Lords; see above, book 2, chapter 17, pp. 262–63 and p. 263, note 4, as well as chapter 19, p. 320, notes a and b. He quotes, with some variation, Blackstone's comments in *Commentaries on the Laws of England,* 1:153.]]

would instantly set themselves above the reach of the law, and soon after ensure the same privilege to their several supporters or dependants.

Personal and independent power being become the only kind of security of which Men would now shew themselves ambitious, the *Habeas Corpus* Act, and in general all those laws which Subjects of every rank mention with love, and to which they look up for protection and safety, would be spoken of with contempt, and <510> mentioned as remedies fit only for Countrymen and Cits:[3]—it even would not be long before they were set aside, as obstructing the wise and salutary steps of the Senate.

The pretension of an equality of right in all Subjects, of whatever rank and order to their property and to personal safety, would soon be looked upon as an old fashioned doctrine, which the Judge himself would ridicule from the Bench. And the liberty of the press, now so universally and warmly vindicated, would, without loss of time, be cried down and suppressed, as only serving to keep up the insolence and pride of a refractory people.

And let us not believe that the mistaken People, whose Representatives we now behold making such a firm stand against the *indivisible* power of the Crown, would, amidst the general devastation of every thing they hold dear, easily find Men equally disposed to repress the encroaching, while *attainable,* power of a Senate and Body of Nobles.

The time would be no more when the People, upon whatever Men they let their choice fall, are sure to find them ready sincerely to join in the support of every important branch of public liberty.

Present, or expected, personal power and in-<511>dependence on the laws, being now the consequence of the trust of the People, wherever they should apply for servants, they would only meet with betrayers. Corrupting as it were every thing they should touch, they could confer no favour upon an individual but to destroy his public virtue; and to repeat the words used in a former Chapter, "their raising a Man would only be immediately inspiring him with views directly opposite to their own, and sending him to increase the number of their enemies."[4]

All these considerations strongly point out the very great caution which

3. *Cits* was a shortened form of the word "citizen," generally used to denote an inhabitant of a town or city of inferior social rank.
4. See above, book 2, chapter 9, p. 190.

is necessary to be used in the difficult business of laying new restraints on the governing authority. Let therefore the less informed part of the People, whose zeal requires to be kept up by visible objects, look if they choose upon the Crown as the only seat of the evils they are exposed to; mistaken notions on their part are less dangerous than political indifference, and they are more easily directed than roused,—but at the same time, let the more enlightened part of the Nation constantly remember, that the Constitution only subsists by virtue of a proper equilibrium,—by a line being drawn between Power and Liberty.

Made wise by the examples of several other <512> Nations, by those which the History of this very Country affords, let the People in the heat of their struggles in the defence of liberty, always take heed, only to reach, never to overshoot, the mark,—only to repress, never to transfer and diffuse Power.

Amidst the alarms that may, at particular times, arise from the really awful authority of the Crown, let it, on the one hand, be remembered, that even the power of the Tudors was opposed and subdued,—and on the other let it be looked upon as a fundamental maxim, that, whenever the prospect of personal power and independence on the governing authority, shall offer to the view of the Members of the Legislature, or in general of those Men to whom the People must trust, even Hope itself is destroyed. The Hollander, in the midst of a storm, though trusting to the experienced strength of the mounds that protect him, shudders no doubt at the sight of the foaming Element that surrounds him; but they all gave themselves over for lost, when they thought the worm had got into their dykes (a).[5] <513>

(a) Such new forms as may prove destructive of the real substance of a Government, may be unwarily adopted, in the same manner as the superstitious notions and practices described in my Work, intitled *Memorials of Human Superstition,* may be introduced into a Religion, so as to entirely subvert the true spirit of it. [[De Lolme's *Memorials of Human Superstition,* which first appeared in 1784, was a revised version of his 1777 *The History of the Flagellants; or, the advantages of the Discipline; being a Paraphrase and Commentary on the Historia Flagellantium of the Abbé Boileau.*]]

5. In 1730 an infestation of "paal worms" *(Teredo limmoria)* threatened the wooden pilings that supported Holland's sea dikes, which were then replaced with stone embankments.

A few additional Observations on the right of
Taxation which is lodged in the hands of the
Representatives of the People. What kind of danger
this Right may be exposed to.

The generality of Men, or at least of Politicians, seem to consider the right
of taxing themselves, enjoyed by the English Nation, as being no more than
a means of securing their property against the attempts of the Crown; while
they overlook the nobler and more extensive efficiency of that privilege.

The right to grant subsidies to the Crown, possessed by the People of
England, is the safe-guard of all their other liberties, religious and civil: it
is a regular means conferred on them by the Constitution, of influencing
the motion of the Executive power; and it forms the tie by which the latter
is bound to them. In short, this privilege is a sure pledge in their hands,
that their Sovereign, who can dismiss their Representatives at his pleasure,
<514> will never entertain thoughts of ruling without the assistance of
these.

If, through unforeseen events, the Crown could attain to be independent
on the People in regard to its supplies, such is the extent of its Prerogative,
that, from that moment, all the means the People possess to vindicate their
liberty, would be annihilated. They would have no resource left,—except
indeed that uncertain and calamitous one, of an appeal to the sword; which
is no more, after all, than what the most enslaved Nations enjoy.

Let us suppose, for instance, that abuses of power should be committed,

---

1. This chapter first appeared in the 1781 edition.

which, either by their immediate operation, or by the precedents they might establish, should undermine the liberty of the subject. The People, it will be said, would then have their remedy in the Legislative power possessed by their Representatives. The latter would, at the first opportunity, interfere, and frame such Bills as would prevent the like abuses for the future. But here we must observe, that the Assent of the Sovereign is necessary to make those Bills become Laws; and if, as we have just now supposed, he had no need of the support of the Commons, how could they obtain his assent to laws thus purposely framed to abridge his authority? <515>

Again, let us suppose that, instead of contenting itself with making slow advances to despotism, the Executive power, or its Ministers, should at once openly invade the liberty of the subject. Obnoxious men, Printers for instance, or political Writers, are destroyed, either by military violence, or, to do things with more security, with the forms of law. Then, it will be said, the Representatives of the People would impeach the persons concerned in those measures. Though unable to reach a King who personally *can do no wrong,* they at least would lay hold of those Men who were the immediate instruments of his tyrannical proceedings, and endeavour, by bringing them to condign punishment, to deter future Judges or Ministers from imitating them. All this I grant; and I will even add, that, circumstanced as the Representatives of the People now are, and having to do with a Sovereign who can enjoy no dignity without their assistance, it is most likely that their endeavours in the pursuits of such laudable objects would prove successful. But if, on the contrary, the King, as we have supposed, stood in no need of their assistance, and moreover knew that he should never want it, it is impossible to think that he would then suffer himself to <516> remain a tame spectator of their proceedings. The impeachments thus brought by them would immediately prove the signal of their dismission; and the King would make haste, by dissolving them, both to revenge what would then be called the insolence of the Commons, and to secure his Ministers.

But even those are vain suppositions: the evil would reach much farther; and we may be assured that if ever the Crown was to be in a condition to govern without the assistance of the Representatives of the People, it would dismiss them for ever, and thus rid itself of an Assembly which, while it continued to be a clog on its power, could no longer be of any service to it. This Charles the First attempted to do when he found his Parliaments grew refractory, and the Kings of France really have done, with respect to the General Estates of their Kingdom.

And indeed if we consider the extent of the Prerogative of the King of England, and especially the circumstance of his completely uniting in himself all the executive and active powers in the State, we shall find that it is no exaggeration to say, that he has power sufficient to be as arbitrary as the Kings of France, were it not for the right of taxation, which, in <517> England, is possessed by the People; and the only constitutional difference between the French and English Nations is, that the former can neither confer benefits on their Sovereign, nor hinder his measures; while the latter, how extensive soever the Prerogative of their King may be, can deny him the means of exerting it.

But here a most important observation is to be made; and I entreat the reader's attention to the subject. This right of granting subsidies to the Crown, can only be effectual when it is exercised by one Assembly alone. When several distinct Assemblies have it equally in their power to supply the wants of the Prince, the case becomes totally altered. The competition which so easily takes place between those different Bodies, and even the bare consciousness which each entertains of its inability to hinder the measures of the Sovereign, render it impossible for them to make any effectual constitutional use of their privilege. "Those different Parliaments or Estates" (to repeat the observation introduced in the former part of this Work) "having no means of recommending themselves to their Sovereign, but their superior readiness in complying with his demands, vie with each other in grant-<518>ing what it would not only be fruitless, but even dangerous to refuse. And the King, in the mean time, soon comes to demand as a tribute, a gift which he is confident to obtain."[2] In short, it may be laid down as a maxim, that when a Sovereign is made to depend, in regard to his supplies, on more Assemblies than one, he, in fact, depends upon none. And indeed the King of France is not independent on his People for his necessary supplies, any otherwise than by drawing the same from several different Assemblies of their Representatives: the latter have in appearance a right to refuse all his demands: and as the English call the grants they

2. See above, book 1, chapter 3, p. 46.

make to their Kings, Aids or Subsidies, so do the Estates of the French provinces call their's *Dons gratuits,* or free gifts.

What is it, therefore, that constitutes the difference between the political situation of the French and English Nations, since their rights thus seem outwardly to be the same? The difference lies in this, that there has never been in England more than one Assembly that could supply the wants of the Sovereign. This has always kept him in a state, not of a seeming, but of a real dependence on the Representatives of the People for his necessary supplies; and how low <519> soever the liberty of the Subject may, at particular times, have sunk, they have always found themselves possessed of a most effectual means of restoring it, whenever they have thought proper so to do. Under Henry the Eighth, for instance, we find the Despotism of the Crown to have been carried to an astonishing height; it was even enacted that the Proclamations of the King should have the force of law;[3] a thing which even in France, never was so expressly declared: yet, no sooner did the Nation recover from its long state of supineness, than the exorbitant power of the Crown was reduced within its constitutional bounds.

To no other cause than the disadvantage of their situation, are we to ascribe the low condition in which the Deputies of the People in the Assembly called the General Estates of France, were always forced to remain.

Surrounded as they were by the particular Estates of those Provinces into which the Kingdom had been formerly divided, they never were able to stipulate conditions with their Sovereign; and instead of making their right of granting subsidies to the Crown serve to gain them in the end a share in Legislation, they ever remained confined to the naked pri-<520>vilege of "humble Supplication and Remonstrance."

Those Estates, however, as all the great Lords in France were admitted into them, began at length to appear dangerous; and as the King could in the mean time do without their assistance, they were set aside. But several of the particular Estates of the Provinces are preserved to this day: some, which for temporary reasons had been abolished, have been restored: nay, so manageable have popular Assemblies been found by the Crown, when it has to do with many, that the kind of Government we mention is that

---

3. For a discussion of this legislation, see above, book I, chapter 7, p. 69, note a.

which it has been found most convenient to assign to Corsica; and Corsica has been made *un pays d' Etats* (*a*).[4] <521>

That the Crown in England should, on a sudden, render itself independent on the Commons for its supplies, that is, should on a sudden successfully assume to itself a right to lay taxes on the Subject, by its own authority, is not certainly an event in any degree likely to take place, nor indeed that should, at this present time, raise any kind of political fear. But it is not equally impracticable that the right of the Representatives of the People might be-<522>come invalidated, by being divided in the manner that has been just described.

Such a division of the right of the People might be effected several different ways. National calamities for instance, unfortunate foreign wars attended with loss of public credit, might suggest methods for raising the

(*a*) An idea of the manner in which the business of granting supplies to the Crown, was conducted by the States of the province of Britanny, under the reign of Lewis the Fourteenth, may be formed from several lively strokes to be met with in the Letters of Mad. de Sévigné, whose Estate lay in that Province, and who had often assisted at the holding of those States. The granting of supplies was not, it seems, looked upon as any serious kind of business. The whole time the States were sitting, was a continued scene of festivity and entertainment: the canvassing of the demands of the Crown was chiefly carried on at the table of the Nobleman who had been deputed from Court to hold the States; and every thing was commonly decided by a kind of acclamation. In a certain Assembly of those States, the Duke of Chaulnes, the Lord Deputy, had a present of fifty thousand crowns made to him, as well as a considerable one for his Duchess besides obtaining the demand of the Court: and the Lady we quote here, commenting somewhat jocularly on these grants, says, *Ce n'est pas que nous soyons riches; mais nous sommes honnêtes, nous avons du courage, & entre midi & une heure, nous ne savons rien refuser à nos amis.* "It is not that we are rich; but we are civil, we are full of courage, and, between twelve and one o'clock, we are unable to deny any thing to our friends."

The different Provinces of France, it may be observed, are liable to pay several taxes besides those imposed on them by their own States. Dean Tucker, in one of his Tracts, in which he has thought proper to quote this Work, has added to the above instance of the French Provinces, that of the States of the Austrian Netherlands, which is very conclusive. And examples to the same purpose might be supplied by all those Kingdoms of Europe in which Provincial States are held. [[De Lolme's French source is Marie de Rabutin-Chantal, Marquise de Sévigné (1626–96), whose letters "to her daughter and her friends" were published in French and in English translation. The work of Josiah Tucker, to which he next refers, is likely *A Brief Essay on the Advantages and Disadvantages, Which Respectively Attend France and Great Britain* (1749), where the discussion of tax rates figured as one of the "principal disadvantages of France with regard to Trade."]]

4. Sovereignty over Corsica, which enjoyed a brief period of independence after 1755, was transferred to France under the terms of the 1768 Treaty of Versailles.

necessary supplies, different from those which have hitherto been used. Dividing the Kingdom into a certain number of parts, which should severally vote subsidies to the Crown, or even distinct assessments to be made by the different Counties into which England is now divided, might, in the circumstances we suppose, be looked upon as adviseable expedients; and these, being once introduced, might be continued afterwards.

Another division of the right of the People, much more likely to take place than those just mentioned, might be such as might arise from acquisitions of foreign dominions, the inhabitants of which should in time claim and obtain a right to treat directly with the Crown, and grant supplies to it, without the interference of the British Legislature.

Should any Colonies acquire the right we mention—should, for instance, the American Colonies have acquired it, as they claimed it, <523> it is not to be doubted that the consequences that have resulted from a division like that we mention in most of the Kingdoms of Europe, would also have taken place in the British dominions, and that that spirit of competition which has been above described, would in time have manifested itself between the different Colonies. This desire of ingratiating themselves with the Crown, by means of the privilege of granting supplies to it, has even been openly confessed by an Agent of the American Provinces (*a*), when, on his being examined by the House of Commons, in the year 1766, he said, *"the granting Aids to the Crown, is the only means the Americans have of recommending themselves to their Sovereign."* And the events that have of late years taken place in America, render it evident that the Colonies would not have scrupled going any lengths to obtain favourable conditions at the expence of Britain and the British Legislature.

That a similar spirit of competition might be raised in Ireland, is also sufficiently plain from certain late events. And should the American Colonies have obtained their demands, and at the same time should Ireland and America have increased in wealth to a cer-<524>tain degree, the time might have come at which the Crown might have governed England with the supplies of Ireland and America—Ireland with the supplies of England

(*a*) Doctor Franklin. [[Benjamin Franklin, in his service as a colonial agent, was based in London during the mid-1760s. His 1766 testimony to the House of Commons occurred at the time that Parliament debated its recent fiscal policy in North America, including the repeal of the 1765 Stamp Act and the adoption of the Declaratory Act.]]

and of the American Colonies—and the American Colonies with the money of each other, and of England and Ireland.

To this it may be objected, that the supplies granted by the Colonies, even though joined with those of Ireland, never could have risen to such a height as to have counterbalanced the importance of the English Commons.—I answer, in the first place, that there would have been no necessity that the aids granted by Ireland and America should have risen to an equality with those granted by the British Parliament: it would have been sufficient, to produce the effects we mention, that they had only borne a certain proportion with these latter, so far as to have conferred on the Crown a certain degree of independence, and at the same time have raised in the English Commons a correspondent sense of self-diffidence in the exercise of their undoubted privilege of granting, or rather *refusing,* subsidies to the Crown.—Here it must be remembered, that the right of granting, or refusing, supplies to the Crown, is the only ultimate, forcible, privilege the <525> British Parliament possess: by the Constitution they have no other, as hath been observed in the beginning of this Chapter: this circumstance ought to be combined with the absolute exclusiveness of the executive powers lodged in the Crown—with its prerogative of dissenting from the Bills framed by Parliament, and even of dissolving it (*a*). <526>

(*a*) Being with Doctor Franklin at his house in Craven-street, some months before he went back to America, I mentioned to him a few of the remarks contained in this Chapter, and, in general, that the claim of the American Colonies directly clashed with one of the vital principles of the English Constitution. The observation, I remember, struck him very much: it led him afterwards to speak to me of the examination he had undergone in the House of Commons; and he concluded with lending me the volume of the Collection of *Parliamentary Debates,* in which an account of it is contained. Finding the constitutional tendency of the claim of the Americans to be a subject not very generally understood, I added a few paragraphs concerning it, in the English Edition I some time after gave of this work; and being now about to give a third Edition of the same, I have thought it might not be amiss to write something more compact on the subject, and have accordingly added the present new Chapter, into which I have transferred the few additional paragraphs I mention, leaving in the place where they stood (pag. 45.) only the general observations on the right of granting subsidies, which were formerly in the French work. Several of the ideas, and even expressions contained in this Chapter, made their appearance in the *Public Advertiser,* about the time I was preparing the first Edition: I sent them myself to that Newspaper, under the signature of *Advena.* I mention this for the sake of those persons who may perchance remember having seen the sketch I allude to. [[To clarify De Lolme's report in this note: many of the materials

I shall mention in the second place, a remarkable fact in regard to the subject we are treating (which may serve to shew that Politicians are not always consistent, or even sagacious, in their arguments), which is, that the same persons who were the most strenuous advocates for granting to the American Colonies their demands, were at the same time the most sanguine in their predictions of the future wealth and greatness of America, and at the same time also, used to make frequent complaints on the undue influence which the Crown derives from the scanty supplies granted to it by the kingdom of Ireland (*a*).[5]

Had the American Colonies fully obtained their demands, both the essence of the present English Government, and the condition of the English People, would certainly have been altered thereby: nor would such a change <527> have been inconsiderable, but in proportion as the Colonies should have remained in a state of national poverty (*b*). <528>

---

for this chapter were first composed before 1775, though they did not appear in his text until the 1781 edition. For his earlier and briefer treatment of this issue, see above, book 1, chapter 3, p. 46.]]

(*a*) For instance, the complaints made in regard to the pensions on the Irish establishment.

5. It is not fully clear to which politicians De Lolme refers in this paragraph. The most likely candidates are William Pitt and his parliamentary allies, who provided the strongest statements in defense of the resistance in North America to the Stamp Act and related tax legislation. But he may refer instead to Lord Rockingham and his Parliamentary Ministry, which secured the 1766 repeal of the controversial tax legislation and the enactment of the Declaratory Act confirming the legislative supremacy of the king and Parliament over the American colonies.

(*b*) When I observe that no Man who wished for the preservation of the form and spirit of the English Constitution, ought to have desired that the claim of the American Colonies might be granted them, neither do I mean to say that the American Colonies should have given up their claim. [[The "claim of the American Colonies" to which De Lolme refers here and in his text (pp. 331–34 above) was the assertion made during the 1765–66 resistance to the Stamp Act that the colonial assemblies in North America (and not the British Parliament) enjoyed authority, with the British crown, to legislate on matters concerning the internal governance of the colonies.]] The wisdom of Ministers, in regard to American affairs, ought to have been constantly employed in making the Colonies useful to this Country, and at the same time, in hiding their subjection from them (a caution which is, after all, more or less used in every Government upon earth); it ought to have been exerted in preventing the opposite interests of Britain, and of America, from being brought to an issue, to any such clashing dilemma as would render disobedience on the one hand, and the resort to force on the other, almost surely unavoidable. The generality of people fancy that Ministers use a great depth of thought, and much forecast in their operations; whereas the truth is, that Ministers in all Countries, never think but of providing for present, immediate, contingencies; in doing which they constantly follow the open track before them. This method does very well for the common course of human affairs, and even is the safest; but whenever cases and circumstances of a new and unknown nature occur, sad blunders and uproar are the consequences. The celebrated Count Oxenstierna, Chancellor of Sweden, one day when his Son was expressing to him his diffidence of his own abilities, and the dread with which he thought of ever engaging in the management of public affairs, made the following Latin answer to him; *Nescis, mî filî, quam parvâ cum sapientiâ regitur mundus* (You do not know, my son, with what little wisdom the World is governed). [[De Lolme cites the maxim of Count Axel Gustafsson Oxenstierna (1583–1654), who served as chancellor of Sweden during the period of the Thirty Years' War.]]

Matters having come to an eruption, it was no longer to be expected they could be compromised by the palliative offers sent at different times from this Country to America. When the Earl of Carlisle solicited to be at the head of the solemn Commission that failed for the purpose we mention, he did not certainly shew modesty equal to that of the Son of Chancellor Oxenstierna. It has been said that, in that stage of the contest, the Americans could not think that the proposals thus sent to them, were seriously meant: however, this cannot have been the principal cause of the miscarriage of the commission. The fact is, that, after the Americans had been once made to open their eyes on their political situation, and rendered sensible of the local advantages of their Country, it was become in a manner impossible to have struck with them any bargain at which either Nation would have afterwards cause to rejoice, or even to have made any bargain at all. It would be needless to say here any thing more on the subject of the American contest.

The motto of one of the English Nobility, should have been that of Ministers, in their regulations for rendering the Colonies useful to the Mother Country,—*Faire sans dire.* [["Actions rather than words."]]

Conclusion.—A few words on the nature of the
Divisions that take place in England.

I shall conclude this Work with a few observations on the total freedom
from violence with which the political disputes and contentions in England
are conducted and terminated, in order both to give a farther <529> proof
of the soundness of the principles on which the English Government is
founded, and to confute in general the opinion of foreign Writers or Politicians, who, misled by the apparent heat with which those disputes are
sometimes carried on, and the clamour to which they give occasion, look
upon England as a perpetual scene of civil broils and dissensions.[1]

In fact if we consider, in the first place, the constant tenor of the conduct
of the Parliament, we shall see that whatever different views the several
Branches that compose it may at times pursue, and whatever use they may
accordingly make of their privileges, they never go, in regard to each other,
beyond the terms, not only of decency, but even of that general good understanding which ought to prevail among them.

Thus the King, though he preserves the style of his Dignity, never ad-
dresses the two Houses but in terms of regard and affection; and if at any
time he chuses to refuse their Bills, he only says that he will consider of
them *(le Roy s'advisera);* which is certainly a gentler expression than the
word *Veto.*

The two Houses on their part, though very jealous, each within their

---

1. The intensity and the vehemence of partisan debate in England were frequently
viewed as a dangerous product of the nation's political system; see, for example, Montesquieu's cautious strictures in *The Spirit of the Laws,* book 19, chapter 27.

own walls, of the <530> freedom of speech, are, on the other hand, careful that that liberty shall never break out into unguarded expressions with regard to the person of the King. It is even a constant rule amongst them never to mention him, when they mean to blame the administration; and those things which they may choose to censure, even in the Speeches made by the King in person, and which are plainly his own acts, are never considered but as the deed of his Ministers, or in general of those who have advised him.

The two Houses are also equally attentive to prevent every step that may be inconsistent with that respect which they mutually owe to one another. The examples of their differences with each other are very rare, and were for the most part mere misunderstandings. Nay, in order to prevent all subject of altercation, the custom is, that when one of the two Houses refuses to consent to a Bill presented by the other, no formal declaration is made of such refusal; and that House whose Bill is rejected, learns its fate only from their hearing no more of it, or by what the Members may be told as private persons.

In each House, the Members take care, even in the heat of debate, never to go be-<531>yond certain bounds in their manner of speaking of each other: if they were to offend in that respect, they would certainly incur the censure of the House. And as reason has taught Mankind to refrain, in their wars, from all injuries to each other that have no tendency to promote the main object of their contentions, so a kind of Law of Nations (if I may so express myself) has been introduced among the persons who form the Parliament and take a part in the debates: they have discovered that they may very well be of opposite parties, and yet not hate and persecute one another. Coming fresh from debates carried on even with considerable warmth, they meet without reluctance in the ordinary intercourse of life; and, suspending all hostilities, they hold every place out of Parliament to be neutral ground.

In regard to the generality of the People, as they never are called upon to come to a final decision with respect to any public measures, or expressly to concur in supporting them, they preserve themselves still more free from party spirit than their Representatives themselves sometimes are. Considering, as we have observed, the affairs of Government as only matter of speculation, they ne-<532>ver have occasion to engage in any vehement contests among themselves on that account. Much less do they think of taking an active and violent part in the differences of particular factions, or the quarrels of private individuals. And those family feuds, those party animosities, those victories and consequent outrages of factions alternately successful, in short, all those inconveniencies which in so many other States have constantly been the attendants of liberty, and which Authors tell us we must submit to, as the price of it, are things in very great measure unknown in England.

But are not the English perpetually making complaints against the Administration? and do they not speak and write as if they were continually exposed to grievances of every kind?

Undoubtedly, I shall answer, in a Society of Beings subject to error, dissatisfactions will necessarily arise from some quarter or other; and in a free Society, they will be openly manifested by complaints. Besides, as every Man in England is permitted to give his opinion upon all subjects, and as, to watch over the Administration, and to complain of grievances, is the proper duty of the Representatives of the People, complaints must neces-<533>sarily be heard in such a Government, and even more frequently, and upon more subjects, than in any other.

But those complaints, it should be remembered, are not, in England, the cries of oppression forced at last to break its silence. They do not suppose hearts deeply wounded. Nay, I will go farther, they do not even suppose very determinate sentiments; and they are often nothing more than the first vent which Men give to their new, and yet unsettled conceptions.

The agitation of men's minds is not therefore in England what it would be in other States: it is not the symptom of a profound and general discontent, and the forerunner of violent commotions. Foreseen, regulated, even hoped for by the Constitution, this agitation animates all the different parts of the State, and is to be considered only as the beneficial vicissitude of the seasons. The governing Power being dependant on the Nation, is often thwarted, but so long as it continues to deserve the affection of the People, can never be endangered. Like a vigorous Tree which stretches its branches far and wide, the slightest breath can put it in motion; but it acquires and exerts at every minute a new degree of force, and resists <534> the Winds, by the strength and elasticity of its fibres, and the depth of its roots.

In a word, whatever Revolutions may at times happen among the persons who conduct the public affairs in England, they never occasion the shortest cessation of the power of the Laws, nor the smallest diminution of the security of individuals. A Man who should have incurred the enmity of the most powerful Men in the State—what do I say!—though he had, like another *Vatinius,* drawn upon himself the united detestation of all parties, might, under the protection of the Laws, and by keeping within the bounds required by them, continue to set both his enemies and the whole Nation at defiance.[2]

The limits prescribed to this book do not admit of entering into any farther particulars on the subject we are treating here; but if we were to pursue this enquiry, and examine into the influence which the English Government has on the manners and customs of the People, perhaps we should find that, instead of inspiring them with any disposition to disorder or anarchy, it produces in them a quite contrary effect. As they see the highest Powers in the State, constantly submit to the Laws, and they receive, themselves, such a certain protection <535> from those laws, whenever they appeal to them, it is impossible but they must insensibly contract a deep-rooted reverence for them, which can at no time cease to have some influence on their actions. And, in fact, we see that even the lower class of the People, in England, notwithstanding the apparent excesses into which they are sometimes hurried, possess a spirit of justice and order, superior to what is to be observed in the same rank of Men in other Countries. The extraordinary indulgence which is shewn to accused persons of every degree, is not attended with any of those pernicious consequences which we might at first be apt to fear from it. And it is perhaps to the nature of the English Constitution itself (however remote the cause may perhaps seem) and to the spirit of Justice it continually and insensibly diffuses throughout all orders of the People, that we are to attribute the singular advantage possessed by the English Nation, of employing an incomparably milder mode of administering Justice in criminal matters than any other Nation, and at the same time of affording perhaps fewer instances of violence or cruelty.

2. Publius Vatinius, a contemporary of Cicero and Julius Caesar who held several important political offices in the years 63–47 B.C.E., was famous for his contempt of the vices and corruption of the Romans.

Another consequence which we might observe here, as flowing also from the principles of the English Government, is the moderate <536> behaviour of all those who are invested with any branch of public authority. And if we look at the conduct of all public Officers in England, from the Minister of State, or the Judge, down to the lowest officers of Justice, we find a spirit of forbearance and lenity prevailing in England, among all persons in power, which cannot but create some surprize in those who have visited other Countries.

One circumstance more I shall observe here, as peculiar to England, which is the constant attention of the Legislature in providing for the interests and welfare of the People, and the indulgences shewn by them to their very prejudices. Advantages these, which are no doubt the consequence of the general spirit which animates the whole English Government, but are also particularly owing to that circumstance peculiar to it, of having lodged the active part of Legislation in the hands of the Representatives of the Nation, and committed the care of alleviating the grievances of the People to persons who either feel them, or see them nearly, and whose surest path to advancement and glory is to be active in finding remedies for them.

Not that I mean, however, that no abuses take place in the English Government, and <537> that all possible good laws are made in it, but that there is a constant tendency in it, both to correct the one, and improve the other. And that all the laws that are in being, are certainly executed, whenever appealed to, is what I look upon as the characteristic and undisputed advantage of the English Constitution. A Constitution the more likely to produce all the effects we have mentioned, and to procure in general the happiness of the People, in that it has taken Mankind as they are, and has not endeavoured to prevent every thing, but to regulate every thing: I shall add, the more difficult to discover, because its form was complicated, while its principles were natural and simple. Hence it is that the Politicians of Antiquity, sensible of the inconveniences of the Governments they had opportunities of knowing, wished for the establishment of such a Government, without much hopes of ever seeing it effected (*a*): nay, Tacitus, the

---

(*a*) "Statuo esse optimè constitutam Rempublicam quae ex tribus generibus illis, regali, optimo, & populari, modicè confusa,"—Cic. *Fragm.* [["(In my judgment,) that is

best Judge of them all, considered it as a project entirely chimerical (*a*). Nor was it because <538> he had not thought of it, had not reflected on it, that he was of this opinion: he had sought for such a government, had had a glimpse of it, and yet continued to pronounce it impracticable.

Let us not therefore ascribe to the confined views of Man, to his imperfect sagacity, the discovery of this important secret. The world might have grown old, generations might have succeeded generations, still seeking it in vain. It has been by a fortunate conjunction of circumstances, I shall add, by the assistance of a favourable situation, that Liberty has at last been able to erect herself a Temple.

Invoked by every Nation, but of too delicate a nature, as it should seem, to subsist in Societies formed of such imperfect beings as Mankind, she shewed, and but just shewed herself, to the ingenious Nations of antiquity who inhabited the south of Europe. They were constantly mistaken in the form of the worship they paid to her. As they continually aimed at extending dominion and conquest over other Nations, they were no less mistaken in the spirit of that wor-<539>ship; and though they continued for ages to pay their devotions to her, she still continued, with regard to them, to be the *unknown* Goddess.

Excluded, since that time, from those places to which she had seemed to give a preference, driven to the extremity of the Western World, banished even out of the Continent, she has taken refuge in the Atlantic Ocean. There it is, that, freed from the danger of external disturbance, and assisted by a happy pre-arrangement of things, she has been able fully to display the form that suited her; and she has found six centuries to have been necessary to the completion of her Work.

Being sheltered, as it were, within a Citadel, she there reigns over a Na-

---

the best constituted form of government, which, in moderation, is compounded of these three constituent parts: the royal, the aristocratical, and the popular." Marcus Tullius Cicero, *De re publica,* II.xxiii.]]

(*a*) "Cunctas Nationes & Urbes, Populus, aut Priores, aut Singuli, regunt. Delecta ex his & constituta Reipublicae forma, laudari faciliùs quàm evenire; vel si evenit, haud diuturna esse potest."—Tac. Ann. lib. iv. [["For every nation or city is governed by the people or the nobility, or by individuals: a constitution selected and blended from these types is easier to commend than to create; or, if created, its tenure of life is brief." Tacitus, *Annals,* book 4, chapter 33; see above, book 1, chapter 3, p. 45, note a.]]

tion which is the better entitled to her favours as it endeavours to extend her Empire, and carries with it, to every part of its dominions, the blessings of industry and equality. Fenced in on every side, to use the expressions of Chamberlayne, with a wide and deep ditch, the sea, guarded with strong outworks, its ships of war, and defended by the courage of her Seamen, she preserves that important secret, that sacred fire, so difficult to be kindled, and which, if it were once extinguished, would perhaps never be <540> lighted again.[3] When the World shall have again been laid waste by Conquerors, she will still continue to shew Mankind, not only the principle that ought to unite them, but what is of no less importance, the form under which they ought to be united. And the Philosopher, when he considers the constant fate of civil Societies amongst Men, and observes the numerous and powerful causes which seem as it were unavoidably to conduct them all to a state of incurable political Slavery, takes comfort in seeing that Liberty has at length disclosed her secret to Mankind, and secured an Asylum to herself.

---

3. De Lolme refers to Edward Chamberlayne's 1669 *Angliae notitia; or, The Present State of England,* part 2, chapter 2, which likened England to "a huge Fortress or garrisoned Town" protected by "a wide and deep Ditch the sea," "the strongest and best built Ships of War," and "abundantly furnished within with Men and Horses."

GUIDE TO FURTHER READING

Modern scholarship has greatly increased our understanding of the historical setting and constitutional theory to which De Lolme's *The Constitution of England* so significantly contributed, but it has not provided any major studies devoted specifically to De Lolme's own work. The two most substantial treatments remain Edith Ruth, *Jean Louis de Lolme und sein Werk über die Verfassung Englands* (Historische Studien, Heft 240; Berlin: Emil Ebering, 1934) and Jean-Pierre Machelon, *Les idées politiques de J. L. de Lolme* (Paris: Presses Universitaires de France, 1969), which also contain information concerning the impact of De Lolme's ideas in, respectively, Germany and France. Briefer and more recent assessments for England include M. J. C. Vile, *Constitutionalism and the Separation of Powers* (2nd ed.; Indianapolis: Liberty Fund, 1998), chapter 5; Mark Francis and John Morrow, "After the Ancient Constitution: Political Theory and English Constitutional Writings, 1765–1832," in *History of Political Thought* (1988), 9:283–302; and David Lieberman, "The Mixed Constitution and the Common Law," in *The Cambridge History of Eighteenth-Century Political Thought,* ed. Mark Goldie and Robert Wokler (Cambridge: Cambridge University Press, 2006).

The larger intellectual context for De Lolme's writing can be pursued through several major interpretations that focus on national debates and political cultures. British and American political theory is illuminated in H. T. Dickinson, *Liberty and Property: Political Ideology in Eighteenth-Century Britain* (London: Weidenfeld and Nicolson, 1977); J. G. A. Pocock, *Virtue, Commerce, and History: Essays on Political Thought and History* (Cambridge: Cambridge University Press, 1985); and Gordon Wood, *The Creation of the American Republic, 1776–1787* (Chapel Hill: University of North Carolina Press, 1969). The case of France receives masterful examination in Keith Michael Baker, *Inventing the French Revolution: Essays on French Political Culture in the Eighteenth Century* (Cambridge: Cambridge University Press, 1990). There is no single definitive study for De Lolme's Geneva, but valuable insight can be gained from two recent contributions to Rousseau scholarship: Helen Rosenblatt, *Rousseau and Geneva: From the First Discourse to the Social Contract, 1749–1762* (Cambridge: Cambridge University Press, 1997); and Bruno Bernardi, Florent Guénard, and Gabriella Silvestrini, eds., *Religion, liberté, justice sur les Lettres écrites de la montagne de J.-J. Rousseau* (Paris: Librairie Philosophique Vrin, 2005).

BIBLIOGRAPHY

De Lolme's Principal Publications

This chronological list is primarily based on the bibliography provided in Jean-Pierre Machelon, *Les idées politiques de J. L. de Lolme* (Paris: Presses Universitaires de France, 1969), pp. 5–7. Information concerning reprintings and subsequent editions of individual works is limited to the period of De Lolme's own lifetime (1741–1806).

Les princes manqués, lettre d'un citoyen à J.-J. Rousseau au du 29 mars 1765 (The failed princes, letter from a citizen to J.-J. Rousseau . . .). Geneva, 1765.

Purification des trois points de droit souillés par un anonyme ou Réponse à l'examen des trois points de droit traités dans les Mémoires des Représentants du 19 mai et 16 octobre 1767 (The purification of three soiled points of law by an anonymous author, or A response to the examination of three points of law in the Memorials of the Representatives . . .). Geneva, 1767.

Réflexions politiques et critiques par un citoyen représentant sur le projet d'arrangement du 25 janvier 1768 (Political and critical reflections on the settlement plan of 25 January 1768). Geneva, 1768.

Constitution de l'Angleterre ou État du gouvernement anglais comparé avec la forme républicaine et avec les autres monarchies de l'Europe. Amsterdam, 1771. Republished Amsterdam, 1774; Amsterdam, 1778; London, 1785; London, 1785; Geneva, 1787; new revised ed., Geneva 1788; republished: Geneva, 1789; Geneva, 1790; new edition (revised according to the 4th English edition), Breslau, 1791.

A Parallel between the English Constitution and the former Government of Sweden; containing some observations on the late Revolution in that kingdom and Examination of the causes that secure us against both Aristocracy and Absolute Monarchy. London, 1772.

The Constitution of England; or, an Account of the English Government; in which it is compared with the Republican Form of Government and occasionally with the Other Monarchies in Europe. London, 1775. Republished Dublin, 1775; Dublin, 1776; London, 1777; 3rd ed., London, 1781; 4th ed. enlarged, 1784.

The History of the Flagellants; or, the advantages of the Discipline; being a Paraphrase and Commentary on the Historia Flagellantium of the Abbé Boileau, Doctor of the Sorbonne, Canon at the Holy Chapel etc. by somebody who is not Doctor of the Sorbonne. London, 1777; 2nd ed., London, 1778; 3rd ed., London, 1782; revised ed., London, 1783.

Memorials of Human Superstition; being a Paraphrase and Commentary on the Historia Flagellantium of the Abbé Boileau, Doctor of the Sorbonne . . . London, 1784. Republished London, 1785.

An Essay Containing a few strictures on the Union of Scotland with England; and on the present situation of Ireland; Being an Introduction to De Foe's History of the Union. London, 1786. Reprinted as *The British Empire in Europe; Part the first, containing an Account of the Connection between the kingdoms of England and Ireland previous to the year 1780. To which is prefixed an Historical Sketch, of the State of Rivalry between the Kingdoms of England and Scotland in former times . . .* London, 1787.

The Constitutions of the Several Independent States of America; The Declaration of Independence; The Articles of Confederation . . . with an Advertisement. London, 1782; new ed., London 1783.

Observations relative to the taxes upon windows or lights . . . To which are added Observations on the shop-tax and the discontent caused by it; Short Observations on the late Act relative to Hawkers and Pedlars; A hint for the Improvement of the Metropolis London. London, 1788.

The Present National Embarrassment considered, containing a Sketch of the Political Situation of the Heir apparent and of the Legal Claims of the Parliament now assembled at Westminster. London, 1788. Reprinted as *Observations upon the late National Embarrassment and the Proceedings in Parliament relative to the same.* London, 1789.

General Observations on the Power of individuals to prescribe by Testamentary dispositions the particular future use to be made of their property, occasioned by the last will of . . . Peter Thellusson of London. London, 1798. 2nd ed., London, 1800.

Works Cited by De Lolme

CLASSICAL SOURCES

Appian of Alexandria. *Roman History.*
Cicero (Marcus Tullius Cicero).
  Philosophical writings: *De amicitiâ; De inventione; De legibus; De officiis; De re publica.*
  Speeches: *De provinciis consularibus; In Pisonem; Pro Plancio; Pro Muraenâ; Pro Rabirio perduellionis reo; Verrine Orations.*
Corpus Juris Civilis. Digest.
Demosthenes. *Against Timocrates.*
Dionysius of Halicarnassus. *Antiquitates Romanae.*
Livy (Titus Livius). *Ab urbe condita.*
Ovid (Publius Ovidius Naso). *Metamorphoses.*
Plautus (Titus Maccius Plautus). *Curculio.*
Plutarch (Mestrius Plutarchus). *Parallel Lives.*
Polybius. *Historiae.*
Quintilian (Marcus Fabius Quintilianus). *Institutio oratoria.*
Sallust (Gaius Sallustius Crispus). *Bellum Catilinae.*
Tacitus (Publius Cornelius Tacitus). *Annals.*
Thucydides. *History of the Peloponnesian War.*
Valerius Maximus. *Factorum ac dictorum memorabilium.*

MODERN SOURCES

Beccaria, Cesare. *Dei delitti e delle pene* (On crimes and punishments). 1764.
Blackstone, William. *Commentaries on the Laws of England.* 1765–69.
Bracton, Henry de (d. 1268?). *De Legibus et Consuetudinibus Angliae* (Of the laws and customs of England).
Burnet, Gilbert. *A History of My Own Time.* 1724–34.
Chamberlayne, Edward. *Angliae notitia; or, The Present State of England.* 1669.
Coke, Edward. *Institutes of the Laws of England.* 1628–44.
———. *Reports of Sir Edward Coke.* 1600–1616, 1658–59.
Comines, Philippe de. *Mémoires de Philippe de Comines* (Memoirs of Philippe de Comines). 1498.
Comings, John. *Digest of the Laws of England.* 1762–67.
Croke, George. *Reports of Sir George Croke, Knight.* 1657–61.

Cunningham, Timothy. *A New and Complete Law-Dictionary, or, General Abridgment of the Law.* 1764–65.

Du Cange, Charles du Fresne. *Glossarium mediae et infimae Latinitatis* (Glossary of medieval and late Latin). 1678.

Ferreras, Juan de. *Historia de España.* 1700–1727.

Fleta: seu Commentarius juris Anglicani (On the common law of England). Ca. 1290.

Fortescue, John. *De laudibus legum Angliae* (In praise of the laws of England). Ca. 1468–71.

Foster, Michael. *Report of some proceedings on the Commission of Oyer and Terminer and gaol delivery . . . to which are added discourses upon a few branches of the Crown Law.* 1762.

Glanvill, Ranulf de (?). *De Legibus et Consuetudinibus Angliae* (Of the laws and customs of England). Ca. 1187.

Hale, Matthew. *History of the Common Law of England.* Ca. 1670; published 1713.

Hénault, Charles Jean François. *Nouvel abrégé chronologique de l'histoire de France* (New general chronological history of France). 1744.

Hotman, François. *Francogallia.* 1573.

Hume, David. *The History of England.* 1754–62. (*The History of England.* Foreword by William B. Todd. 6 vols. Indianapolis: Liberty Fund, 1983–85.)

Jacob, Giles. *A New Law-Dictionary.* 1729.

James VI and I. *Speeches.* 1566–1625.

Johnson, Samuel. *A Dictionary of the English Language.* 1755.

Junius [pseud.]. *Letters of Junius.* 1769–72.

Littleton, Thomas. *New Tenures.* 1481.

Lyttleton, George Lord. *Letters from a Persian in England to His Friend at Ispahan.* 1735.

Machiavelli, Niccolò. *Istorie fiorentine* (History of Florence). 1525.

Mézeray, François Eudes de. *Abrégé chronologique de l'histoire de France* (A general chronological history of France). London, 1668.

Middleton, Conyers. *A Treatise on the Roman Senate.* 1747.

Montesquieu, Charles-Louis de Secondat, Baron de. *Considérations sur les causes de la grandeur des Romains et de leur décadence* (Considerations on the causes of the greatness and decline of the Romans). 1734.

———. *De l'esprit des lois* (The spirit of the laws). 1748.

More, Thomas. *Utopia.* 1515.

Oldmixon, John. *History of England, During the Reigns of the Royal House of Stuart.* 1729.

The Parliamentary or Constitutional History of England; being a faithful account of all the most remarkable transactions in Parliament. . . . 1751–61.

Pope, Alexander. *An Essay on Man.* 1733.

Robertson, William. *History of Scotland.* 1758.

Robinson, John. *An account of Sweden; together with an extract of the history of that kingdom.* 1694.

Rousseau, Jean-Jacques. *Du contrat social* (The social contract). 1762.

———. *Lettres de la montagne* (Letters from the mountain). 1764.

Ruffhead, Owen. *The Statutes of the Realm, from Magna Charta to the End of the Last Parliament.* 1769.

Rushworth, John. *Historical Collections of Private Passages of State.* 1659–1701.

Sévigné, Marie de Rabutin-Chantal, marquise de. *Lettres de Madame de Sévigné: de sa famille et de ses amis.* Paris: Hatchette et cie, 1862–66.

Smith, Adam. *An Inquiry into the Nature and Causes of the Wealth of Nations.* 1776. (*An Inquiry into the Nature and Causes of the Wealth of Nations.* Edited by R. H. Campbell and A. S. Skinner. 2 vols. Indianapolis: Liberty Fund, 1982.)

Spelman, Henry. *Reliquiae Spelmannianae: The Posthumous Works of Sir Henry Spelman Kt.* 1723.

Swift, Jonathan. *History of the Last Four Years of the Queen.* 1758.

Temple, William. *Introduction to the History of England.* 1695.

Tucker, Josiah. *A Brief Essay on the Advantages and Disadvantages, Which Respectively Attend France and Great Britain.* 1749.

United Kingdom. Parliament. *A Collection of the Parliamentary Debates in England.* . . . 1739–42.

United Kingdom. Parliament. *A Collection of State-Trials and Proceedings upon High-Treason and Other Crimes and Misdemeanours.* . . . 1730–35.

Wood, Thomas. *An Institute of the Laws of England.* 1720.

INDEX

Act of Union (between England and Scotland): *Essay Containing a few strictures on the Union of Scotland with England; and on the present situation of Ireland* (1786), De Lolme, xvii; parliamentary seats since, 56, 158n; Scottish legislation regarding monarchy prior to, 265n

acts of Parliament (written or statute law), 84, 86, 105, 113, 160–66. *See also* Act of Union; Bill of Rights; Charter of Forests; *Confirmationes Chartarum;* Coventry Act; Habeas Corpus Act; Insolvent Debtors Act; Magna Carta; Merton, Statute of; Military Tenures Act; Regulating Act; Settlement, Act of; Statute of Marlebridge; treason; Triennial Act

Adams, John, ix

Adolphus Frederick (king of Sweden), 321n

Aelius, 96

Albizzi, 142

Alexander the Great, 206

Alfred the Great, 23

Amalphi, discovery of Justinian's *Pandects* at, 81

ambassadors: immunity from prosecution, 252n; king's power to send and receive, 63

America. *See* United States

Amuraths (sultans), 296

Anglo-Saxon England, 23–24

Anne (queen of England), 248n, 252n, 263n, 265n, 266, 269–70

Antiochus and Popilius, 272n

appeal of murder, 74n

Appian, 236n

Appii, 191

Appius Claudius, 96

Aquilius, proconsul of Syria, 236

Archimedes, 154

aristocracy. *See* lords

Aristotle, 317n

armed forces. *See* military

Arthur, Duke of Britanny, 30n

assembly, right of, 285–86

Athens, 141, 142n, 156n, 188n, 227, 253n, 276

Augurs, 189n

Aula Regis, 28, 60n, 86, 90

axes and *fasces,* 157n, 221

Bacon, Francis, 243, 247n

Bajazets (sultans), 296

balance of powers. *See* equilibrium theory

barber of Piraeus, 188n

Barebones, Praise-God, 282n

Barebones Parliament, 280, 281n

Beauchamp, Francis Ingram Seymour Conway, Lord, 92, 93n

Beccaria, Cesare, 130n

Littleton, Sir Thomas, 85
Livy (Titus Livius): on Antiochus and
Popilius, 272n; on civil law, 96n; on
execution of laws in Rome, 232,
233n; on republican government and
popular assembly, 173n, 180n, 187;
on revolutions and popular disturbances in Roman history, 221, 223n,
225n, 226n, 227; on right of resistance, 219n; on unity of executive
power, 150–51n
locomotive faculty, right of, 80
Long Parliament, 50, 201
lords: removal of overly powerful subjects from office by monarchy, 269–
71; Scottish, parliamentary rights of,
158n; solidity of monarchy, effects
on great men of, 284–85; unity of
executive power and, 145–49
Lords, House of: civil judicial capacity
of, 248–49; criminal trials of lords
temporal in, 129n, 249; execution of
laws for liberty of subject by, 248–
49; impeachment of king's ministers
by, 76–78; loss of liberty prevented
by institution of, 314–15; members
of, 57, 58; relationship to House of
Commons, 157–59; royal prerogative
of adding members to, 262–63, 319–
20, 323–24n. *See also* Parliament
Lords of the Articles (Scotland), 164n
Lords Spiritual, 57
Lords Temporal, 57
Louis IX (king of France), 27n
Louis XI (king of France), 30n, 37n,
42, 118n
Louis XIII (king of France), 30n
Louis XIV (king of France), 331n
Louis XV (king of France), 272n,
273n, 282n
Louis XVI (king of France), 282n
Low Countries. *See* Netherlands

luxury and liberty, 317n
Lyttleton, George, Lord, 214–15n

Machiavelli, Niccolo, 78, 142n, 227
Magna Carta (*Magna Charta,* "Great
Charter"): executive power and, 152,
239, 324; historical background, 35–
37, 40; initiative or exclusive right of
proposing laws, 311; innocence, pre-
sumption of, 294; monarchy of
England, nature of, 273; private lib-
erty and, 87; resistance, right of,
214–16; revolution resolved in favor
of liberty by, 226, 228–29
Manlius (Marcus Manlius Capitoli-
nus), 219
Mansfield, Lord, 128n
Marius (Gaius Marius), 141, 142n
Marlborough, John Churchill, Duke
of, 149n, 269–70
Marlebridge, Statute of, 37
Mary, Queen of Scots, 270, 271n
Mary I (queen of England), 47
Mary II (queen of England), 53–54n,
76n
Mathews, Admiral, 299n
Matilda (queen of England), 82n
Maupeou (French chancellor), 272n
Mayne, Admiral, 299n
Megacles, 141, 142n
Memmius (Gaius Memmius), 234,
235n
Memorials of Human Superstition
(1784), De Lolme, xvii, 326
Merton, Statute of, 37
metapolitics, 275n
Mexico, 312
Mèzeray, François Eudes de, 27n, 29–
30n, 41n
Middlesex elections controversy,
293n
Middleton, Conyers, 189n

This book is set in Adobe Garamond, a modern adaptation by Robert Slimbach of the typeface originally cut around 1540 by the French typographer and printer Claude Garamond. The Garamond face, with its small lowercase height and restrained contrast between thick and thin strokes, is a classic "old-style" face and has long been one of the most influential and widely used typefaces.

Printed on paper that is acid-free and meets the requirements of the American National Standard for Permanence of Paper for Printed Library Materials, z39.48-1992. ∞

Book design by Louise OFarrell
Gainesville, Florida
Typography by Apex Publishing, LLC
Madison, Wisconsin
Printed and bound by Edwards Brothers, Inc.
Ann Arbor, Michigan